T0154814

Giving Life,
Giving Death

STUDIES IN VIOLENCE, MIMESIS, AND CULTURE

SERIES EDITOR
William A. Johnsen

The Studies in Violence, Mimesis, and Culture Series examines issues related to the nexus of violence and religion in the genesis and maintenance of culture. It furthers the agenda of the Colloquium on Violence and Religion, an international association that draws inspiration from René Girard's mimetic hypothesis on the relationship between violence and religion, elaborated in a stunning series of books he has written over the last forty years. Readers interested in this area of research can also look to the association's journal, *Contagion: Journal of Violence, Mimesis, and Culture.*

ADVISORY BOARD

René Girard†, *Stanford University*
Andrew McKenna, *Loyola University of Chicago*

Raymund Schwager†, *University of Innsbruck*
James Williams, *Syracuse University*

EDITORIAL BOARD

Rebecca Adams, *Independent Scholar*
Jeremiah L. Alberg, *International Christian University, Tokyo, Japan*
Mark Anspach, *École Polytechnique, Paris*
Pierpaolo Antonello, *University of Cambridge*
Ann Astell, *University of Notre Dame*
Cesáreo Bandera, *University of North Carolina*
Maria Stella Barberi, *Università di Messina*
Alexei Bodrov, *St. Andrew's Biblical Theological Institute, Moscow*
João Cezar de Castro Rocha, *Universidade do Estado do Rio de Janeiro*
Benoît Chantre, *L'Association Recherches Mimétiques*
Diana Culbertson, *Kent State University*
Paul Dumouchel, *Ritsumeikan University*
Jean-Pierre Dupuy, *Stanford University, École Polytechnique*
Giuseppe Fornari, *Università degli studi di Bergamo*
Eric Gans, *University of California, Los Angeles*

Sandor Goodhart, *Purdue University*
Robert Hamerton-Kelly†, *Stanford University*
Hans Jensen, *Aarhus University, Denmark*
Mark Juergensmeyer, *University of California, Santa Barbara*
Cheryl Kirk-Duggan, *Shaw University*
Michael Kirwan, SJ, *Heythrop College, University of London*
Paisley Livingston, *Lingnan University, Hong Kong*
Charles Mabee, *Ecumenical Theological Seminary, Detroit*
Józef Niewiadomski, *Universität Innsbruck*
Wolfgang Palaver, *Universität Innsbruck*
Ángel Jorge Barahona Plaza, *Universidad Francisco de Vitoria*
Martha Reineke, *University of Northern Iowa*
Tobin Siebers†, *University of Michigan*
Thee Smith, *Emory University*
Mark Wallace, *Swarthmore College*
Eugene Webb, *University of Washington*

Giving Life, Giving Death

Psychoanalysis, Anthropology, Philosophy

Lucien Scubla
Translated by M. B. DeBevoise

Michigan State University Press · *East Lansing*

Copyright © 2016 by Michigan State University Press; *Donner la vie, donner la mort: Psychanalyse, anthropologie, philosophie* copyright © 2014 Éditions Le Bord de L'eau

♾ The paper used in this publication meets the minimum requirements of ANSI/NISO Z39.48-1992 (R 1997) (Permanence of Paper).

Michigan State University Press
East Lansing, Michigan 48823-5245

Printed and bound in the United States of America.

22 21 20 19 18 17 16   1 2 3 4 5 6 7 8 9 10

LIBRARY OF CONGRESS CATALOGING-IN-PUBLICATION DATA
Names: Scubla, Lucien, author.
Title: Giving life, giving death : psychoanalysis, anthropology, philosophy /
Lucien Scubla ; translated by M. B. DeBevoise.
Other titles: Donner la vie, donner la mort. English
Description: East Lansing : Michigan State University Press, 2016. | Series: Studies in violence, mimesis,
and culture | Includes bibliographical references and index.
Identifiers: LCCN 2015033655| ISBN 9781611862089 (pbk. : alk. paper) | ISBN 9781609174941 (pdf) |
ISBN 9781628952674 (epub) | ISBN 9781628962673 (kindle)
Subjects: LCSH: Psychoanalysis and anthropology. | Philosophical anthropology.
Classification: LCC GN508 .S252313 2016 | DDC 128—dc23 LC record available at
http://lccn.loc.gov/2015033655

Book design by Charlie Sharp, Sharp Des!gns, Lansing, MI
Cover design by David Drummond, Salamander Design, www.salamanderhill.com.
Cover artwork is *The Tempest* by Giorgione (Giorgio da Castelfranco), ca. 1510, 31" × 29"
oil on canvas, located at Accademia, Venice.

Michigan State University Press is a member of the Green Press Initiative and is committed to developing and encouraging ecologically responsible publishing practices. For more information about the Green Press Initiative and the use of recycled paper in book publishing, please visit *www.greenpressinitiative.org.*

Visit Michigan State University Press at *www.msupress.org*

Slaves of death, men envy and fear women, mistresses of life. Such is the primitive and primordial truth that a serious analysis of certain myths and rituals reveals. Myths, by reversing the real order, attempt to conceive of the world's destiny as male destiny; rituals, the stage on which men act out their victory, are used to ward off, to compensate for the all-too-obvious truth that this destiny is female.

PIERRE CLASTRES

The most important things are done through tubes. First proofs: the generative organs, the writing pen, and [the] rifle.

GEORG CHRISTOPH LICHTENBERG

There is perhaps today no more firmly credited prejudice than this: that one *knows* what morality really consists in.

FRIEDRICH NIETZSCHE

Contents

Preface

What now remains of the Oedipus complex, a century after *Totem and Taboo* first appeared? Neither the myth supposed to illustrate it, nor the clinical data supposed to lend credence to it, nor the ethnographic facts marshaled to extend its field of application have succeeded in giving it a firm basis. Indeed, the canonical "Oedipal triangle" exhibits two signal weaknesses: in insisting on sexuality at the expense of procreation, it reduces the mother to a libidinal object, a source of incestuous desires rather than a giver of life; and in attributing spontaneously cannibalistic and murderous impulses to children, it makes them responsible for most, if not all, of the violence visited upon them by adults.

Yet, as ethnology attests, the transmission of life constitutes the pivot of both systems of kinship and rites of initiation, and the struggle for control over procreation is at the heart of the rivalries that set men not only against women but also against themselves. It is around women, guardians of life, that society organizes itself for the sake of its own perpetuation, and that the institutions responsible for containing social conflict develop, by means of a balance, often a very subtle one, between feminine and masculine principles.

Paradoxically, however, anthropologists no less than psychoanalysts reject the idea of characterizing women by their power to give life. Structural anthropology sees women as objects of exchange, allowing various segments of society to establish alliances with one another, rather than as the bearers of continuity among generations; feminist anthropology sees women as objects of male domination, from which they can escape only by freeing themselves from the burden of procreation. Even though everyone knows that women bring children into the world and that men do not, not only the human sciences but modern Western thought as a whole, to which these sciences give expression, are determined to ignore this female prerogative and the original asymmetry of the sexes.

The present work attempts to describe a few of the major aspects of this refusal and to trace their cultural roots—to measure the distance, as it were, separating aboriginal Australians, for example, who assign a mother-in-law to a little boy at the moment of his birth, from those Westerners (admittedly a small, though not insignificant, minority), who refrain from giving him a specifically male first name so that he will be free to choose his gender later. It is an intellectual voyage among a great variety of peoples, as well as an x-ray of the contemporary Western world.

When Saint Paul wrote that there is neither Jew nor Greek, neither slave nor free, neither male nor female, he did not mean to deny that these differences exist—only to subordinate them to the primary quality of being a child of God, supposed to be common to all human beings. The intellectual avant-garde of our age rejects the religious character of this assertion while, literally, preserving its content: it demands that nature be substituted for God; calls upon science to prove that there are neither peoples nor sexes, only human beings and communities and genders, all of them socially constructed; and awaits perhaps the day when technology will be able, by the use of cloning and artificial wombs, to bring forth the world of indistinguishable, and in every respect equal, individuals that it seems to long for.

Although I present facts and advance hypotheses that are not in keeping with the mood of the times, my aim in this book is not polemical. To the contrary, I should like to join with Spinoza in proclaiming: *Non ridere, nec lugere, neque detestari, sed intelligere.*

Composed on the occasion of the centenary of *Totem and Taboo*'s publication, this book looks to rehabilitate the spirit that animates that book; that is, an anthropology that seeks to identify a common source for family and religion, rather than to dissociate the elementary structures of kinship from the elementary forms of religious life; that conceives of the family in terms of an irreducibly tripartite structure, not as a relationship between two partners who may or may not elect to have a child; and that attempts to understand how rites manage to join violence and the sacred—in other words, the gift of death and the gift of life.

In undertaking to address three related and intertwined problems involving the relations between male and female, the individual and the group, and the transmission of life and of culture, naturally I do not claim to resolve them all, or even any one of them completely; only to present a great many facts and a certain amount of analysis that may help point the way to a resolution.

Acknowledgments

Chapters 1 and 2 constitute a reworked and expanded version of an article entitled "Psychanalyse et anthropologie: Un rendez-vous manqué?" that appeared in 2011 in the *Revue du MAUSS*, no. 38: 65–86. Chapter 4 is a revised version of an article that appeared the following year in issue no. 39 of the same journal (79–100) under the title "De l'échange de femmes' au don des femmes: Le déni de la procréation dans l'atome de parenté." Chapter 13 contains several pages from "Le symbolique chez Lévi-Strauss et chez Lacan," an article published in 2011 in issue no. 37 of the same journal (223–39). The contents of these three articles are reproduced with the permission of the editors of the *Revue du MAUSS* and of its publisher, Éditions La Découverte.

Chapter 11, "Hiérarchie de sexes et hiérarchie des savoirs, ou Platon chez les Baruya," is a modified version of an article that appeared under the same title in 2002, in issue no. 9 of the journal *Cités* (13–24). It is reproduced with the permission of the editors of this journal and of Presses Universitaires de France.

The first part of chapter 15, "Auguste Comte's Lesson, or The School for Wives," is taken from an article published in 1981 under the title "Philosophie, procréation, religion" in issue no. 2 (506–16) of the journal *Le Temps de la réflexion*, now defunct. This material is reproduced with the permission of Éditions Gallimard, which retains the copyright.

The second part of this same chapter, "Rituals of Transmission and Male Violence," is a reworked version of an essay that appeared in 2001 under the title "Mimétisme, violence et éducation: Quelques aspects de la relation maître-disciple" in a volume edited by Maria Stella Barberi and published by Desclée de Brouwer, *La spirale mimétique: Dix-huit leçons sur René Girard* (234–46).

.   .   .

My thanks to the editors and publishers who have so kindly allowed me to reproduce all or part of these articles.

I am especially grateful to Alain Caillé for having suggested that I undertake this work in the first place, for having accepted several draft chapters for initial publication in the *Revue du MAUSS*, and for closely monitoring their subsequent development. Thanks also to Marika Moisseeff for her warm encouragement, and to Sylvie Malsan for her careful preparation of the final manuscript.

Finally, with regard to the present English version of the book, I am grateful to William Johnsen for sponsoring its appearance in the series he directs for Michigan State University Press, and especially to Malcolm DeBevoise for his very fine and faithful translation.

It goes without saying that I assume full responsibility for the work as it stands, and for whatever imperfections may remain.

CHAPTER ONE

Freud and the Oedipus Legend

P sychoanalysis and anthropology became known to each other almost at once, and for a long time they went forward together, without, however, ever really getting to know each other. The history of their development, growing up side by side, is above all the story of a missed opportunity. And yet all signs seemed at first to foretell a mutually rewarding relationship. Psychoanalysis appeared at a time when anthropology was in its ascendancy, and shared its ambition to develop a human science no less robust than the natural sciences. Freud, a contemporary of the great early figures of religious ethnology, was an attentive reader of William Robertson Smith, James Frazer, and Émile Durkheim, but also, as we know from *Totem and Taboo*, of less famous authors and more specialized works as well. His intellectual curiosity and his interest in the customs of exotic peoples were nourished by what appeared in principle, at least, to be a compatibility between the postulates of cultural evolutionism, then dominant in anthropology, and those of the psychoanalytic theory that he was then in the process of formulating. For just as he regarded the unconscious as the infantile part of the human psyche, and mental illness as a fixation on the most remote human past, anthropologists attributed the same type of magical behavior and prerational thought to primitive peoples, children, and madmen. Thus Ernest Jones, for example, held that psychoanalysis and folklore studied survivals of the past—individual in the one case, collective in the other—in complementary ways (see Jones 1951, 5). Fortified by Blondel's social psychology and Piaget's genetic psychology, this "archaic illusion," as Claude Lévi-Strauss was later to call it, persisted in the thinking of psychoanalysts, whereas ethnologists had abandoned evolutionism early on, under the influence first of the diffusionist and then of the functionalist schools. Not until the 1930s was it finally agreed that, among primitive and savage peoples (to use the terminology of the period) on the one hand, and civilized peoples on the other, children are to be distinguished from adults; in each case, some are of sound mind, others not (see Lévi-Strauss [1949c] 1969, 84–97). Freud, even if he was more clear-sighted in this regard than his eminent contemporaries,[1] nonetheless helped to sustain the common misconception by giving it the support of psychoanalysis.

But this is a relatively unimportant point. More disturbing is Freud's inability to profit from his ethnographic learning in order to compare his own hypotheses with much more numerous and varied empirical findings than he could draw upon from clinical experience. Anthropology, though it furnished him with a sort of laboratory where he could test the principles of psychoanalysis and, if need be, amend them, remained for him first and foremost a new territory to be annexed. So convinced was he of being right that he felt sure facts could not help but confirm his ideas. The truth of the matter is that Freud always behaved as a conqueror, eager to push the frontiers of his empire to their furthest possible extent. This can be seen already in his earliest works. Taking a longer view, we can see that his attempt to conquer the human sciences unfolded in three stages.

Freud and the Conquest of the Human Sciences

Psychoanalysis, strictly speaking, is a medical technique intended to heal persons suffering from neuroses. But Freud did not mean for it to be reduced to a therapeutics, a method for treating illness. He regarded it also, and perhaps primarily, as the opening pages of his *Introductory Lectures on Psycho-Analysis* (Freud [1915–1916] 1963) suggest, as the first scientific theory of mental life. Reflex psychology having proved to be no less incapable than behavioral psychology of explaining mental disorders of any kind, it fell to psychoanalysis to provide psychiatry with the psychological basis it lacked. Although psychoanalysis manages only—or at the very most—to treat neuroses, Freud believed it could supply a general explanation of all mental disorders, not only different forms of neurosis, but also perversions, of which neuroses are the negative, as it were, and psychoses. The apparently modest promise of psychoanalysis as a therapeutics was therefore compensated for by an immense theoretical ambition. This was the first stage of conquest.

The second stage moved from psychopathology to a general theory of mental life through the analysis of dreams and parapraxes, which is to say normal phenomena that structurally resemble psychoses in the first instance, and neuroses in the second, and therefore constitute a natural link between the normal and the pathological. This extension was decisive. The appearance of *The Interpretation of Dreams* in 1900 and then *The Psychopathology of Everyday Life* the following year is generally agreed to mark the moment when psychoanalysis achieved the status of a well-formed and independent discipline. All the elements of what is customarily called the "first Freudian topic" (the distinction between the unconscious and the preconscious, between primary and secondary processes, between primal repression and "after-pressure" [*Nachdrangen*], and so on) were now in place.

It then remained, in a third and final stage, to stake a claim not only to human psychology, but to all cultural and social phenomena, by setting forth a psychoanalytical theory of religion, science, art, economics, and so on. From 1907 onward, Freud lay siege to this new territory by publishing, in the journal *Imago*, a series of studies on the prohibition of incest, on taboos, and on totemism that a few years later, in 1913, he was to collect in *Totem and Taboo: Resemblances between the Psychic Lives of Savages and Neurotics*. In the second sentence of his preface, he clearly announces his intention, implicit in the work's subtitle, to apply "the point of view and the findings of psychoanalysis to some unsolved problems of social psychology" (Freud [1913] 1955, 13:xiii). Bring me facts, he seems to say, and I will make a theory out of them.[2] Although he had read Durkheim, who insisted on the specifically social character of human relations, Freud was not interested in the social institutions described by ethnologists. It is as though he considered the culture of different societies to be reducible to facts of collective psychology, which themselves are reducible to individual processes, to which psychoanalysis alone held the key. Dragged down to the level of individual psychology, ethnology has nothing of its own to teach us. It is merely a training ground for psychoanalytic theory.

In view of the immensity of the territory to be conquered, Freud thought to surround himself with young disciples having expertise in the various fields it encompassed as well as the enthusiasm required to carry out the missions assigned to them. Otto Rank (1884–1939) published *The Myth of the Birth of the Hero* in 1909, and then, two years later, a work on the Lohengrin legend (see Rank [1909] 2004; Rank 1911). In 1914, Theodor Reik (1888–1969) began work on a series of four studies—on the practice of couvade, the rites of puberty among primitive peoples, the Kol Nidre declaration, and the sounding of the shofar in the Jewish rites of Yom Kippur—that were collected five years later in a volume to which Freud contributed a preface: *Ritual: Psycho-analytic Studies* (see Reik [1919] 1931). In 1920, Géza Róheim (1891–1953), an ethnologist by training, published an article in *Imago* on marriage rites, and then embarked upon an extensive round of field studies in Oceania, Africa, and North America whose principal objective was to refute Bronisław Malinowski's arguments against the universality of the Oedipus complex (see Malinowski 1927). Then there was Ernest Jones (1879–1958), author of a very detailed article on superstitions relating to salt that appeared in 1912. Following Freud's break with Jung, Jones became the zealous guardian of psychoanalytic dogma and took it upon himself to spread the good word among anthropologists in the United Kingdom,[3] while railing against Malinowski on his own account.[4]

The interest shown by the founder of psychoanalysis and his lieutenants in ethnology is therefore undeniable. To them we owe writings whose erudition rivals that of Frazer, and which have the power to stimulate the thinking of researchers still today. Moreover, they undertook original work that enlarged the scope and enriched the documentary basis of anthropology. It is therefore tempting to believe that their good intentions and their respect for ethnography have not been reciprocated. Indeed, among anthropologists from Kroeber to Malinowski and Lévi-Strauss, psychoanalysis seems to have aroused mainly reservations and criticisms, if not disdain or outright hostility. Even the so-called culture and personality school, which brokered a fruitful exchange of ideas between Adam Kardiner and ethnologists such as Ralph Linton, Ruth Benedict, Margaret Mead, and Cora DuBois, seems to have taken from Freud hardly anything more than the importance of the earliest manifestations of infantile anxiety and, consequently as well, of the educational systems that arouse or repress them, that give them free rein or channel them in this or that direction.[5] There can be no doubt that the attitude of most anthropologists was rather distant, nor that it was encouraged by an excessive division of labor that tended to isolate disciplines from one another. But it was not necessarily due to any principled rejection. As I have already suggested, and as we shall see later, looking at specific cases, it is rather more on the side of Freud and his disciples that closed-mindedness and rigidity are to be observed.

Malinowski's testimony is significant in this regard. He had fallen under the spell of Freud's theory at once, and even if its obscurities and occasionally specious arguments soon led him to temper his enthusiasm, he nonetheless recognized that psychoanalysis had made a significant contribution to the knowledge of human nature, and that its hypotheses had helped him work out his own ideas (see Malinowski 1927, vii–x). At the same time, he deplored the inability of Freudian analysts to welcome anything coming from ethnology and the social sciences—neither fresh data or new insights that would force them to revise their system or to reconstruct it on a larger basis, nor even information that promised to strengthen its fundamental postulates: "Curiously enough," he writes, "though sociology and anthropology have contributed most [of the] evidence in favour of psycho-analysis, and though the doctrine of the Oedipus complex has obviously a sociological aspect, this aspect has received the least attention" (1–2).

Instead of seeking the genesis and form (or forms) of the Oedipus complex in the interactions between parents and children, which vary from one culture to another, the Freudian approach simply decrees that a somehow preestablished Oedipal structure determines a priori the nature of these interactions at all times and in all places. Assigning primacy to conflicts and to intrapsychic mechanisms,[6] while assuming in advance the completeness of psychoanalysis, it could not help but regard any external theoretical contribution as superfluous. Corresponding to the atomism of the Freudian subject, then, is a sort of autism in the theory itself. This is why psychoanalysis has no other possible relation to anthropology than that of master to servant. It asks only that anthropology confirm its own hypotheses by furnishing new examples that it then undertakes to explain with reference solely to its own concepts. To be sure, the theoretical corpus of psychoanalysis was in a state of perpetual flux during Freud's lifetime, the result of his constantly changing conception of the unconscious, the theory of impulses (or "drives" [*Trieb*]), and the typology of mental disorders. But it was, so to speak, always the same cards that were endlessly being reshuffled. One searches in vain in Freud's writings for a single concept or a single hypothesis borrowed from ethnography—apart from the notion of taboo, or at least the term.

Occasionally, however, under the influence of his anthropological reading, Freud managed to collect his wits, shake off his radical individualism, and recognize, if only for the length of a paragraph, the primacy of the collective over the individual. Thus, for example, in a neglected passage of *Totem and Taboo* devoted to affirming yet again the existence of a structure common to the major neuroses and great cultural productions, he astonishes us by inverting the usual relations, of anteriority and dependence, between them:

> Neuroses exhibit on the one hand striking and far-reaching points of agreement with those great social institutions, art, religion, and philosophy. But on the other hand they seem like distortions of them. It might be maintained that a case of hysteria is a caricature of a work of art, that an obsessional neurosis is a caricature of a religion and that a paranoiac delusion is a caricature of a philosophical system. The divergence resolves itself ultimately into the fact that the neuroses are asocial structures; they endeavour to achieve by private means what is effected in society by collective effort. (Freud [1913] 1955, 13:73)

By comparison with psychoanalytic orthodoxy, the reversal of perspective is spectacular. Culture here is no longer a prolongation of neurosis and the ego's defense mechanisms by collective means, but a primary and sui generis reality; now, by contrast, it is neurosis that is derivative, an individual byproduct, a crude caricature of culture. Illness is alienating because it makes the subject a stranger to the culture of his group. It results from a failure of the individual, whether due to internal or external causes, to adapt himself to the norms and the cultural symbolism of his environment. Religion, for example, is not an obsessional neurosis that has been enlarged to the scale of an entire people or of humanity as a whole; it is the obsessional neurosis that is a deformed version of religion, because it is purely private.

In this rare and precious passage, Freud reasons as Lévi-Strauss was to do a few decades later in comparing the child, the primitive, and neurosis, as part of a larger inquiry into the unity of mankind and the diversity of cultures. Culture and illness operate on the same materials, precisely the ones that are available to every child in working out his own relationship to nature and society. But while culture uses these materials to create a structurally stable synthesis regulated by norms of collective behavior, the child cobbles them together to produce an anomic synthesis that is much more precarious and purely individual.[7] Unfortunately, this flash of lucidity on Freud's part, a trace of which still remains in the preface he wrote to Reik's book (see Reik [1919] 1931, 10–11), was to have no further consequence—as though, fearful of being seduced by the sirens of culturalism, he had repented a moment of weakness and promptly returned to the fold of psychoanalytic orthodoxy, repeating his canonical definition of religion as universal neurosis loudly and clearly in *The Future of an Illusion* (Freud [1927] 1961). Even for a psychoanalyst, revising one's own beliefs is a very difficult thing.

And yet Freud, to his credit, continued to navigate cautiously among contradictory hypotheses, not hesitating, even once analytic theory had officially been constituted, to bring together in his writings evidence and ideas that could not easily be reconciled, either with the theory or with one another. Thus, in his autobiographical study, he curiously juxtaposes the notion of obsessional neurosis as a private, deformed religion with the definition of religion as a universal obsessional neurosis (see Freud [1925] 1959, 20:66–67). René Girard has shown in *Violence and the Sacred* that one finds the same type of inconsistency in his theory of the Oedipus complex—where the son's identification with the father is described sometimes as prior to the rivalry, sometimes as subsequent to it; sometimes as the source of rivalry, sometimes as its consequence—and in the scenario he imagines of the murder of the father of the primitive horde, which likewise juxtaposes, in an ambiguous manner, two different processes (see Girard [1972b] 1977, 169–222). Nevertheless, as Girard notes, this fundamental honesty on Freud's part serves to moderate his dogmatism and makes his works fascinating to read, precisely because of the tensions they contain. Freud's exaggerated confidence in the ability of psychoanalysis ultimately to overcome every difficulty led him to advance speculations that a more circumspect author would have passed over in silence or crossed out on rereading what he had written. Freud did no such thing, hoping one day to produce a conclusive synthesis that in the end eluded him.

The fact remains, however, that with his crucial decision to replace the theory of trauma by the theory of fantasy in the etiology of neuroses he became convinced that he had finally gotten to the bottom of the matter, and that henceforth, having laid a solid foundation for any future psychology that could plausibly claim to be scientific, he could argue on the basis of a few incontrovertible propositions. Yet substituting fantasy for trauma amounted to giving primacy to the subjective over the intersubjective, to imaginary relations and interactions with others over actual relations and interactions, and also to recognizing the priority of the "individual myth of the neurotic" and of theories of infantile sexuality over the collective mythology of peoples.[8] It amounted, then, to diminishing society in relation to the individual, culture in relation to psychology. I need hardly point out that, from such premises, it was virtually impossible that psychoanalysis and anthropology should ever meet on equal terms.

But we shall see that far from strengthening his discipline, Freud's hegemonic attitude helped to weaken it. What he took to be the very foundation of psychoanalysis was in reality its Achilles' heel. The guiding principles of psychoanalysis, which he thought could be inferred from his clinical data, prevented him from incorporating information from other much more numerous and much richer sources. Ethnographic data suggest an interpretation that is diametrically opposed to the one he gives of relations between generations and between the sexes, which play a crucial role both in the organization of human societies and in the structure of the Oedipus complex. For each of these sets of relations, psychoanalysis gives the impression of playing against type by inverting the natural order of things. Whereas it claims to reveal a hidden reality in helping us to go back from the conscious to the unconscious, in fact it recycles old myths without deciphering them, obscuring instead of clarifying them, and thus works to conceal under the cloak of science things that human beings have always preferred to leave unclear. Nowhere is this more true than in the canonical exposition of the two great doctrinal pillars I have just mentioned, the etiology of neuroses and theories of infantile sexuality. We need therefore to pause here for a moment.

In his first studies on hysteria, Freud explained the neuroses of his female patients by reference to a traumatizing event that they claimed to have experienced during childhood, of having been sexually abused by an adult, generally their own father. The more cases of this kind that he examined, however, the more improbable they seemed to him, and he changed his mind: the reported episodes were in fact imaginary; only the infantile fantasy of seduction was real—and so powerful that it was liable to leave indelible traces in a patient's psyche, to the point that it could be mistaken afterwards, and in perfectly good faith, for a real event. A small but significant detail is enough to arouse suspicion about this theoretical revision: it was not until Freud had conceived and published it that he was able to recognize, in later editions of his earliest works, that it was not an uncle, as he had written at first, but in fact their own father whom his patients accused of molesting them. It is as though he found it comforting that his new hypothesis doubly exculpated the father of the accusation of incest, on the one hand by rendering this act purely imaginary, and on the other by imputing the idea of sexual seduction, and even the initiative for it, to the child rather than the adult.

Oedipus Complex or Laius Complex?

Children, as everyone will agree, are not little angels. But even if one accepts that everything that is fully manifest in the adult is already present in outline in the child, it does not follow that, like shamans who accuse children of sorcery, one can blame them for any kind of misbehavior, and in this way shield adults from the same charge. But that is just what Freud does when, taking things the wrong way around, he exempts psychoanalytic theory from all challenge. Whether it is a question of sexual seduction, as here, or of cannibalistic impulses associated with the oral stage, or of murderous tendencies associated with the Oedipus complex, he manages always to regard as primary infantile behaviors that are more plausibly seen as reactionary, phantasmic attitudes brought about by the quite real aggression of adults. As the ethnopsychiatrist Georges Devereux points out in a genuinely positivist spirit—though, it is true, he can hardly be accused of being overly fond of psychoanalysis—it is never the child, but always the father or the mother who exclaims "You look good enough to eat"; and, if it is not actually rare that children are eaten in time of famine (in Australia, "it was deemed preferable to kill a useless baby than a useful dingo hunting dog"), one never hears of famished children who kill their parents and eat them (Devereux [1970b] 1980, 127, 129–30). Whereas "law and public opinion penalize parricide infinitely more severely than infanticide, . . . [statistics] tell a very different story: throughout the course of history, infinitely more children have been killed either before or after their birth by their parents than parents have been killed by their children" (128); indeed, "for every parricide or matricide there are probably millions of cases of abortion or infanticide . . . ; for every incestuously raped mother, there are thousands of children seduced by adults" (117).

Psychoanalysis nevertheless approves, and in this regard even reinforces, the assumptions of criminal law and common behavior. In asserting that the desire to kill one's father is especially pronounced, it lends authority to the idea that this desire must be subdued by the most violent means. As we shall see later in connection with Reik's work, this idea can be used to justify the practices of peoples who, if psychoanalysis is to be believed, carry out preemptive reprisals against children. Moreover, whereas most legal systems hold the adult wholly responsible for sexual intercourse with a child, the same idea tends to rationalize the attitude of adults who excuse their clumsiness or misbehavior by placing all blame on the child. As one ethnologist (someone who is very sympathetic to psychoanalysis but who nevertheless pays due regard to factual evidence) observes, whereas the Freudian theory of the "family romance" postulates that all children dream of having different parents than the ones to whom they were actually born, on the islands of New Guinea and New Britain one finds myths and customs of abandonment and adoption that show the desire of parents to substitute other children for the ones they have actually produced themselves (Juillerat 1995). Nor is this theme foreign to our own oral traditions. In folktales such as "Thumbelina" and "Hansel and Gretel," we also find parents who try to do away with their children.

One may therefore be tempted simply to reject the nodal complex of psychoanalysis, at the risk of causing the whole edifice to totter. But we must be careful not to throw out the baby with the bath water. The Oedipus myth itself is much richer and more complex than the truncated story to which orthodox psychoanalysis ended up reducing it. Even if we restrict our attention to the aspects that interested Freud, it is evident that the myth does not describe only a son inexorably doomed to kill his father, or a father fated to die at the hand of his son—still less a son who is doomed to sleep with his mother, or a mother who is destined to be defiled by her son. Note that it is Laius, and not Oedipus, who is responsible for initiating violence. Two misdeeds are attributed to Laius. First, he rapes the young Chrysippus. Second, in order to escape the curse that this crime brings upon him, he tries to take the life of his own son by piercing his feet (according to one version of the myth) and then abandoning him on a mountainside. Parricide (more exactly, regicide) and incest (more exactly, marriage to the queen) are, from the psychological point of view, secondary and almost accidental elements. They can be considered necessary elements only insofar as they are canonical components of the royal ritual of accession and what Marie Delcourt calls the legend of the conqueror: the pretender to the throne eliminates his rival and marries the queen or princess (see Delcourt [1944] 1981).

A myth proves nothing, of course. And, of course, it demands to be deciphered. Nowhere is this more obvious than with the Oedipus corpus, which exhibits numerous variants and itself contains several successive layers of interpretation. Nevertheless, if Freud's Oedipus complex, which rests on an arbitrarily abridged version of the myth, has no privileged hermeneutic status, neither is it a mere variant of the myth, so that one would have only to study its formal relationship to all the other variants, as Lévi-Strauss maintained (see [1958a] 1963, 218). If indeed the whole of the corpus needs to be taken into account, it is not for the purpose of treating it as a closed system, shut in on itself. One must try to unravel its various strands, first by making an inventory of them and ordering them hierarchically, and then comparing them, as Delcourt and Devereux do in their own ways, with what can only be called "reality," that is, with those practices that are actually attested in human societies. Now, on this view of the matter, just as infanticide and pedophilia precede parricide and incest, so too what Devereux calls "Laius and Jocasta complexes" appear to be logically both prior to, and more fundamental than the Oedipus complex. The former thus entail the latter: far from being the expression of primal impulses, the "Oedipal" attitudes of children have a reactive character.

Despite this important modification, Devereux is very careful not to upset psychoanalytical orthodoxy, though less, it would seem, from scholarly caution or tactfulness than from an excess of modesty, or perhaps fear of committing a sort of intellectual parricide or regicide. Rather than sharpen his critique, he chooses to blunt its edge and pleads extenuating circumstances on Freud's behalf. It is because psychoanalysis had adopted the adult's point of view from the outset, he charitably says, that the Oedipus complex was discovered well before that of Laius or of Jocasta. But this error of perspective, if that is what it really is, is altogether excusable, for in spite of its derivative character the Oedipus complex is in no way "secondary," in the figurative sense of the term. It is not a contingent response, but a necessary and universal reaction to the complexes from which it issues, and so loses none of its explanatory force (see Devereux [1970b] 1980, 117–18, 120).

Whatever its psychological motivations may have been, this overly deferential criticism had the disadvantage of blurring what was at issue, and of defusing, if not actually evading, serious debate. So anxious is the ethnopsychiatrist to pass for a "rigorously Freudian analyst" that, while recognizing "the priority of the counter-Oedipal impulses of parents by comparison with the Oedipal attitudes of children, whose release they trigger" (as Roger Bastide puts it in his preface to Devereux 1970a, xiv), neither Devereux nor, as it happens, his spokesman Bastide feels the need to unburden himself of a paradoxical vocabulary, consecrated by usage, that stands the actual order of things on its head. Now, the same is true of the cannibalistic impulses ascribed to children, which Devereux, for his part, considers to be posterior to the cannibalistic impulses of parents, and particularly of the mother, though no one really knows, when all is said and done, whether they are real or wholly imaginary. Even in passages where he plainly contradicts received psychoanalytic wisdom, Devereux goes out of his way to treat Freud with the respect owed to a tutelary figure, and here and there goes so far as to appeal to his authority.[9] What is more, he never systematically develops his main argument. It is laid out fragmentarily in several essays that cite to one another, each one consisting of a collection of more or less disparate "cases" and "observations" whose common features are sometimes hard to discern. It may therefore be doubted that psychoanalysis had already, as Devereux asserts, discovered the Laius and Jocasta complexes, much less worked out their implications.

Femininity and Maternity

However this may be, the way in which Freud and the majority of his disciples address the relationship between the sexes is still less satisfying than the way in which they conceive of the one between generations. We need to bear in mind that the libido is supposed to develop by passing through three infantile stages—oral, anal, and phallic, respectively—until finally, with the onset of puberty, reaching the genital stage. If Freud calls the third stage phallic, rather than genital, it is not only because, prior to puberty, the child is not yet capable of procreating. It is also, and above all, because the theory of infantile development, which holds that children of both sexes, and not only boys, were all originally endowed with an imaginary organ having a masculine connotation, is an essential element of Freud's conception of the Oedipus complex and of the fantasies that are inherent in it. The idea that every woman is a little boy to begin with (see Freud [1932] 1964, 22:126–30) makes it possible to explain each of the forms, masculine and feminine, of the Oedipal triangle. For it is the discovery that girls do not possess, or, more exactly, no longer possess a phallus that arouses and feeds in the boy's mind the fantasy of castration, and thus gives rise to his attitude of fear and hostility toward a father who is capable at any moment of robbing him of his precious organ and so of reducing him, too, to a mutilated being. In the little girl, it is the awareness of being deprived of a phallus that triggers feelings of hostility toward her mother, whom she blames for having caused her to suffer this defect, and that orients her libido toward her father, in the hope of obtaining from him the marvelous appendage that she lacks, or its symbolic equivalent, as would be the case were she to have a child by him. Plainly, the phallic theory was essential in order to provide a more solid foundation for the male Oedipus complex, but above all in order to justify the existence of a corresponding female Oedipus complex. This is why Freud constantly defended it and clung to it, for example in the fifth of the *New Introductory Lectures on Psycho-Analysis*, published in 1932 and dealing with "femininity" (see 22:112–35), which, in our time, would be enough for him to be tried for aggravated male chauvinism.[10]

In depicting man as endowed with something more and woman with something less, psychoanalysis simply adopted (more blatantly even than in the case of the difference between generations) a virtually universal dichotomy and embroidered it with a few additional motifs on a transcultural canvas. While imagining that it was going back from the conscious to the unconscious, it did nothing more than ratify perfectly explicit collective representations, which various peoples, primitive and civilized alike, have deposited in innumerable binary classifications that resemble one another in many respects. Thus in a famous table of contraries, Pythagorean in origin and assembled by Aristotle (see *Metaphysics* A.5 [986ᵃ]), the male principle is, as almost everywhere, associated with goodness and light, and the female with evil and darkness.[11] By devising new refinements to contrast masculine and feminine in his own fashion, as positive/negative, fullness/emptiness, and so on, Freud unwittingly demonstrated the power of an immemorial tradition that he managed also to perpetuate by modernizing it.

And yet even a cursory examination of initiation rites attested in any region of the world, together with the myths associated with them, suffices to show that men and women have never been fooled by this tradition. They have always known and felt in their heart of hearts, whether they implicitly recognized or openly acknowledged it, that it is not men, but women who are marked by the plus sign, as it were, who are endowed with enhanced being because they have the privilege of carrying and bringing children into the world, and because they are, for this very reason, the guardians of life. It is men, by contrast, who suffer from a lack, which they try, for better or for worse, to compensate for by claiming for themselves a monopoly on belligerent behavior and the majority of ritual activities. Freud, in picturing the child as a phallic substitute, inverts both the natural and the cultural order. In reality, the affirmation of manhood substitutes for the capacity to procreate with which women have been equipped. In pretending to have the power to make male youths born again—youths whom they have symbolically killed in rites of initiation and transformed into fierce warriors—men almost invariably mimic, while at the same time they transpose, feminine activities of which they are thereby shown to be envious. Initiating fathers are mothers of substitution. Indeed, it is for this very reason that paternity is a matter of importance in most societies. Women are well aware of this, however, or guess as much, and they do not always make a secret of it. Among the Baruya, they greet the claim of men to beget warriors with derision, fabricating grotesque scarecrows as part of a ceremony parodying male rites of initiation.

They thus show themselves, on this point at least, to be far more lucid than Freud and all his fellow psychoanalysts put together.

Indeed, it is astonishing that this open secret should have escaped the great majority of observers and theorists. Not only psychoanalysts, for whom the standard Oedipal triangle reduces the mother to a libidinal object that father and son fight over for the right of possession and, in the female version of the complex, to a rival of the daughter, who, owing to an odd sort of detour, is alone recognized as capable of bringing forth children; but also, with only a few exceptions,[1] anthropologists of all persuasions, who, while they are in no way unaware of what is going on, give the impression of closing their eyes to a fact of life so banal that it hardly merits a moment's attention. Only a few isolated voices, notably male—Francis Martens (1975), for example, and especially Pierre Clastres—have dared to say, frankly and plainly, that femininity resides above all in maternity, and that this attribute, which is specific to her, makes woman and not man the stronger sex. "The essential property of women," Clastres writes in one of his last essays, "which integrally defines their being, is to assure the biological, and beyond that, [the] social reproduction of the community: women bring children into the world. Far from [being] consumed object, or exploited subject, they are producers of those whom society cannot do without: namely, children, as the tribe's immediate and distant future" (Clastres [1977] 1994, 194).

In the primitive societies studied by Clastres, man is essentially a warrior, hunter, and sacrificer. He is a "being-for-death," whereas the woman, as mother, is a "being-for-life" (ibid., 195). But this opposition, which may be marked by taboos (the prohibitions, for example, against men touching women's baskets and against women touching men's bows [see Clastres, 1966]), transcends cultural differences, as the ethnologist clearly grasps. It has a natural foundation that culture serves only to modulate. Demography demonstrates that, from the moment of conception, the female is much more firmly attached to life than the male. There are more stillbirths among male than among female children, and, although about 105 boys are born for every 100 girls, by the end of the first year of life, solely as an effect of naturally occurring rates of infant mortality, the number of girls will have overtaken that of boys their age; moreover, this advantage will be preserved and added to throughout their lives. Of course, these statistics may be modified by the incidence of female infanticide and, in our own time, selective abortion, but it is precisely the gap observed in relation to the natural norm that makes it possible to detect and measure the extent of such practices in populations that prefer to conceal them. The same is true of adult behaviors, which evidently have an effect on mortality rates, but which confirm that, all other things being equal, women are more long-lived than men. The statistics concerning suicide are no less illuminating. Durkheim was the first to rigorously demonstrate that suicide may vary as a function of various social factors, but he was obliged to recognize a fact that stood out from the masses of data he analyzed: no matter which parameter is considered, it is always the case that fewer women take their own lives than men: "To every woman [who kills herself] there are on the average four male suicides" (Durkheim [1897] 1951, 72). Yet Durkheim does not choose to dwell on this remarkable phenomenon, and one may easily guess the reason why: it cannot be fitted into his explanatory framework. He mentions it only in passing, in a chapter devoted to the possible relationship between suicide and madness, and does not even include it in the very detailed table of contents (nine pages in a small font) that accompanies his work.

It is well to recall these things in order to avoid being intimidated by certain dissenting voices that, while they have the merit of rejecting the Freudian model of femininity, maintain that there is no difference in principle between men and women, and insist on their complete interchangeability, which they confuse with equality of rights; in order to avoid being bewitched by theories of gender that, in holding sexual orientation to be indeterminate, construe the social differentiation of masculine and feminine as an arbitrary construction aimed only at legitimizing extant power relations. These antinaturalist fantasies are outlandish outgrowths of existentialism and of the opposition, dating back to the Sophists, between *phusis* and *nomos*. It is nevertheless futile to deny the existence of a distinctively human nature and to set the given against the constructed. For it is in the very nature of being human that we belong to the species *Homo faber*. And if some of our constructions are more solid than others, it is precisely because we are neither masters of essences nor lords of forms. No more than a saw can be made out of wool, to borrow Aristotle's image (*Metaphysics* 8.4 [1044ᵃ 29]), or salad greens grown by tearing off their leaves, as the Chinese proverb has it, no human society can be made out of undifferentiated individuals who construct their gender apart from norms of any kind and solely by virtue of their own goodwill.

Since art does nothing more than imitate nature, as Aristotle famously said, there is good reason to believe that if the artificial womb prophesied by some and devoutly wished for by others is one day realized, it will no more take the place of natural wombs than the computer has caused (or ever will cause) the human brain to disappear.

CHAPTER TWO

Procreation and Headhunting

Fatherhood among the Marind

Stéphane Breton, in an article influenced by psychoanalysis, studies a practice described by Jan van Baal[1] that well illustrates what may be called the Clastres thesis, for the very manner in which ritual gives fatherhood its full value in this case implicitly reveals the primacy of feminine power. This example will detain us for quite some time, as much because of its intrinsic interest as because of the reactions it has provoked among those who have commented on it.

Let us look at the facts of the matter. Among the Marind-anim of Irian Jaya (the western part of New Guinea), a man fulfills his paternal responsibility by giving a name to his children, but he can do this only by setting out to cut off the head of a man from a neighboring tribe, whose very last words (or last mumblings) will constitute this name. The club he must use to crack the skull of his victim, before asking his name and decapitating him, is made of a stone disk attached to a shaft and is supposed to represent a couple copulating. The disk itself represents the pudenda of an old woman, Sobra, to whom the invention of headhunting is ascribed (see Breton 1999, 84–90).

These details are significant. They make it clear that this act of male belligerence is the equivalent of female reproductive capacity. What is more, they amount to an implicit recognition of the subordination of the masculine to the feminine. Not only do women bring children into the world, they are also the inventors of headhunting, which confers on men the status of paternity and, by virtue of just this, constitutes a male substitute for gestation.

All this, of course, is suggested rather than stated. But in representing the ritual of headhunting as a sort of gift that women once made to men long ago, the Sobra myth takes things the wrong way around. It obscures the fact that, in reality, it is men who try to deprive women of their reproductive functions, through a form of symbolic predation. Among the Marind, it is not the ability to bear children that allows a woman to accede to motherhood; only marriage makes this possible. Thus the newborn child of a young unmarried woman, conceived during the ritual orgies that the Marind organize on many occasions, is put to death at once (see Breton 1999, 87). A married woman, by contrast, becomes a mother solely by virtue of the fact of her marriage, before even conceiving a child. Her marriage does not really involve anything more than a change of name. Following a common practice, known as teknonymy, she is henceforth called "mother of ——," where the blank is to be filled in with the name that her husband will have chosen for their future child. At the origin of childbirth, then, there is no female capacity for begetting, only the initiative, taken by a man, to go out and bring back someone's head, and with it a name. In this way he becomes a father. That is not all. When a woman marries, she is offered up, in the course of a ritual orgy, to all the men of her husband's clan or phratry, even before her husband has been able to have sexual relations with her (see 86). Without anything actually being said, it is a way of asserting, Breton notes, that a woman is able to conceive and bear children in her womb through this collective action alone. It is only owing to the intervention of men, in other words, and specifically of a father, that women can enjoy the condition of maternity. For the Marind, in a society without father or husband there would be neither mother nor children.[2]

The accession of a man to fatherhood, and consequently of a woman to motherhood, therefore unfolds in two stages, for it comprises two complementary rites, each of which is necessary without being sufficient. It is necessary first that the husband go away in search of a head and a name, enabling him to confer particular rights on the child to be born; next, that a group of male relatives perform a collective rape, the source of life and fertility, so that his wife can have a child. But these two successive male predatory acts, individual in the one case, collective in the other, are in a sense concealed by a notional exchange of services between the representatives of the two sexes. Headhunting is thought of as a sort of gift sponsored by Sobra, in the name of all women, that allows each man to become a father, and the collective appropriation of the reproductive power of women by the male group as a gift in return, of fertility and of life, that will aid the married woman in becoming a mother. Exclusively male predation—tendentiously regarded as the only legitimate form of accession to parenthood[3]—is thus disguised as an exchange of gifts between men and women. The mythic representation nonetheless implies the tacit recognition, by the male part of the community, of being fundamentally subservient to its female part.

Lacanian Interlude: The True Name of a Lack and the Difference between the Sexes

Stéphane Breton, for his part, because he seeks primarily to understand how society contributes to the "definition of the subject," is less interested in the relations between men and women than in the expression of the individual and collective aspects of male rites and in the relations that come to be created through them between subject and object. The subject, he holds, is mutually codetermined in relation to a "separate object"—in the event, the trophy brought back from headhunting and the name that is attached to it, so that it can be transmitted to another. The naming ceremony makes both the adult who transmits the name truly a father, and the child who receives it truly human. This rite, he says, is governed by a "principle of individuation," and puts "the final touch on a joint effort" that, without it, would be "incomplete" (Breton 1999, 87). In reality, however, as we have just seen, it is the communal rape that is supposed to put the final touch on the marriage by giving corporeal existence to a child whose father, for his part, has previously chosen the mother and the child's name. Nevertheless, since the father-child relation presupposes that a trophy will have been brought back from a headhunting ritual, and since the appropriation and the transfer of the woman's reproductive capacities to the father are not the doing of the father himself, but of the male group as a whole, Breton can with some reason infer from this example, and from another structurally similar example, two things: on the one hand, that "the object defines the subject" (103), and on the other that "the unconscious is not solipsistic, but social through and through" (111). Though he employs the vocabulary of psychoanalysis, he thus directly takes issue with psychoanalytic orthodoxy, which tends, to the contrary, to dissolve the collective in the individual.[4]

And yet Breton does not seem to see that his empirical findings entitle him to challenge the "androcentric" conception of the difference between the sexes no less forcefully than the psychoanalytic orthodoxy inherited from Freud. On this point, he limits himself to substituting an intellectualized version of castration, due to the Lacanians, for that of the Freudian vulgate, criticized by the Lacanians for its naiveté though they retain its male bias.[5] If the theme of castration appears in the mythology of the Marind, it is less, he says, in the way of a singular event than as a figure of an "original absence." Castration in this mythology does not signify the loss of a real object, but that of an "object that by definition is *lacking*." This organ therefore cannot be the penis, the male organ, but the phallus, which designates "something that is conspicuous by its absence" and of which the penis is only one of many illusory reifications. Supposing this to be true, two questions at once arise. If the phallus and the penis really are so different, why should they be confused so frequently? And, more generally, why should this sexual symbolism exist in the first place? Why should the phallus be the preeminent signifier of an original absence?

Breton himself does not raise these questions. An allusive reminder of Freudian dogma seems to him sufficient. "Obscured by the reification of the penis, and of the mythological substitutes that are forever being severed," he says, "is a dread of the apparently neutered genitalia of the woman" (Breton 1999, 92; full text of this passage given in n. 5). And yet, in the ethnography on which he relies, no evidence of such a dread is to be found, nor anything else that would support such a claim. The Sobra myth shows that, for the Marind, the female genitalia are neither a wound, the sign of a neutered body, nor the signifier of a lack, of something missing; to the contrary, they are the source of life and the origin of the world—which, after all, is at least as credible as the theory of infantile urges imagined by Freud.

As for the naming ceremony, to which we must come back one last time, it too can be seen to point in the same direction once the basis for it has been examined a bit more carefully. Breton himself mentions it in the sentence immediately before the one I have just quoted and commented on. Curiously, however, he fails to see that the details he assembles here spoil the image he is about to present of the mutilated genitalia and the dread they inspire. In the course of the ceremony, he recalls, the father does not transmit to his son an organ or an object, but instead a symbol "whose resemblance"—and this is the crux of the matter—"to the notion of a 'name true,' designated among the Marind by the female genital organs, cannot be ignored." To decipher this sibylline remark and show that it falsifies the claim he now proceeds at once to assert, one has only to recall what Breton has just told us, a few pages before, about the "name true" and its relationship to the feminine. From the ethnographic account, we know that, in the course of their initiation rites, the novices learn a secret language that is supposed to reveal to them the real name of things. This by itself is in no way exceptional, but the Marind seem to attach much greater importance to it than other peoples, and in this regard to display a combination of sophistication and zealousness that is distinctive enough to attract the attention of a Lacanian anthropologist. "The mythological names," Breton says, "fit together in accordance with the formula of a nested esotericism offering a ritual name the possibility of being eclipsed by a higher-order name. All this is governed by the quest for what they call the 'name true,' *pa-igiz* (a generic term designating the names given by fathers to their children), which itself is a 'name true.' Mixed up with the mythological origin of things, this truth is expressed by a word designating the female genitalia. Behind the name there emerges the source, the womb" (ibid., 88).

In other words, no secret name is necessarily the actual name of what it is supposed to designate, for behind this name there may be another name, and so on. But the chain of secret names, unlike the signifying chain of the Lacanians, has a final link, so that the quest for the actual name is not perpetuated indefinitely: it reaches an endpoint in the name of the female genitalia, the origin of all names, and "behind the name there emerges the source, the womb." The naming ritual therefore does indeed imply the female sex organ, only in this case not as something mutilated but rather as the source of life, not as something that inspires dread but instead as something that arouses envy. The wound, if it is in fact a wound,[6] is sustained by men, frustrated by their inability to do what their female mates are capable of doing, namely, to give birth. The constitutive, and supposedly phallic, symbol of paternity is neither an imaginary penis nor a pure signifier of something lacking, but instead an idealized womb.

Incompleteness of the Human Being or
Missing Part of the Male Subject?

The conclusion Breton draws therefore seems to me inadmissible. "According to the Marind," he says, "man is defined by a *missing part*. This part can complete the subject, if such a thing is possible, only on the condition that its purely symbolic character is doubly attested: it cannot be kept to oneself, it must be transmitted" (1999, 92). This assertion suffers from several purely logical defects. It attributes to a particular group of people a general conception of man and society that is not explicitly present in it, but which its ethnography seems to corroborate, and which in reality is due to Breton himself, as the argument of his article as a whole makes clear. Two levels of analysis are confused here: that of the observer and that of the object observed. This is all the more damaging since an indigenous theory, where one exists, forms a part, no less than customs and institutions do, of the phenomena that anthropological theory must explain. Furthermore—and this is essential for our purposes—Breton's assertion has the additional defect of conflating two distinct propositions having neither the same reference nor the same meaning. For in drawing out the implication of the naming ritual, only by abolishing the fact of sexual difference, it treats as characteristic of people in general, of the human subject, a trait peculiar to the male of the species, whose true nature it moreover fails to indicate. It thus sets up as a universal proposition—true or false, but in any case unproven—a more specific proposition, grounded in experience but still poorly defined.

Formulated more prosaically, but also more explicitly, these two propositions amount to the following. Among the Marind, as among all other peoples, human beings, male and female, are finite creatures. Since their desires always exceed their capacities, they are subject to want. From this it follows that they are neither masters nor possessors of life; they have the power only to bring children into the world and to raise them. This is the first proposition. But whereas women give life to children, men can only give them names and other cultural goods, which is to say symbolic capital. The "missing part" of the male subject is nothing other than the ability to give birth, which he does in fact lack. One may even say, to use the Lacanian idiom, that the ability to give birth is an "original lack," since none of a man's male ancestors has ever possessed it, and that it will be perpetuated indefinitely, since none of his male descendants will ever be able to enjoy it. Only substitute symbols can populate male lines of descent—where, if one wishes to look for it there, the characteristic property of the Lacanian "signifying chain" may be found. This is the second proposition.

Is there a link between the two propositions? Could it be that the second one is only a particular, male version of the first, one among many other possible ones, and one that indeed might have a female counterpart? This cannot be ruled out.[7] But Breton has not demonstrated such a link, and the ethnography on which he relies does not permit it to be established. In making the unwarranted claim, by way of conclusion, that human beings in general "suffer from an irremediable incompleteness" (1999, 112), he ignores the evidence that he himself has assembled, that it is always and only the male subject[8] who suffers in this way, since the male has never been and never will be pregnant—unless one day a uterus can be surgically grafted onto him, as certain feminists, whose hopes may one day be fulfilled by advances in medical technology, have recommended. In passing surreptitiously from the particular to the universal, from the male sex to the human species, Breton does away with the dialectic of fatherhood and motherhood, which none-theless constitutes the heart of the ethnography he lays out, and thus misses an authentically universal truth: the asymmetry of the sexes, whose irreduc-ible character the Marind remind us of by the very manner in which they try to disguise it, by converting it into a form of exhibition. What Breton calls "the spectacle of things"—thus the title of his article—is, among other things (but above all), a staging of this primary and fundamental asymmetry. In all societies, no matter how men conceive of female procreation, they must face up to this indisputable truth: it is women who bring children into the world and thus assure, first and foremost, the survival of the group and the continuity of generations.

From the Privilege of Giving Birth
to the Burden of Procreation

Was there any need for such a long detour to end up at such a trivial result? Certainly not—except for the purpose of showing how even fine and cul-tured minds, in the presence of this basic truth, may yet be moved to bring all the resources of their learning and intelligence to bear on the task of getting around it, or else drowning it in a sea of generalities. In the belief that they are exposing the sources of vernacular strategies and theories, they construct new variants from them, using similar procedures. But this very activity tells us as much about the reality it fails to grasp as about the assumptions that prevent it from doing so. For if anthropology congratulates itself on having escaped ethnocentrism, it is itself culturally situated; it professes axiological neutrality without being able to cease being normative. Thus it is that, in our own day, anthropology is often a companion of the Western tendency to neglect procreation or even to denigrate it.

In attaching importance to sexuality, at the expense of procreation, psychoanalysis helped to promote this tendency and to legitimize it. In principle, and by definition, a mother is a woman capable of giving birth and of transmitting this power to her daughter. No more than there can be a child without a mother, there cannot be a mother without a child. But in classical Freudian theory, the mother is before everything else a libidinal object and the seat of a lack, or deficiency, which she transmits to her daughter and for which the child is merely a palliative, nothing more. In Lacanian theory,[9] more generous and more egalitarian than Freudian theory, this lack is more equitably distributed between the two sexes, which has the effect of concealing their true asymmetry and favoring the male point of view. In both cases, men and women are sexual beings, but the child is not, strictly speaking, a constitutive element of the difference between the sexes.[10] In postulating an equivalence in principle among all sexual orientations, the practitioners of gender theory take one more step toward freeing sexuality from any link with procreation.

Among the Marind, almost every social institution grows out of a concern for producing descendants and of managing relations between the sexes to this end. It is not in order to satisfy sexual impulses, but instead to enjoy the status of fatherhood, that men cut off heads, forcing themselves to travel a hundred kilometers, if need be, in order to find an appropriate victim. The ritual orgies themselves, which are an aspect of the same process, have a social, not a libidinal, function: "They caused much weariness in the participants, who took part only because they answered to a higher necessity" (Breton 1999, 86).

But in the West, and above all in the "enlightened" and "liberated" circles of the intelligentsia, procreation, and especially motherhood, which elsewhere is considered an enviable privilege, tends to be regarded as a lowly occupation, a heavy burden, if not actually an obscene activity[11] that should for this reason be proscribed or else shared between the two sexes until it can be safely entrusted to artificial insemination and mechanical incubators.[12] Curiously, very few ethnologists seem to notice this. Among authors writing in French, Marika Moisseeff, whose fine article (2000) wittily and perceptively describes the customs of the Dentcico (an anagram of "Occident"), is a happy exception.

Moreover, the ethnography of the Marind, punctuated by gang rapes, warlike expeditions, and the like, poses another problem. Western anthropologists today, whether they are directly exposed to these brutal practices or only made aware of them through the accounts of earlier authors, are accustomed to say and think that there are not savage and civilized peoples, only different peoples, and thereby repress or conceal the feelings of repulsion that these practices cannot help but inspire in them. Accordingly, anthropologists describe things in theatrical terms, as matters of staging or, as in the case of Breton, of spectacle. The aesthetic perspective serves as a defense mechanism. Lévi-Strauss's four-volume work *Mythologiques*, filled with musical themes, names of plants and flowers, and other bucolic flourishes, and equipped with an index expurgated of any terms having a violent connotation, is a model of the genre. And yet to gloss over the bloody character of headhunting—to act as though it were, for a father, an innocent way of discovering a name for his child, and thus of gaining entry to the realm of symbolism—instead of calling attention to the fact that, almost everywhere in the world, killing is the male equivalent of giving birth, dying on a battlefield the equivalent of dying in labor, and so on, is to turn a blind eye to the very real violence committed by human beings. This form of denial, this refusal to try to unravel the intimate relations, attested in every part of the earth, between ritual and violence, between the gift of life and the gift of death, is all the more awkward since whatever speculative appeal psychoanalysis may have is indissociable from the prospect it holds out of restoring to anthropology the feelings and the impulses that structuralism, in the intellectualized version given it by its leading exponents, has ceaselessly worked to repress (see Green 1999; Gillison 1999).

CHAPTER THREE

The Guardians of Dogma

Jones, Malinowski, and the Maternal Uncle

f we come back now to the disciples with whom Freud surrounded himself in order to bridge the gap between psychoanalysis and anthropology, it will become apparent that things went downhill from the very beginning. In spite of his dogmatism, the author of *Totem and Taboo* had nonetheless hesitated, it will be recalled, between opposite ways of conceiving the relationship between psychological disorders and civilization, and consequently between the individual and society. One might therefore have expected the young and brilliant minds he had gathered around him to undertake original research on possible links between the generative mechanisms of mental illness and the ones at work in the formation of cultures, and, armed with fresh documentary materials, to set out to rethink the whole Oedipal problem from top to bottom. But not at all. Far from taking their teacher's doubts seriously and showing a willingness to modify his doctrine in the light of new evidence, they almost always made mechanical or purely exegetical use of his hypotheses, accepting all of them together instead of separating the true from the false; commenting on them instead of submitting them to empirical test; appending them to ethnographic descriptions instead of weighing their validity against these descriptions. It was as if Freudian theory, now and forever more, constituted a body of principles and proofs so coherent that not a single one could be removed without threatening the entire edifice with collapse; a set of propositions so well established that none of them could be grasped without immediately being assented to, and that any criticism would be bound to rest on errors or misunderstandings.[1]

A century later, then, one has the impression of looking back on a series of missed opportunities, a waste of energy and time that might have been more profitably employed at a time when so many fine minds had fervently embraced the ambition of conquering the human sciences. But in rereading the writings of this period, one also has the sense that the zeal (or, less charitably, the juvenile enthusiasm) and the curiosity that animate them, the profusion of ideas and intuitions they display, the wealth of information that spills out from the interpretive framework erected to contain it—that all these things, which some might regard as the very signs of scientific maturity, have a much greater chance of giving wings to a new generation of researchers than the fragmented studies and the lack of theoretical perspective that are typical of our own time. The American cultural anthropologist Alfred Kroeber, for example, without having changed his mind about the deep misgivings about psychoanalysis he had expressed earlier in his career, was forthright in giving Freud credit for uncovering important aspects of human nature, for asking the right questions, and for his incomparable theoretical ingenuity (see Kroeber 1920, 1939). Despite their dogmatism and their lack of originality, Freud's disciples are also worthy of our consideration, particularly with regard to a number of crucial points whose significance for the most part escaped them, but which almost in spite of themselves they did much to elucidate.

The Art of Deciphering Symbols, or Jones between Bouvard and Pécuchet

We owe to Ernest Jones a study of the superstitions relating to salt and related substances, "The Symbolic Significance of Salt" (Jones 1951, 22–109), written in the style of Frazer and impressively documented. But in seeking to explain all the factual evidence amassed in support of the idea that salt symbolizes sperm, he arbitrarily privileges one of the terms of the comparison. The advantage of doing this is far from clear. Over the course of many pages he makes one think rather of Bouvard and Pécuchet, the characters in Flaubert's eponymous novel who collected all sorts of reputedly phallic objects: "They collected whippletrees from horse-carts, chair legs, door bolts, pharmacists' pestles. When someone came to see them, they asked, 'What do you think this looks like?' and then divulged the mystery. And if the person protested, they shrugged their shoulders, out of pity" (Flaubert [1881] 2005, 99).

Jones reasons as a student of technology who errs through anthropomorphism might. It is not because human beings have three sorts of teeth that they created three sorts of tools having the same functions. It is because, for geometric reasons, there are only three possible modes of percussion (punctiform, linear, diffuse) between a tool and a material, and therefore only three fundamental modes of action on the material (piercing, cutting, grinding), that human beings have necessarily been equipped with three types of teeth, and so have created three types of tools to perform these same operations. Or, to take another example, closer to our subject, it is not because the same Magdalenian object—a staff made from the antler of a reindeer, bulbous and pierced with a hole at one end—has successively been regarded by anthropologists as a ritual object (baton), an accessory of hunting and war (arrow straightener and assegai launcher), and, more recently, an instrument of sexual pleasure (dildo) that this last hypothesis turns out to be the right one, even if it is possible that no researcher would have dared to publish it, or even to conceive of it, before Freudian ideas became commonplace. Psychoanalysis has succeeded in enlarging its field of inquiry, but nothing more. In this case we are dealing with three mutually compatible functions—and there is nothing exceptional about this case.

Those who are committed to a dogmatic interpretation of sexual symbolism forget that mankind is not an empire within an empire, and that the creativity of nature, like that of mankind, which is a modality of it, is subject to very strong constraints. As René Thom observes: "If dynamic geometric forms representing sexual processes are encountered in so many objects of animate and inanimate nature, it is because these forms are the only structurally stable ones in our space-time that realize their fundamental function as the union of gametes after spatial transport. One might almost say that these forms preexist sexuality, which is perhaps only their genetically stabilized manifestation" (Thom [1972] 1977, 97). It is true that Jones was sometimes aware of the limits of his work. "It need hardly be said that demonstration of the sexual origin and meaning of the materials used in a given religious ritual," he modestly conceded in an essay published in 1912, "is far from explaining even the unconscious basis of that ritual" (Jones 1951, 93). But a few years later he seems to have forgotten this scruple. In a lecture of 1928 that revisited certain aspects of his earlier study, he mentions the custom of throwing rice at weddings. While noting that confetti was now often used in place of rice, he presents the matter as though the strictly sexual symbolism that may be ascribed to the grains of this marsh grass is the key to everything: "It would doubtless be agreed that the rice in this context represents the idea of fertility, and the act of throwing it the corresponding wish in respect of the bridal couple. Psycho-analysis would say that the rice is an *emblem* of fertility, but a *symbol* of seed; and they would mean by this that investigation of the unconscious would show that it was the idea of seed there from which all the other acts and thoughts proceeded" (11).

In reality, neither the emblematic significance attributed to rice nor the unconscious sexual symbolism that Jones imagines he has detected in it can help make sense of this custom, for the same type of ritual behavior is found elsewhere, in other contexts. We know, for example, that in ancient Greece, before sacrificing an ox, grains of barley were thrown at it, or sometimes leaves. The parallelism with rice and confetti is striking, and in the Greek case, at least, there is no mystery: a ritual stoning, itself more or less harmless in effect, inaugurates a series of increasingly violent acts leading to a fatal result—the ox is lashed with grains of barley, then shorn of its coat, then knocked to the ground and its throat slit (see Burkert [1966] 2001, 11–12). The comparison with the Greek rite is even less incongruous as, in the case of marriage, it sometimes occurs that stoning actually takes place among the two families in attendance: "[A] combat breaks out between the two groups. Stones are thrown, and many heads are battered. The scars and wounds . . . [serve] as proof of the wedding contract" (Franz Boas, quoted in Girard [1972b] 1977, 248; also in Lévi-Strauss [1958b] 1973, 204). It may even be that a man dies—"a sign that the newlyweds will never part" (Boas, quoted in Lévi-Strauss, ibid.). Far, then, from imparting clarity, Jones's supposed psychoanalytic explanation prevents us from seeing a true problem that goes beyond the particular case in question: why on earth is it necessary to make a pretense of stoning in rites as important as marriage and sacrifice?

Moreover, from the point of view of psychoanalysis itself, which is to say of the relationship between the conscious and the unconscious, there is no reason to grant sperm a special status. To judge from ethnographic accounts, sperm does not necessarily have to be concealed or disguised by the mental apparatus. Jones omits to say, or else is unaware, that sperm figures in certain rites no less explicitly than urine, which he considers a more respectable substitute and of which he furnishes many examples. Thus, among the Baruya of New Guinea, for example, sperm is orally transferred from elders to the young in the course of initiations, for it is supposed to give men the power to create warriors without the aid of women, and, once transmitted from husband to wife during the first days of marriage, to give the future mother the ability to breastfeed her children (see Godelier [1982] 1986). If the ingestion of sperm by novices in the course of initiation must remain a secret act, it is by no means an unconscious one: the novices are sworn not to divulge the secret. Once again, the crux of the matter is an attempt by males to assure themselves of the most complete control possible over procreation—an attempt that is itself often tacit, but not unconscious or repressed. Here we find ourselves not so much in the symbolic and hermeneutic sphere as in the world of human beings, faced with the practical details of how they interact with one another.

No doubt Jones himself took these interactions into account, seeing them as evidence of a contest between members of the two sexes,[2] and even among men themselves, as we will see shortly, for control over the children of their group. But he had no intention of leaving it at that. Anything that did not come under the head of sexual theory or that could not be fitted into the standard Oedipal framework seemed to him to be secondary, if not in fact altogether marginal. His interpretation of systems of matrilineal descent (see Jones 1951, 145–73) is no less instructive in showing how difficult it was for psychoanalysis to learn from ethnography, because of its fear of having to modify basic principles. Jones's interpretation is, above all, a reply to Malinowski: an effort to protect analytic orthodoxy.

Oedipus Complex and Matrilineal Regime: The Conflict of Interpretations

Bronisław Malinowski, the great ethnologist of the Trobriand Islands, nonetheless attached a great deal of importance to what Freud chose to call the "Oedipus complex." He objected only that this convenient term, adapted to

Western societies, should be used to refer to a configuration more general than the one Freud described and capable, too, of assuming other forms as a function of the kinship system. Thus in Trobriand society, where in accordance with the system of matrilineal descent the maternal uncle has responsibilities that in our society are reserved to the father, one does in fact find the two components of the complex—a desire for the death of an adult relative and incestuous sexual desire—but otherwise directed. It is toward his maternal uncle, who belongs to the same clan as he does, and not toward his father, who belongs to another clan, that the Trobriand boy has hostile feelings, and it is his sister, not his mother, whom he desires sexually and who is the object of the strictest taboo. Freud therefore rightly detected a universal structure, but studied only one of its variants, which he wrongly took to be the only one possible. The Oedipus complex proper is evidently a later form that appeared with patriarchal societies threatened with extinction.[3]

As often happens in the other sciences, Malinowski did not dispute Freud's discovery, but rather proposed a more general version of it. His goodwill and sense of scholarly decorum were not to Jones's liking, however. As far as Jones was concerned, the Freudian model in its accepted form was universal. Strictly speaking, there can be no matrilineal variant of the standard model; to the contrary, it is on the basis of this model that the existence and the properties of matrilineal systems and of their avuncular complex are to be explained. Such systems are merely "a mode of defence against the primordial Oedipus tendencies" (Jones 1951, 170) and, more particularly, a way to *deflect the hostility felt by the growing boy towards his father*" (159; emphasis in the original). The same is true of feigned ignorance—otherwise known as denial—of the role played by the father in conception, which both expresses this hostility and protects its object against it. This argument, the psychoanalyst believed, sufficed to settle the question. His verdict was plain, and exempt from any further appeal: "On Malinowski's hypothesis the Oedipus complex would be a late product; for the psycho-analyst it [is] the *fons et origo*" (170). To this the anthropologist replied, in effect, that he had been misunderstood. He did not contest the universality of the Oedipus complex, only the explanatory power that psychoanalysis attributed to it. This complex of drives and affects, this "correlated system of sentiments" (Malinowski 1927, 178) is indeed present in all societies, but it is not, for all of that, the source and the sufficient reason of the kinship systems within which it is deployed.

Their disagreement was fruitless in the end: Jones lacked the means to reconstruct the matrilineal system on the basis of the classic Oedipus complex, Malinowski the means to deduce his particular version of the Oedipal triangle of the matrilineal structure. Indeed, whether the rule of descent is matrilineal or patrilineal, bilinear or cognatic, all peoples, despite a few apparent exceptions,[4] prohibit the union of a mother and son, of a father and daughter, of a brother and sister. There is therefore no mechanical link, in one direction or another, between the mode of descent and the prohibition of incest. In *Totem and Taboo*, Freud had moreover already noted that the matrilineal regime as such was not opposed to the union of a father with daughter, nor the patrilineal regime with that of a mother with son, and yet both were proscribed (see Freud [1913] 1955, 5 n. 1).

Jones gives the impression of trying to evade this difficulty. Approaching the Oedipus complex with an eye not to its sexual component, but rather to its aggressive aspect, he is almost exclusively interested in preventing the possibility of "father murder." But this concern is groundless. For while matrilineal descent, together with the exogamy rule, has the effect ipso facto of statutorily separating a son from his father, it nevertheless does not physically keep the two of them apart. Malinowski's findings demonstrate this clearly. Among the Trobriand Islanders, one finds very strictly monitored avoidance behavior, only there it involves brother and sister, who are kept apart from each other from earliest childhood (see Malinowski 1927, 10). By contrast, a boy maintains close relations with his parents, and particularly with his father, whom he regards as a playmate. Not only is there physical proximity between them, but also complete intimacy. The father is thus his most distant relative statutorily, and the closest affectively. Exactly the opposite obtains in respect of the person exercising parental authority, the maternal uncle, who is genealogically the closest relative, but affectively, and even geographically, the most distant. Indeed, the rule of patrilocal residence, which, in combination with the taboo governing relations between brother and sister, obliges a married woman to leave her matrilineal group and go live with that of her husband (figure 1), has the effect that the maternal uncle and the uterine nephew always belong to distinct residential units.

If now we consider the matter from the point of view of preventing incest, Jones's hypothesis appears to be still more untenable. For while a matrilineal regime could spare the father Laius's fate simply by making him an affinal,

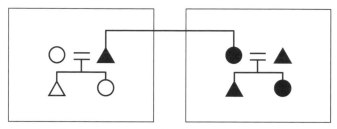

FIGURE 1. Matrilineal Descent and Patrilocal Residence

or even a stranger, it cannot completely protect the mother against the fate of Jocasta; indeed, if the risk of incest were really as formidable as Freudian orthodoxy imagines, the opposite would be true. One would therefore expect to find elaborate precautionary measures instituted in order to lessen this danger. We find nothing of the kind, however. Only the sister is subject to a strict rule of avoidance behavior. As for the mother, she is protected only by the exogamy rule, which also applies to her daughter. Why does her daughter benefit from this supplementary precaution when it should have been intended exclusively for her own benefit? Moreover, to the extent that the father is not a relative, in this case there is nothing in the matrilineal principle itself that would erect a barrier against an incestuous relationship with his daughter. The temptation of giving into this illicit desire is all the greater, Malinowski observes, as there is a taboo that strictly prohibits the brother and the maternal uncle from "tak[ing] any interest in her sexual affairs, . . . [and so], strangely enough, [it is] her father who is her guardian as regards matrimonial arrangements." And yet, "sexual intercourse between the two is considered in the highest degree reprehensible, though it is never given the name of *suvasova*, which means breach of exogamy" (Malinowski 1927, 72). There is a good reason for this: the prohibition that falls upon them is specific; in no way does it derive from either the mode of descent or the law of exogamy.

However one looks at the matter, then, the conclusion is the same. With all due respect to Jones, the matrilineal regime could not be a defense mechanism against the Oedipal impulses that psychoanalysis attributes to children. If a boy were spontaneously led to sexually desire his mother and to kill his father, nothing peculiar to the matrilineal structure would serve to counteract the propensity to incest and parricide. What the Trobriand example shows is the utter gratuitousness of this kind of interpretation. It is futile to object that sexual and murderous impulses have been displaced, redirected in this case toward the sister and the maternal uncle. Nothing in the description given by Malinowski justifies such a concession to psychoanalysis. The ethnographic facts suggest instead that the relationship psychoanalysis postulates between desire and prohibition should be stood on its head. In this regard we will be justified in criticizing Jones more harshly than Malinowski himself did. Malinowski noted that Jones's analysis amounts to making the maternal uncle a scapegoat (see ibid., 138). But why should the son need a scapegoat if his relations with his father are altogether peaceable? And why should the son reorient toward his sister Oedipal impulses that originally were directed toward his mother, and that, in the event, are the object of a less rigorous taboo? Surely it is simpler and more natural to suppose that, if he happens to manifest hostile feelings toward his uncle and to dream of incest with his sister, it is in reaction against the severity with which the one exercises his authority over him, and against the strictness of the taboo that has separated him since birth from the other. As for temptations to incest between father and daughter, Malinowski argues that these temptations are increased, rather than diminished, by virtue of the fact that they are prohibited between two persons who are not subject to the law of exogamy (72). Trobriand ethnography, by demonstrating the derivative and reactive character of the so-called Oedipal impulses, which we have already established on other grounds, plainly invites us to generalize this argument.

The Maternal Uncle: Substitute, Partner, or Rival of the Father?

Still, even if Jones is totally mistaken, Malinowski's explanation is not wholly satisfying. In showing that the prohibition of incest cannot be reduced to rules of descent and exogamy, he does no more than draw our attention to the complexity of social systems and suggest that they are more or less independent of the impulses and other mental phenomena with which Freud and his disciples tried to identify them. He does not manage to uncover their mechanisms, even for the Trobriand case alone. He finds it curious, for example, as we saw earlier, that it falls to the father to supervise the arrangements for the marriage of his daughter. Without claiming to be able to do any better, I should like nonetheless to make one further point in this connection. From Malinowski's account we know that, among the Trobriand Islanders, a man is chiefly concerned with the two members of the following generation who are closest to him: in the collateral line with the son of his sister, over whom he exercises, and then to whom he transmits, male authority over the matrilineal group to which they both belong; and in the direct line with his own daughter, who, by virtue of the prevailing mode of descent, belongs to another matrilineal group, but for whose marriage he is responsible in order to perpetuate the group's existence. Here once again we find a male ambition, the like of which we have already encountered among the Marind, to exert control over female procreation.

Jones allows us to take two further steps in this direction. He has both the virtue and the honesty of pointing out a pair of unsettling and even paradoxical facts, without, however, seeing that one is squarely opposed to his interpretation of matrilineage, and that the other must lead us to reconsider the whole Oedipus problem. The first is a reaction, noted also by Malinowski, that one could scarcely have expected to find in a society that denies the role of the father in conception. "A Trobriander," he observes, "is horrified at resembling his mother, brother, or sister; i.e., those who are thought to be his only blood relatives, and he is intensely insulted at the mere suggestion; he maintains, on the contrary, that he is the physical image of his father" (Jones 1951, 155). But this supposed resemblance between a son and his father evidently stands in contradiction to the uterine descent rule and the denial of any genetic link between them. But by the same token it utterly nullifies, if there were still any need to do so, the prophylactic effect that these things, in making a stranger of the father, are supposed to have in suppressing Oedipal impulses.

The second datum is observed in the patrilineal society of the Maori people of New Zealand, and reported by Edward Sidney Hartland thus: "When a child dies or even meets with an accident with fatal results, the mother's relatives, headed by her brother, turn out in force against the father. He must defend himself until he is wounded. Blood once drawn the combat ceases; but the attacking party plunders his house and appropriates

everything on which hands can be laid, finally sitting down to a feast provided by the bereaved father" (quoted in Jones 1951, 166). For Jones, this
violent episode confirms the Freudian thesis: "The father is thus punished
because his repressed hostile wishes have come true and the child has met
with harm" (166).

These "repressed wishs" are the famous counter-Oedipal drives whose
specious character we have already noted. Men, once they have become
adults, and knowing that they had previously desired the death of their
father, dread falling victim in their turn to the hostile feelings of their own
children; indeed, this fear may even push them to take preemptive action.
Thus, in spite of their name, counter-Oedipal impulses can manifest themselves even before the Oedipal impulses they are supposed to answer. All this
is purely conjectural, of course, but Jones believes it is supported by Reik's
work (see [1919] 1931, 27–166) on couvade and rites of initiation, matters
that I shall take up in a later chapter. And yet it does not explain the attitude
of the maternal uncle, who, strictly speaking, does not punish the father, but
avenges an injury and demands reparation for the harm he has suffered. The
death of the child puts everything in focus. Whereas the supposed Oedipal
and counter-Oedipal impulses that set father against son are purely hypothetical, and the paternal family plays no apparent role in the matter, there
is no mistaking the very real rivalry that exists between the two brothers-in-
law—a source of hostility where one would have expected to find amicable
relations between one who gives a woman and one who takes her.[5] How then
does it come about, in both a patrilineal society such as that of the Maori
and a matrilineal society such as that of the Trobrianders, that the mother's
brother can act as though he were always, by right, the legitimate guardian of
his sister's children?

Jones sees in the behavior of the uncle the vestiges of an ancient matrilineal social organization. Leaving aside the ad hoc and, more than this, the gratuitous character of this explanation,[6] even if one were to rehabilitate the old
evolutionist theory that every society initially passes through a matrilineal
stage, it would amount only to exchanging one question for another. For in
that case it would be the primacy of matrilineage that needs to be explained.
And Jones, as we already know, casts no light on this point.

CHAPTER FOUR

The Atom of Kinship, or the Absent Mother

n fairness to psychoanalysis, it must be recognized that anthropology itself has not always helped to clarify matters. In rejecting evolutionist theory, dismissing its vain pretensions and all its works and claiming to lay a foundation for the scientific study of ethnology while dispelling the unpleasant odors and miasmas of the past, anthropology not only hurt itself through an undeniable excess of youthful enthusiasm; it turned away from real problems and, at the same time, erected something very much like taboos around them. By placing all modes of descent and systems of kinship on the same level, by treating them as so many different but equivalent means of organizing family and social life, it not only diminished the importance of problems associated with historical succession and mutual influence among these different systems, but abjured any morphogenetic perspective, and indeed any consideration of the logical priority of one system in relation to another. This was particularly true in the case of structuralism.[1]

The fashion in which Lévi-Strauss treats the avuncular relationship, which is to say the relationship between maternal uncle and uterine nephew, is altogether exemplary. In a very famous essay devoted to this question, "Structural Analysis in Linguistics and in Anthropology" (1945) (reprinted in Lévi-Strauss [1958a] 1963, 31–54), he begins by objecting to the theories of his predecessors, notably among them the evolutionist theory endorsed, as we have just seen, by Jones. Lévi-Strauss observes, quite rightly, that if the privileged relationship between uncle and nephew in a patrilineal regime was merely a survival of an old matrilineal form of organization, it is not clear either why it should have been so widespread or why it often had a religious character, as Hocart showed, and as may be seen still today from the phonetic resemblance of the words *zio* and *Dio* in Italian and of *tio* and *Dios* in Spanish. The important place accorded the maternal uncle by the majority of kinship systems suggests that it does not depend on the mode of descent but on a feature that is common to all of them. What, then, is this universal feature, of which the uncle is the most manifest witness and even the canonical representative? For the author of *The Elementary Structures of Kinship*, who conceives of every marriage as an alliance between givers and takers of women, the answer is readily apparent. If the maternal uncle is present in all systems of kinship, it is owing to his role as a wife-giver.

Recall that, for Lévi-Strauss, every matrimonial alliance can be described as an exchange of women arranged by men who are, respectively, givers and takers of wives. This exchange is either bilateral and "restricted" to one or several pairs of partners (where A gives to B and B gives to A, while C gives to D and D gives to C, and so on) or unilateral and "generalized" to some indeterminate number of partners (A gives to B, who gives to C, who gives to D, and so on). The simplest form of restricted exchange is the exchange of sisters. The simplest form of generalized exchange is one in which a brother gives his sister in marriage to another man, who himself gives his own sister to a third man, and so on. In both cases, the future maternal uncle of the children is the wife-giver.

Now, if this is so, it will not do to say simply that every system of kinship rests on three types of relation: alliance (between husband and wife), descent (between parents and children), and shared parentage (between brothers and sisters). For the elementary family of our civil law, comprising a father and a mother and their children, includes these three types of relation without involving the transaction between wife-giver and wife-taker on which marriage is supposed to be based. It follows that this family unit, as it is commonly called, and which certain anthropologists still take to be the basic unit of every society, cannot in fact constitute the true element, or "atom," of kinship. The atom consists instead of a man (the wife-giver), his

Elementary Family   Atom of Kinship

FIGURE 2. Classic Elementary Family and "Atom of Kinship" according to Lévi-Strauss

sister, and his sister's husband (the wife-taker), and the child that issues from their union. This is a necessary consequence of the prohibition of incest and of the exogamy rule. Once the problem of the avunculate, as it is known, has been properly posed, it is immediately resolved. "Thus we do not need to explain how the maternal uncle emerged in the kinship structure: He does not emerge—he is present initially. Indeed, the presence of the maternal uncle is a necessary precondition for the structure to exist" (Lévi-Strauss [1958a] 1963, 46).

A Curious Omission

This solution is every bit as elegant as it is plausible. At first sight it does not seem vulnerable to any objection in principle. By contrast, the analysis and typology of atoms of kinship, which form the heart of Lévi-Strauss's essay (see ibid., 37–46), exhibit a peculiarity that few commentators seem to have noticed. Lévi-Strauss seeks to show that the customary attitudes of people toward one another form a system, to which the members of the unit of kinship are subject, and which are always in a kind of balance, similar to the equilibrium of positive and negative forces in atoms of matter.[2] Whether it is a question of relations between members of the same generation or of intergenerational relations, a positive (or free) relation always balances a negative (or antagonistic) relation. If the relation between brother and sister is antagonistic, the relation between husband and wife is free, and vice versa; if the relation between uncle and nephew is negative, the relation between father and son is positive, and vice versa. For reasons of stability, there are therefore only four possible elementary forms, which, represented with the aid of an obvious symbolism, are as follows: (+ − and + −), (+ − and − +), (− + and + −), and (− + and − +). Moreover, Lévi-Strauss holds that these variants do not depend on the mode of descent, but are attested in both matrilineal and patrilineal societies. Let us suppose that this is so. There remains a curious omission. Whereas Lévi-Strauss gives the impression of taking into account all of the possible relations obtaining between any two members of his elementary structure, in fact he leaves out two of them, and not the least significant ones for a typology of systems of attitudes: the mother-child relation (more specifically, in his model, the relation between mother and son) and the relation between brother and husband of the sister.

The Canadian ethnologist Pierre Maranda was the first, as far as I know, to notice this anomaly and to attempt to remedy it. But having done so in the course of a rather tedious article in which he tries to apply the "canonical formula of myth" to the atom of kinship (see Maranda 1963), his perceptiveness seems to have been almost wholly unappreciated. This is all the more regrettable since, despite an immoderate taste for formalization that general readers are apt to find intimidating and specialists beguiling, Maranda's structuralist piety was placed in the service of fundamental problems and enlivened by profound intuitions (see Scubla 1998, 140–51). Even if his reasoning in this case needs to be modified somewhat (see 149–50), he is not wrong to suspect a discrepancy between certain formal properties of the unit of kinship and the modeling of them proposed by Lévi-Strauss. In the elementary quartet consisting of three adults (one of them a woman) and a child, Maranda notes that the child has a "particular importance" and even constitutes the pivot of the structure; in Lévi-Strauss's model, the woman figures only as a spouse, possible or forbidden as the case may be, but not as a mother of the child. Thus Maranda insists on restoring this bond of descent to its rightful place alongside the relation of exogamy, and even "posing the problem of the unit of kinship on the basis of procreation rather than of the taboo of incest" (Maranda 1963, 817).

Now, this amendment is crucial. It amounts to turning Lévi-Strauss's theory of kinship, which accords priority to exogamy over procreation, and to marriage over descent, upside down. The elementary structures of kinship that Lévi-Strauss describes in his book of this title constitute a theory of the elementary structures of marriage. For Lévi-Strauss, marriage is not a way of assuring and perpetuating a line of descendants, but of creating social bonds by means of exchange between groups and lineages; consanguinity is a way of renewing and reinforcing the structure of exchange by transferring matrimonial debts from one generation to the next. On this view, procreation is not a primitive fact, but rather a secondary feature of the system, and so the presence of the child in the atom of kinship, far from being something obvious, stands in need of justification. For "if the relationship between 'brothers-in-law' is the necessary axis around which the kinship structure is built," Lévi-Strauss asks, "why need we bring in the child of the marriage when considering the elementary structure?" From the synchronic point of view, its presence is superfluous. Nevertheless, he argues, "the child is indispensable in validating the dynamic and teleological character of the initial step, which establishes kinship on the basis of and through marriage. Kinship is not a static phenomenon; it exists only in self-perpetuation. Here we are not thinking of the desire to perpetuate the race, but rather of the fact that in most kinship systems the initial disequilibrium produced in one generation between the group that gives the woman and the group that receives her can be stabilized only by counter-prestations in following generations" (Lévi-Strauss [1958a] 1963, 47). The child is therefore only a means of transferring a debt, and so of reactivating the system of exchange in each successive generation.

Lévi-Strauss is obviously not unaware that the reproductive faculties of women are the sine qua non of the survival of human communities. Unless I am mistaken, he explicitly acknowledges this at least once, in a passage that unfortunately I am no longer able to locate. But at the time when the essay in question was composed, this aspect of the matter seemed to him manifestly irrelevant to the theory he was developing of kinship, which, as I say, is almost exclusively a theory of marriage. In *The Elementary Structures of Kinship,* he reduces consanguinity to the hereditary transmission of a genetic heritage, which is to say, in the terms of his celebrated dichotomy, to a fact of "nature," before which "culture," he says, is "powerless" (Lévi-Strauss [1949c] 1969, 30). He contrasts it with marriage, which nature imposes on men as well, but this time without determining it, and which is therefore subject to cultural norms. And so if anthropology, according to a definition that goes back to

Kant, is the study of that which is peculiarly human in human beings, that is, the study of culture, it follows that marriage is wholly within its province, whereas patterns of descent and consanguinity, representing the animal part of mankind, come solely under the head of biology.

Next, in distinguishing the "exchange of women," which is to say matrimonial alliances, from the exchange of economic goods, Lévi-Strauss maintains that these scarce goods ("commodités rarifiées," as he calls them, an odd piece of *franglais* [Lévi-Strauss (1949b) 1967, 43; cf. (1949c) 1969, 37]), which are also, in their way, part of the province of anthropology, have value only insofar as they satisfy erotic longing and economic need. As to their procreative advantages, he has nothing whatever to say. He does go on at some length about the miserable life of unmarried Bororo men and their unfortunate counterparts in other societies, deprived of sexual gratification and domestic comforts (see Lévi-Strauss [1949c] 1969, 38–40), but he is silent on the matter of a family without descendants, or a society that, for want of children, finds itself incapable of ensuring its own survival.

It is surprising, moreover, to see him justify marriage here by a rationalist and individualistic sort of *Homo œconomicus* calculus, especially in the midst of a lengthy description of marriage as a social categorical imperative; of exchange as a basic fact of the human condition, and not the result of two complementary transactions; of reciprocity as an a priori synthesis of self and others, and so on (to recall the formulas he was soon to employ in criticizing Mauss's analysis of the gift [see Lévi-Strauss 1950]). Mauss himself, in a lecture reprinted in the *Manual of Ethnography*, was no doubt a shrewder judge when he quoted an old French saying: "A father can feed ten children; ten children cannot feed a father" (Mauss [1947] 2007, 103). The meaning of this proverb is plain. One must give to one's own children what one has received from one's father. One does not make a gift in order to benefit oneself from a future counter-gift, but to sustain the flow of life, to satisfy the obligation that falls upon each person to pass on the life that he has received by procreating in his turn and by taking care of his progeny. Lévi-Strauss does not see that it is much more probably the human necessity of prolonging this vital flux, rather than doing whatever rules qua rules may require, that underlies the prescriptions he studies.[3]

The Arbitration of the Psychoanalysts

To decide between the theories advanced by Maranda and Lévi-Strauss, let us start off with a problem raised by Lévi-Strauss that, while it furnishes proof of his talent as a theorist, also exposes the limits of the structural theory of kinship and, as a consequence, throws into relief the incisiveness of the modification suggested by Maranda. Lévi-Strauss quite rightly wonders whether or not the atom of kinship, as he defined it and in all the many variants he studied, is the only possible basic unit. Might not the same relations be observed among other terms than the ones that are proper to his atom? "Could we not conceive of a symmetrical structure, equally simple, where the sexes would be reversed? Such a structure would involve a sister, her brother, brother's wife, and brother's daughter. This is certainly a theoretical possibility. In human society, it is the men who exchange the women, and not vice versa" (Lévi-Strauss [1958a] 1963, 47).

Quite so. From the formal point of view, it is a matter of indifference whether men exchange women or women exchange men. Diagrams of kinship, and the mathematical formulas associated with them, have the same properties on either assumption (see Héran 2009). In principle, then, there could be a counterpart to the usual atom of kinship. In fact, however, no such alternative exists, for it is women and not men who are the object of matrimonial exchange.[4] What is surprising here is not Lévi-Strauss's response to the question that he asked himself. It is to see him pass at once, without any further qualification, from bold speculation to timid incuriosity. He simply bows down before a phenomenon as obvious as male control of matrimonial exchange, as if it were a raw datum, external to the problem at hand. Having shown that the atom of kinship does not depend on the mode of descent, it does not occur to him to seek any sort of connection between the undeniable historical fact that it is men who exchange women, and not the opposite, and a still more obvious natural fact, namely, that it is women, and not men, who bear children. The great merit of Maranda's revision, however clumsy it may be in other respects, is that it tries to establish a connection between exogamy and procreation, and indeed, suggests that the former may be understood in terms of the latter.

The psychoanalysts, for their part, were bound to point out the omission of the mother-son relationship in the atom of kinship. It was nevertheless not until the mid-1970s that this lacuna was explicitly, and independently, indicated by André Green and Francis Martens (both clinical specialists, influenced by Lacanian thought, who were also very keen on structural anthropology), the first in a session of Lévi-Strauss's 1974–1975 seminar at the Collège de France, the second in an article that appeared at the same time in the journal *L'Homme*.

Green begins by recalling that the atom of kinship combines three kinds of relationship (consanguinity between brother and sister, marriage between husband and wife, and direct descent between parents and children), and then makes two proposals aimed at reestablishing the balance between exogamy and procreation. He recommends, first, a finer discrimination than the one made by Lévi-Strauss among the three types of relationship in question, distinguishing between descent and consanguinity instead of putting them both on the side of nature. Descent, he says, is an intermediate term between (natural) consanguinity and (cultural and social) marriage: "If the relationship between brothers-in-law is essentially founded on marriage, might one not suppose, by contrast, that the brother-sister relationship, called consanguinity, derives from the fact that they come from the same mother, which signifies a more 'biological' relationship, this term being understood less in its absolute sense than as a counterpoint to the wholly social character of the exchange relationship . . . ? Descent would therefore represent the integration of these two orders" (Green [1977] 1983, 87).

Apart from its own interest, this first remark is notable because it remedies the defect of Lévi-Strauss's atom of kinship by introducing, prior to the exchange relationship that is supposed to govern it, the mother of the "wife-giver" and his sister, which is to say the woman from whom they are both issued. This explicit reminder of the basis of consanguinity is all the more opportune—and this second remark, Green says, is the more important of the two—since the mother as such does not figure in the atom of kinship. One does indeed find a mother there, but she occurs in it only in her capacity as sister and wife. The atomic model, "while it symbolizes the most complete possible set of relations between the terms uniting the elements, omits one of them . . . : [the relation] between mother and child" (ibid., 88).

Unwilling to entertain the possibility that Lévi-Strauss might be mistaken, however, Green notes in passing that this major omission in the system of relations "is perhaps the very reason for its existence." The equilibrium of the system, in other words, is incompatible with simultaneously taking into account woman's dual status as mother and wife, so that "the atom of kinship encompasses the relationship [between mother and child] without ever directly aiming at it, but obliquely instead, through its ambient influence" (Green [1977] 1983, 88). Lévi-Strauss has left out nothing: his model is not incomplete; it describes an elemental core of relationships that could be formed only by excluding the relationship between mother and child.

In making this concession to Lévi-Strauss, disposing of the difficulty he has just pointed out by means of a clever formula having no explanatory power, Green prevents himself from getting at the truth he was just beginning to uncover. Having noticed the absence of a maternal figure at two successive levels of Lévi-Strauss's schema, he sketched a maternal lineage orthogonal to the relationship of exogamy, and suggested that this latter relationship was subordinate to it. But instead of emphasizing the vertical line of uterine descent, retracing it in ink, so to speak, and showing how the relationship between brothers-in-law is organized around it, he now abandons the approach altogether, preferring to transform the atom of kinship in such a way that it would be compatible with the Oedipus complex, by causing the positions occupied by the father and the maternal uncle to coincide (see ibid., 93–94)—so completely, in fact, that in the end, thanks to a formal and abstruse bit of legerdemain of the sort that was popular at the time, both Lévi-Strauss and Freud emerge unscathed.

The Uterine Triangle

In spite of Green's conciliatory gesture, Lévi-Strauss, rather than try to evade the difficulty, took up the challenge. He well knew that of the six relationships involved in the atom of kinship, two are not taken into account in his so-called system of attitudes: the relationship between mother and child, to which Green had explicitly called attention, and the relationship between brothers-in-law, which he himself had neutralized at the outset but which Jean-Marie Benoist put back into play, in the discussion that followed Green's presentation, by recalling (in a way reminiscent of Malinowski) that the figure of the maternal uncle suggests the need to broaden and deepen the Oedipus theory in view of its disproportionate emphasis on the relationship with the father.[5] Nevertheless, while the anthropologist is to be congratulated for not avoiding debate on these questions, his responses, important and instructive though they are, can hardly be considered satisfactory.

If he has not introduced the mother-child relationship, Lévi-Strauss explains, echoing Laplace, "it is because I have no need of that hypothesis." For, he adds—shifting from "I" to "we," as if he were taking cover under the authority of the ethnological community—"in the majority of cases, the societies that we study" do not subject this relationship to strict norms, whereas they do this systematically in the case of the ones included in the model. This is a most welcome thing, he remarks condescendingly, for these societies thus leave room for the psychoanalyst (quoted in Green [1977] 1983, 100). Curiously, to judge from the transcript of the discussion, no one in attendance seems to have dared point out the weakness of this argument, when a single example, probably well-known at the time, would have sufficed to refute it. Among the Baruya, whom I discussed earlier, the son is subject to a very strict avoidance taboo with regard to his mother for the entire term of his initiation and lasting until such time as he has fathered at least three children. Only then can he once again speak to her directly and eat in her presence (see the intervention by Godelier in Piattelli-Palmarini et al. 1978, 3:144–45).

It is hard to believe that Lévi-Strauss was unaware of this sort of thing. The real reason why the mother is not present ex officio in his element of kinship is much more profound than the one given, for it has to do with his very conception of systems of kinship. We know that for Lévi-Strauss, contrary not only to Freud but also to other anthropologists, the incest prohibition is not a primitive datum but a consequence of the exogamy rule. It is not because a man ought not marry his sister or his daughter that he must give them in marriage to another; it is because a brother or a father is obligated to give, the one his sister, the other his daughter in marriage to another that they cannot take them as wives for themselves. Having granted this much, however, a considerable difficulty arises: whereas a son is similarly prohibited from marrying his mother once she has become a widow, it would seem incongruous to justify this prohibition on the basis of an obligation to give her in marriage to another. Hence the emphasis on the brother-sister relationship in the atom of kinship at the expense of the mother-son relationship—this even though some societies authorize the marriage of brother and sister, and even though, conversely, all societies prohibit sexual relations between mother and son, considered everywhere to be the outstanding case of incest,[6] except in the structural theory of marriage, which assigns it a secondary place. It is therefore not ethnography but Lévi-Strauss's system, by its very nature, that has no room for the mother as such in an elementary kinship structure. Since it is hard to see this, however, Lévi-Strauss managed by artful maneuvering to steer clear of danger.

The relationship between brothers-in-law is also omitted in the system of attitudes by which the atom of kinship maintains its equilibrium. But neither Green nor anyone in the audience noticed this. Nobody pointed out that Lévi-Strauss passes over it in silence when he enumerates the relationships that, in his view, societies "normalize," that is, strictly codify. Here again, it is impossible to agree with Lévi-Strauss. One has only to recall the highly ritualized scene reported among the Maori by Jones, in the course of which the uncle, on the death of his nephew, comes to demand an explanation from his nephew's father. We will look at a still richer variant of the same scenario, among another people, shortly.

For the moment, if we are to understand Lévi-Strauss's position, we must come back to the structural theory of kinship. The primacy it accords to the brother-sister relationship over the mother-son relationship has the immediate consequence, to recall a formula already quoted, that "the relationship between 'brothers-in-law' is the necessary axis around which the kinship structure is built" (Lévi-Strauss [1958a] 1963, 46). Why therefore does it not appear in the system of attitudes, which constitutes the dynamic component of the atom of kinship? One possible response is to say that, *to the very extent that this relationship is what makes the structure possible*, the relationship is not a particular component of it. On this view, the complementary relationship between wife-giver and wife-taker serves the sole purpose of opening up and creating a kinship space in which other relationships can then be combined. It would also explain Lévi-Strauss's claim, quoted earlier as well, that there is no need "to explain how the maternal uncle emerged in the kinship structure: He does not emerge—he is present initially. Indeed, the presence of the uncle is a necessary precondition for the structure to exist" (46). The uncle is there from the first, not in the capacity of an element, as one would have been inclined to suppose, but as a "precondition," which is to say only as a wife-giver, who is necessarily correlated with a wife-taker. As Gillian Gillison puts it (see 1987, 167), he does not figure in the atom as an individual but as a sign; not as someone related to a child through the child's mother, but as a symbol of matrimonial exchange. This is just what Lévi-Strauss himself says in response to the exchange I mentioned earlier between Benoist and Green: "When I spoke of [the maternal uncle], I didn't mean that he played a role in the structure of kinship as such. It happens that, in the simplest structures known to us, it is convenient to use the maternal uncle, but only insofar as he represents wife-givers" (quoted in Green [1977] 1983, 103).

It is nevertheless strange, to say the least, to say that the uncle as such plays no role in the structure of kinship. What becomes then of the avuncular relationship, the point of departure for the whole inquiry? And of the atom of kinship, which was supposed to dispel the mystery of this relationship? The discussion that follows only deepens our perplexity. Earlier, replying to Green with regard to the mother, Lévi-Strauss had taken refuge in the point of view of traditional societies; but now, reacting to Benoist's comment, it is Lévi-Strauss who adopts the perspective of modern societies: "In our society—the one that psychoanalysts argue from— . . . at bottom it is the wife—the future mother—who herself represents the group of givers: she gives herself. . . . Moreover, the role played elsewhere by the maternal uncle may be confused with hers, according to a certain folklore of the nineteenth century, I'm not sure how far it has any real foundation, reinforced by her own mother—the mother-in-law—but they are doubles of each other" (quoted in Green [1977] 1983, 103–4).

Exit the maternal uncle, then, and along with him the question of his relationship to his brother-in-law within the atom of kinship, the brother-in-law having now become superfluous as well. For if the wife gives herself, and if her own mother is nothing more than her double, there are no longer, strictly speaking, givers and takers, nor, as a consequence, any structural theory of kinship left to apply. In taking refuge in the point of view of modern society, Lévi-Strauss gives the impression of fleeing his own preferred terrain, of abandoning his own frame of reference while leaving the questions at issue unresolved.

He nonetheless says one last thing that allows him, for better or for worse, to save his conception of matrimonial exchange, if not for modern society as a whole, at least for Western society toward the end of the century before last, and that also points the way, though he does not realize it, to a

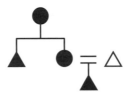

FIGURE 3. The Uterine Triangle and the Atom of Kinship

solution: "However much [credit is to be attached to the folklore I mentioned a moment ago], if we ascribe ethnographic value to the literature of the nineteenth century and to vaudeville, it is evidently the mother-in-law who personifies the group of wife givers" (quoted in Green [1977] 1983, 104).

In other words, although our civil code assigns to the father the right to grant or to refuse his daughter's hand to another man, in reality it is her mother who enjoys this power. Paternal power is a secondary and reactive trait. But if such a thing is attested in both modern and premodern society, are we not dealing here simply with a particular modality of a universal trait? For Lévi-Strauss has just successively mentioned three possible representatives of the class of wife-givers: the maternal uncle, the wife herself, and her mother. Here we find the three members of the uterine triangle sketched by Green when he observed that the brother and sister of the atom of kinship have in common the fact of being issued from the same mother. We may well wonder, then, whether this triangle is not the germ of any system of kinship formed on the basis, not of exogamy, but of procreation; and, indeed, whether it is not the basic structure of Lévi-Strauss's atom of kinship, which is easily reconstituted by adjoining to it, first, the son of the sister (who is also the uterine nephew of her brother), and only then, by way of conclusion, the husband of the sister (who is also the father of this child)—in that order, so as to make clear that the status of giver of children, reserved for women, is prior to that of giver or taker of wives, almost always reserved for men.

And yet it never occurred to either the psychoanalyst or the anthropologist—the one determined to detect the presence of an Oedipal structure, the other wedded to the primacy of marriage—to explore this possibility. As it happens, however, it did occur at just this time to one author, the Belgian scholar Francis Martens, someone with a foot in both camps, that it would be a good thing to call attention at long last to a fact that was known to everyone but ignored or disregarded, probably for this very reason, by the sleuths of the unconscious and by all those who believe that the only knowledge worth the name is knowledge of that which is hidden, namely, that "maternity and paternity are in no way—on the phenomenal level—symmetrical. The main biological fact of the matter is obvious: *it is the woman who brings children into the world*. It is with her—and with her alone, initially—that the mystery of generation is associated" (Martens 1975, 161). The mother, as a parent, is so designated by nature, whereas the father is "a product of culture." Even if anthropology is probably justified in rejecting the hypothesis of a primitive matriarchy, or at least the idea that every society passes first through a matrilineal phase, it is nonetheless true that uterine relationships logically precede agnatic relationships. It would therefore be no less serious an error than the one committed by the old evolutionist theories if, supposedly with the sanction of linguistics, one were to regard the nomenclatures of kinship as systems of purely arbitrary signs, and matrilineal and patrilineal descent as two conventional, wholly equivalent ways available to human societies, now and forever more, of coding the genealogical relations that bind their members to one another.

This salutary reminder has nonetheless gone largely unheeded, surely not because of the author's jovial (though sometimes impulsive) manner, but for having been couched in a Lacanian idiom that blunted its force and, more importantly, for having been almost entirely eclipsed by an overriding concern on Martens's own part to reconcile Lévi-Strauss's theory of exchange with Freud's theory of incest. What should be front and center is thus pushed into the background. Indeed—and this is not an insignificant detail—the heart of the argument, having to do with the dissymmetry between maternity and paternity, is not even touched on in the final summary that Martens himself gives (see ibid., 174). He nonetheless manages to develop several convergent lines of evidence that jointly lend support to the idea that the atom of kinship must be conceived on the basis of procreation, since it is women who bring children into the world. This circumstance has the consequence of establishing an irreducible difference between the sexes: between the mother, whose identity is certain, and the father, always uncertain.[7] From this it follows at once, though this fact is not sufficiently stressed, that there is a difference of status between two persons of the same sex that confers a genealogical advantage, as it were, to the maternal uncle over the father. Indeed, "the maternal uncle is, in the generation preceding ours, the *only* male ascendant of whom we may be certain" (168), and conversely, the uterine nephew is, for the mother's brother, the closest male descendant of whom he can be certain. Thus the matrix of any system of kinship: the avuncular relationship is immediately assumed, prior to any consideration of matrimonial exchange.[8]

So vital is this basic uterine structure that it preserves its full force even in the kinship nomenclature of a society where the paternal right is clearly asserted. Martens, relying on Benveniste's classic study (see Benveniste 1969), gives an example from ancient Rome to show that father and mother do not form a symmetrical pair. Whereas *mater* denotes the female parent, *pater* denotes her husband: *Pater is est quem nuptiae demonstrant.* Implicit in the term *pater familias* is not a genealogical bond, but a relationship of authority grounded in law. What is more, *mater* refers to a quite specific person, whereas *pater* is a generic term applied not only to the father and to his brothers, but also to the members of a phratry, even to immortal beings (Jupiter, for example, and later, in Christian Rome, God the Father). The word *filius*, for its part, is originally associated with the idea of feeding or suckling (*nourriture* in French), not descendance. Etymologically, the newborn infant (*nourrisson*) is related to the foster father (*père nourricier*). Indeed, all the children of several brothers are designated by the same term, *sunus*, meaning offspring; it was in order to pick out the one in whom he took a particular interest that the father added to *sunus* the term *filius*. But these rather relaxed relationships on the paternal side are never found on the maternal side, where the maternal uncle (*avunculus*) and the uterine nephew (*nepos*) are, by contrast, well-specified categories.

The terms used to refer to them nevertheless have something strange or even paradoxical about them, since *nepos* is employed both for grandson and nephew, and *avunculus* is the diminutive of *avus*, paternal grandfather. These two problems may appear to be distinct, but Benveniste elegantly resolves them by means of one and the same solution (see ibid., 1:225–35). If we suppose it to be a rule that a man marries his patrilateral cross cousin, which is to say the daughter of his father's sister, then it follows, as the reader can easily verify (see figure 4), that the paternal grandfather is also a maternal great uncle, and his grandson is the uterine nephew of his own uterine nephew.

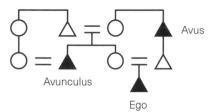

FIGURE 4. The Maternal Great-Uncle (*avus*) and Maternal Uncle (*avunculus*)

One therefore has a generational chain linking men through women, such that each man is the *avunculus* of the one who comes after him and the *nepos* of the one who comes before. The grandson and nephew, though they do not belong to the same generation, are both descendants, via a female parent, of the grandfather.

Benveniste notes, moreover, that the grandson is often called "little grandfather." This is the meaning, for example, of the Old French word *ave-let*, itself evidently a diminutive deriving from Latin *avus*. Here Benveniste reminds us that many societies regard the grandson as a reincarnation of the grandfather and identify alternate generations with each other. But he leaves it at that, without connecting these details with the ones he has just examined. Martens, for his part, despite the precedence he accords to genealogical association through a female parent, contents himself with rapidly noting the properties of patrilateral marriage pointed out by Benveniste. Martens prefers to concern himself with the marriage of a man to his matrilateral cross cousin, an elementary form of generalized exchange made famous by Lévi-Strauss[9]—with, in other words, the marriage of the uterine nephew with the daughter of the maternal uncle, despite the fact that, in his analytical framework, this young woman is primarily of interest for being the daughter of the uncle's wife.

Yet it suffices to combine Martens's matrilineal perspective with Benveniste's patrilateral point of view in order to take another step in the same direction. Whereas a man's son is, in the first place, the son of the man's wife, his grandson—the son of the daughter of his sister (that is, the issue of marriage to a patrilateral cross cousin)—is, two generations later, the only male descendant to whom he can be sure of being related. This grandson is therefore his replica in the sense just indicated, a "little grandfather" (see

Scubla 1985a, 56–57). On this view of the matter, patrilateral cross-cousin marriage is not only, as the classical theory of marriage would have it, the simplest way for a matrimonial debt contracted by the present generation to be repaid by the next generation (see Fox 1967, 202–6). It is also, and above all, a very effective way for men to exercise a right of supervision over their descendants.

The Maternal Uncle and the Redemption
of the Uterine Nephew

That control over procreation is indeed the crux of the matter, here as elsewhere, receives further confirmation from two important pieces of ethnographic evidence cited by Martens. Societies may be more or less permissive with regard to sexuality, but in all those in which sexual freedom is very great, procreation is strictly regulated. This is true of the matrilineal society of the Trobrianders as well as of the patrilineal society of the Rukuba of Nigeria. In both societies it is considered to be of the highest importance that birth be legitimate, which is to say that a father, and not merely a male parent, can be clearly identified, that is, institutionally assigned to the child. In the case of pregnancy outside marriage, abortion and infanticide are generally the only acceptable options (see Martens 1975, 163). This shows once more that one of the strongest and most constant human desires is to have the greatest control possible over a function that, by its nature, eludes human beings for the most part, and that involves a more or less concealed rivalry between the sexes in attempting to appropriate children for one's own purposes.

But this tense and potentially combative relationship between father and mother, and, by extension, between men and women, is accompanied by a no less pronounced antagonism among members of the male sex, only this time between brothers-in-law, or rather between the husband and his wife's brother, between father and maternal uncle. As Martens observes, "relations between nephew and maternal uncle—which are both affective and juridical—always place the maternal uncle in competition with the father" (ibid., 166). Indeed the maternal uncle, as we have seen, directly participates in the element of kinship, whereas the father is an intruder. The status of the former as a wife-giver, far from putting him at the center of the system, as Lévi-Strauss would have it, tends to put him on its periphery, for to say that he gives his sister in marriage to another man amounts to saying that he renounces the child of this sister, to the advantage of this other man,[10] though their child is the sole representative of the following generation to whom he can be sure of being related. Even if this gift, or this renunciation, is repaid or compensated in some way, it engenders a more or less deep and lasting hostility toward the beneficiary, as many ethnographic accounts testify.

The conflictual relationship between the two men among the Gimi of New Guinea has been well brought out by Gillian Gillison (1986).[11] In this patrilineal society, the maternal uncle is explicitly perceived as a person who threatens the life of the child. To remove the danger that the uncle embodies, it is necessary that he be appeased by means of ritual gifts when his nephew is given a name, when the nephew falls sick or is wounded, has his first haircut, undergoes initiation, and so on. "All these obligatory 'gifts' [made by the child's father and other agnates] are called the 'head of the child.' When the mother's brother receives them, he is said to 'eat the head of the child'" (Gillison 1986, 43).

This expression, which Gillison thinks "probably reflects a truth of the past" (ibid.), shows in any case that the life of the child is seen as belonging by right to the uncle, who in this regard behaves like the jealous divinity of the Old Testament, the God who demands that the firstborn be redeemed (see Exodus 13:11–16; Numbers 3:40–51). The gifts presented to him are sacrifices intended to turn him away, to hold at bay the capacity for violence that he carries within him, in keeping with the definition of sacrificial rites formulated by Girard ([1972b] 1977) and already implicit in Mauss.[12] The properly sacrificial character of the avuncular relationship is manifest. When the nephew dies, his matrilateral relatives arm themselves and go to his home. One of the members of the patrilineage of the deceased fastens a pig to a stake, so that the mother's brother, in his fury, may kill it with an arrow. "'The pig,' an informant explains, 'is the head of our brother, and killing it calms the rage in [the uncle's] belly. Were it not for the pig, we would be obliged to fight one another'" (Gillison 1986, 43–44 n. 2).

Thus we end up back at the religious character of the avuncular relationship, pointed out at the outset by Lévi-Strauss, then promptly forgotten and, ultimately, denied any place in his model of the atom of kinship. From the fact that this quality reappears once the mother-child relationship is recognized, and from the conflictual relationship between the brothers-in-law that flows from it, we see that we have not lost our way. All these elements are related. This is why Lévi-Strauss's model must be revised.

Instead of reasoning in terms of the binary relations (or pairs of individuals) included in the atom of kinship, as Lévi-Strauss does, no doubt it is preferable, and no less consistent with the structural method, to consider ternary relations (or triads of individuals) first. There are four triads in all. Let us begin with the nuclear family (mother, father, son), which, in spite of certain relativist claims to the contrary, seems to be universal, or at least attested in all known societies (see Murdock 1949, 23–40; also Todd 2011). Lévi-Strauss shows that underlying this triad is another one, on which it depends, associated with marriage ("giver" brother, "given" sister, "taker" husband), seldom found in the West but still common in many other societies. Martens identifies two still more fundamental triads: a primordial matrilineal triad (brother, sister, sister's child), which constitutes the basis of the atom of kinship, and a potential patrilineal triad (brother, sister's child, sister's husband), marked by the rivalry of the two men for possession of the sister's child and culminating in the pact in which the nuclear family originates—a pact whose primary purpose is plainly to determine the respective rights of the maternal uncle and the father of the mother's child. This sequence of triangular relationships may indeed constitute the deep dynamic structure of the atom of kinship.

CHAPTER FIVE

Incest of the Second Type

Impasses and Issues

n according primacy to alliance over descent, the structural theory of kinship favors symmetrical relationships. Descent and alliance rest on opposite principles: if A is an ancestor of B, B cannot be an ancestor of A, whereas if A is related by marriage to B, B is thereby related to A. Even in societies that tend to conceive of the succession of generations as a cyclical process, the relationship of ascendant to descendant remains asymmetric since the grandson is considered to be a replica (or reincarnation) of the grandfather, but the reverse is not true.[1] By contrast, even in systems of generalized exchange, which distinguish between "givers" and "takers" of women, relatives by marriage nevertheless occupy equivalent places since, in the rounds of exchange, each one is alternately in the position of giver and taker.[2] The notion of exchange and the principle of reciprocity, pillars of structural theory, imply symmetry.

Lévi-Strauss himself nonetheless notes that two phenomena, apparently correlated with each other, manifest "the basic asymmetrical relationship between the sexes which is characteristic of human society" (Lévi-Strauss [1949c] 1969, 117). On the one hand, "it is men who exchange women, and not vice versa" (115). On the other hand, though in principle all things are both possible and formally equivalent, the modes of matrilineal and patrilineal descent, like the modes of matrilocal and patrilocal residence, are in fact unequally distributed. There are, he says, very few systems that are both matrilineal and matrilocal (117).[3] But it needs to be kept in mind that, for him, one is dealing here with a fact external to the system of exchange. By themselves, the diagrams representing alliances are perfectly neutral; one can interpret them as depicting both exchanges of women performed by men and exchanges of men performed by women. The latest and most perceptive commentator on Lévi-Strauss, François Héran, in what he calls a critical history of structural reason (an elaboration of the ideas contained in his brilliant 1996 doctoral thesis on "figures" and "legends" of kinship), is at pains to emphasize that the masculine asymmetry identified by Lévi-Strauss is part of a legend and not a figure; in other words, it is a matter of commentary and interpretation, and has nothing to do with the intrinsic properties of the structural model itself (see Héran 2009).

In the Footsteps of Lévi-Strauss: Françoise Héritier and the Omaha Alliance System

It is in this intellectual context that the originality of the work of Françoise Héritier, Lévi-Strauss's successor at the Collège de France, becomes apparent. Her work is not limited to extending the argument of *The Elementary Structures of Kinship* while retaining the idea that exogamy is the source, and not the consequence, of the prohibition of incest; it tries at the same time to rethink the structures of exchange and reciprocity in the light of a "principle of male dominance," regarded now not as an external variable but as an endogenous principle. Structural anthropology is indebted to Héritier for three important contributions in particular: the modeling of so-called "semicomplex" alliance systems; the incorporation of the "differential valence of the sexes" in kinship systems; and the discovery of the structuring effects of a principle of "non-combination of the identical."

These three contributions have a common origin: the study of relationships between individuals of the same sex and individuals of different sexes within systems of kinship called "Crow" and "Omaha," both of which observe a principle of non-redoubling of alliances, which is to say a rule that prohibits a person from marrying into a lineage where a close relative has already taken a husband or wife. Héritier's whole theoretical approach to anthropology grows out of fieldwork conducted among the Samo of the former Upper Volta (now Burkina Faso), a patrilineal society with an Omaha system in which she meticulously collected a very great number of genealogies and compared alliance rules with the marriages that were in fact contracted over the course of several generations.

It is generally agreed that her most significant findings are stated in a work modestly entitled *The Practice of Kinship*. Published in 1981, it is by itself enough to assure her place among the great theorists of kinship. In analyzing the matrimonial proscriptions of the Samo and comparing the theoretical possibilities of alliance they entail with the record of actually concluded marriages, Héritier made an unexpected discovery: the rules of a semi-complex system are perfectly compatible with the exchange of sisters, that is, with the simplest form of restricted exchange that can be encountered in an elementary system.

Lévi-Strauss had conceived of semi-complex systems, on either the Crow (matrilineal) or Omaha (patrilineal) model, as situated midway between elementary systems of the Kariera or Aranda type, which assign to each individual a well-determined class of potential spouses (for example, marrying a cross cousin rather than a parallel cousin), and complex systems, which permit the free choice of a spouse beyond a small circle of excluded candidates, immediate family members and other close relatives. Like complex systems, semi-complex systems lay down only matrimonial prohibitions; but because these prohibitions are very numerous and bear upon entire lineages, they restrict the choice of a spouse more strongly than complex systems. Lévi-Strauss nonetheless believed (see [1949c] 1969, 459–77) that the number of possible alliances was still so great as to constitute an insurmountable challenge to ethnologists. Héritier, marshaling empirical evidence in support of a splendid flash of insight, that the Samo were equipped with a sort of "Aranda super-system" (1981, 122), proved that semi-complex systems are only an extension of elementary systems.[4] This was undeniably a major achievement for the structural theory of kinship (see Héran 2009, 144–48, 154–56).

The analysis of semi-complex systems led Héritier to advance several general hypotheses that have not met with the same approval from the anthropological community, whether because they seemed to be invalidated by accepted facts, or because they were not formulated precisely enough to be confirmed or disconfirmed, or because their implications have yet to be fully appreciated, or because, in a few cases, they have been flatly rejected.

Incest of the Second Type

The matrimonial proscriptions of the Crow and Omaha systems are in large part rules against renewing alliances. Among the Samo, for example, while a man cannot marry a woman of his father's patrilineage (a classic exogamy rule in a patrilineal regime), he is also forbidden to marry a woman of his mother's patrilineage, that is, to perpetuate within this lineage an alliance already concluded by his own father. This type of rule suggested to Héritier the idea that the principle of non-redoubling of alliances could be the consequence of a more general principle, of non-combination of identical things, which a considerable body of research suggests may extend well beyond kinship relations (see Héritier 1979, 233–39).

No doubt, as we shall see in a later chapter, the division of labor between the sexes furnishes the best illustration of this ingenious idea. Héritier, for her part, was chiefly concerned to detect beneath the non-redoubling rule what she calls "incest of the second type" (ibid., 221), to which she subsequently devoted an entire work (see Héritier [1994] 1999). This phrase concealed an ambition not only to uncover the prohibited sexual and matrimonial relations that had eluded her predecessors, but also to work out, on the basis of these relations, a new and more general definition of incest. The current definition is not thereby made redundant, but instead becomes a special case. According to the new definition, "It is no longer a question of the connection between two blood-relations of different sexes in a prohibited sexual relationship, but of the *connection between two blood-relations of the same sex who share the same sexual partner*. It is these blood-relations of the same sex, brother/brother, sister/sister, father/son, mother/daughter, who find themselves in an incestuous relationship by virtue of their common partner and who are exposed to its dangers" (Héritier 1979, 219; emphasis in the original).

On this view, incest consists in two persons having a threefold identity: of gender, of kinship, and of sexual partnership with a common third party, whether related by blood or not. The classic forms of incest found in the

Oedipus complex, between mother and son or father and daughter, have not disappeared; they have been redefined, the first as a relationship between a father and son sharing the same woman, the second as a relationship between a mother and daughter sharing the same man. In the Oedipus triangle, the canonical incestuous couple is no longer Oedipus and Jocasta, but Oedipus and Laius. The prohibition no longer applies so much to a heterosexual relationship between two relatives as to the indirect relationship that is implied by it, for now it is aimed at "a homosexual relationship between blood relatives, mediated by a common sexual object" (ibid., 230). It is these two people, of same rather than different sex, whom incest puts at risk.

In support of this original concept of incest, seemingly paradoxical by comparison with the usual definition, Héritier gives several remarkable examples. I shall recall here only the first one of them. The Baule (or Baoulé) people of Africa do not only proscribe sororal polygyny and sororate; they also forbid a man from having sexual relations with two sisters or two uterine cousins. When this supplementary rule is violated, the two women are subjected to a rite of purification that includes a sacrifice. The victim, a kid or sheep, is symbolically split lengthwise to reestablish the distance that existed between them before the incestuous acts. But—a crucial detail—the man is in no way involved in this lustration ceremony (see Héritier 1979, 219).

By bringing out in a very clear way the distinction between the status of the two women, on the one hand, and that of the man, on the other, this example perfectly illustrates the definition of incest of the second type. By itself, it suffices to show the importance of a type of relationship that classical theories had neglected. Héritier, following Pierre Étienne (whose ethnography she relied on), was surely right to draw the attention of anthropologists to its existence and to inquire into its scope and its characteristic features. But can we therefore see it as the very essence of incest and as a paradigm of sexual and matrimonial prohibitions?

Prohibition of Incest or Prevention of Rivalry?

As several commentators have remarked,[5] Héritier herself neglects or even dismisses a line of inquiry that the ethnography of the Baule in particular should have suggested to her: rivalry between co-wives or co-mistresses, which the prohibition of marriage and sexual relations with sisters and cousins seeks to avoid and purification ceremonies are meant to ward off. "The relationship of rivalry plays, in the constitution and functioning of the Baule matrimonial system, a role every bit as important as the relationships of shared parentage [*germanité*] and alliance do" (Étienne 1975, 8).

Furthermore, Étienne expressly distinguishes between close relatives and potential rivals. Polygyny is a means of assuring that one will have many descendants. The ideal of a Baule man is to be able to number among his dependents not only the children of his wives but also those of their sisters (see ibid., 20). Nevertheless he must be careful that rivalry does not penetrate within the circle of blood relations. This is why sororate is forbidden (16), for, it is said, one cannot be both sister and rival (22), and why postmortem jealousy of a deceased sister is dreaded.

Étienne himself tends to treat the possibility of conflict between rival sisters as a secondary rationalization of the logic of matrimony. "It is no doubt true," he writes, "at the level of sexual fantasies; but this first truth masks another: always this same principle of non-redoubling of alliances" (ibid.).

Héritier dutifully echoes this sentiment—virtually word for word, in fact (see Héritier [1994] 1999, 157)—except that she does not consider the abstract rule of non-redoubling to be the ultimate reason for the prohibitions. Nevertheless she tries to justify it by means of a theory meant to make its significance more readily grasped.

Before even examining the nature of this justification and the problems that it raises, one may wonder whether it is really necessary at all, at least in the present case. Do we not already have everything we need in the way of a satisfactory explanation? Rivalries bring quite real dangers, not only imagined ones. This is why all societies take care to prevent them or else to ritualize their expression. In Leviticus (18:18), as among the Baule, sororate is proscribed in order to avoid rivalry between sisters.[6] In many societies, vengeance is erected into an institution ("vindicatory system") to contain clashes among rival groups and to prevent them from degenerating into massacres (see Verdier 1980). For rivals there is always a risk that competition will eventually lead to armed confrontation, with murderous consequences. By definition, rivals occupy symmetrical positions: since each is the double of the other, they are potential enemies. The principle of non-redoubling can therefore be seen as a precautionary principle intended to prevent the proliferation of individual rivalries.

Nathalie Heinich was the first, to my knowledge, to postulate an organic link between the prohibition of incest of the second type and the fear that a confusion of social positions may give rise to lethal animosity (see Heinich 1995, 948–49; Fine 2013, 111). The work of Bernard Vernier reinforces her hypothesis by showing that this prohibition varies as a function of social status. "One does not touch the wives of blood relations," Agnès Fine notes, "for to do so would be to introduce theft and war among them. In the same way, one does not introduce rivalry and war into another free family. But one is allowed to transform sisters or a mother and her daughter into rivals if they are slaves or foreigners whose interests are unimportant" (Fine 2013, 101–2).

The purification ritual of the Baule lends further support to this idea. To put a sacrificial victim to death, more particularly by splitting it in two, is a classic way of preventing or expiating an incestuous relationship.[7] But it is also, in a deeper sense, a way of putting an end to conflict. In dividing the sacrificial victim into two distinct pieces, the ceremony separates rival groups and places them at a safe distance from each other; it reestablishes a boundary that stops them from encroaching upon each other (see Garine 1980, 97). For the operation is not only symbolic, it is cathartic. In deflecting violence toward a ritual victim, or toward the god that is supposed to claim it, sacrifice provides an outlet: it pacifies enemy brothers and potential rivals; undoes the deadly bonds that had been created, or that risked being created, between them; removes the danger brought about by transgression of a taboo.

Among the Baule it is therefore plausible to suppose that the restorative sacrifice is performed by the two women, and not by their male partner, because they alone are in danger of becoming rivals. However this may be, the hypothesis suffices to completely explain the prohibition and the ceremony that compensates for its violation, both of which are intended to avert the danger of intrafamilial rivalry. What is more problematic, by contrast—though this is not a defect of the hypothesis, quite to the contrary—is the incestuous character of the prohibited relations that the hypothesis seeks to challenge. In the case we are interested in here, the prohibition does not bear so much on a particular type of sexual relation as on the conflict that such relations are liable to provoke (indeed, there are no sexual relations, strictly speaking, between the two Baule sisters or female cousins, but we need not

pause here to consider specific instances). Nor is there really any sexual relationship between father and son in this reformulation of classic maternal
incest in terms of incest of the second type. In both cases, the prohibition
constitutes an obstacle to the emergence of hostility between two women or
between two men sharing the favors of the same person. Generally speaking,
most of the taboos studied by Héritier have in common the effect of blocking
rivalry. One may therefore wonder why this property should not suffice to
explain all of them. There would no longer be any need for a unitary theory
of incest that enlarges the classic definition; one would be left instead with
a preliminary sketch of a general theory of the prohibitions aimed at preventing interfamilial conflict, and notably conflict arising from incestuous
relations. The scientific interest of this enterprise would be in no way less,
but it would be a different enterprise, for it would not seem to promise any
new insight into incest itself. Héritier had something else in mind, however.
Her ambition was to construct a general theory of incest that would be both
more comprehensive, by encompassing a new class of facts overlooked by the
usual definition, and more powerful, by giving a fuller account of the facts
already noticed by this definition.

Incest of the Second Type and the "Mechanics of Fluids": Explanation or Rationalization?

Taking certain vernacular explanations as her guide, Héritier cataloged and
systematically analyzed various local theories of bodily fluids and the humors
that underlie them. On comparing the ways in which different societies treat
corporeal substances, depending on whether they are common to the two
sexes (such as blood and urine) or distinctive (such as milk and sperm), the
idea occurred to her of trying to rehabilitate a "materialist"—and therefore,
to her mind, a more scientific—interpretation[8] of the rules and prohibitions
governing the lives of men and women. A good part of her lectures at the
Collège de France, and of the writings she published during the same period,
are devoted to developing this idea. Together they constitute a minutely
detailed compendium of popular and scholarly conceptions, drawn from the
most diverse societies throughout the history of mankind, of the functioning
of the human body, of the relations between the sexes, and of the relations

human beings maintain with the cosmic and social components of their environment. Imposing order on so vast a mass of data, detecting invariants, extracting the principles of a dialectic of hot and cold, dry and wet, and so on—seeking, in other words, to formulate the laws of what might be called (as materialism demands) a "mechanics of fluids," yet one that is grounded in the last analysis (as structuralism demands) on a combinatorics of sameness and difference—naturally required considerable effort. In spite of the ambivalent interaction between the material and the symbolic (see Heinich 1995, 947; Godelier [2004] 2011, 355, 361), this critical inventory is in itself very useful, a patient and highly suggestive exploration of the ways in which associative chains are formed and become intertwined with one another. But did Héritier actually succeed in doing what she set out to do? Did she realize her theoretical ambitions by providing the key to incest of the second type? Permit me to say at the outset that, like the majority of those who have examined the matter, I doubt it very strongly.

Let us confine our attention to two examples that may stand for many more, and that must themselves be compared with each other: the Oedipal incest of a mother and her son, on the one hand, and that of sisters or uterine cousins having sexual relations with the same man, on the other. In each case the incestuous relationship involves two blood relations of the same sex, on the one hand a son and his father, and on the other, two sisters or two cousins. In each case the prohibition is intended to protect them from the injury that would be caused through a combining of identical things, that is, an encounter of two substances too alike to be able to enter into contact with each other. These are the premises of the theory of incest of the second type, and the doctrine of bodily substances on which it is supposed to rest.

Yet if one naively applies the theory, a dual difficulty is immediately apparent. In the first case, there is indeed an encounter between two like substances, the sperm of the father and that of the son, in the mother's womb; but it is the two men, and not the woman in whose body the pernicious commingling occurs, who are imagined to be in danger. In the second case, as the purification ritual attests, it is assuredly the two female blood relations who are liable to be harmed, but the commingling of substances that is supposed to cause the harm does not occur; although both women come into contact with the seed of the same man, there is no direct contact between like substances.

In order to avoid these difficulties without having to amend the theory of bodily fluids, there is no choice but to make less naive use of this theory, even at the risk of falling into sophistry. One must hold that it is through the mother, as intermediary, that the sperm, or more simply, the body of the father, may be hurtfully conjoined with that of his son; and that it is likewise through the common partner of the two women that their vaginal secretions, or more simply, their respective bodies, undergo the same sort of noxious conjunction. Now, of these two types of possible admixture, substances in the one case, bodies in the other, Héritier chooses the latter—with the result that bodily fluids no longer have any specific role. In prohibiting the redoubling of alliances, one prohibits "the meeting of identical flesh through a common partner" (Héritier [1994] 1999, 157). But who does not see that this merely dresses up the avoidance rule in a new vocabulary, without the least gain in understanding?[9] However one views the matter, the "materialist" costume is superfluous. The only way to judge the scope and validity of Héritier's theory will therefore be by examining incest of the second type in its simplest form.

Testing the Theory against the Facts

In this connection, from the moment her seminal article appeared, Héritier's theory ran up against a considerable obstacle. Whereas the Baule proscribe sororate and sororal polygyny, other peoples tolerate it or even recommend it. The same is true for levirate and fraternal polyandry. It is hard to see, then, how incest of the second type can claim to be a universal principle. To get around the problem, Héritier advanced a weakened version of the principle of combining of similars. It remains universal in the sense that the combining of similars is never a matter of indifference, sometimes being systematically encouraged, sometimes systematically prohibited (see Héritier 1979, 232). But even in this attenuated form, which already deprives it of a good part of its explanatory power, its inadequacy is shown by the fact that the Baule, though they strictly prohibit sororate, practice levirate without, however, absolutely prescribing it (see Étienne 1975, 16). A rule whose application is manifestly incomplete can hardly be regarded as a fundamental principle.

In retrospect it is clear, considering the impasses into which Héritier was led by her initial hypothesis, and despite the considerable resources of talent and knowledge she devoted to salvaging it, that her project of constructing a new anthropology of incest, both more fundamental and more general than the orthodox theory (see Héritier [1994] 1999), was bound to fail. There is no alternative but to concur in this regard with the sometimes severe but reasoned and complementary judgments of Maurice Godelier ([2004] 2011, 335–63), François Héran (2009, 552–65), and Bernard Vernier (2009), to which I refer the interested reader.[10] I will say only a few words about the two examples we have taken as our guide. They seem to me to go to the heart of the matter because the two cases are not in fact symmetrical; in reality, they belong to two distinct registers. Neither one being reducible to the other, they cannot be united under the category of incest of the second type.

The reason is that there is an essential difference between them. Not only are there on one side two women sharing the same man, and on the other two men sharing the same woman; in the Baule case, the two sisters or cousins are related, but their common partner has no family bond with them. In the canonical form of classic incest, not only are the father and son related, but their potential common partner is also the mother of the son. This decisive point becomes altogether marginal in the unitary theory proposed by Héritier, however, because it no longer matters. In laying emphasis on the relationship between the father and the son, rather than between the son and the mother, this new conception of incest prohibitions—whether one interprets them, as Héritier does, in terms of substances needing to be kept separate and harmful encounters needing to be avoided, or, as other authors do, in terms of rivalry to be prevented and potential conflicts to be averted—reduces the mother to a mere sexual object shared or coveted by two related persons. Her generative character is obliterated once more, as in Freud's Oedipal triangle and in Lévi-Strauss's atom of kinship.

And yet it is in just this capacity, in all societies, that the mother is the object of a strict taboo. When a woman becomes a widow, there is no longer any carnal contact to be dreaded between her and both her son and her husband, nor any possible rivalry between son and father. Even so, she cannot take her son as a second husband, and sexual relations between them continue to be forbidden. Are we to say that the taboo weighing upon them somehow persists through a kind of inertia? In that case the taboo would have to be endowed with exceptional force, and a father and son should always and everywhere be expressly forbidden to have sexual relations with the same woman, whoever she might be. But this is not the case. Among the Hittites, for example, this type of dual relationship was prohibited with family members or with free persons, but permitted with slaves or with prostitutes (see Vernier 2009, 194).

The fact that a father and his son can share the same prostitute is essential. It shows that the theory of humors, or corporeal contact, does not explain the prohibition of incest of the second type or, a fortiori, the taboo that we are interested in here. Fear of rivalries, which dual relations threaten to unleash, is a much more plausible explanation, especially in a case such as the one cited by Vernier, for, unlike a relative or a woman of high social status, a slave or a prostitute could not be the object of a serious conflict between two free men. But it is of no help whatsoever in trying to understand the absolute character of the taboo involving the mother and son; indeed, it weighs upon the son even in the event he is born after the death of his father. We therefore must seek the reason for it, and for its deterrent power, elsewhere. Treating it as one case among others for which a general explanation can be given is plainly a nonstarter. It constitutes a unique case, and no doubt owes its singular quality to the fact that while a man may have several sisters or several female cousins, he can have but one mother. The union of a man with the person who brought him into the world has a regressive character; because it reverses the process of birth, which by contrast separates the son from his mother, it is, and remains, the archetypal form of incest, the one whose prohibition is universal and that endures when prohibitions falling upon more distant relatives disappear, one after the other.

If this is so, we must give up regarding the prohibition of incest as a mere consequence of the exogamy rule, and recognize its priority instead.[11] Moreover, and without relinquishing the ambition of discovering general rules, it is certainly necessary to abandon the idea of subordinating all sexual relations to a single principle. Tempting though it may be to subsume Oedipal incest with the mother and the dual relationship of a man with two sisters under the same category, Héritier has unfortunately failed to do this, and it is probably impossible. By contrast, the Baule case and many other similar ones studied by Vernier seem to be amenable to a unified explanation, namely, that these relations are prohibited in order to avoid conflicts between close relatives and members of the same social class. Thus it is that the Hittite laws I just mentioned forbid a man from having relations with two sisters if he is married to one of them, but permit him to do so if this is not the case and if they live in different places, or else if they reside in the same place and they are foreigners or slaves (see Vernier 2009, 191–200; Fine 2013, 1101). One could, like Freud ([1913] 1955, 13:144) and Girard ([1972b] 1977, 221), interpret prohibitions based on exogamy in the same manner: men must marry outside the familial or local group in order to prevent the most closely related women from quarreling. In fact, in the majority of societies where there is no state, but instead what Raymond Verdier calls a vindicatory system, one observes two interdependent taboos governing sexual relations. Together they create a sense of communal identity, with one taboo regulating homicide and vengeance, the other incest and marriage. One both fights and marries one's adversaries: one trades plunder, blows, and murders with them while also exchanging women (see Verdier 1980). In every case the aim is to forestall rivalries and internal conflict by moving violence and anything that might give rise to it outside the community.

That the prohibitions of incest and of homicide should have the same field of application seems paradoxical to us, for they have evolved in modern societies in inverse relation to each other: the scope of the former prohibition tends to be limited to the elementary family, and that of the latter to be extended to humanity as a whole. Governments today grant the individual total freedom in choosing a mate, so long as this person comes from outside one's immediate family (within which sexual relations themselves are nevertheless not always the object of statutory regulation or penalty);[12] by contrast, they reserve to themselves the right to arbitrate conflicts as well as a monopoly on legitimate violence. The advent of the state therefore causes exogamy proper to disappear, while at the same time, in confiscating vengeance (to use Verdier's strong expression), it takes away from the individuals and groups the right to do justice themselves. In this context, the prohibition against taking one's spouse from within the elementary family, which neither the "civil pact of solidarity" nor "marriage for all" was able to abolish, or had not yet succeeded in eliminating, attests in its way to the primary and specific character of Oedipal incest.

The lesson of all this is easily drawn. The two examples we have considered, Oedipal incest and the dual relationship involving two sisters, show first of all the sui generis character of Oedipal incest, for it cannot be deduced from either a theory of exogamy (contra Lévi-Strauss) or a general theory of incest that also includes a dual relationship with two related persons (contra Héritier). But they also suggest the possibility of constructing, on the basis of this second example and of similar cases, a general theory of sexual prohibitions and exogamy rules inspired by Freud's *Totem and Taboo*, which is to say a theory that takes seriously the idea that "sexual desires do not unite men but divide them" ([1913] 1955, 13:144), and that it is therefore necessary to guard against this danger by means of specific prohibitions. It follows that so-called incest of the second type represents neither a plausible generalization of classic incest nor, strictly speaking, a second form of incest, even if there is indeed something common to all the facts that it is supposed to bring together, namely, the impossibility of combining close kinship with sexual intimacy.

As for the explanation of prohibitions that Héritier's hypothesis purports to furnish by means of a theory of humors, it too must be renounced, not because, as some have objected, this theory is substantialist, rather than symbolic or structural, in nature (see Heinich 1995, 947; Héran 2009, 556), but because the Hittite examples analyzed by Vernier suffice to invalidate it, and because it adds nothing to our understanding. It is probably a rationalization of certain avoidance rules, sufficiently widespread to warrant notice, but one that would have to be elucidated in its turn, instead of being erected into an explanatory principle. In this regard I cannot follow Agnès Fine, who in her excellent critical study of Vernier's work tries diplomatically to rescue part of the theory of humors by arguing that it is corroborated by several African examples.[13] There is no need to resort to such an argument in order to recognize the scientific value of Héritier's work. As Maurice Hocart reminded the anthropologists of his time, science is not a matter of always being right. It is a matter of devising concepts and hypotheses, which he likened to levers, that make it possible to acquire "power over facts,"[14] to order the data yielded by fieldwork, to clarify them and open up new lines of inquiry. Now, this is manifestly the case with the notion of incest of the second type and the theory of humors. Even if they have not justified the hopes that their author placed in them, they furnished her and many others with an Ariadne's thread, a lever for moving masses of facts—and, in the first place, the desire to try. There can be no doubt that they helped to renew interest in kinship and inspired research that has enriched our knowledge. Hypotheses that prove to be immensely fruitful, even if in the end they are disconfirmed, do much to advance the cause of science.

To this I hasten to add that there is no need to throw out the baby with the bath water, which is to say the very principle of non-combination of identical things. Though it has its source in the theory of humors, it need not suffer the same fate. It will continue to be valuable, I believe, not only in clarifying the nature of incest but also, as we shall see later, in shedding light on other, no less important relationships.

CHAPTER SIX

The Brother-Sister Relationship and the Principle of Male Dominance

The structural theory of alliance treats differences between the sexes as a symmetric relationship, which is to say a relationship whose terms are interchangeable. If one conceives of alliance as an exchange, it is a matter of indifference whether one says that men exchange women or that women exchange men. We have become accustomed to adopting the male point of view in speaking of matrilateral marriage, where a man's preferred spouse is the daughter of his mother's brother, and of patrilateral marriage, where it is the daughter of his father's sister. But both the perspective and the vocabulary can be reversed. For a woman, the first type of marriage is patrilateral since her spouse is the son of her father's sister, and the second is matrilateral since it involves the son of her mother's brother.

From Lévi-Strauss's point of view, this symmetry between the sexes also obtains between brother and sister, and not only, as one may be tempted to suppose, between two brothers or two sisters, which is to say within pairs of siblings of the same sex, whose symmetry seems more obvious.[1] What distinguishes the brother-sister relationship from the other two is that it constitutes the pivot of the exchange relationship and the atom of kinship. In structural theory, the atom of kinship rests entirely on "the idea that the *brother-sister* relationship is identical with the *sister-brother* relationship, but

FIGURE 5. The Equivalence of Same-Sex Siblings in Contrast to That of Different-Sex Siblings (Lévi-Strauss)

that these both differ from the *brother-brother* and the *sister-sister* relationships, which are identical with one another" (Lévi-Strauss [1949c] 1969, 128). Indeed, in many kinship systems, parallel cousins—the issue of same-sex siblings—are likened to brothers and sisters and, consequently, forbidden to marry, whereas cross cousins—the issue of a brother and a sister—are considered potential (perhaps even preferential) spouses.[2]

The matrimonial rules of semi-complex systems agree with this perspective, taking into account only the opposition between cross and parallel relatives, that is, between heterogeneous and homogeneous pairs, without regard for their constituent terms: in both cases, men and women are subject to the same redoubling restrictions. But is that enough to establish that cross relatives, like parallel relatives, are symmetrical? Françoise Héritier raises the question, and with good reason. In attempting to answer it, she appeals chiefly to two properties of the terminology of kinship, one quite general, the other characteristic of Crow and Omaha systems.

From the Asymmetry of the Sexes to the Principle of Male Dominance

It has been customary since Lowie and Murdock to distinguish among terminologies of kinship according to the way in which they classify and name cousins. By this criterion, confining ourselves to the relevant cases, there are only four possibilities.[3] The first consists in applying the same terminology to cousins and to siblings—in other words, in not differentiating between the cousins either of brothers or of sisters. The second, by contrast, distinguishes cousins from siblings by the use of specific terms, as our system

FIGURE 6. The Equivalence of Same-Sex Siblings in Contrast to the Asymmetry of Different-Sex Siblings (Héritier)

of kinship does. The third likens parallel cousins to siblings, reserving specific terms for cross cousins. The fourth, by contrast with the preceding case, likens cross cousins to siblings, reserving specific terms for parallel cousins. Héritier notes that while the first three cases are observed in many places, the last one, though it is structurally possible,[+] is nowhere attested (see Héritier 1981, 19, 39–42). One may therefore infer, she says, that cross relatives are instinctively, and in principle, regarded as more distant than parallel relatives. Indeed, it is a *"fundamental law of kinship* that cross solidarity is never stronger than parallel solidarity, and a *cross relation between individuals or groups is never the implicit basis of equivalence or identity"* (38; emphasis in the original).

The tendency to group siblings and parallel (rather than cross) relatives together, and the disinclination to do the opposite, that is, group siblings and cross (rather than parallel) relatives together, naturally leads us to ask what makes members of the one set similar and members of the other fundamentally dissimilar. Héritier believes that a clue may be found in the terminology of the Crow and Omaha systems. These have the peculiarity of treating the cross relation, which is to say the brother-sister relationship, as a generational difference: a son-mother relationship in the Crow (matrilineal) system, a father-daughter relationship in the Omaha (patrilineal) system. This brings out very clearly the distance between the two terms of a cross relation, that is, between two persons who are related since they are siblings, but who are seen as dissimilar because their sex is different. It therefore becomes necessary to revise the sibling classification proposed by Lévi-Strauss to say that whereas pairs of same-sex siblings are always symmetric and similar to one another, pairs of different-sex siblings are asymmetrical and dissimilar. It is this trait that separates parallel from cross relatives (see ibid., 47).

This asymmetry, far from being a secondary property, is regarded as the organizing principle, the womb of kinship systems: "The asymmetrical brother-sister relationship is the basic element of the whole structure of kinship, for everything is included in it. It contains not only the difference of sex, but all the other things as well: the necessity of marriage with other similar units, the act of procreation from which it is issued and the ones that follow, the choice between principles of descent, the crossing of the collateral lines that come out from it, the relative relationship of primogeniture" (Héritier 1981, 47). This seems to me entirely correct. Indeed, Héritier is doubly right, not only in correcting the structural theory of kinship by stressing the asymmetry of the brother-sister relationship, but also in locating marriage in its proper place, between "the act of procreation from which it is issued and the ones that follow," which is to say by subordinating alliance to reproduction. But she seems not to see that these two things are one and the same; and as a result of failing to identify the exact nature of the asymmetry she detects in kinship terminologies, she is led to seek the reasons for it outside the field of kinship, in the realm of dominance relationships. For an insufficiently analyzed and still undetermined asymmetry she is prepared, in other words, to substitute a unilateral inequality: domination of the feminine by the masculine.

It is true that, in assimilating degrees of collaterality to degrees of descent, the terminologies of Crow and Omaha systems reveal what could be called "a *directed relationship of sexual dominance*" (ibid., 48; my emphasis); but it is no less true that this orientation changes when one passes from one system to the other. For while in an Omaha system the cross relation "is equivalent to a father/daughter paternal relationship," in a Crow system it "is theoretically equivalent to a mother-son maternal relationship" (48). Héritier herself would be the first to admit that the manner in which she describes this reversal—in setting a true equivalence against an equivalence that is only "theoretical"—betrays a certain uneasiness. As an ethnographer of the Samo, she starts off from the Omaha point of view, where male dominance appears to be implicit in the terminology since the sister is supposed to be the daughter of her brother. But Héritier is obliged to recognize that a Crow system, interpreted in the same fashion, adopts a diametrically opposed perspective, since now the brother is considered to be the son of his sister. To minimize the reversal by suggesting that in this case it is purely theoretical evades the issue in a way that has the effect of discrediting the whole argument from terminologies. This is why she finds it necessary to resort to a "second, more general reason" in order to explain the asymmetry of the cross relation, namely, "the existence of a massive bias in favor of male domination" (49). But this amounts to appealing to an external factor to account for a property that was supposed to be inherent in the relationship. At bottom, Omaha systems do nothing other than give an original form of expression to a principle that one way or another, whether it is tacitly or explicitly acknowledged, whether it is affirmed or denied, underlies the whole of human behavior. They plainly state a universally accepted norm of subordination of female to male that is supposed to rest on the innate superiority of men to women, and that could be described in various ways: in some systems, as a difference of generations; in others, as a difference between older and younger within generations; in still others, as a difference between wet and dry, and so on.

Asymmetry of the Sexes and the Female Privilege of Giving Birth

Be this as it may, is it really the final word? It seems simpler to search for the source of the principle of male domination in the desire of men to compensate for the female privilege of bringing children into the world—indeed, institutionally or symbolically, to appropriate women's reproductive capacities (see Scubla 1982, 1985b, 1991). The dominance principle is a reactive, not an original principle. It represents an attempt to reverse the asymmetry in favor of the male sex.

What essentially distinguishes parallel from cross relations is not the difference between the sexes in and of itself, but its link with procreation. As figure 7 shows, in a homogeneous pair, two sisters or two brothers always have the same "valence" (or value, which is to say relative strength or weakness), whether because both of them inherit, or neither one of them inherits, the power that their mother had of bringing children into the world. A brother and sister, by contrast, have opposite values, since the daughter alone receives from her mother the power to procreate—unless, of course, her brother were to receive a uterus transplant, a fantasy contemplated by certain feminists that amounts to a symmetric and inverse version

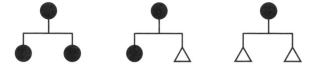

FIGURE 7. The Ability to Have Children, Differential Strength of the Sexes, and
Classification of Siblings

of mythical narratives according to which women originally possessed the
cultural prerogatives of men.

I certainly do not mean to suggest that Héritier is unaware of this way
of looking at the matter. Curiously, however, she seems to have deliberately
avoided any mention of it in explaining what she means by the "differential
valence of the sexes." At the risk of weakening her own argument, she says not
a word about it in the text itself of *The Practice of Kinship*, alluding to it only
in a note that refers the reader to an article she had published earlier in an
Italian encyclopedia.[5] In more recent writings, notably an article in which she
summarizes her work on kinship, she has been more explicit. "The earliest
men," she says, "found themselves faced with a disconcerting mystery, . . . the
exorbitant privilege enjoyed by women of giving birth to both sexes. . . . It was
necessary to explain this privilege, as well as the reason why from one form
another form could emerge, why women could give birth to boys. . . . There
resulted from this a remarkable state of affairs, remarkable because of the
reversal that it implied: the taking by the masculine part of humanity of both
the initiative in procreation and responsibility for it" (Héritier 2000, 35).

Two important notions are put forward here, of (feminine) "privilege"
and (masculine) "reversal." Male dominance is no longer a primitive fact: it
results from the reversal of a prior asymmetry. It serves to compensate for the
feminine prerogative of bearing children, by "domesticat[ing] the privilege
that women enjoy of giving birth to the two sexes" (ibid., 36). Héritier even
goes so far as to say that here we find "the thing to which everything else is
moored" (36). Everything else—which is to say systems of kinship, with all
their prescriptions and prohibitions.

But there are still several possible ways, it would seem, of thinking about
this mooring and how kinship systems and matrimonial practices come to
be secured. In the passage I quoted a moment ago the reader will have noted

that Héritier does not characterize the difference between the sexes by reference simply to the fact that women, and not men, give birth to children, but still more importantly to the fact that they have the power to give birth to boys, which is to say to children who differ from themselves in respect of their sex. This is an essential point to her way of thinking, and one to which she often returns: "Women reproduce themselves identically, but they have the extravagant capacity to produce bodies different from theirs, [whereas in order to] reproduce themselves identically, a man is *obliged to pass through a woman's body*" (Héritier [2002] 2012, 18, 23; emphasis in the original).

When all is said and done, it is this "issue of sameness and difference" that Héritier sees as the heart of the matter, and as being at the root of the differential valence of the sexes, particularly as it is embodied in the brother-sister relationship. The same tension between like and unlike, between same and different, is also the source (see Héritier [1994] 1999, 201–38) of the "mechanics of fluids" (239–64) that defines incest of the second type. It is the cornerstone for all perceptions and behaviors relating to kinship.

The implications of this hypothesis can be worked out only if we remove an ambiguity first. Are sameness and difference, like and unlike, true structuring principles, constitutive of reality itself, or are they only conceptual tools that allow us to analyze it? For if we are dealing merely with intellectual categories, it is hard to see how they could by themselves be the source of familial institutions and of social organization as a whole, rather than simply the source of the thoughts and perceptions that accompany them. But if we are dealing with organizing principles, it would be necessary to show how their combinations and arrangements make it possible to reconstruct, step by step, all human institutions, actions, and productions. Héritier herself does not make so fine a distinction, and indeed often gives the impression of hesitating between these two positions.[6]

The "earliest men," she says, were disconcerted by the birth of boys and did not cease to search for the mysterious reason "why from one form another form could emerge." Surely it is more plausible to suppose that our most distant ancestors were chiefly preoccupied with the birth of girls, which is to say with the precarious position of groups in which women were few, and the necessity in such a case of somehow obtaining, from a more fortunate group, the women needed for their survival. As Lévi-Strauss writes, "savage peoples have clearly and constantly been faced with the simple and brutal choice,

powerfully expressed by Tylor, 'between marrying-out and being killed out'"
(E. B. Tylor, "On a Method of Investigating the Development of Institutions" [1889], quoted in Lévi-Strauss [1949c] 1969, 43)—the choice between
more or less voluntarily and peacefully giving up women, on the one hand,
and having them violently taken away through wars of extermination on the
other.[7] It is in terms of this fundamental experience that we must think about
what Héritier very happily calls the "domestication" of women's reproductive
functions.

In concentrating from the first on the birth of boys and on the enigma
that it posed to the human mind, in laying emphasis at the outset on the
general philosophical issue of sameness and difference, she not only favors
an intellectualist version of the origin of institutions; she also distracts attention from the thing that constitutes the very foundation of the brother-sister
asymmetry, namely, the ability to give birth, which the daughter possesses
but the boy does not.[8] Already challenged in this crucial respect by the theory
of incest of the second type, women find their own most distinctive capacity—the power to assure the survival of the group by producing not only
boys but also, and especially, girls, which is to say potential mothers—once
again devalued.

It is as though Héritier could not bring herself to explain the difference
between the sexes directly, in terms of their asymmetric relation to procreation. But why? For fear of giving too "naturalistic" a definition of femininity? Her theory of humors and her professed allegiance to materialism give
reason to doubt it; if anything, they seem to point in the opposite direction.
However this may be, her reluctance to take a strong stand on this point
had the consequence that she failed to push her criticism of Lévi-Strauss's
classification of siblings as far as she should have done. Recall that, for Lévi-
Strauss, the three possible pairs of siblings—two brothers, two sisters, a
brother and a sister—are all symmetrical, but the third stands opposed to the
other two because it alone is capable of furnishing a basis for matrimonial
exchange. Héritier takes issue with this on the ground that the brother-sister
relationship is in fact asymmetrical, but she retains the idea that the two pairs
of same-sex siblings are not only symmetrical but equivalent. This is the case
in her magnum opus of 1981, and it remains true twenty years later when,
recapitulating her thinking about kinship, she says once more that a cross
relative is more distant than a parallel relative (see Héritier 2000, 24). Now,

as figure 7 shows, if the asymmetry of the brother-sister relationship is really based on a woman's capacity to become a mother, rather than to be the object or partner of a matrimonial exchange, the two pairs of same-sex siblings not only cease to be equivalent, they are dramatically different.[9] Although both are symmetric, they occupy diametrically opposed positions equidistant from the asymmetric pair, which figures as the middle term of the triad. It is no longer possible, under these circumstances, to hold that a parallel relative is necessarily closer than a cross relative.

From the Elementary Structures of Alliance to the Elementary Forms of Kinship

Laurent Barry (2008) provides us with an additional proof on this point. His work gives a precise measure of the relative closeness of first cousins for several societies in which kinship is organized according to either a uterine or an agnatic principle.[10] These degrees of proximity are calculated on the basis of two kinds of information: customary rules concerning marriage, and statistics obtained by analyzing recorded marriages. Depending on whether the degree of kinship is more or less close, marriage between cousins may be prohibited, tolerated, authorized, or preferred. By combing through marriage lists and scrutinizing genealogies it becomes possible to compare prescriptions with actual practice. Barry's study, in assembling a sufficiently large and reliable mass of data for a number of societies to allow general conclusions to be drawn, has given renewed impetus to the study of kinship.

Recall, first, that four types of cousins are distinguished: matrilateral cross cousins (MCC), patrilateral cross cousins (PCC), matrilateral parallel cousins (MPC), and patrilateral parallel cousins (PPC). Figure 8 represents a man and his sister with their ascendants, flanked by their four types of cousins: the daughter of the mother's brother (MCC) and the daughter of the father's sister (PCC), these two being cross cousins; and the daughter of the mother's sister (MPC) and the daughter of the father's brother (PPC), these two being parallel cousins.

Recall, too, that Lévi-Strauss constructed his theory of alliance on the basis of the dichotomy between parallel and cross cousins, the latter representing exogamy, the former endogamy. Let us consider a society consisting

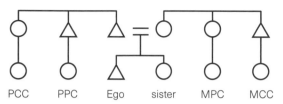

FIGURE 8. Male Ego's Sister and Four Types of Cousin

of two exogamous moieties. As the reader may easily verify, whether membership in a half is transmitted through men or through women, that is, by either patrilineal or matrilineal descent, parallel cousins, like brothers and sisters, belong to Ego's half, whereas cross cousins belong to the other half; the former are therefore not marriageable, while the latter are eligible to be considered as spouses. Hence Lévi-Strauss's interest in dual organizations of this type and their various ramifications, and, a fortiori, in peoples who explicitly use the same term to designate a sister and a female parallel cousin while reserving a specific term for the female cross cousin (a term, moreover, that in some cases has the meaning of a potential wife)—in short, in societies that directly incorporate an exogamy rule in their segmentary structure and in their kinship terminology. But this is also the source of the enigma that confronts Lévi-Strauss in the case of so-called Arab marriage, which is to say the difficulty, if not the impossibility, that structural theory encounters in trying to explain the preferential union of a man with his female patrilateral parallel cousin (PPC)—a type of marriage practiced not only in the Arab world but also in certain other societies equipped with a patrilineal clan or lineage system, where such marriage therefore exhibits a character almost as endogamous as that of another stumbling block for structural theory, the custom of marrying one's own sister, recorded in ancient Egyptian dynasties.

Now, Barry has shown—and this is an essential result—that, in spite of their patrilineal structure, societies practicing Arab marriage have a kinship system organized on the uterine model (see Barry 2008, 232ff.) Moving from the closest to the most distant relatives, Ego's sister and female cousins are ordered in the following manner: Ego, sister, MPC, PCC, MCC, PPC. The MPC is the closest of the four cousins; the cross cousins occupy an intermediate rank; and the PPC is the most distant. This is why the latter is, by law and in fact, the preferential spouse. Accordingly, Arab marriage is in its way a form of exogamy as well.

In societies equipped with a system of agnatic kinship, such as the Han in China (see ibid., 636ff.), things are obviously reversed. There the two female parallel cousins exchange their respective places, and one observes the following order: Ego, sister, PPC, PCC, MCC, MPC. But the overall structure remains unchanged; as in the preceding case, cross cousins occupy the middle position, and the parallel cousins are disjoint and diametrically opposed. These facts, numerous and well established, by themselves constitute an unchallengeable refutation of Héritier's claim: parallel relatives are not necessarily closer than cross relatives.

The symmetry between these two cases nevertheless is not seen as confirming the primacy that I attribute to the uterine principle. For Barry, as for the structuralists, who are grateful to him in this regard (see Héran 2009, 565), the uterine principle and the agnatic principle are but two possible ways among others of organizing kinship independently of any genetic or biological constraint (see Barry 2008, 164). Kinship, in Barry's view, is a social construct intended to divide human beings into two categories: immediate relatives, endowed with a common identity, and potential relatives by marriage, known as affines. The definition and transmission of this identity are bound up with the difference between the sexes, but they vary from one society to another since they do not depend on the intrinsic properties of one sex or the other, but instead on the role that each society assigns them in the formation of identity (see 171). The fact of the matter—Barry does not say this, but it is clearly implied by his argument—is that vernacular theories of the difference between the sexes and of their function in the transmission of kinship have a marginal role in this connection: they try merely to justify, without explaining, the systems in which they are found and of which an exhaustive survey can be made a priori. Parental identity can be transmitted exclusively through either one of the two sexes, and therefore either by the female pathway (uterine principle) or by the male pathway (agnatic principle), and also through the two sexes, who thus contribute to it either in identical ways (cognatic principle) or in distinct ways (parallel principle). Moreover, it may or may not be extended to affines; in the affirmative case this occurs by means of one of the modalities just mentioned. There are therefore, in total, twenty (four times five) fundamental types of kinship group and possible affinity (see 210). Without having to appeal to considerations of another order than that of a combinatoric based on the existence of two sexes and the distinction between immediate family and relatives by marriage, one can thus construct a theory of kinship and exogamy[11] that is much more general than the classic structural theory.[12] Without having to abandon the classic definition of incest, one obtains a "unified theory of the prohibition of incest" that brings together the prohibitions of a "first type" (concerning blood relatives) and those of a "second type" (concerning relatives by marriage) (209).[13]

Must we leave it at that, then, going no further than to recognize a de jure equivalence between different principles of kinship and between the configurations that result from their combination? Probably so, if we proceed initially by detaching kinship relations from all the other aspects of social life with which they are entangled in order first of all to derive a pure theory from them. Not only is this process of abstraction legitimate, it also is no less necessary in anthropology than it is in the other sciences, and kinship theorists are to be given credit for undertaking it. But once one puts kinship systems back in the context of the actual lives of human beings, and of the broader cultural life that these systems help to organize, one can no longer pretend they are interchangeable, which is to say independent of the natural characteristics of the human beings whose relations they govern and of the social institutions these systems shape.

As Barry himself emphasizes, no society can conceal the primary proximity of children to the mother who has borne and often nursed them (see 2008, 195). He stresses also the great importance of male couvade and circumcision rituals, which, among the Merina of Madagascar, counterbalance the principle of uterine kinship and the eminent place the woman is recognized to occupy in procreation (see 363). In this particular case, the desire to compensate for a female privilege by means of a male prerogative is explicit. But it may be wondered, more generally, whether the patrilineal descent system and the patricentric organization of societies that, like the Malagasy people, practice Arab marriage do not betray a concern of this sort, whether or not it is openly acknowledged. Enlarging the perspective still further, one might even conjecture that, whatever may be the principle serving to define parental identity, every human community recognizes in one way or another, if only half-heartedly, the primacy of the mother-child bond and the crucial role played by women in assuring its reproduction and survival. The system of the Han in China, though it is agnatic, cannot be considered an exception. The Han are not unaware that it is above all thanks to women that the flow of life is replenished and carried onward. Barry does not lay sufficient emphasis on this point, it seems to me. Catherine Capdeville-Zeng, a student of Chinese systems, concurs. She remarks that Barry "fails to comment on a fact that he himself mentions, namely, that a woman transmits her blood to her daughter. Surely this is a major fact, for it shows that uterine lineages do indeed exist alongside male lineages" (Capdeville-Zeng 2010, 446). Indeed, the specific role of female lineages could not be more plain.

One might regard these female lineages as a counterpart, in systems governed by an agnatic principle, to the male lineages that are abundant in systems governed by a uterine principle—and so also as evidence of the "palindromic" character of the Arab and Chinese systems, laid end to end (see Barry 2008, 189, 755). But I believe that the inference of symmetry is specious in this case. The complementarity of the sexes, as it is observed in human societies, is probably not a primitive datum, but the result of an adjustment to a preexisting and primordial asymmetry favoring women. It is thus that I would interpret the use of the patronymic in most cognatic societies today. By giving the father's name to a family, it is implicitly recognized that the family's perpetuation depends chiefly on its female component. In this regard, I would argue, cognatic systems display the same features as other systems; despite appearances to the contrary, they do not depart from the common rule, nor do they violate their own egalitarian principles, as our era is inclined to imagine, regarding patronymy as an intolerable anomaly. However this may be, it is certain that the asymmetry inherent in the difference between the sexes prevents the logic of agnatic systems from being pushed as far as that of uterine systems. The agnatic equivalent of Na society is unknown. Whereas a society without father or husband can in fact exist, it is very hard to imagine a society without mother or wife, even if recent technological advances and institutional adaptations that increasingly have the effect of separating procreation from sexuality seem to embrace this dream, seeing in it the promise of attaining a better world—indeed the best of worlds.[14]

We are now therefore in a position to restate the conclusion of the preceding chapter in a stronger form. The brother-sister relationship is fundamentally asymmetric, and it does in fact contain everything else, as Héritier insists, because the sister does not figure in it only as an object of matrimonial exchange, but above all as a potential mother and guarantor of the continuity of the group. The fact that even in patrilineal societies the maternal uncle often occupies a more important place than the paternal uncle proves not only that a cross relative may be closer than a parallel relative (see Héran 2009, 549); it points to something more profound, namely, that procreation, of which the woman is the principal vector, is the organizing principle of kinship groups. In recentering kinship on procreation, and in the process extending Héritier's work in an original way, Laurent Barry has succeeded in constructing a much more general theory than the one developed by Lévi-Strauss. Françoise Héritier, for her part, has therefore not only helped to complete structural theory, she has also shown the way for others to go beyond it.

CHAPTER SEVEN

Conceptualizing Difference or Dissolving Hierarchy?

From Asymmetry to Parity

Though she often speaks of the "differential valence of the sexes," Françoise Héritier has never really taken it seriously. She has never committed herself to characterizing it in terms of the function, peculiar to women, of conceiving children—in terms of a property that, whether or not it is actually what she calls a "thought-blocker" (something that sets a limit to what the human mind is capable of imagining), constitutes in any case a crucial constraint for every human society. Yet indeed it is this natural, and until now irreducible, fact that establishes the asymmetry of the sexes from the very beginning, and confers upon women—the point cannot be insisted upon often enough—an exceptional value for the survival of every human community. Curiously, however, Héritier scarcely mentions[1] the preponderant place that belongs to women by their very nature, and that all human societies recognize in one way or another, as we are emphatically reminded by such legendary episodes as the abduction of the Sabine women, or by compensatory practices that seek to avoid bloody reprisals by permitting an injured party to obtain from his adversary a woman capable of procreating, which is to say by permitting him to reconstitute his "life-capital"[2]—scenes in which are manifested not only male violence and domination, but also the final recognition of their powerlessness to control life, of which women are the guardians.

This reluctance, indeed aversion to the idea of taking a simple fact of nature as a criterion for the difference between the sexes is a paradox of contemporary thought. One swears only by the body, reduces the soul to a phantom and the mind to a function of the brain or to an emergent property of the interaction of brains, but at the same time one refuses to distinguish individuals, the sexes, or peoples by any physical characteristic whatsoever. In anthropology in particular, discriminating terms tend to be regarded as discriminatory; the word "race" has now become taboo, and the term "gender" is often substituted for "sex," which may itself soon be banished from the language. It is as though the egalitarian ideology of our time fears recognizing any distinctions among human beings other than the ones produced by chance events of history, arbitrary social conventions, or the contingent choices of individuals.

Even if Héritier's language is rather measured in this regard, it does not go against the mood of our time. It may have helped even to sustain it, as her two volumes on the difference between masculine and feminine (Héritier 1996; [2002] 2012) seem to suggest. This is all the more striking in view of the fact that in the first of these (which bears the subtitle "Thinking about Difference") she begins with a discussion of her theory of bodily fluids (see Héritier 1996, 9), apparently without fear of being accused of "substantialism." Despite its theoretical ambition,[3] this work does not study so much the difference between the sexes as the inegalitarianism that is its companion in most societies, a rather vast sample of which Héritier rapidly surveys. As the subtitle is meant to make clear, her subject is the perception—tacitly hierarchical and masculine—of sexual difference.

One must be alert to the dual shift that occurs here, explicitly, in the assimilation of the object with its image, and implicitly, in the assimilation of the concept of difference with that of inequality. It is less a matter, then, of examining attitudes toward sexual difference than of drawing up an indictment of sexist attitudes,[4] with the result that anthropological analysis veers off into political combat. Instead of concentrating on sexual difference itself, attention is turned toward male dominance and the reasons that are supposed to justify it, which, it is held, the anthropologist must at least "expose to view, for want of being able to eradicate them" (ibid.). But in doing this, one risks not only confusing the thing itself with biased perceptions of it, but also, and more damagingly still, believing that the weakness of the naturalistic arguments advanced in favor of male supremacy suffices to refute any naturalistic conception of the difference between the sexes.

While Héritier herself does not commit this paralogism, she nonetheless charts a course that will bring her closer and closer to gender theorists, even if she manages to avoid embracing their radical constructivism. She does not imagine that the supposed masculine and feminine traits always refer to intrinsic properties of men and women, but neither does she maintain that they are purely conventional labels, like the grammatical gender of words, applied by human beings; to the contrary, because it is a question of categories invented by men for the purpose of dominating women, these traits presuppose an inborn difference between the two sexes. The fact remains, however, that this difference and even this primary asymmetry are rarely defined in her work, and tend to become ever more evanescent with the passage of time.

An Evolving Argument: From a Private Female Domain to the Principle of Male Dominance

In the first volume of *Masculin/féminin* (Héritier 1996), it is not until the ninth chapter, which is to say not before the reader has come to the last third of the book, that the difference between the sexes is explicitly associated with procreation. The last pages of this chapter are particularly important, for, as far as I am aware, they are the only ones in Héritier's entire work to clearly and simultaneously state the three following propositions: what characterizes women and distinguishes them from men is not sexuality but fertility;[5] the domination of women by men is intended above all to control, and indeed to appropriate, this fertility;[6] and since fertility by its very nature creates a domain reserved for women, it can only lead by way of compensation to the formation of a domain reserved for men.[7] It will have been noted that the last two propositions are not equivalent, the one being couched in terms of inequality, the other in terms of complementarity. Faced with the female privilege of carrying children and bringing them into the world, men react in two different ways: either by attempting to turn the hierarchy to their advantage through the creation of institutions capable of managing the "life-capital" represented by women and their reproductive capacities, or by arrogating to themselves a privilege that is symmetrical to one of theirs, such as hunting and making war.[8] In the first case, one enters into rivalry and competition with the aim of achieving a dominant position; in the second case, into a search for balance between complementary, though not necessarily hierarchical, responsibilities,[9] which must be kept separate if conflict is to be avoided. Anticipating what in the next chapter I call "Testart's law," Héritier suggests that the principle of this separation is to be sought in the opposition between menstrual blood, involuntarily shed by women of childbearing age, and the blood of the warrior, voluntarily shed by men on the field of battle (see Héritier 1996, 234–35).

This chapter no doubt represents Héritier's most serious attempt to analyze the difference between the sexes and its social consequences on the basis of their natural foundation. It nonetheless cannot be considered part of the book's main argument, for it is neither the conclusion of the preceding chapters nor the premise of a concluding chapter. In reproducing an article first published almost twenty years earlier, in 1979, it constitutes instead a vestige of what by now was a rather remote phase of the author's thought. The original article does not appear to have served as a point of departure for subsequent investigation; to the contrary, it is a synopsis of positions from which her thinking was progressively to distance itself—as though she had been unable to resist the fashions of her time. The reason for this, I believe, has to do with weaknesses that were apparent on first publication, and that came to seem still more disabling in the years that followed.

Héritier does not make as sharp a distinction as I myself have done, in summarizing her argument, between the two ways that are available to men to counterbalance the female privilege of fertility, namely, subordination and complementarity, the one consisting in an attempt to turn the reproductive power of women to male advantage, the other in opposing to it a symmetric male prerogative and power. Héritier treats the matter as though the latter were an extension of the former; she does not dissociate subjection and complementarity, that is, subordination of the feminine to the masculine, on the one hand, and, on the other, the creation of a private domain reserved for men. In general, she seems to assume there were always only two possibilities, male domination and equality of the sexes, a hierarchy favorable to men and perfect parity between men and women. The idea that any other relations might have existed between masculine and feminine—of complementarity, for example, or even of hierarchy—is never entertained. The idea that it might be permissible, or even necessary, to distinguish in order to unite, as it were, seems to be totally excluded, as though the act of discrimination were considered, at least in the present instance if not also in principle, illegitimate. This tendency is more apparent in the second volume of *Masculin/féminin*, published in 2002, but it can be glimpsed already in the first volume, and particularly in its oldest chapter.

This chapter has yet another weakness, of undervaluing, or even neglecting, the primordial supremacy that bringing forth children confers on women over men; of acting as though the native difference between the sexes were only the occasion, for the male part of humanity, to impose its will on the female part. In this connection Héritier reminds us that the hypothesis of a primitive matriarchy, which is to say of a society originally controlled by women, was refuted long ago, and moreover that no example is known of a society, ancient or modern, equipped with matriarchal institutions. In all the societies attested by history or ethnography, power is exerted by men. It is only in the myths recounted to young men in the course of initiation rites that male prerogatives are described as issuing from a revolution that had abolished a prior matriarchal regime. In the beginning, it is related, women possessed all authority, and not least the power to supervise initiations; but whether they tried to dupe the male community (according to an Ona myth) or proved to be incompetent in the performance of their duties (as in a Buruya myth), men rose up in revolt and took matters into their own hands. A Dogon myth rests on the same scenario; many others could be cited as well (see Héritier 1996, 216–17). Evidently the convergence of these accounts is not proof of their historical veracity; their function is neither to describe nor to illuminate the past, Héritier says, but to "legitimize the existing social order" (218). Nevertheless they are highly significant. Specious though their justification of a male-dominated society may be, it has the virtue of recognizing that the existing order "rests on an original act of violence committed against women" (218). It is this last point that holds her full attention. "The myth explicitly declares that every culture, every society is founded on sexual inequality and that this inequality is an act of violence" (218).

The myth nonetheless will not support so cynical an interpretation. It does not amount to a claim by males to have the right to exert arbitrary

and absolute authority over females. The original matriarchy to which the
myth refers, even if it has no historical reality, cannot be regarded solely as
a justificatory fable. Its mention, at the outset of the mythical account, is a
way of recognizing and expressing the logical priority of a female power (to
give life) over a male power (to organize social institutions). Héritier does
not grant sufficient importance to one very revealing detail of the Baruya
myth in particular: it is in the women's menstrual hut that the men rob them
of the ceremonial objects used in initiations (see Héritier 1996, 217). What
better way of acknowledging the compensatory character of the private male
domain—of recognizing, without actually saying so, that this domain is a
substitute for gestation? Novices are imagined to have died in the course of
their initiation and then to have been reborn, without the help of women, by
means of specifically masculine powers alone. How better to suggest that the
rite is the male equivalent of the female prerogative of childbirth? But Héritier, who a bit later rightly appeals to this notion of compensatory equivalence
in contrasting the warrior's blood with menstrual blood (see 233–34), does
not seize the opportunity it presents for revisiting the Baruya example—with
the result that, in the very chapter in which this crucial idea might have been
able to be developed, perhaps even to the point of supplanting the idea of
domination, it is just barely touched on, and indeed passes almost unnoticed.
It is as though this negligence had irreversible consequences, a missed chance
that could never be redeemed; in the rest of the work, the idea of compensatory equivalence occupies an increasingly modest position, and in places
seems actually to disappear.

By the end of the first volume of *Masculin/féminin*, we are able to look
back over the road traveled since the time of the earliest chapter. The whole
private male domain is now conceived and described as an anomaly, as a
"bastion" to be "stormed" and "toppled," or else conquered (ibid., 296–97,
301). The vocabulary is suited to evoking a war between the sexes, not
their complementarity. The purpose has become more militant, whereas
the anthropological analysis that is supposed to support it—and this is the
point that interests us here—has paradoxically become weaker. To show that
the principle of male dominance is still active in modern societies, Héritier
recalls that the Catholic Church still refuses to allow women to be ordained
as priests (see 296–99). The arguments advanced by religious authorities to
justify this refusal, she remarks, are confused and inconclusive. This is quite

true, at least to judge from the statements reported by an evening newspaper, which apparently constitute her sole source of information (see 297–98). But she herself proposes an obscure explanation resting on a presumptive relationship between the word of God and sperm that conflates two distinct problems: the ordination of women and the celibacy of priests. "Male chastity and preaching go together" (298), she confidently asserts, although this assertion, which betrays a certain confusion between the Catholic priest and the Protestant pastor, is not true in either case.

The Catholic priest is not primarily a preacher, but a sacrificer. In the course of what is traditionally called the "sacrifice of the Mass," he reenacts the original sacrifice of Christ, put to death on the Cross. During the rite he enters into very intimate contact with the blood of Christ, and this is why a woman, bearing the mark of menstrual blood, could not perform such an office: the blood of sacrifice, no more than blood spilled in war, cannot be allowed to come into contact with menstrual blood. Here we have a matter of general principle, attested in all societies. The Catholic priest, like every sacrificer, is necessarily a man. As for the celibacy that this imposes upon him, it may be seen, among other things, as an additional precaution aimed at keeping the blood of holy sacrifice apart from menstrual blood. By contrast, the Protestant pastor is primarily a preacher and not a sacrificer. The Protestant service is neither an efficacious sacrifice, as the Catholic Mass purports to be, nor even a symbolic sacrifice,[10] but a commemoration of the Last Supper, which is to say Christ's last meal. This is why the pastoral function, whether it is a question of preaching the Gospel or of leading a service of worship, can be performed by a woman as well as by a man, who moreover may be married to one another, and therefore under no obligation of sexual abstinence.[11] This is a more plausible explanation, and indeed the very one that Héritier herself would have given if she had remained faithful to the spirit of her earlier work.

The Anthropologist and the Citizen:
From Descriptive to Normative Discourse

The second volume of *Masculin/féminin*, subtitled "Dissolving Hierarchy," is intended as an extension of the first. Héritier had wanted to give it the subtitle "Solutions [plural] of Hierarchy," a play on the different meanings of the word "solution" (see Héritier [2002] 2012, 11). That the will of the publisher should have prevailed instead is understandable, for, quite apart from any commercial or other reasons that might have told in its favor, the wording that was finally agreed upon perfectly describes the content of this work. It is an exercise in advocacy, a collection of essays on subjects as varied as contraception, cloning, medically assisted procreation, prostitution, excision, and various forms of female submission or enslavement, with the sole and avowed objective of denouncing and, if possible, eradicating every form of male domination, abolishing every private male domain. The volume also has the peculiarity of taking as its principal documentary basis the press, "considered as a shared source of information, knowledge, and perceptions, none of these less trustworthy than the evidence obtained from field work" (29; for references, see 395–404). I shall therefore say a few words about these aspects of the work before examining its basic argument.

Obviously there can be no objection if an anthropologist wishes to place her talent and her pen in the service of this or that cause. But if she intends to do it ex officio, as it were, on the strength of her professional reputation as an anthropologist, how does she manage to move from judgments of fact to value judgments, from objective observation to normative prescription? Traditional anthropology, which is essentially descriptive, eliminates the very possibility of passing from one register to the other by postulating the relativity of norms, which is to say by reducing norms to a particular class of facts. Since each culture has its own values, all values are formally equivalent. Anthropologists can do no more than note their plurality and their manifest incompatibility—for example, the incompatibility between the egalitarian principles of modern societies and the hierarchical principles of other societies; they cannot regard one society as preferable to another.

In practice, however, anthropologists often have two ways of talking: one relativistic, when they are describing exotic societies, while taking care to avoid making any value judgment; the other evolutionist, when they reckon, or even decree, that such and such a measure represents a civilized advance or a harmful regression in the case of their own society. No such complaint can be directed against Héritier. For her, cultural relativism is neither a cardinal truth nor an absolute principle; it is an argument invented by ethnologists during the twentieth century to combat the naive ethnocentrism of Western societies, and a methodological rule permitting the various solutions devised by human societies for coping with universal problems to be compared.[12]

Universalist anthropology nevertheless encounters its own theoretical and practical difficulties. How are we to know whether a universal trait is the necessary effect of a law or a contingent product of history? And how are we to assure ourselves that it may be abandoned or altered without harm, or that, to the contrary, it needs to be preserved? Descartes used to say that he had learned more about the human condition by associating with people of different customs than by reading philosophers; but despising those "confused and anxious people" who are "always thinking up some novel reform" (Descartes [1637] 1999, 13), he likened institutions and customs to a road whose meandering path seems in large part arbitrary, but which has been traveled for so long by so many and become so smooth from constant traffic that the convenience of continuing to follow it outweighs the trouble of taking a more direct but more arduous route. Who can say whether this is the voice of wisdom or pusillanimity? Shrewd pragmatism or stubborn conservatism?

Claude Lévi-Strauss's way of meeting these difficulties is scarcely more satisfying. Conservative and cautious in dealing with peoples among whom he was an outsider and whom he rightly feared upsetting, Lévi-Strauss believed that he could act as a critic—indeed, a revolutionary—within his own society because, as an insider, he risked destroying less. But this is to forget that the internal dynamic of a society may be a deadly one, and that the decline and disappearance of a civilization probably depends as much on endogenous factors as on exogenous factors. What is more, it leaves the fundamental question, which is not only practical in nature but also theoretical, unanswered.

Héritier does not directly address such problems, but neither does she pretend they do not exist. Even where she most strenuously takes issue with the principle of male dominance, she often suggests that, though vanquished in one place, it may yet rise up again elsewhere in a new form (see, for example, Héritier 1996, 301). Obviously this is not a contradiction. The dominance principle might have a status analogous to that of a physical law such as gravity. One cannot do away with gravity, but that does not mean one is fated to be its plaything. Gravity does not prevent birds from flying or human beings from inventing the airplane and the parachute, or even from slowing down the motion of the earth by rising above its surface. The male dominance principle may likewise be a force to be mastered rather than eliminated. It is a pity that Héritier did not take advantage of the opportunity presented by her second volume in order to consider essential questions of this sort.

The volume as a whole is characterized by an utter absence of theoretical curiosity. Bringing together a group of essays written in a way that suggests they were originally intended to guide government policymakers in France, it seems to be an outgrowth of Héritier's service as a member of the National Consultative Ethics Committee for Health and the Life Sciences. Evidently her readers, at least in the first instance, were interested in having the benefit of expert advice and practical recommendations, without getting bogged down in philosophical controversies. The need to avoid all unnecessarily technical detail explains not only the scarcity of citations to the scholarly literature but also, by contrast, the abundance of materials drawn from journalistic sources. One may well understand the constraints under which Héritier was obliged to operate, while at the same time regretting that she could not have allowed herself a bit more leeway. There is certainly nothing wrong from the point of view of ethnology with this way of proceeding; after all, reading the newspaper with the detached perspective of an anthropologist is an exercise that has long been recommended to students. And yet it is not one that everyone is good at. It is a much simpler matter to observe an exotic society than one's own; to be able to look at one's own society and analyze it objectively, one must find the right distance. As we saw a moment ago with the example of the ordination of women as priests, however, this is not always easy to do. The ethnologist is continually at risk of behaving like an advocate rather than a judge, of taking sides instead of refereeing, of participating in public debate instead of studying its motivations, of going down into the arena instead of remaining seated above in the gallery.

Indeed, the exercise is seldom successful,[13] and even Françoise Héritier, whose voice is almost always the voice of a scholar, does not manage to avoid the risk I have just mentioned. Sometimes reinforcing, sometimes qualifying the dominant discourse, her method in this work more often resembles that of a mediator seeking to create a consensus in support of a compromise measure than that of a theorist concerned to formulate principles that may turn out to be mutually incompatible, or that may in fact be undiscoverable. By the same token, naturalistic and cultural theories of the difference between the sexes are almost never considered on their own merits, which is to say as systems of ideas whose explanatory power can be estimated and compared only by first carefully examining their premises and their internal consistency. They are treated instead as raw data, as matters of opinion or intuitive conceptions—more or less plausible, more or less respectable, more or less shared—rather than being jointly and systematically analyzed. Hence the need to try somehow to reconcile them.

The following lines show how rather vague and apparently unobjectionable statements allow divergent points of view to coincide without, however, being granted the same legitimacy: "Maternity is not in itself a natural phenomenon; it is the object of a constant social construction that defines its rules and obligations. Yet one cannot overlook its biological dimension, if only in view of the time devoted to the bringing into the world and the feeding of children (above all when they are fed at their mother's breast)" (Héritier [2002] 2012, 364). In spite of their apparent obviousness and the author's conciliatory tone, these two sentences are by no means as innocent as they seem; diplomatically, but nonetheless unambiguously, they decide in favor of the constructivist point of view.

One might have supposed that maternity, despite its juridical—and therefore conventional—aspects, is first and foremost a natural phenomenon. But this would be to adopt the point of view of the ordinary person, who regards menstruation, pregnancy, childbirth, and lactation as self-evident signs of maternity and the characteristic traits of femininity (see ibid.). Héritier treads very carefully here, while showing preference to the advocates of conventionalism, who are the first to be allowed to speak, in the name of science, and whose argument will carry the day. "Maternity, they tell us, is not in itself a natural phenomenon." Note these two words, "in itself," which seem to weaken the claim being made without really altering its meaning.[14] For if maternity is not in itself a natural phenomenon, but something that is socially constructed, nothing prevents it from being diluted in an indeterminate sort of parenthood, open to all without distinction as to sex. It is true that Héritier seems to dismiss this possibility. One cannot, she says, evade the "biological dimension" of maternity. But here again her purpose is ambiguous. For the rest of the essay shows that this corrective is above all a concession to what used to be called the man in the street, who persists in characterizing maternity in terms of pregnancy and childbirth—a concession that is all the more difficult to avoid making as biomedicine itself, though today it has at its disposal genetic criteria for distinguishing between male and female, has never abandoned the popular point of view (see ibid.). In short, it is more a kind of opinion than a fact of nature that obliges modern science to consider the asymmetry of the sexes, rooted in gestation, as an irreducible datum.

The other essays of this second volume of *Masculin/féminin* are of the same temper. While praising Simone de Beauvoir, Héritier nonetheless refuses to liken maternity to a burden and to call for voluntary sterility (see Héritier [2002] 2012, 357). But neither does she accept the "valorization of woman as mother," which very quickly would have the effect of confining women to purely domestic tasks (137). She objects, with greater justification, to the notion of maternal instinct, which, she says, "throws an animalic veil" over a "social state that is a matter of choice" (387), and relegates women to the side of biology, the better to reserve for men "the honors of the symbolic" (364). Maternity, no matter which side one approaches it from, whether nature or culture, invariably impresses her as an occasion offered to men to exert domination over their female companions,[15] to reduce them to a "resource" so that men can reproduce themselves (128–29), to punish them in the event of sterility (58), and in any case to deny them access to the political and symbolic worlds (200–201).

The female ability to give birth, although undeniably a "privilege" (see especially 131, 201), has thus become a "handicap" (201). This is why Héritier, though she recognizes a "functional asymmetry" between the sexes that it would be absurd to "evade" or try to "disguise" (353; see also 364 and the back cover of the book), ends up taking back with one hand what she gives with the other by arguing for the perfect equivalence of maternity and paternity. Even though she considers these two conditions to be markers of social status, and not facts of nature, anything is grist for her mill. She looks to biology to settle the matter. By establishing the "shared role played by male and female gametes in conception" and therefore "a common male and female responsibility for procreation" (204–5), modern science unambiguously places maternity and paternity on the same level.

Peripatetic Interlude: Aristotle, Women, and Monsters

For Héritier, the principal obstacle to the equality of the sexes is in no way due to their intrinsic properties; it arises exclusively from fanciful conceptions of their anatomical and physiological differences, instilled and propagated by the earliest theories of sexual reproduction. However baseless these notions may have been, they endured and became an integral part of the Aristotelian theory of generation; and since this theory was the bridge between ancient natural philosophy and modern biological science, it comes in for vigorous and sustained criticism from Héritier.[16] This criticism relies on a detailed reading of the relevant texts. A few preliminary remarks will therefore be necessary if we are to appreciate both its value and its limitations.

Aristotle held that every natural or artificial object can be decomposed into matter, a passive principle, and form, an active principle. It is thus that, depending on the form they are given, milk becomes butter or cheese (through the action of churning or fermentation), wool becomes a rug or a coat (through the action of spinning and weaving), wood into a bed or a table (through the action of cutting and joining), bronze into a vase or a statue (through the action of casting and modeling), and so on. Like many Greek thinkers of his time, and also as many other societies have done, Aristotle calls the active principle male and the passive principle female. Nevertheless—and this is a point that Héritier omits to mention—the female is not therefore supposed to be inert. Matter, Aristotle says, desires form, as the female desires the male (see *Physics* 1.9). The fact remains that, for him, as later for Freud as well, woman is characterized by an inherent incompleteness,[17] and feminine desire aims chiefly at making up for this deficiency. In this sense Aristotle likewise stands on its head what I have regarded, from the beginning of the present work, as a natural hierarchy of the sexes. Yet Héritier, who objects to any form of hierarchy between the sexes, does not challenge Aristotle's doctrine on this ground. What seems reprehensible to her in Aristotle is the definition of femininity as a sort of monstrosity, and, conversely, monstrosity as an "excess of the feminine."[18]

She concentrates the whole of her attention on a part of the treatise *On the Generation of Animals* devoted to a problem that was not original with Aristotle, but that his theory of procreation could not help but deal with. If the female furnishes the matter and the male contributes the form, how does it happen that the son of a man does not always resemble his father but may resemble his grandfather, or another male relative, or even his mother? And how does it happen, more generally, that a man may beget not only boys but also girls? Finally, how can it be that human beings sometimes give birth to monsters, which is to say to beings that are neither wholly human nor animals of another species?

These questions have one thing in common, that procreation is not reducible to mere reproduction. Aristotle, quite naturally—and this is to his credit—seeks to find a single answer for all of them, and, if possible, one that will be more satisfying than the replies that had been given by those who came before him. It then occurs to him to try to resolve all three enigmas by working out the implications of a simple idea: by virtue of the fact that the male morphogenetic principle is liable to be more or less active during insemination and gestation, its capacity to beget offspring will vary, depending on its degree of strength or weakness, over a whole gradation of forms ranging from exact replicas to monstrosities. From this general explanation, however, Héritier retains only one element: the fact that the conception of girls and the formation of monsters are supposed to be due to common causes. That amounts, she says, to likening femininity and monstrosity, so that monstrosity begins with the birth of a girl and culminates with an excess of the female principle in relation to the male principle. She thus transforms an epistemological virtue (the concern not to needlessly multiply hypotheses) into a moral fault, or, at the very least, an antifeminist prejudice.

The situation is more complicated than she imagines. Material and formal causes are not the only ones at work here. One must also take into account the final causes to which they are subordinated, as Aristotle himself expressly does (see *On the Generation of Animals* 767[b] 8–15). The process of generation is not a competition between male and female; if the active male principle attempts to impose a form on feminine matter, it is because it is acting in the service of a norm; it seeks to perpetuate the species of which it is supposed to be the canonical representative.[19] This is why the birth of a girl instead of a boy, although it has for an efficient cause a "failure of the masculine," as Héritier quite justly writes ([1994] 1999, 260),[20] is absolutely not the anomaly that she makes it out to be (see 261; 1996, 195, 198). Her commentary mixes the true and the false, for she fails to consider the final causes from which modern thought takes pride in having freed itself since the Galileo-Cartesian revolution. The birth of a girl, unlike that of a monster, is not a failure of generation. The one is the fruit of a "natural necessity" (Aristotle, ibid., 767^{b} 8–10); the other is "necessary accidentally" (767^{b} 13–15). This distinction is crucial.[21] It means that men beget girls through the action of internal factors, which is to say spontaneously and with the purpose of reproducing their species, whereas, in the event they produce monsters, it is through the action of external factors that accidentally disturb the natural (which is to say spontaneous and purposeful) development of the embryo. This is why a woman is in no way a monster; she is a natural creature whose development, from the perspective of this theory, is incomplete but not impaired. Aristotle is very clear on this point. He says that monstrosity begins not with the birth of a girl, but with that of a child, male or female, who resembles none of the members of his or her family and who therefore figures as an intruder or stranger.[22] It is the deviation from an ancestral norm that constitutes the first step toward monstrosity.

In short, women and monsters have only one thing in common: they both owe their existence to a weakness of the male morphogenetic principle, whether because during the process of gestation this principle does not manage to fully stamp the female material principle with its imprint, or whether it fails to offset the disruptive effects of exogenous factors. In the one case, this relative impotence is a way of permitting the natural process of gestation to attain its proper ends; in the other, it is a deficiency permitting the disruptive phenomenon to exert its deleterious power upon the natural process of gestation. The feminine and the monstrous, respectively the products of these opposed dynamics, therefore cannot be compared with each other. There is between them a difference of kind, not of degree. It is a mistake to believe that, for Aristotle, the feminine is a sort of vestibule leading to the monstrous, and that monstrosity is merely an excess of femininity. Considering that her reading of *On the Generation of Animals* is on the whole scrupulous and fair, it is all the more regrettable that Héritier should fall into this error at the end, and that, in her most recent writings, Aristotle's thinking about the difference between the sexes should be reduced to a caricature.

Because her attention is riveted on the hierarchical aspect of sexual difference, Héritier does not notice that female and male, matter and form have complementary, not competitive, roles in the task of perpetuating the species.

For it to be fertile, the relationship between the sexes must be harmonious (see Aristotle, ibid., 767^a 16, 24). On the one hand, there is no matter that is totally amorphous and passive, or, to the contrary, stubbornly disobedient; nor, on the other hand, is there any form capable of molding matter according to its own rule and desire. The matter-form relationship is more subtle than certain classic examples would lead us to believe, such as that of wood, which, depending on whether it is fashioned by a woodworker, a carpenter, a cabinet maker, and so on, seems to be a material capable of receiving the most various shapes. In reality, every kind of matter already has a form and, by virtue of just this fact, may or may not be capable of receiving other forms. As Aristotle himself famously put it, one cannot make a saw out of wool. The world is therefore filled with a multitude of forms, joined to one another and hierarchically arranged between pure matter and pure form, which themselves may only be ideal terms. Just as matter desires form, as female desires male, so too form desires matter, which individualizes it and gives it reality. For there are no forms separate from matter.[23] Form resides wholly in the activity of "informing," through which it imparts shape, while at the same time actualizing the potentialities of matter. The contribution of both principles, male and female, is therefore necessary. In the case of gestation, it is notable that Aristotle often compares the action of the male seed to that of rennet, which transforms milk into cheese—milk rather than water or any other substance in this case, for the action of the formal principle has nothing magical about it; it must be given a suitable material to work on. Could it be any clearer that embryogenesis is a collaborative undertaking, the female share of which is crucial? Héritier mentions this comparison (see 1996, 197), as it happens, but without noticing that it undermines the Manichaean view of the difference between the sexes that she attributes to its author.

Other nuances of Aristotle's text seem to escape her as well. The definition of the male as "that which generates in another" and of the female as "that which generates in itself" (Aristotle, ibid., 716^a 13–15) points to an asymmetry favoring the latter, for while the necessity that the two sexes come together in order to procreate is implied, it stresses the dependence of the male on the female. As for the observation that "in man males are more often born defective than females" (775^a 4–5), it attributes to the male sex an intrinsic frailty that has subsequently been confirmed by the modern demographic study of infant mortality. Notwithstanding the errors to which ancient authors inevitably were liable, we nonetheless find in Aristotle a wealth of acute observations and ingenious hypotheses. In our own time, no less powerful a thinker than René Thom was of the opinion that Aristotle's biology was much richer and, in many respects, more scientific than Darwin's, or indeed than the modern theory of molecular biology.

Denying Natural Differences

In this connection, it seems to me plain that the fixity of the ovules and the motility of the spermatozoa, and the necessary activation of the former by the latter, shows the usefulness of the distinction Aristotle makes between a female material principle and a male motor principle. Present-day biologists who describe the phenomenon in terms that Aristotle himself would not have disavowed presumably feel much the same way. But the convergence of ancient and modern opinion does not weaken Héritier's conviction; to the contrary, she sees this intellectual affinity as an additional reason to combat what remains for her an archaic and prescientific view of sexual difference (see Héritier 1996, 20, 203–4). The point at issue here may seem relatively insignificant, but in fact the opposite is true, since generally she is averse to recognizing the least natural difference between men and women.

Although Héritier avoids "involving [herself] in the conceptual debate concerning categories of sex and gender" (ibid., 21), and although she admits the existence of a "functional asymmetry" between the sexes (Héritier [2002] 2012, 363), she will have nothing to do with experiments and data that unmistakably reveal differences between men and women. No research of this kind can possibly meet with her approval. Studies that seem to recognize an innate superiority of the male sex, in any domain whatsoever, are naturally accused of feeding the hierarchical model that she seeks to expose and demolish (see 46–47); generally speaking, to judge both from what she says and what she does not say, her suspicions are aroused by the attempt to establish a stable correlation between either sex and a particular type of activity or performance. No matter that an observed difference may be innate or acquired; that the sexes may excel at doing different things; that a differential trait may be valuable or unimportant—anything that may seem to constitute a durable and objective marker of masculine and feminine she rejects as null and void. To a psychologist who shows that men accomplish certain tasks more easily than women by virtue of physical and intellectual abilities that are part of their biological inheritance, but that might ultimately be a consequence of the immemorial apprenticeship instituted by the division of labor between the sexes, she objects that it is precisely this division of labor that needs to be explained, rather than uncritically accepted as a primitive fact and explanatory factor (see 42–44). Her argument is easily disposed of, of course, for if the sexually differentiated division of labor, though not uniform, varies very little from one people to another, as empirical investigation confirms, one can only conclude that a general pattern of organization has spontaneously imposed itself on all peoples and that it therefore has, by definition, a natural basis.[24] But nothing seems capable of shaking her conviction that all supposedly observed dissimilarities are either illusory or the product of contingent and arbitrary differentiation.[25] Even experiments showing that the activation of cerebral areas differs according to sex in both rats and humans, and therefore independently of any cultural conditioning, seem to her contestable (see 44–45).

It comes as no surprise, then, that she should have nothing to say about older observations that invite us to take the hypothesis of innate differences seriously. She passes in silence over the work even of an ethnologist as undogmatic as Marcel Mauss, who, while emphasizing the fact that every society teaches its members what he calls "body techniques," noted that men and women nonetheless naturally perform certain feats that seem to be peculiar to their sex and remain invariant (see Mauss [1936b] 1950, 373); and also of one as rigorous as Irenäus Eibl-Eibesfeldt ([1973] 1976), who undertook to generalize Mauss's intuitions, in effect producing a systematic inventory of the schemas of innate behaviors that showed, for example, that the interests and games of girls spontaneously differ from those of boys in all cultures (see Eibl-Eibesfeldt [1976] 1979, 40–43).

What is more, Héritier totally ignores the fact that all the relevant evidence indicates that women are physiologically more robust than men, and therefore are, in fact, the stronger sex. This is true whether we consider demographic data accumulated over several centuries, which indisputably prove that women at all ages enjoy a lower rate of mortality than men, or whether we consider more recent research in immunology, establishing that their immune system is stronger and more diversified than that of men, probably owing to the fact that during pregnancy it must protect the health of both the mother and the embryo (see Gualde 2004). Héritier thus deprives herself of sound arguments for criticizing egalitarian theories, while at the same time fending off charges that she sees no sexual differences whatsoever (see Héritier [2002] 2012, 206–7), which her own denials nonetheless tend to encourage. In the last analysis, what is there besides the asymmetry of the sexes? Unlike Aristotle, she never gives a simple, neutral, and objective definition of it. Often mentioned but forever elusive, since it is always ignored whenever it rears its head, this asymmetry is destined ultimately to be dismissed as a piece of make-believe.

Embracing Imaginary Differences

Héritier does not describe the difference between the sexes in itself, but instead the singular perception that men are supposed always to have had of it, namely, as an "extravagant" phenomenon, bearing the mark of "scandal," "mystery," and "injustice." This theme recurs like a leitmotif throughout the second volume of *Masculin/féminin*.[26] What the masculine mind finds disconcerting is not the simple fact that women bring children into the world, but the dual scandal that accompanies this privilege. On the one hand, there is a logical mystery: women's extraordinary talent for producing not only sameness by giving birth to girls, but also for producing the opposite by having boys;[27] on the other, a physiological mystery, compounded by a sense of injustice, since women can reproduce themselves identically whereas men are incapable of it.[28] From this arises the domination of women by men, an attempt to reestablish equilibrium, or rather to invert a hierarchical relationship to their advantage,[29] by substituting for the fantastic idea of female prerogatives the very real subjugation of women to a male world—indeed, by reducing women to mere purveyors of boys, to a "material" suited to reproduction of a male world.[30]

There is a good deal of truth to this picture, but it has the defect of blurring the boundaries between the real and the imaginary, between the essential and the accidental. It rightly defines the masculine in terms of the feminine, for it is accurate to say that "men fear women" (Héritier [2002] 2012, 59) and their powers. But Héritier omits to say that this fear is not entirely without foundation. Indeed, the difference between the sexes is not neutral, but intrinsically hierarchical; resting as it does on fertility, it immediately gives women an advantage. One may therefore perfectly well conceive of a female empire in which men play a minimal role in its perpetuation, no less modest than that of rennet in the making of cheese. The like of this is seen in insect societies, in which the males are eliminated after having fertilized the females; it is also part of what is true about the myth of the Amazons. By contrast, a male empire in which the roles are reversed is a pure chimera—and this even though men may be tempted to reduce women to mere reproductive resources,[31] and even though the killing of female infants is much more widespread than that of male infants, for these two tendencies lead to a contradiction. In any viable society, men must content themselves at the least with preferring the birth of a boy to that of a girl; at the most, with desiring "a son at any cost" (25).

Such is the fundamental and primary asymmetry that nature imposes on the human species. To reproduce themselves, human beings need the cooperation of the two sexes, but their functions are not the same: since fertilization takes place solely in women's bodies, it makes women the principal depositories and guardians of life, if only by virtue of the relatively long period of length of gestation and its uniparous character. All peoples are familiar with this cardinal truth and grant it a privileged place, as their rites and their myths testify. But in reading Héritier, one often has the impression that this primary asymmetry is an illusion—and moreover that this illusion has been dispelled owing to the discovery of the mechanism of reproduction. It is all the more curious, then, that the fantastic asymmetry supposed to be the source of male domination derives all of its force from this very real asymmetry, of which it is a deformed image. For men assuredly cannot give birth to boys in the same way that women can give birth to girls; and yet their female counterparts, whatever men may imagine, are no more capable than they are of reproducing themselves by parthenogenesis.

This way of approaching the difference between the sexes, by promoting an imaginary asymmetry to the detriment of a veritable asymmetry, leads to a neglect not only of their most distinctive trait but also of the unavoidable fact of their complementarity, which, partly omitted, partly denied, ends up being wholly ignored. Héritier, quite remarkably, has next to nothing to say about this indispensable complementarity; only in a roundabout way, and then mainly in the pages devoted to reproductive cloning, does she consider the question at all. For example, when she compares the two possible forms, female and male, of the "unisexual utopias" that cloning makes it possible to bring about, she notes that, given the current state of technology, the former would be much more easily realized than the latter (see [2002] 2012, 152–53, 227–29): whereas the male population could totally disappear once "a few straws of semen to renew the species from time to time" have been preserved, the female population, even if reduced to the rank of ovule donors and embryo carriers,[32] could not be done without.

Héritier's manifest interest in cloning is all the more understandable since, in her view, "women's liberation" began only with the advent of contraception. Accordingly, anything that serves to dissociate sexuality more sharply from procreation strengthens the promise of still greater liberation. Indeed, if male domination actually has the origin that she assigns to it, it will be eradicated once men can beget boys as women beget girls. Parallel cloning of men and women would make each of the genders autonomous. Although for the time being it remains an impossibility, it would be the ideal solution to the problem of escaping from what she frankly calls the "straightjacket imposed on mankind, as on the majority of animal species, by the constraints of sexual reproduction" (ibid., 235). Everything considered, however, it is not an outcome she desires—though not because cloning in itself seems to her "prejudicial to the dignity of the individual human being" (234), but because it would deprive human societies of their most distinctive characteristic. For by making kinship groups independent of one another, it would favor self-segregation and, as a consequence, cause the institution of matrimonial alliance to disappear—the very thing that, according to Lévi-Strauss, forms the basis of social ties. On this view, from which Héritier does not dissent, marriage is the womb of culture and, ultimately, the source of mankind's humanity.

Forgetting Symbolic Differences

It will be clear by this point, then, that nothing in her analysis of the difference between the sexes has caused Héritier to modify her allegiance to the structural theory of alliance. As in her other writings, sexual difference is

reduced to an alterity required for the formation of a social framework based
on exchange and reciprocity. The asymmetry of male and female, although
quietly acknowledged, never appears under its own colors, as it were, but
always in the guise of an inequality arbitrarily instituted by men. It is one of
the most constant products of human history, to be sure, but nevertheless
a contingent one, not an architectonic principle upholding an irrefragably
symbolic order.

Along with the structural oppositions of right and left, pure and impure,
sky and earth, and a few others, the opposition between male and female
occupies a favored place among the asymmetric relations that underlie
institutions as diverse as dual organization, sacred royalty, and rites of initiation. But apart from her fine earlier study of the dualistic system of the
Samo (see Héritier 1973), Héritier pays scarcely any attention to the way in
which societies actually apply these structural principles. It is as though she
encountered the same difficulty Lévi-Strauss did in making sense of a difference whose terms are not reversible. Indeed, Lévi-Strauss always saw it as
an anomaly[33] that the constitutive moieties of dual organization are almost
always designated by pairs of asymmetric terms, such as up and down, older
and younger, day and night, higher and lower, and so on. Given that the moieties of a community are exogamous and that the exogamy rule obliges every
person, male and female, to seek his or her mate in the other half, this terminological hierarchy seemed to him contrary to the principle of reciprocity
that governs matrimonial alliances and that, to his mind, constitutes the very
essence of social ties (see Lévi-Strauss 1944). This is why he was inclined to
suspect dualist societies of concealing inegalitarian relations under the veil
of reciprocal exchanges of goods and services (see Lévi-Strauss [1955] 1961,
230; [1958a] 1963, 124) and of thus creating "misleading institutions" ([1955]
1961, 231), or at least of almost always embedding a tripartite structure in an
apparently dual structure (see [1958a] 1963, 132–63). In the case of Bororo
society, it is easy to see that the solutions proposed by Lévi-Strauss are not
satisfactory, and also to draw, from his own ethnographic data, a better explanation for the asymmetry of moieties, as well as of the myths and rites that
are associated with it.[34] This is not the place to recapitulate the argument.[35] If
the Bororo example nonetheless deserves a moment's attention, it is because
it also implies a conception of the difference between the sexes that is much
more complex than the one described in *Masculin/féminin*.

The Bororo village forms a great circle, the center of which is occupied by the men's house and the circumference by family houses. It is therefore structured by a "concentric" principle, to use Lévi-Strauss's term, between a sacred male center, forbidden to women, and a profane periphery where adults of both sexes and their children reside. The spatial organization of the village therefore reveals at once the precedence of the male pole; at the heart of the village, the place reserved for the men's ritual dances significantly bears the name "bororo," whereas the profane female space is situated some ways from this sacred area, near the edge of the forest. Nonetheless, while there is no common house for the women corresponding to that for the men, it must be noted that the individual huts on the periphery are personal property and passed down from mother to daughter. Moreover, the concentric structure of the village is bisected by a diametric opposition, that is, by a line cutting straight across the village that divides it into two facing halves of equal importance, each comprising the same number of clans. These moieties are matrilineal (which is to say that the child of a couple always belongs to the mother's moiety) and exogamous (which is to say linked by matrimonial unions, each man having to look for a mate in the other moiety). But they also exchange many mutual services, since each great ritual requires the cooperation of the two moieties. This is notably the case with the naming ceremony, which takes place when the child is six or seven months old; the name is chosen by the members of the maternal clan, and the rite is mainly performed by a brother of the mother and a sister of the father (which is to say by two persons who, like the parents themselves, represent both the two moieties and the two sexes, but who, unlike the parents, must be unmarried).[36]

Let us come back to the question of marriage. Lévi-Strauss, as we have seen, always interprets marriage as an exchange of women. Among the Bororo, the residence rule is matrilocal. In other words, when a woman marries, she remains in her mother's house, whereas the man leaves his maternal home, located in the moiety opposite, to join her. In Lévi-Strauss's terms, it is as though women exchange men rather than the other way around. Among the Bororo, husbands move from one woman's house to another, and consequently from one female descent line to another—not wives from one male descent line to another, lines that in this case are absent or have, at most, a virtual existence. If certain informants are to be believed, this is one of the meanings of the well-known saying "the Bororo are *arara*," which the married men repeat in self-mockery, comparing their lot to that of the red parrots whose plumage they use for ritualistic purposes: shorn of their brightly colored feathers, the birds fly miserably among the houses of the village.

In this subtle arrangement of relations between males and females, Bororo society may be seen to exhibit a complementarity of the sexes next to which the requirement of absolute and unqualified equality insisted upon in modern societies seems quite simplistic. One might say, of course, as Lévi-Strauss himself does, thinking of the great male rites celebrated in the center of the village from which women are excluded, that in this society "the real participants are the men," whereas the women, coming in from their huts on the perimeter, are "predestined [to be no more than] spectators" (Lévi-Strauss [1955] 1961, 228). Looking at the matter more closely, however, one sees that this is an altogether specious male point of view, and that the perspective must be reversed. Among the Bororo it is the women—givers of life, guarantors of the perpetuation of lineages, and owners of the houses— who represent the stable element of the society, whereas the men's activities, whether they take place in the center of the village, between the natal hearth and the conjugal home, or in the secrecy of the men's house, are only, in the eyes of their female companions, and perhaps also in their own eyes, a sort of restlessness—futile for the most part, and on the whole a pathetic spectacle.[37]

Héritier would not have had to renounce her allegiance to structuralism altogether in order to profit from these observations and to resituate her study of the relations between masculine and feminine in a more general framework of systems of binary oppositions, which, as Robert Hertz and his most faithful followers have shown, organize not only the classificatory operations of human thought,[38] but social reality itself (see Tcherkézoff 1983; [1991] 2000). It is a pity she did not, for it might have helped to offset to some degree her determination to reduce structuralism to a theory of exchange and a kind of materialism that do not really express its essence.[39] Her mentor, Lévi-Strauss, himself often turns attention away from the heart of the matter by likening structures to mental categories,[40] and by neglecting the rites and institutions in which their morphogenetic power is most apparent.[41]

Hocart, for his part, showed that all institutions have a ritual origin.[42] Ritual, because it brings people health and salvation, is fundamentally a source of life. It therefore implies the cooperation of a male and a female

principle, that is, a man and a woman, or their divine counterparts, performing (or imagined to perform) an act of impregnation:

> A complete ritual requires two parties, male and female. These need not be
> a man and a woman, for the two parties come together as god and goddess,
> and a god and a goddess may be represented otherwise than by a man and a
> woman. In modern India a male and a female idol may be bedded together,
> in Vedic India a dead stallion and the queen. There is a Vedic rite of mating
> the king with the earth symbolically. (Hocart 1952, 190–91)

In sacred monarchies and chieftaincies, the ritual couple is a king and queen.
The king marries the queen on the day of his coronation. This marriage is
not a superfluous detail of the enthronement ritual, but instead a constitutive
element of it; originally, in fact, it was nothing other than this,[43] so that when
the king took secondary wives, he could do it without ceremony, as ordinary
mortals did (see Hocart 1954, 76). The royal marriage is a sacred act that
unites not only a man and a woman; like the whole of the royal ritual of
which it is an essential part, and which aims to ensure the general prosperity
and the order of the world, it possesses both a social and a cosmic dimension.
Accordingly, it reunites the two sides of society (sea and land, east and west,
right and left, summer and winter, and so on), as well as heaven and earth
and the celestial and terrestrial divinities, of whom the king and queen are
representatives (see Hocart [1936] 1970, 262–90).

We have just seen that these two representatives are not necessarily
human beings. Hocart adds that they are not necessarily of different sexes
either. But that does not alter the nature of the ritual relationship. It is still
necessary that one of the partners embody the male principle, the other the
female principle: "In the royal consecration of the Igalas [of Southern Nige-
ria] . . . one man lies on top of the other and they 'go through the motions';
the new king is then born from under the skirt of the man who takes the
woman's part" (Hocart 1952, 191).

The best known and best documented case is that of the Lovedu (see
Krige and Krige 1947). Since the nineteenth century, the office of rainmaker
was no longer held among them by a king, as is generally the case in Africa,
but by a queen. The royal office nonetheless remains masculine, and the basic
structure of the ritual pair unchanged. During her enthronement, the queen

does not take a husband, but, like the king, receives wives. There is nothing homosexual about this institutional union; it is a totally chaste relationship meant to perpetuate the canonical form of sacred royalty. The queen represents the male principle, her wives the female principle. The office is one thing, the holder of the office something else entirely. The system is formally the same in the Académie française when the post of permanent secretary is held by a woman, who in the performance of her duties becomes *le* (and not *la*) *Secrétaire*. In the same way, a male soldier who mounts guard (*monter la garde* in French) becomes *la* (and not *le*) *sentinelle*.

These last examples notwithstanding, the modern Western mind tends increasingly to situate itself at the extremes of traditional thought. In all the cases just considered, traditional thought is organized in terms of the difference between masculine and feminine, a structuring principle to which it gives maximal extension by carefully distinguishing between offices and their holders, which is to say between institutions and individuals. The modern mind, by contrast, ignores this distinction when it urges the legalization of same-sex marriage, and, conversely, lays emphasis upon it when, confusing the individual and his office, it advocates the use of terms such as *auteure* and *écrivaine* (rather than the usual masculine forms, *auteur* and *écrivain*) to designate female authors and writers.[44] In traditional thought, the difference between the sexes is seen as a relation of complementarity that may serve as a model throughout one's life; to the modern mind, by contrast, it is an incubator of inequality that threatens to pervert the social order. If a fear of undifferentiation is liable to lead in the one case to the invention of imaginary differences, a passion for equality may just as well lead in the other to the denial of real differences.

Anthropological Insight or Statist Ideology?

Héritier treats gender theory with great caution. Her feminism is in any case much too reasonable to be considered at all extreme. Thus she advocates "the equality of status, not the isomorphism or undifferentiation" of male and female (2000, 36), and argues on behalf of "a society in which difference and asymmetry will be the foundation, not of hierarchy, but of genuine harmony" (Héritier [2002] 2012, back cover). As a practical matter, however, she lays down only one rule to be followed in seeking to achieve this result: perfect parity of the two sexes in every walk of life. She suspects the idea of complementarity of "disguising" a relationship of dominance and of resting on an idealization of the heterosexual couple (see 364). Accordingly, she recognizes only equivalent and interchangeable individuals, whose relations, being equal, cannot help but be harmonious. This amounts to taking back with one hand what she gives with the other, for the desired harmony would not in fact be based on difference and asymmetry, but would presuppose instead the disappearance of all asymmetry and all difference.

By this point there is virtually nothing left of what Héritier had earlier called the "differential valence of the sexes"—as though, sensitive to the criticism of those who saw this expression as covering up the nakedness of male domination, or even of offering an excuse for it (see Fine 1998), she continued to employ the phrase while slowly and almost imperceptibly emptying it of any real content. The asymmetry of the sexes, no matter that she went on paying lip service to it, ended up losing all architectonic and symbolic function. It was now neither a primary constitutive fact of human nature, like the difference between generations or the shortness of life, nor an organizing principle of the cultural order, like the asymmetry of left and right, or of sacred and profane. Without any reality of its own, it was no more than the fading reflection of a certain idea, the imaginary foundation of male domination. Its apparent universality is therefore deceiving, an illusion that may be expected to vanish once women are finally recognized not as women, but as human beings and, in the last analysis, as individuals and citizens.

Héritier's recent expressions of support for same-sex marriage confirm this impression of a change in her thinking.[45] Earlier, in connection with cloning, she had worried about the possible disappearance of the "dual reference, paternal and maternal" (Héritier [2002] 2012, 226). But now she feels that a law authorizing marriage between persons of the same sex need only be consistent with the "requirements of its time."[46] But how are we to know what a time is, and how are we to know what its requirements are? In the course of human history, generally it is events that have determined the common perception of living in a particular time and not the other way around: thus we speak of the era of the Crusades, of the age of discovery or of colonization, and so on; generally it is human activities that mark off an era, no matter that environmental constraints may alter its course as well, by lengthening or shortening the seasons of sowing and harvest, for example. When it is a question of internal causes and endogenous processes, however, we speak instead of stages, such as the stages of life, or the stages in the progress of a disease, or (in the case of nineteenth-century evolutionist theories) the stages of development of a civilization. Beneath an apparently harmless exterior, the reference to the requirements of a time turns out to conceal much stronger ontological implications than one might have suspected at first. It supposes a universal and absolute time, not the temporality peculiar to a particular society—as relativist, and even evolutionist, theories imagined in ascribing to different peoples either divergent or convergent dynamics, but in any case dynamics that are endowed with specific rhythms susceptible, at the very most, to relative comparisons, but not to being ranked in relation to some absolute standard. It is one thing to observe, by comparison with a given society, that another society does not yet use the bow, or, to the contrary, already possesses the rifle; but it is quite another to be surprised, by referring to some temporal norm external to all societies, that one can still, at a given time t, continue to have such-and-such a custom or refuse such-and-such an innovation. On the basis of what overarching point of view could one really know the requirements peculiar to this time t?

There can be no doubt that universal constraints do in fact exist. The most incontestable of these is demographic: in the absence of a sufficient rate of fertility, a population is doomed to decline and, eventually, to disappear. This circumstance implies a number of local constraints that vary in space and time. In particular, if it wishes to survive, a society having a very high rate of infant mortality has no choice but to condemn contraceptive practices that "trick" nature, and to treat abortion as a criminal offense. Once improved hygiene and more effective medicine have considerably reduced mortality, however, new measures must be adopted, only now to guard against the danger of excessively rapid population growth. It becomes necessary to encourage contraception, indeed to make sure it is effective through the use of techniques that are more reliable than older methods. This is what happened in many countries, notably France, that decriminalized abortion after the Second World War. And yet in view of the variety of modern methods, and especially the widespread availability of chemical techniques of contraception, it was not necessary, from a strictly demographic point of view, to make abortion the favored procedure for limiting births. The creation of a right to abortion was but one cultural choice among other possible choices. Although abortion is indeed a very effective way of reducing the birth rate,[47] its selection seems to have depended on considerations other than effectiveness.[48]

This notion of choice is essential. French historians and geographers, notably Lucien Febvre and Pierre Gourou, have long insisted that civilizations are neither created ex nihilo nor are they simply the products of geographical, economic, or historical determinism: "Necessities, nowhere. Possibilities, everywhere. And man, master of possibilities, judges their use: this is to place him henceforth in the foreground through a necessary reversal: man and no longer the earth, nor the influences of climate, nor the determining conditions of places" (Febvre [1922] 1970, 257). Structuralism served both to temper the somewhat overly Promethean character of such claims and to make the notions of possibility and choice more precise. For Lévi-Strauss, just as elementary particles can form stable configurations by arranging themselves in accordance with the possibilities offered by Mendeleev's table, so too human beings can constitute coherent societies by grouping themselves in accordance with the possibilities offered by an "ideal catalogue" that structural anthropology undertakes to reconstruct. Not all imaginable configurations are therefore realizable: just as there is only a finite number of possible atomic forms, so too there is only a finite number of possible cultures from among which societies are bound to choose; and even if the prohibition against combining identical things discerned by Héritier was not devised for this purpose, it represents a further step in the same direction to the extent that it is formally similar to Pauli's exclusion principle, which determines possible atomic structures a priori and takes their stability into account.

It must be acknowledged that the ambitious program structuralism set for itself remains unfulfilled. Indeed, it seems no longer to enjoy even the virtues of a regulative ideal in the eyes of those who first conceived it. Responding to a journalist who had asked her about the possibility of two persons of the same sex marrying, and in this connection about what an anthropologist considers to be possible or impossible in family institutions, Héritier recently mentioned the existence of "thought-blockers," that is, external constraints restricting what can be imagined to be possible; but since in addition, and unavoidably so, she grants human beings an unforeseeable and potentially unlimited capacity for innovation, she can only be interpreted as referring to temporary obstacles, contingent products of history that survive through inertia, albeit precariously, for they are purely ideal and lack any efficacy of their own.[49] Thus it is that, for the time being, as she points out, same-sex marriages respect the civil and canonical prohibitions of classical marriages; but if it is true that the prohibition of incest is indissociable from exogamy, as Lévi-Strauss is supposed to have proven, if it is a survival of "archaic times" when marriage was an alliance between two families, why should it continue to restrict the choice of a spouse when marriage is now conceived as being founded exclusively on love and individual choice?[50] Is it still one of the "requirements" of our time? If it is, how can we know it to be so? How can we explain why it should be so?

If one gives the notion of a requirement its full weight, the problem seems insoluble. But Héritier manifestly intends the word in a much weaker sense. By the requirements of a given time she means nothing other than the majority aspirations of the moment, which need not be coherent and may in fact be the result of the vagaries of arithmetic. Public opinion may both cling to an old rule, out of habit, and subscribe to a new one as a matter of fashion. How can one detect, from among their changeable and inconstant states, the operation of true thought-blockers and ineliminable constraints? From Descartes to Rousseau and then on to Schumpeter, it has long been known that the opinion of the majority is, by itself, nothing more than the opinion of the majority, and that it is therefore not for this reason alone legitimate and salutary.[51] Héritier is not unaware of this. After suggesting that a decision may be "beneficial" so long as it corresponds "to the conscience and will of a majority," she adds that "[it] must nonetheless be subject to fundamental and internally consistent ethical requirements: [it must] satisfy as far as possible individuals and their needs, taking into account all possibilities, cognitive as well as technological, but never to the detriment of others, however distant they may seem to us" (interview in *Marianne*, 4 February 2013).

There are therefore other requirements as well, no less imperative than those of a given time. But if this is the case, from what does their authority derive, and how do people reach agreement with one another? Is not the weak version of Kant's categorical imperative[52] that is offered to us here every bit as unstable as the convention of heterosexual marriage or the prohibition of incest,[53] which might be supposed to be immutable but which the requirements of a time seem fully capable of abolishing? We have just seen that the legalization of contraception, which was meant to put an end to abortion, in reality prepared the way for its becoming commonplace. All the more reason, then, to expect that same-sex marriage will lead on to surrogate motherhood: first, because lawmakers in France, whether or not they are conscious of the symbolic value of the term, have insisted on calling this new institution "marriage" and not "civil union"; next, because if marriage can be reduced to a private contract—approved by the state, to be sure, but founded solely on subjective elements (love and the free choice of consenting adults)—it is hard to see why surrogate motherhood should not constitute a private contract every bit as legitimate as the one formalizing marriage, of which it is the natural complement, and therefore no less in keeping with the presumptive requirements of its time.

The ambiguity of the notion of a requirement casts further doubt on its legitimacy. So-called fundamental requirements, if any really exist, cannot help but be problematic, since there seems to be no obvious way of establishing either their nature or the means of determining it. The status of the requirements of a time is no less uncertain. Taken as designating a product of history, the expression seems improper; what is more, it can be taken in two different senses. For a disciple of Nietzsche or Pareto, it designates the aspirations of a dominant elite at a particular time—aspirations that the elite finds itself able or feels itself authorized to impose on all.[54] The manner in which political and media elites in France have almost unanimously treated the question of same-sex marriage is a good illustration of this point of view;[55] what used to be a subject of farce suddenly became a manifest right that it was idiotic, sacrilegious, or even criminal to contest. But this aspect of the matter, fundamental though it may be, does not suffice to explain the drafting and then the approval of the proposed legislation. The new law may also pass for a requirement of its time inasmuch as it is a product of the individualist and egalitarian dynamic that has shaped Western society, especially in France, since the Revolution.

This dynamic of the modern state is characterized by a tendency to dissolve all intermediate bodies and all traditional forms of social attachment, and to recognize individuals only insofar as they are citizens, which is to say members of the state. The preamble to the Constitution of 1791 gives a striking picture of this tabula rasa policy:[56] referring to the Declaration of the

Rights of Man of 1789, it begins by stripping individuals of all the differences that they are supposed to have inherited and reducing them to mere possessors of rights, and then, on the basis of these rights alone,[57] reconstructing society as a whole from the ground up. Héritier's feminism is a direct descendant of this radical individualism; it obliterates in its turn all attachment to sex, demanding that a woman be recognized not as a woman but simply as a person and a citizen. Marcel Gauchet, having shown in an analysis of the Declaration of 1789 published on the occasion of its bicentennial (Gauchet 1989) that the text resembles an axiomatic system whose apparent simplicity prevents all of its implications from being immediately perceived, surmised that since we are not yet in a position to appreciate the full extent of its consequences, it may still hold some surprises in store for us. Same-sex marriage, required in the name of the equality that all citizens enjoy as a matter of principle, corroborates Gauchet's conjecture. By making available to persons of the same sex an institution that one might have thought was reserved for heterosexual couples, the modern legislator completes the preamble to the Constitution of 1791, for he devalues the difference between the sexes just as the Constitution had devalued the difference between noble and commoner. The difference between the sexes, like hereditary titles, now has only a private value.[58] Héritier, in expressing her unqualified support for the new law concerning marriage, seems to have come at the end of a long inquiry into the opposition between masculine and feminine to believe that this opposition has no contemporary social relevance. But what really is the nature of this conclusion? For the journalist interviewing her, it is the fruit of the expertise of an eminent anthropologist whose opinion he has solicited. From the perspective of an outsider, however, not only is the situation different, the roles are reversed: the journalist is an ethnographer and his interlocutor is an ideal informant, exactly the sort of person he hopes to encounter in the field, well versed in the rites and myths of her society (in this case the practices and the ideology of the modern Western world) and willing to reveal their most important features.

These features are, on the one hand, individualism, and, on the other, its corollary, the almighty power of the state and its schools, which are supposed to bring individuals the true freedom they lack by rescuing them from every kind of differentiating social influence, notably that of the family, and imposing on them the most perfect possible equality in every area of life. It is striking to note that in the second volume of *Masculin/féminin* (see [2002] 2012, 282), one of the rare practical measures advocated by Héritier to remedy male domination is the rewriting of all textbooks, from primary through high school level, in order to purge them of sexist clichés and prejudices. This sort of advice would appear to have had the ear of politicians who in the preceding legislative session had already mandated the teaching of gender theory in schools, and whose zeal was now redoubled in an attempt to eradicate, from nursery school (whose name in French, *école maternelle*, would itself now have to be changed in order to dispel any sexist connotation) onward, all forms of differential treatment of girls and boys in respect of clothing, games, and so on. Echoing a paradox first found in Rousseau's *Émile* but now doing double duty as a contradiction, it is only with a great deal of artifice that one can contemplate destroying differences held to have been artificially constructed by earlier generations. In Rousseau, it is a question of recovering an original state of nature supposed to have been buried beneath the artifice of civilization—a very doubtful assumption, but nonetheless well suited to the task of legitimizing the paradox of an educational system having to resort to artifice in order to hear the voice of nature and allow itself to be guided by it. Here, by denying any natural difference between the sexes, one could at most only substitute one artificial construction for another, at the risk, however, of considerably enlarging the share of artifice that education can accommodate while pretending at the same time to eliminate it.

But the state is not only a coercive power. It is also a tutelary power, a substitute for divinity as well as for nature, likewise thought to have been vanquished by the finest modern minds. Maurice Godelier is fond of summing up what he learned from the Baruya in a single phrase: a man and a woman are not enough to have a child. In the Western religious tradition, it was common for a couple (and still is for some couples) to speak of the children that God had given them. Christianity tends to present the two aspects, divine and human, of the transmission of life separately, but it nevertheless considers them to be related. Thus the virginal conception of Christ does not do away with the need for Joseph to be with Mary. Similarly, to say that a woman has given three children to her husband does not deny the divine origin of this gift. Whatever one's view of this may be, in the case of same-sex marriage everyone will agree that a man and a man, or even a woman and a woman, are not enough to have a child. If marriage is not reducible to a private contract, it is therefore not only a matter of love and choice but also a way of obtaining from the state and/or the market a kind of procreation that nature does not indiscriminately grant to all. In the case of same-sex marriage, the state is unavoidably called upon to play the role of the Holy Ghost, or of the stork, in the reproduction of children. This is why it seems difficult to dissociate medically assisted procreation and surrogate motherhood from marriage between persons of the same sex. It is easy to see why a politician might be led for tactical reasons to decouple the two things; it is much harder to see why an anthropologist might be led to do this for theoretical reasons.

CHAPTER EIGHT

Testart's Law

Division of Labor and Sexual Identity

Often symmetric and sometimes mimetic, conflicts opposing individuals to other individuals, lineages to other lineages, and nations to other nations may seem to suggest that the identity of an individual or a group is an exclusively relational property. To an outside observer, the more adversaries believe that they differ from one another, the more they resemble one another; the more they imagine they have a distinctive identity of their own, the clearer it is from the similarity of their behaviors that they are deceiving themselves. René Girard has shown that this shared illusion of defending an autonomous personal or social identity is an essential element of tragedy,[1] and that this undivided solidarity of the self and the other is so inseparably a part of the human condition that it altogether resists interindividual analysis and requires instead an "interdividual" psychology.[2] On this point, as on so many others, mimetic theory agrees with structuralist *doxa*,[3] which holds that two opposed terms are co-determining: neither one has an intrinsic value, only a positional value.[4]

No doubt there is a great deal of truth in this. Reality is a web of relations, not a mere juxtaposition of terms. In chemistry, the properties of a simple body are determined by its valence, which is to say by the bonds that it is capable of forming with other atoms. It is, for example, in the multiple combinations of carbon with hydrogen, oxygen, nitrogen, and so on that the potentialities of a carbon atom manifest themselves; its nature may be said to be jointly determined by all these various relations. But it does not follow that, like the "value" of a word in the Saussurian sense of the term,[5] "[w]hat characterizes [it] most exactly is being whatever the others are not" (Saussure [1916] 1983, 115). All the elements in Mendeleev's table differ from one another, yet each of them has original properties. The same is true in the human world. The genius of a Newton in science or of a Mozart in music depends upon the era and the civilization in which each one came to maturity, for their works could not have been composed apart from them. If they had been born in other times or in other places, their talents would have counted for nothing: in a society without writing or elaborate string instruments, and above all without a sufficient division of tasks and functions, without astronomers or mathematicians, without choirmasters or full-time musicians, their talents would have remained undeveloped and wholly unknown, even to themselves. As Hocart showed ([1936] 1970, 294–99), the specialization of functions gives birth to, or at least precedes, the specialization of skills and talents; thus, in the Fiji islands, "it was not self-assurance, memory, and the gift of speech that gave rise to a herald caste, but the function of herald that created a need for men of that type" (295). This in no way implies that the idea of a native gift, individual or generic, is illusory: not everyone who enjoys a privileged upbringing can hope or aspire to become a Newton or a Mozart, for neither one of them was the product solely of birth and social circumstances, however favorable these may have been. With all due respect to radical constructivists and all those who consider the power of education to be unlimited, there is indeed one natural and irreducible datum, namely, that "culture" and "nature" cannot be totally foreign to each other. Culture does not write down an articulated system of differences on a blank slate, any more than it magically extracts this system from an undifferentiated mass of people; instead it "recruits" and "selects" those individuals and groups that are best suited to perpetuate it, and in this way adjusts the divisions peculiar to a particular social order to the potentialities furnished by nature.[6]

Modern thought nevertheless remains profoundly allergic to the idea that human institutions might have a natural substrate on which their lines of force are traced out, as it were. It readily admits that external constraints, due to the scarcity of available natural resources and to competition from

other species, impose limits on human activities, but it is loath to recognize
the existence of internal determining factors, of norms that are inherent in
human nature.[7] The case of marriage is exemplary. One might suppose that
this institution, though it may assume various forms, has at least a natural
basis—that is, a material cause in the Aristotelian sense of the term—in the
union of a man and a woman. For contemporary relativism, however, this
amounts to an illusion, since heterosexual marriage is only one possible case
among others; moreover, humanity does not consist of individuals endowed
with a native and well-determined sexual identity—men and women, in
other words—but only of beings provided with a socially constructed gender
and a sexual orientation that can change over time. And so just where one
imagined that constant identities could be discerned there turn out to be
only contingent attachments.

Sexual relativism in this case seems to have taken over from linguistic relativism, which had long been looked to as a model and a norm for the whole
of the human sciences. Having appeared at the moment when linguistic relativism was increasingly showing signs of weakness, even of losing credibility
within the field of linguistics itself, sexual relativism is in a way a substitute,
indeed an avatar, by virtue of the place that it assigns to the category of gender.
But whereas the one was fashionable among scholars, who alone were aware
of the linguistic "turn" (soon to become the linguistic "mirage"), with the
other we are witnessing something quite different, an academic tendency that
spilled over into the public sphere and then, having first gained currency in
the world of politics, went on to make its influence felt in social institutions
of all kinds. Has relativism therefore carried the day? Is the idea that humanity
naturally consists of men and women as gratuitous as the claim that the sound
continuum is cut up in a variety of ways by human phonological systems, or
the light spectrum by different systems of color classifications? Or could it
be that this idea is in fact more much robust than these two constructivist
dogmas, which have not stood up to empirical scrutiny?[8]

The Law of Blood: Hunting, Sacrifice, and Procreation

Let us therefore put this question to the test, framing it again in terms of the
archetypal theme of the division of labor. Anthropologists agree that most,

if not all, societies consider certain tasks to be properly masculine and others properly feminine; the division of labor by sex, in other words, is universal. Nevertheless, the relativists insist, the distribution of tasks between men and women is purely conventional, because it varies from culture to culture: in some cultures hunting is an activity reserved for men, but in others women are allowed to take part; here pottery is feminine and weaving masculine, but there it is exactly the opposite; here women are kept away from all the major rituals, but there they can make sacrifices, and so on. Only the principle of a sexual division of labor is universal, then, whereas its modalities are infinitely variable and arbitrary—thus the received wisdom among anthropologists. But is it really true?

If one were to add to the list of examples I have just given, while limiting oneself to enumerating facts—a great many facts perhaps, but chosen at random and without any other aim than to form some impression of their variety—it would be easy to convince oneself that one has verified, or even proven, the relativist thesis. Science consists, however, not in collecting facts, but in explaining them; at a minimum it requires that refutable predictions be formulated,[9] that is, propositions of the type "if p, then q" that bear not so much on the facts themselves as on the relations that unite them.[10] If one reconsiders the question of division of labor in this perspective, a much different picture emerges. It will now appear, to the contrary, that all societies distribute the activities of the two sexes in accordance with universal principles.

The proof of this was given almost thirty years ago by Alain Testart in a very detailed study of hunter-gatherer societies (see Testart 1986a). Testart showed that in every society, if hunting is the prerogative of one of the two sexes, it is always a male prerogative; if the two sexes are allowed to hunt, but the kill is reserved to only one of them, killing is always done by men and never by women. If women, like men, are permitted to kill game, but only one of the two sexes is authorized to use weapons that draw blood, it is exclusively men who enjoy this right, whereas women may employ only methods of killing that do not involve bloodshed, such as clubbing or smoking out wild animals.

This series of refutable propositions undeniably constitutes a law in due and proper form. Notwithstanding that they are corroborated by the whole of the ethnographic literature that Testart has examined, they may yet be modified or actually invalidated by the discovery of new facts. Furthermore, the distribution of tasks whose various forms are claimed to be invariable rests on a simple principle: in every instance it is a matter of maintaining a more or less great, but never negligible, distance between menstrual blood, involuntarily shed by women, and the blood of the slain quarry, deliberately shed by the hunter. These two kinds of blood may be in close proximity to each other, but never mixed. To avoid their being combined, the most cautious societies prohibit women from taking part in hunting altogether; others, by contrast, allow them to use arms that draw blood, but nonetheless never during menstrual periods or just after they have given birth (this is notably the case among certain Eskimo groups, in which women are permitted to harpoon seals except during their periods [Xavier Blaisel, personal communication]); in still other societies, it is only after the onset of menopause that they are allowed to engage in sanguinary activities. These different cases, which Testart himself does not explicitly address,[11] make it possible to refine the formulation he gave of the law, and confirm that the heart of the matter is indeed the incompatibility of menstrual blood, lost by women of childbearing age, with the blood of animals of prey, drawn during the hunt. All hunter-gatherer societies prohibit the mixing of these two kinds of blood; they differ only in respect of the more or less restrictive measures they employ to prevent it.

Although he is interested mainly in subsistence activities in a particular type of society, Testart is not unaware that the law of separation of different kinds of blood is not restricted to the practices of hunter-gatherers; it is corroborated, he says, by "a great amount of data from other societies [concerning] the exclusion of women from the trades of war, butchery, and surgery, and their quite general exclusion from [offices involving] blood sacrifice" (Testart 1988, 715). The case of the sacrificial rite deserves rather more than this cursory mention, for it is well documented and shows that the principle governing hunting activities in hunter-gatherer societies also structures the ritual activities of humanity as a whole. In all known societies, where ritual activities are reserved to one of the two sexes, it is always men who hold a monopoly on them. Where women can exercise some ceremonial functions, but not all, the ones proscribed are associated with rites involving blood, and notably sacrifices, which are forbidden to them (so that, as we saw earlier, even in the Catholic religion, only a man can celebrate the "sacrifice of the Mass" and afterward become a priest). Where women can conduct sacrifices, but without the two sexes being equally authorized to perform all the ritual operations, the killing of the victim always falls to men (as may be seen, for example, in the case of the Thesmophoria, an ancient Greek festival presided over by women in which a man is nonetheless granted entry for only a few instants: he cuts the victim's throat and withdraws the moment the act is done [see Detienne and Vernant 1979, 208]). Where, finally, women can perform blood sacrifices, this is forbidden to them during the menstrual period or the period of impurity that follows childbirth (see Journet 1987, 241–46).

To my knowledge, no counterexample has been adduced to disconfirm this general explanation. Kristofer Schipper, an authority on Taoism, once during a public debate presented me with what he maintained was an invalidating case of female sacrifice in China, conclusively established by his own book (Schipper 1982) and a later work by Brigitte Berthier (1988). Yet neither one contradicts Testart's law. The first shows only that the Taoist religion has strong feminine connotations, which is not contrary to the law in question since, if one generalizes it by extending it to cover ritual, it implies that ritual is to men what procreation is to women (see Scubla 1982, 122–38; 1985b, 359–74), a theme we have already encountered. In the next two chapters, dealing with the couvade and initiations, I shall give fresh examples of male rituals clearly bearing "feminine" traits. The second reference turns out to be no more telling. To be sure, in one of the legends studied by Berthier, Chen Jinggu and other female divinities perform sanguinary operations of all types, not necessarily confined to ritual (murder, castration, sacrifice);[12] but there is no evidence that, in real life, women enjoy the same liberty as men in this regard or, in particular, that they can make blood sacrifices during worship services for which they have direct responsibility. In any case, Berthier is silent on this point.[13] It is nevertheless notable that Chen Jinggu herself twice refuses motherhood and finally dies, following an abortion—as if she had to choose between shamanism and procreation (as Berthier herself perceptively remarks [see 1988, especially p. 295]). In this respect Jinggu resembles Diana in Roman mythology, who no doubt owes her status as goddess of the hunt to the fact that she is a virgin. Even in the divine world, sanguinary practices and childbearing seem to be incompatible. In the absence of any proof to the contrary, Testart's law therefore remains undisturbed; and now that it has been extended to imaginary beings, there can scarcely be any doubt that it touches on the very essence of male and female identities.

If to this one adds that the other sanguinary practices mentioned by Testart—war, butchery, surgery—are probably all, like hunting itself, ritual in their origin,[14] the cumulative effect is to suggest a simple explanation of all these things and of the law of blood separation that governs them. It looks very much as though the cultural, and more precisely the ritual, prerogatives that had been assigned to men came to compensate for the natural privilege held by women with regard to procreation—as though hunting and sacrifice are to men what parturition is to women; as though the blood of the slain animal and of the sacrificial victim, which is to say the blood associated with two activities vital to the health of society (nourishment and religion), are to the male sex what menstrual blood, signifying the fertility on which the group's survival depends, is to the female sex. Bruno Bettelheim ([1954] 1962), in a study of "symbolic wounds" that attracted notice at the time of its publication, gave several examples illustrating this hypothesis. Despite a notable change of tone in the preface to the second edition,[15] however, his psychoanalytic training had led him to lay stress on sexuality at the expense of procreation, and on the supposedly symmetric and reciprocal attitudes of the two sexes rather than on their inborn asymmetry, which is to say on the desire of each of them to have the sexual attributes of the other rather than on the male desire to counterbalance the original female privilege of giving birth. Nevertheless it was a step in the right direction, though in the event it had scarcely any effect on the intellectual climate of the day (a significant detail: the French edition of Bettelheim's work included two critical essays, one by André Green, the other by Jean Pouillon—formidable intellects, to be sure, but evidently more concerned to preserve the integrity of Freudian thought and structural anthropology than to support and develop the author's central thesis).

Testart, for his part, unless I am mistaken, never refers to Bettelheim, whose style of interpretation has in any case little in common with the Marxist strain of Testart's thinking. For Testart, the phenomena in question come under the head of what he calls an "ideology of blood"; they are therefore secondary phenomena that do not belong to the infrastructure, but instead to the superstructure of social organization, even if they do have a real impact on the mode of production of the societies in which they manifest themselves. In his book on the sexual division of labor he limits himself first to showing that this ideology is found among all hunter-gatherer peoples, and then to describing its effects and its principal modalities. In slightly later writings he suggests that the law of blood separation may be seen as a particular form of the prohibition against combining identical things, whose very general character had been demonstrated by Françoise Héritier.[16] That enabled him to avoid having to deal with psychologizing explanations, which have always gotten a bad press among sociologists and anthropologists. In his most fully elaborated work, *Des mythes et des croyances,* he reformulates the law of blood separation as a prohibition against "putting *S* with *S*," where *S* plays the same role as a variable in an algebraic equation, in this case representing any substance endowed with symbolic value, not only blood (*sang* in French), but also saliva (*salive*), salt (*sel*), and so on (see Testart 1991, 10–11, 19–23). With regard to the example discussed earlier, it still remains to be explained—since after all it does not go without saying—why menstrual blood and the blood of the hunt (or that of sacrifice), that is, the blood *involuntarily* shed by women and the blood *deliberately* shed by men, which in the one case flows from one's own person and in the other one causes to flow from another person, should be held to be the same, or equivalent; failing this, the formal principle invoked to account for their mutual exclusion could not operate. Following the example of Odile Journet (1987), whose fine study of female rites likewise relies on Héritier's principle, it becomes necessary to closely examine the relations among sanguinary effusions, which is to say the spilling of blood that figures in sacrifice, acts of violence, and procreation. Moreover, while it is quite legitimate to condemn psychologism, which refuses to recognize the autonomy of society and the symbolic world, it would be absurd to construct an anthropology that overlooks the biological and mental characteristics of human beings. After all, a civilization is not made of persons without qualities, but of beings of flesh and blood, endowed with needs and drives, memory and reason, emotions and passions.

Before we examine the omissions in Testart's work on the sexual division of labor, as well as places where the argument is weaker than it need be, I should mention an important aspect of his monograph that reveals its full richness and lends additional force to the law that he has discerned. His inquiry does not bear solely on hunting in the narrow sense, but on the practical activities of hunter-gatherers in general, and the techniques and technologies associated with these activities. They include all those operations that occur after the hunt itself, such as the cutting up of the slain animal, the treatment of the skins, the conservation of the meat, and so on; gathering in its various forms, not only collecting what lies on the ground but also the harvesting of plants with a sharp tool, extracting roots and tubers with a spade, felling trees whose fruits hang too high above the ground to be readily picked, and so on; manufacture and repair of the weapons, tools, and utensils needed to perform these various tasks and operations, and so on. Adopting the concepts introduced by Leroi-Gourhan to describe and classify technological objects (see 1943, 43–58),[17] he shows that in all the activities in which the two sexes can engage, weapons and tools are distributed over an explicit or implicit range of application organized around two poles: one masculine, characterized by "hurled and pointed percussion" (as in the case of the spear and the arrow, in particular, which draw blood); the other feminine, characterized by "pushed and diffuse percussion" (as in the case of the scraper and the millstone, which carry no risk of drawing blood). There emerges from this a set of homologies, and a strikingly coherent way of looking at the problem as a whole:

> It will be seen how far we are from the idea that men hunt and women gather. Men hunt only insofar as they hurl missiles that pierce and perforate. Women take part in other forms of hunting. Similarly, women practice gathering only in the form of picking up, digging, or detaching fruit from a plant by hand (without percussion), or with a stick (diffuse percussion, which in this case is hurled but not piercing), or with a knife (pushed percussion, which is piercing but not hurled). But gathering that involves the use of a tool such as the ax (hurled linear percussion) is masculine. The same law governs all such activities depending on the nature of the technological movements they employ. . . . Men pursue activities involving linear or pointed hurled percussion, whereas women pursue ones involving diffuse pushed percussion. (Testart 1986a, 68–69)

There can scarcely be any doubt that Testart has penetrated to the heart of the matter. The objection was once put to me that the needle and the weaving spindle, despite their form and their mode of percussion, are nonetheless instruments having a feminine connotation in the West. It is easily answered: the dressmaker's needle is used in a piercing manner, to be sure, but it is directly inserted, not hurled; and the distaff, in spite or possibly because of its form, is traditionally opposed to the spear—further evidence that it is not so much (or not only) the form of the instrument as its mode of percussion that is the salient point. One might liken the weaving spindle to a spade, an instrument that is also typically feminine in certain parts of the world, but employed in a diffuse pushed manner. Recall, too, that when Sleeping Beauty accidentally injures herself with her spindle, a sort of spear, in effect, that draws her blood—and this, by no means incidentally, at the age when she had just begun to menstruate—she falls into a sleep that resembles death, as if she had violated a taboo of the same kind as the one that forbids a Guayaki woman from touching the bow of a warrior (see Clastres 1966). Everything considered, the validity of Testart's law seems to me firmly established. It is one of those rare laws, in due and proper form—indeed perhaps the only such law—in which anthropology can take pride.

In illuminating subtle points of correspondence between the respective attributes of the two sexes, the functions assigned to each one, and the formal and dynamic properties of the technologies these involve, Testart's law also has the virtue of inviting us to go beyond male envy of the procreative capacities of women (which nonetheless it does not deny) and inquire into the ultimate reason for the distribution of tasks between men and women. This reason cannot have anything to do with the anatomy or the physiology of the sexes, of course, even if there is a resemblance between male and female sexual organs and objects such as the bow and arrow, on the one hand, and the basket, on the other (see ibid.), or between the emission of sperm and hurled percussion, on the one hand, and the fixity of the ova and pushed percussion on the other. Just as the sexual attributes of men and women cannot explain the form of their weapons and their tools, which evidently are subject to specific technical constraints, so too they cannot account for the structure of their social and ritual organization, for which we must assume other specific constraints. The fact remains that if they do not causally determine one another, it is not by chance, but indeed by affinity, that all these things (technological objects and institutions and rites, as well as the men and women who have created them) are in agreement with one another; it is because they all conform to universal principles and because they are distributed in accordance with the general schemas that govern all natural and cultural phenomena.

One might therefore be tempted to demand, in the manner of René Thom, for example, that a discipline such as topology provide the ultimate explanation for this set of formal oppositions and correspondences, of which the difference between the sexes is only a particularly prominent example.[18] In that case the final, primitive reason for the sexual division of labor would transcend all at once the more specific and secondary reasons given by biology, psychology, and sociology. But this would only tell us what we already know, namely, that far from being an artificial and arbitrary phenomenon, the distribution of tasks is a fundamentally natural phenomenon, which is to say one that develops spontaneously in all societies, in accordance with the same principles, without therefore being uniform and immutable.[19]

Challenges to Testart's Law: False Problems
and Fundamental Questions

In spite of its intrinsic interest and the rigor with which it has been established, Testart's law has not had the audience it deserves. To judge from the reviews that greeted its publication and from the general neglect that followed,[20] it seems not to have attracted any real interest in academic circles, and, within the anthropological community itself, to have run up against, if not outright rejection, then at least massive indifference.[21] It is true that it appeared at a time when ethnology was undergoing a profound crisis, affecting not only anthropology proper, which is to say research into transcultural invariants and universal laws, but ethnography itself, suspected of being merely one among a number of forms of literature, having no more scientific value than the novel: reality, like theory, was becoming indistinguishable from fiction. But this unfavorable situation does not explain everything. The epistemological crisis of anthropology and its intellectual excesses[22] were themselves the effect, I believe, of a more profound malaise. It was supposed that ethnology, in throwing light on the diversity of customs, had allowed the West to look at itself with greater detachment. Scientific description was considered to be an instrument of social and political criticism, in which the Australian aborigine, the Dogon, and the Nambikwara now took over from Montesquieu's Persian. But this same instrument very quickly proved to be a double-edged sword, apt to reveal not only the motley assortment of possible cultural forms but also the existence of anthropological invariants diametrically opposed to the core individualist and egalitarian values of modern Western society—hence, by way of reaction, and of defending these threatened values, the promotion of a constructivist and ultra-relativist anthropology holding all observable distinctions between human beings to be purely conventional, and more or less obliquely indicting classical ethnology for condoning traditional forms of domination, whether religious, political, economic, or sexist.

A few years prior to the appearance of Testart's monograph, an article by Paola Tabet (1979) on the division of labor among hunter-gatherers, reprinted almost twenty years later in a collection of essays whose title translates as "the social construction of sexual inequality" (Tabet 1998), well testified to this state of mind—while also, it must be conceded, showing by its wealth of documentation and its measured tone that this intellectual position is not inconsistent with solid research and sound argument. Examining a series of revealingly selected passages in the literature, Tabet takes issue with anthropologists as different as André Leroi-Gourhan, Raymond Firth, and Bernard Arcand for describing the distribution of tasks between the sexes in terms of complementarity and harmonious cooperation. The truth of the matter, she maintains, is that men, by systematically forbidding women the use not only of weapons but also of the most useful tools, have been able to keep their mates in a state of subjugation, indeed of absolute domination. By reflexively adopting the male point of view, and in spite of their undeniably scientific intent, these authors, who may fairly be regarded as forming a representative sample of their discipline, have painted an unduly idyllic picture, giving only a very partial and biased view of things as they really are, and thus leaving to others the task of constructing an anthropology that for once "will be one not of men but of [all of] humanity" (Tabet 1979, 51).

Tabet is right to say that the distribution of labor between the sexes, too often treated as something in no need of further discussion, requires more detailed description and, above all, a proper explanation. But the one she proposes is plainly unsatisfactory. For if inequality and, more generally, the differentiation of the sexes, considered in the light of the technologies they are respectively permitted to exploit, were solely a social construction, why should they always operate in the same manner? Why should it always be the man, and not sometimes the woman, who possesses the weapons of war and the hunt? What one actually observes is altogether contrary to what one would have expected: war is always a masculine affair. Moreover, while men do in fact enjoy a monopoly on weapons, they do not make war on women, only on other men. Is it because their sole interest is in intimidating and dominating their mates, or are there other reasons for this universal affinity between belligerence and the male condition? It is striking to note that, in a work that nonetheless displays due diligence in analyzing an impressive mass of information, these basic questions are not addressed directly, or even touched on.[23] Anything that might suggest a difference in principle between masculine and feminine is rejected out of hand. Since reality nonetheless confronts us with recurrent and insistent differences, which therefore cannot be the product of chance, they can only be explained as consequences of some relation of force, no doubt one of considerable importance in the history of humanity, but, in the last analysis, a contingent and arbitrary phenomenon just the same.

Under these circumstances, and considering the mood of the time, it was most unlikely that Testart's law would have any hope of being warmly received; at most, it could have expected to be politely ignored when it was not simply dismissed with a shrug—and this in fact is what occurred, to judge from the reactions, very few and far between as far as one can tell, that it aroused in the anthropological community following its publication. In a review for a Canadian journal, Chantal Collard reduced Testart's essay, in effect, to a not terribly original synthesis of the earlier work of Murdock, Leroi-Gourhan, and Tabet, combined with a tendency to neglect or even twist facts that do not suit his hypothesis (see Collard 1987). As Testart observed in response to her criticisms (see 1987c), Collard did not bother to notice the central and original idea of his analysis, which is not so much the prohibition against women using arms designed to draw blood as the obligation to keep menstrual blood separate from other sorts of blood. This point is enough to invalidate the counterexample she claims to have found in his essay: among the Batak of Malaysia, women are indeed permitted to use blowpipes—but not, as Testart had made quite clear, for the purpose of killing a wild animal. Collard's review, obviously the result of a hasty and careless reading, would scarcely deserve to be mentioned were it not representative of a very widespread mistrust of all general propositions, and of the rather desperate attempt to which it gives rise, in the name of science, to seize upon any apparent counterexample. This sort of intellectual laziness is typical of the flabby and unrigorous relativism that I lamented at the beginning of the present chapter.[24]

The review by François Héran (1986), which appeared in the *Revue française de sociologie*, is an altogether different matter. Unlike Collard, he gives the impression of having actually read Testart's book, whose structure and main arguments he does a good job of summarizing, and whose originality he is at pains to emphasize. But that only throws into clearer relief a curious resistance, implicit in Collard's review and manifest in this one, to the idea that is at the heart of the work: the "ideology of blood," to use Testart's Marxist vocabulary, or, to give it a more neutral and precise expression, the prohibition against mixing menstrual blood and animal blood. This resistance does not really come as a surprise to anyone who is familiar with Héran's later work and his habit of stressing the symmetry displayed by structuralist diagrams of kinship, in which there are indeed two different sexes, only in two perfectly permutable positions. The very manner in which a critic as fair-minded as Héran dismisses the inconvenient asymmetry introduced by menstrual blood is nonetheless astonishing, and reveals the existence of a veritable taboo among a sizable segment of the small world of anthropology on even mentioning menstrual blood. From the following it will be clear what I mean.

On looking over the three parts of Testart's monograph, Héran approves of the first and the last; but having decided that the middle part is incompatible with the two others, he postpones his examination of it until the end of the review. He endorses unreservedly the first part of the work: contrary to what has long been believed, it is not the strenuousness of hunting, together with the comparatively slender physique of women, or their reduced mobility during pregnancy, that has caused such activities to be reserved for men, since their mates are allowed to take part in hunting in certain societies, and since the tasks involved in gathering that are generally assigned to them often demand as much, if not more, physical strength and exertion as those involved in hunting; in reality, the hindrances that disqualify women for certain tasks and make these tasks a male monopoly are properly seen to be "social," not "natural." Héran also unreservedly endorses the general classification of technologies, and their distribution between the two sexes, that Testart presents in the third part. "In a few perspicuous tables," Héran writes, "[the author] exposes to view, not a strict sexual dichotomy of movements and tools, but a graduated division between two poles, two types of movements and tools, which can be classified in the light of the typology of techniques for manipulating utensils of various kinds elaborated by Leroi-Gourhan" (Héran 1987, 714).

This schema, he adds, has three principal virtues. First, between the masculine pole, characterized by hurled pointed percussion, and the feminine pole, associated with pushed diffuse percussion, it ranges over a whole gamut of movements and instruments, neutral or mixed in character, that allow different societies to modulate the division of tasks as a function of the technological or economic requirements peculiar to them. Second, owing to this very flexibility, the division of activities cannot be explained by appeal to differences of physical strength or skill, thus confirming the results of the first part. Finally, and most importantly, "it is clearly structuralist," for "while the proposed table may often be interpreted as setting in opposition hard materials, on the one hand, fashioned by men for the most part, and soft materials, on the other, fashioned by women for the most part, it is not a question of separating two [types of] substance but rather of bringing out an opposition between two types of behavior" (ibid., 715). Higher praise could not be imagined.

By contrast, Héran unceremoniously dismisses Testart's central thesis, which is to say the fundamental explanation of the sexual division of labor by the incompatibility of animal blood and menstrual blood—a "curious" claim, in his view, and one that comes as "a considerable surprise" to the reader because it is at odds with the rest of the book. The arguments that he brings to bear against it, however, are so feeble that, to an impartial observer, it is rather Héran's categorical rejection of what he calls Testart's "hematocentrism" that seems surprising, more a product of passion than of reason. His first and chief complaint is directed against the "substantialist" character of Testart's thesis, which is seen as contrary to the structuralist inspiration of the work as a whole (ibid.). But this argument is specious, for the notions of substance and structure are no more antithetical than those of matter and form in Aristotle, from which they are in any case descended. Moreover, in the bipolar structuralist table drawn up by Testart, the opposition of two kinds of blood, flowing from a wound in the one case, spontaneously in the other, is implicit since, on the male side, the weapons and tools reserved for men are indeed those that cause blood to be shed, and, on the female side, women, who do not have the right to use them, have by contrast the singular experience of seeing their own blood flow periodically in a spontaneous manner. If any doubt still remains about the contrast between these two kinds of blood, it suffices to recall that in the very few societies in which women are permitted to hunt with arms that draw blood and to make blood sacrifices, these activities are expressly forbidden to them during their menstrual period. The fact that Testart himself does not employ this decisive argument in his essay might have been an extenuating circumstance in judging Héran's fairness had his criticism been more measured. What I wish to point out here is precisely the peremptory fashion in which Héran dismisses the hypothesis in question: for him, agreeing in this regard with Collard, it goes without saying that the sexual division of labor cannot depend on differences between the sexes, on the native attributes of men and women. On this crucial point, then, his examination is limited to confirming a prior prejudice. But his second objection is no sounder than the first. The ideology of blood, Héran says, may be a justification of locally and intermittently observable practices, but one has a hard time seeing "by what miracle" it could be common to all hunter-gatherer societies—still more since Testart gives only a very few examples of taboos explicitly prohibiting contact between a woman and the blood of a slain animal (see ibid., 715–16). It was a simple matter for Testart to explain to Héran that ideology, in the sense in which he intends the term, may "reside in deeds and practices no less than in speech" (Testart 1988, 716), and that it is indeed what one observes in most societies of this type. More generally, since the ideology Testart has in mind affects all the sanguinary practices of the majority of known societies, the reason for this is readily grasped: far from being an arbitrary interpretation, the principle of keeping different kinds of blood separate has served as the basis for the sexual division of tasks in the human species as a whole. Héran is all the less justified in rejecting it as he proposes no alternative explanation.

Testart's Vacillation

In spite of their lack of substance, the criticisms directed against Testart nonetheless have the value of exposing certain weaknesses in his own reasoning, or at least in its presentation. Owing not only to the way in which he lays out the argument and characterizes the "ideology of blood," but also to a number of inappropriate comments and damaging omissions, Testart inadvertently invites misunderstanding and even lays himself open to the charge of inconsistency that Héran shrewdly saw could be brought against him.

Let us once more begin at the beginning. Having shown that women are allowed to hunt in certain societies and that, no matter what anyone may say to the contrary, they are therefore physically capable of doing so, Testart very logically concludes that neither their own constitution nor economic reasons can explain why they are typically prohibited from engaging in this activity; only ideological reasons, which thus are seen to be stronger than economic rationality, can account for such a prohibition. So far so good. But at this point, most unfortunately in my view, Testart cannot resist taking a potshot at his adversaries: "The woman gives life, the hunter takes life; the two are opposites, and therefore separate. Foolishness of this sort would scarcely be worth mentioning were it not for the fact that it reappeared in a recently published work on the question of women" (Testart 1986a, 25–26).

Foolishness, certainly—or rather, error, if from the proposition in question one were to infer that women are always and everywhere excluded from taking part in hunting activities; but at the same time, and above all, it is the keystone of Testart's own ideology of blood, for which he hardly prepares the reader by making this contemptuous remark. For in attributing exclusively to men the use of weapons and tools designed for shedding blood, this ideology undeniably assigns them the status of givers of death, just as, in refusing to allow women the use of them because they are already stained by menstrual blood, it acknowledges their status as givers of life. Separating blood deliberately shed by some from blood spontaneously spilled by others and distinguishing between the giving of death and the giving of life amount to the same thing; depriving the law of incompatibility of this clear and simple interpretation runs the risk of reducing the ideology of blood to an arbitrary intellectual construction.

Testart seems himself to have been aware of this defect when he came to write *Le communisme primitif*, which, with the aid of Marxist categories, or least in using them as a means of expression, presents original views on the classic questions of exogamy and totemism, and develops the notion of an ideology of blood in new and important ways. After recalling that the economic basis of hunter-gatherer societies consists of two fundamental processes of production, a "masculine process of production, hunting, whose product is meat" and "a feminine process of production, whose product is the human being in its sexual aspect" (Testart 1985, 221), he goes on to say:

> Because the [different] bloods must be kept separate, it cannot be the same worker who works in the two processes; because the process having to do with childbirth can only involve the woman, it is the man who, as a consequence—social and ideological consequence of premises that take note of a physiological reality—is the hunter. The fact that there are *two* processes is therefore not contingent; this fundamental economic duality corresponds to the other essential duality posed by primitive communist society [i.e., the society of hunter-gatherers], the opposition between the sexes, an irreconcilable opposition because grounded in nature, in blood, and which manifests itself through the radical separation of male and female worlds. (ibid., 470)

This passage represents an essential step in the right direction. In his essay on the sexual division of labor, completed in 1982, Testart sought to show that this division did not have a natural foundation, but instead was social in its origin. Applying Lévi-Strauss's dichotomy of nature and culture (see Testart 1986a, 19–20) in conjunction with the basic assumptions of structuralism, he treated the ideology of blood governing this division as a totally autonomous symbolic construction (see 27). By the time he finished his treatise on primitive communism, several years later, he had changed his mind: now the ideology of blood rested on a "physiological reality," on an opposition of the sexes "grounded in nature." It is not ideology, in other words, but primarily nature itself that establishes menstrual blood and pro-creation as primordial markers of the difference between the sexes. Even if ideology develops a symbolism that is peculiar to it, "the natural character-istics of the female sex" are no longer conceived of as a mere "pretext" for elaborating its main themes (27), but as the very basis for them.

Unfortunately, this welcome rethinking of the problem was short-lived—the step forward was soon followed by two steps back. Stung by the convergent criticisms of Collard (see Testart 1987b) and Héran (Testart 1988), the one having reproached him for being obsessed by menstrual blood, the other for yielding to substantialism, Testart retreated to the position that, in his model, only the relation of opposition between the two kinds of blood matters, and not the terms of the relation, which are reversible: primacy is no more to be accorded to menstrual blood over animal blood than to animal blood over menstrual blood.[25] But this formal reversibility must not cause us to forget the natural asymmetry of the sexes, that is, the fact that it is the woman, and not the man, who is directly and irreducibly marked by the sign of menstrual blood, and therefore identified with the gift of life. Testart himself, a few years later, finally came around to the view that the law of blood incompatibility should be considered as a particular form among others of the prohibition against "putting S with S" (see Testart 1991), which had the effect of wholly obscuring the original asymmetry. Certainly this formalist perspective allowed him to discern a number of important homologies and to make a more fertile analysis of mythico-ritual structures than classical structuralism had managed to do, but only at the price of two crippling concessions: to parry the charge of substantialism, he artificially detached ideologies and symbolic systems from the natural properties of human beings in which they are rooted; to parry the charge of hematocentrism, he turned his back on an essential anthropological truth, obliterating what he himself had helped to bring to light in the first place.

Rather than surrender without a struggle, it seems to me that Testart had every reason to embrace the challenge of defending the naturalism and substantialism his detractors abhorred, while at the same time showing that this can be done without reductionism—on the condition of rehabilitating, as I have more than once recommended be done, the Aristotelian conception of nature. In this way it becomes possible to dispense with the false opposition between nature and culture without falling into the trap of what nowadays is called "naturalization," a crude piece of scientism promoted by philosophers and cognitive scientists over the last several decades that reduces nature to the very partial image of it given by classical physics. I shall have a few more words to say about this in the next chapter.

Nor should there be any fear of putting the issue of menstrual blood at the heart of anthropology, on the ground that it had led the pioneers of the discipline astray. For, as the whole of ethnography testifies, killing is equivalent to procreating in most societies; killing for a man is what giving birth is for a woman. By shedding blood on the field of battle, in hunting, or in sacrificial rites men try to compensate, for better or for worse, for the privilege that women possess, so long as they experience menstrual periods, of bringing children into the world. In giving death to an enemy, prey, or ritual victim, men take imaginary revenge on their mates: among the Araweté, for example, only a man who has acquired the status of a murderer is assured of attaining immortality, whereas the woman, no matter that she transmits life and assures the continuity of the community, is summoned to a certain death (see Viveiros de Castro 1996, 89).[26] Male dominance is only an exaggerated version of these attempts at revenge. There is indeed a fundamental rivalry between the sexes that is probably universal, but it does not necessarily take the form of dominance relationships.

Infrastructure or Superstructure?

The notion of ideology of blood raises another problem. In Testart, the term "ideology" presents two faces, so to speak, one structuralist, the other Marxist. To define the sexual division of labor as an "ideological phenomenon" is to maintain, as we have just seen, that it is not amenable to a "naturalist approach" (Testart 1986a, 29). This is the structuralist aspect of the matter. For an author who subscribes to Marxist principles, it is also to affirm that, in the societies in which it is found, this phenomenon does not belong to their infrastructure but solely to their superstructure. And yet, though it is a social rather than a natural phenomenon, still it is not an economic phenomenon—even if, like everything that comes under the head of superstructure, it is supposed ultimately to depend on the way in which the social relations of production determine the development of productive forces. It is this aspect that Testart explores in his work on primitive communism.

But Testart's point of view entails theoretical complications, without any gain in explanatory power, to the extent that the division of labor observed in hunter-gatherer societies obliges him to grant ideology a much greater influence than orthodox Marxist theory does. We have already seen this to be the case with the sexual division of labor, whose structuring power manifestly exceeds the capacities of a strictly ideological phenomenon, which is supposed to have only a secondary, reactive effect on the infrastructure of the society that constitutes its material base. And it is still more true of the social division of labor encountered in Australian totemic societies, which Testart examines once again in his book on primitive communism. In these societies, he remarks, there is no economic division of labor; men and women do, of course, carry out different tasks, but neither among men nor among women are there any persons who specialize in a particular task; each man is expected to perform every kind of labor considered to be masculine, each woman every kind of labor considered to be feminine. Societies are nonetheless not homogeneous; they are divided into totemic clans, each having specific competences, notably with regard to rites for the multiplication of animal and plant species (*intichiuma*); each clan is responsible for the fertility of a particular species, yet the ritual labor performed for its multiplication does not benefit only the restricted circle of its own members, it benefits the whole of the community. We are therefore indeed dealing here, in these societies, with a social division of labor, but one that presents a paradox for Marxist theory, for it is not of an economic, but of a ritual nature—or, as Testart would prefer to put it, an ideological nature:

> Every individual, in his capacity as a hunter, will succeed one day in killing a kangaroo (assuming that he is physically capable of it and that no prohibition prevents him from doing so); to the contrary, the totemic institutions are such that only members of the kangaroo clan are capable of bringing about the magical increase of the kangaroo species. This amounts to saying that, in the economy, there is no social division of labor, whereas the totemic system of the *intichiuma* is recognizably a social division of symbolic production. It is therefore evident that the interdependence of social groups is more pronounced in the totemism [of the society] than in its economy; the communitarian aspect of the society is more prominent in its ideology than in its economy. (Testart 1985, 283)

Exploiting the resources of dialectic, Testart has no trouble resolving the paradox of a superstructure that is more complex than the economic infrastructure of which it is usually supposed to be a reflection. Far from refuting the received view, the totemic system actually strengthens it. For in orthodox Marxist doctrine, he holds, ideology is not a mere reflection, but instead a distorted expression of the system of productive forces and social relations of production that constitute the material base of society; and indeed this the case here, since "totemism projects onto the symbolic order a social division that does not exist in reality" (ibid., 284). "This *false* representation of productive forces," he goes on to say, "nonetheless *agrees with* the relations of production: it insists on cooperation, on interdependence; it creates imaginary socialized productive forces. The totemic representation makes the economy look much more primitively communist than it really is" (284; emphasis in the original).

In this passage, the perverse effects of the very term "ideology" are quite clear, since totemism is reduced to a set of representations and images projected onto a symbolic world. One thus loses sight of the fact that the productive system and totemic rituals do more than create imaginary social divisions and illusory symbolic productions. They actually structure human society; they equip it with real institutions, by dividing it into exogamous clans capable of sustaining complex relations of exchange and rivalry, of cooperation and competition, with one another. What Testart discovers here, as Durkheim and Hocart did before him, is the priority of religious institutions in relation to economic institutions and, more generally, the ritual origin of all social organization. But scarcely has he glimpsed this truth than he hastens to repress it by demoting ritual to a place alongside ideology. With all due respect not only to Marxists but also to economists of all persuasions, it needs to be recognized that "population first condenses round the centre of ritual, not round shops" (Hocart [1936] 1970, 251); that towns were religious centers before they were commercial centers; that the church square is much older than the marketplace, and the temple much earlier than its merchants—who, moreover, in the beginning, were only minor ritual auxiliaries, mere purveyors of sacrificial victims. All of modern thought, steeped in economism, has become immune to this idea. Testart does no more than conform in his own manner to the ambient tropism; his efforts to escape the clutches of a truth he cannot bring himself to face recall the treasures of intelligence that were expended in a vain attempt to reconcile Marxist orthodoxy with Freudian and Lacanian thought, or with structuralist anthropology. These intellectual contortions long ago lost their allure, but without the discredit that now attaches to them having in the least weakened the hold of economics over the sciences of man and of society.[27]

Male Spaces, Female Spaces

Testart's misjudgment in this regard is all the more regrettable as the study of the sexual division of labor, which has no satisfying economic explanation, greatly profits from likewise being examined from the point of view of the ritual organization of society. An article by Elli and Pierre Maranda describing the structure of residential space (*fera*) among the Lau of Malaita (Maranda and Maranda 1970) very clearly shows why. Their article is entitled "The Skull and the Womb," for the village space is structured around two poles, embodied in the one case by the skulls of ancestors buried alongside the sacrificial victims immolated by men, in the other by the huts occupied by menstruating women and the part of the village reserved for childbirth. The agglomeration as a whole is laid out in the form of "a rectangle or an ellipse with two foci, male and female respectively, each one forbidden (*abu*) to the members of the other sex" (835). Between these two sacred areas, male and female, stretches a profane space common to the two sexes, which itself, like the agglomeration as a whole, bears the name *fera*; located in this space are "the *luma*, grass huts where the women sleep while they are not having their periods, with their younger sons and unmarried daughters," while adolescent boys have individual huts and adult men sleep in the men's house located in the male area" (836).

It will be plain, then, that every society rests on an increasingly pronounced separation of the sexes, since with the passage of time boys grow farther and farther apart from the female world. But this separation begins very early among the Lau, for the *luma*, like the *fera* as a whole, is itself divided in three parts, with a side for men, a side for women, and a common space between. This tripartite structure corresponds point by point with the one described by Testart in his table of the sexual division of activities among hunter-gatherers, with a male pole, characterized by hurled pointed percussion, a female pole, characterized by pushed diffuse percussion, the two of them separated by a neutral intermediate zone, accessible to both sexes. But whereas this structure was an abstract metaphorical space, here we are dealing with a palpable configuration, implanted in the earth itself and organizing in space and time, according to their sex, the entire life of the individuals of a community.

It is tempting to interpret the fact that the term *fera* designates both the entire village space of the Lau and the mixed, profane part situated between the sacred male and female areas as the sign of a more egalitarian society than that of the Bororo, among whom, it will be recalled, the word *bororo*, referring to their village, is applied more particularly to an area reserved for dancing in the male sacred space. At least two things serve to temper this impulse, however. If the two diametrically opposed areas are mutually taboo (*abu*), each one for members of the other, each one nonetheless represents a particular modality of the sacred: the sacred of the female pole, *sua*, being "negatively marked," and the sacred of the male pole, *mamana*, positively marked (Maranda and Maranda 1970, 841). Furthermore, the opposition of male and female corresponds to that of high and low: the male part of the village is always upstream, the female part downstream (835). Inside her *luma*, a woman can neither suspend an object nor lay a fire on a raised platform, "by virtue of the principle that the high belongs to men" (836); for the same reason, "she is also forbidden to climb the trees that grow in the *fera*" (836). Even in the common space, supposed to be profane and neutral—"unmarked," as the Marandas say, *mola* in the vernacular language—taboos recall the supremacy of male over female.

As one would expect, since their article is written in homage to Lévi-Strauss, the Marandas lay emphasis on a set of structural oppositions, but without thereby eliminating either their hierarchical character or their substantive content. The crux of the matter is the opposition of the blood shed by women while giving birth or during their menstrual periods and the blood shed by men. Each of these two kinds of blood may be either baleful or beneficial, a source of death or a source of life. The primary source of the sacred and of the prohibitions that are associated with it—of what the people of Malaita call *abu*, a word that moreover also means "blood"—is blood that ritual is unable to contain: "blood intentionally spilled from an opening made with a weapon of aggression" or "blood uncontrollably lost from a natural opening" by women (ibid., 847). From the very fact that menstrual blood is spilled involuntarily, it is more especially dangerous and thus confers on the female sacred (*sua*) its negative connotations. But because menstrual blood is also a sign of fertility, it is ultimately from the act of giving life that women's *sua* comes, just as men's *mamana*, despite its positive connotations, nonetheless comes from the act of taking away life. In other words, life kills if it is given badly, and death vivifies if it is given well (838). Consequently there is a perfect parallelism between the bringing of a child into the world by a woman and the sacrificial offering made to one's ancestors by a man:

> The only man who is really equivalent to a woman in labor is the priest.... Now, the sacerdotal act is first and foremost the [sacrificial] immolation of a man and/or a pig to ancestors whose skulls lie in a ditch in the most marked place in the sanctuary.... Only a woman about to give birth can enter the maternity quarter ... where, without other aid than the presence of a woman engaged by her husband to bring her nourishment, she gives birth on bare rocks dedicated to this purpose. Only the officiating priest can enter the sanctuary ... where, with the aid of one or two assistants ordered by him to bring victims, he sacrifices to the ancestral spirits on bare rocks dedicated to this purpose. (Maranda and Maranda 1970, 838)

What is more, this ritually prominent symmetry—of a woman giving birth and a man sacrificing—does not imply that the two things are strictly equivalent or interchangeable. In reality, one is logically prior to the other, which is only its inverted image. And the birthing quarter of the village is far from being an "inverted sanctuary," as "the indigenous axiom of male predominance" would have it; the Marandas' study shows that, to the contrary, it is the male sanctuary that represents an inversion of the female sacred quarter (ibid., 847–48). Behind the proclaimed supremacy of the male over the female, one cannot help but perceive, when all is said and done, an implicit recognition of the superiority of the feminine gift of life over the masculine gift of death. This lesson can be extended to cover Australian totemic rites: like hunting, ceremonies to ensure the multiplication of plant and animal species are performed by men, who, through a sort of self-sacrifice, spill their own blood in order to assure the reproduction of natural species (see Durkheim [1912] 1995, 330–55). Ritual is neither a pointless extravagance nor a gratuitous game of life and death; it is a source of life whose model and purpose is procreation and the perpetuation of society.

Third Sex or Ritual Mediation?

Among the Lau of Malaita, the sexual identity of each human being is determined at birth; each one is assigned at birth a course of development that
is at once spatial, temporal, and social, within a residential unit whose very
structure helps to shape and strengthen it. Obviously not all societies enforce
such fixed rules for determining the respective places of male and female;
ethnography shows, to the contrary, that relations among men and women
are characterized by great variability. In the preceding pages I have asked
whether or not this variability is limited, whether or not the diversity of the
forms that the male-female relation can assume is compatible with the presence of invariants and, if so, which ones—but without challenging the very
existence of the two terms of the relation, in other words the universal bipo-
larity of masculine and feminine. Over the last few decades, however, and
within a widening circle of social scientists, this traditional fashion of dealing
with the problem has come to be regarded as grossly naive and prescientific.
It no longer suffices to show, as Margaret Mead did, that the sexual division
of labor "reveals more about culture than about nature," nor to inquire, as
Simone de Beauvoir and her followers did, into "the origin and the universality of male domination"; now it is considered to be necessary to call into
question not only the respective status of the two sexes and the nature of
their relations, but more profoundly, the very dichotomy of male and female
as well, and to go so far as to mount "an epistemological critique of the dualistic conception of gender in which classical logic, Judeo-Christian ideology,
and scientific rationalism confine us" (Saladin d'Anglure 2012, 143).

The sponsor of this "libertarian" program, Bernard Saladin d'Anglure, is
a specialist on the Inuit and a self-proclaimed disciple of Mauss, from whom
he has borrowed in particular the notion of a "total social phenomenon," that
is, the idea that a close interdependence obtains among the different aspects
(familial, religious, economic, and so on) of human life, which the various
social sciences try to study separately and which anthropology itself tends
to compartmentalize. While praising Mauss's famous essay on the seasonal
variations of Eskimo societies (1906) for throwing light on their "dual mor-
phology," communitarian and religious in winter (families living together
in large houses), individualist and secular in summer (families dispersed in
private tents), Saladin d'Anglure regrets that he remains "the captive of a

reductive explanation, dualistic and seasonal, of their social life" (ibid., 144). One can free oneself from this unduly narrow ecological and binary conception, he says, if one notices, on the one hand, that the opposition of the sexes is in this case more decisive than that of the seasons, and on the other hand, and above all, that this cardinal opposition discloses the existence among the Inuit of a median position, which is to say a "third sex," or "third gender," that makes it possible to escape from the dualist straitjacket.

In support of this last point, which constitutes the main thrust of his paper, and the only one I shall discuss here, Saladin d'Anglure makes two principal and complementary arguments. The first one is associated with the system for assigning proper names that prevails among the Inuit. When a child is born, he or she is supposed to be the reincarnation of an ancestor and so is given the name borne by this ancestor, or, more exactly, a name chosen from among the ones of recently deceased ascendants that are still available.[28] It may therefore happen that a boy receives the name of a female ancestor, or a girl that of a male ancestor; this poses no onomastic problem, for personal names, having no gender, can be assigned indifferently to children of both sexes and therefore pass from one sex to another. Nevertheless—and this is the crucial point—since the personality of the child is determined by the name it is given or, more precisely, by the sex of the forebear from whom it receives the name and of whom it is the reincarnation, transvestism and the learning of tasks ("the use of kinship terms, of the cutting and dressing of hair, of clothes and finery, of tools and technologies, of gestures and body postures") normally reserved for the other sex become obligatory when the child does not have the same sex as its namesake (ibid., 146, 150).

The second argument aims to demonstrate that this state of affairs, far from being hypothetical or merely rare, is, or used to be, rather widespread if not actually common. Indeed, for the Inuit, the ideal family ought to comprise at least one boy to help his father, and a girl to assist her mother. When nature does not spontaneously achieve this equilibrium of the sexes, recourse is therefore frequently had to adoption, or, if this was impossible, to the "inverted socialization" permitted by the choice, in this case deliberate, of an eponym of the desired sex, "particularly when the first children were girls" (ibid., 151).

Saladin d'Anglure then goes on to mention two details that are essential to grasping the import of this custom: "The daughter, elder or younger, was

thus often inversely socialized until her first menstruation, which was celebrated as if she had killed a large wild animal (whereas normally it would
have been pretended that she had had a son); from this day on she had to
wear feminine clothes. Symmetrically, in a sib of boys, a younger son was
often dressed and socialized as a girl until he killed his first large wild animal; he had then to cut his tresses and dress as a boy" (ibid., 151–52). It will
therefore readily be seen, first, that this cross-dressing is generally temporary
and, unlike adoption, does not allow the ideal equilibrium of the sexes to
be established within the "family atom"; second, that the equivalence of
shedding animal and menstrual blood is observed among the Inuit as everywhere else.[29]

Of course, for the young people who are forced to undergo this sudden
change of identity at puberty, it is a particularly painful ordeal, and all the
more so as they must confront it alone, without the support of their closest relatives, who, rather than try to help them, continue to use "the kinship
terms required by the eponym." How is such an attitude to be explained?
The answer, according to Saladin d'Anglure, unfolds in two stages, during
and after adolescence:

> The fact of having been subjected to another reality than the one of their
> childhood constituted a very real crisis for these adolescents, punctuated
> by clashes and rebellions. It was only slowly and gradually that they man-
> aged to acquire the abilities of people of their sex, and throughout their
> lives they remained marked by their early education and by the overlapping
> of gender boundaries. This overlapping had become a component of their
> personality, and made them a class apart, which I have proposed calling
> the "third social sex" or "third gender." They were generally held in high
> esteem for their polyvalence, their autonomy, and also for a particular
> power of mediation that expressed itself notably in the religious domain."
> (ibid., 152)

The rest of the article makes it clear that Saladin d'Anglure considers
the last quality to be the most significant of the three. Inverted socialization,
practiced from birth, and the crisis of sexual identity, instigated at puberty,
may be likened to tests of initiation whose purpose is to determine which
persons have a vocation to be a shaman. Those who, for better or for worse,

regain their native sexual identity are reunited with the lot of ordinary men and women; those who conserve a split personality thus show their aptitude for shamanism: "If, in the Inuit cosmogony, the difference between the sexes is primary ... and helps to conceptualize other differentiations, then an individual socialized from earliest childhood in the straddling of this boundary becomes, as an adult, a boundary-straddler who is capable of straddling all boundaries. Is this not the definition of the shaman, one who must know how to straddle not only the boundary between genders, but also that of the animal world and that of the supernatural world ... ? Inverted socialization is therefore, if not a sufficient condition, at least a necessary condition for the shamanic calling" (ibid., 154).

One could not put it better. Shamans are ritual mediators, and like all who hold this type of office, whether they belong to the human species, as do sacred kings, or to the animal world, as does the pangolin, the scaly anteater worshipped by the Lele of the Kasai,[30] they combine contrary predicates and/or perform actions (sacred kings are often incestuous and cannibals) that make them singular, even monstrous beings, apart from ordinary categories or, if one prefers, astride several of them. An exemplary case is that of the king of the sacred grove at Nemi—at once slave and king, priest and murderer, sacrificer and sacrificial victim: it was Frazer's genius to realize that he was the archetype of all such ritual figures. The sexually ambiguous Inuit shaman is no more than an original variant, a particular instance of this type.

This is why, invaluable though the information collected by Saladin d'Anglure among the Inuit undoubtedly is, it in no way obliges us to enlarge our supposedly narrow Western categories in order to make room for a "third sex" or "third gender." Indeed, all the facts that he marshals and analyzes point in the opposite direction. Let us review them briefly. The Inuit consider the dichotomy of the sexes to be a model for all other oppositions. While the names they give to their children have no gender, and therefore are equally well suited to a boy or a girl, the names nonetheless carry the sex (and not the gender) of their last bearer. It is, in fact, the sex (and not the gender) of the eponymous ancestor that determines whether the education that will be given to the child is masculine or feminine; and this difference in education shows that the Inuit, like other hunter-gatherer peoples, distribute tasks, behaviors, and activities between two categories, feminine and masculine. The child who has received an education contrary to his sex regains his native and true sexual identity at puberty.[31] Finally, equilibrium between the sexes is desired in all families, which ideally comprise a boy and a girl, themselves images of the father and the mother, respectively.

There is nothing in any of this that could possibly call into question "scientific rationalism," "classical logic," or "the Judeo-Christian ideological heritage." The Inuit theory of the conception and development of the fetus (ibid., 147–48) obviously does not coincide with that of contemporary embryology, but the Inuit themselves distinguish, as do our biologists, two sexes and two sexes only. The fact that, up to a certain point, their shamans combine masculine and feminine identities does not undermine the biology of the sexes any more than the existence of the pangolin invalidates classical taxonomies; still less, then, could it overthrow scientific rationality itself. Nor is classical logic, which remains the backbone of this rationality, in the least threatened by the paradoxical properties of the shaman, on the one hand because it can be freed, if need be, from the constraint of the principle of excluded middle,[32] and on the other hand because, from the Aristotelian theory of the syllogism to Craig's interpolation theorem,[33] the notion of a middle term—and therefore of mediation—occupies a central place in it. As for Judeo-Christian thought, it is not less complex than Inuit thought; indeed, Jesus combines in his person two opposite natures, the one divine, the other human, and by virtue of just this he is the Mediator par excellence, the intermediary between God and humanity, and at the same time, in Pascal's phrase, the "model of all conditions," which is to say the mediator between all human beings. It is true that Christ represents the male face of the divine, whose female counterpart is the Church, conceived of as his mystical bride; but the God of the Old Testament, to which trinitarian Christians remain faithful, is himself prior to male and female. This point is clearly stated in a well-known biblical verse, too often recalled, however, only by its opening words. It must be read in its entirety: "God created man in the image of himself, in the image of God he created him, male and female he created them" (Genesis 1:27 [New Jerusalem Bible]). Since God created man in his image and since he created them male and female, so it is that God brings together and transcends both masculine and feminine—as, in this verse, he brings together and transcends singular and plural. On closer examination, then, neither scientific thought nor Western religious thought turns out to be incapable of grasping the subtleties of Inuit thought; still less do they constitute a prison from which Inuit thought would help us escape.

If the transvestism and the shamanism of the Inuit in no way imply the existence of a third sex or of a third gender, they do nonetheless show that the horizontal relations of exchange and cooperation, of rivalry and competition, that grow up among human beings cannot represent the whole of society or, a fortiori, the whole of reality, but instead require the existence of a transcendent third party. This truth is given visual expression by a fine diagram that attempts to incorporate social and religious life in a complete summary of Inuit cosmology. It has the form of a circle lying in a horizontal plane and surmounted by a half-circle lying in a vertical plane, which cuts it diametrically. Shamanic mediation is performed along an ascending line whose origin is at the center of the circle (see Saladin d'Anglure 2012, 155). I believe that this picture is fundamentally correct. While it comprises elements peculiar to Inuit culture, its structure is probably universal. More than thirty years ago, Régis Debray conjectured that every human society could be represented by a cone whose base is "solid" and whose area is "imaginary." "A group," he said, "is not a circle, a plane limited by a line all of whose points are equidistant from a center, for the fixed point of the group is not internal to its plane. The center of a community is an apex . . . which means that all its component line segments (from the perimeter of the base to the apex) point in the same direction. Their convergence describes the lateral area of the group" (Debray [1981] 1987, 257).

The image described by Debray is therefore very close to the one traced out by Saladin d'Anglure for Inuit society, and it could be illustrated by many similar examples. In the Bororo village, the two complementary structures—diametric and concentric—analyzed by Lévi-Strauss correspond to the two orthogonal planes of the Inuit model, and the sacred center of the village can be seen as a projection of the apex of the cone imagined by Debray in the horizontal plane (see Lévi-Strauss 1958a, 152). The Inuit may well be remarkable for their singular traits, but these traits are nonetheless universal—molds, as it were, in which their culture has been given form.

CHAPTER NINE

Nature and Culture

The Return of the Sophists in Western Thought

The traditional pillars of the Western view of the world, whether scientific or religious, are therefore more robust than they may seem. Contemporary Western thought, by contrast, at once individualist and egalitarian, enamored of diversity and hostile to distinctions, exhibits weaknesses and inconsistencies that popular ethnology and its bogus relativism have made still more disabling. The opposition of nature to culture, now one of the intellectual reflexes of all decent people, or more exactly of all half-educated people, well illustrates this state of affairs. Used by Lévi-Strauss as a convenient shorthand with which to introduce his ideas about kinship in 1949, it was then naively adopted by professors of philosophy, and, finally, became a dogma promoted by authors with no firsthand knowledge and very little ethnographic background.[1] By an irony of history, however, just when his work was thought to provide "scientific" support for reinstating the distinction between nature (*phusis*) and law (*nomos*) first made by the ancient Sophists,[2] Lévi-Strauss himself felt the need to reconsider certain bald and injudicious claims in the first edition of *The Elementary Structures of Kinship* (see Lévi-Strauss [1962b] 1966, 251–52; [1983] 1985, 34; 1984, 28–30), almost to the point of repudiating them in the preface to the second edition (see Lévi-Strauss [1949b] 1967, xvi–xvii; [1949c] 1969, xxix–xxx).

Lévi-Strauss's earliest statements in this connection nevertheless continue to be very influential within the profession. They express what remains for the majority of anthropologists today a fundamental (albeit generally unspoken) assumption—an axiom, in effect, a proposition that is thought to be in no need of justification. This is all the more remarkable as the criterion used by Lévi-Strauss for separating nature and culture rests on an easily detected fallacy that his successors seem somehow scarcely to have noticed. All the more likely is it, then, that this negligence reveals something about the mood of the time, and that there are lessons to be learned from it. We will do well to pause here for a moment.

The Specious Criterion of Universality and Norm

Here is how Lévi-Strauss describes what he calls the "double criterion of norm and universality," which permits the ethnologist to isolate cultural elements from natural elements among the phenomena he observes within human societies: "Wherever there are rules we know for certain that the cultural stage has been reached. Likewise, it is easy to recognize universality as the criterion of nature, for what is constant in man falls necessarily beyond the scope of customs, techniques and institutions whereby his groups are differentiated and contrasted. . . . Let us suppose then that everything universal in man relates to the natural order, and is characterized by spontaneity, and that everything subject to a norm is cultural and is both relative and particular" (Lévi-Strauss [1949c] 1969, 8).

The strict line of demarcation that this famous passage appears to institute between nature and culture is in fact misleading. Lévi-Strauss proposes two different criteria for separating the share of nature and the share of culture in human life, each of which is defined with the aid of two opposed predicates. According to the first criterion, nature is characterized by spontaneity, and culture by the quality of being subject to a norm; according to the second criterion, the universal is the mark of the natural order, the particular that of the cultural. In speaking of a "double criterion of norm and universality" Lévi-Strauss closely associates them, as if they were interchangeable. But it is here that the shoe pinches, for in considering spontaneity and universality, on the one hand, and norm and singularity, on the other, to be equivalent he excludes a priori the existence of both natural differences and universal norms. Now, this is manifestly contrary to what we know to be true. In the human species, natural differences undeniably do exist; indeed, they constitute the very subject matter of what used to be simply called anthropology,[3] before the creation of a specific discipline called physical anthropology or, more recently, biological anthropology. And there are also undeniably universal norms, or transcultural principles—such as the prohibition of incest, dear to Lévi-Strauss, or Testart's law—the inventory of which is still far from complete (see Scubla 1988). The two criteria amalgamated by Lévi-Strauss are therefore not equally well instantiated. What is more, it is evidently the first one, and not the second, that is correct: the distinctive mark of nature, as we have known since Aristotle, is not universality but spontaneity; and what really distinguishes nature from culture is the distance between two modes of transmission, biological heredity and external tradition—a classic opposition, stated in exactly these terms by Lévi-Strauss himself ([1949c] 1969, 8) only a few lines above the passage I am commenting on here. Far from clarifying things, then, this passage only confuses them.

Lévi-Strauss's paradoxical attitude is easily explained. The double criterion of universality and norm is a rhetorical gambit aimed, first, at making the incest prohibition, a universal rule, appear to be exceptional in uniting two supposedly contradictory properties; and then at showing that it resolves the very contradiction it is seen to contain if one assumes that the prohibition itself embodies the passage from nature to culture, or, what comes to the same thing, the intervention of culture in nature—the intervention, that is, of a human institution, the basis for all later institutions, which, owing to its universality, simultaneously uproots all of mankind from the order of nature and causes it to enter into the order of culture, which is to say of the norm (see ibid., 24).

Apart from the defects I have already mentioned, and the question-begging that unavoidably accompanies any attempt to establish the singularity of an institution when it has been assumed from the first, this brilliant exercise[4] has the harmful consequence of putting norms, and therefore culture, outside of human nature, when human beings are, by their nature and in their essence, cultural beings. As Aristotle said, man is by nature a political animal. Here again the ancient philosopher may serve us as a guide, so long as we are willing to read him attentively. His formula is well known, but the phrase "by nature" is often omitted, and it is this phrase that gives it its full meaning. For Aristotle, it will be recalled, "nature" signifies both spontaneity and finality; to say that man is by nature a political animal is therefore to hold that human beings spontaneously come together and form successively larger communities, until a state of society is reached in which they are able to develop all of their natural potentialities: a society sufficiently large to be economically self-sustaining, sufficiently organized to be stable, and sufficiently differentiated to accommodate persons engaged in specialized pursuits such as science and mathematics—what, in other words, the Greeks called a *polis*, literally, a city. On the ancient view, one is not born human, one becomes human; and one can fully become human only within communities that allow all of the potentialities of human nature to flourish and endure. Similarly, the acorn is not born an oak; it becomes one only in the course of a long process in which its nature, as an oak, unfolds as a function of the possibilities and constraints of its environment. Human beings have more possibilities, but this does not mean that human culture is an exception in nature; it is not, as Spinoza put it, "an empire within an empire." And if this is so, one must therefore cease to place norm in opposition to spontaneity. Culture is not external to human nature, it is the realization of it, as the full-grown oak is the finished form of the acorn.

Is it possible even for a moment to believe that Lévi-Strauss was unaware of all this? In the second edition of *Elementary Structures*, he remarks that hunter-gatherers were often called "natural," or savage, peoples—as if culture, which was denied to them, began with agriculture and the habit of fixed settlement, and civilization with urban life. Seeking to soften a contrast that he himself had helped both to harden and sharpen, he then goes on to conjecture that it might be more ideological than scientific:

> By this hypothesis, the contrast of nature and culture would be neither a primeval fact, nor a concrete aspect of universal order. Rather it should be seen as an artificial creation of culture, a protective rampart thrown up around it because it only felt able to assert its existence and uniqueness by destroying all the links that lead back to its original association with the other manifestations of life. Consequently, to understand culture in its essence, we would have to trace it back to its source and run counter to its forward trend, to retie all the broken threads by seeking out their loose

ends in other animal and even vegetable families." (Lévi-Strauss, [1949c] 1969, xxix–xxx)

Lévi-Strauss speaks here in the conditional mood, which saves him the trouble of having to repudiate his own theory and rewrite the whole of the introduction to his first great work. But there can scarcely be any doubt that he is saying what he really thinks. Nor is there the slightest question that a vitalist and neo-Aristotelian attempt "to understand culture in its essence" is nearer to what is wanted than the cognitivist perspective of researchers who seek to naturalize anthropology with the aid of a materialist theory of mind. But this fine phrase, without actually constituting a hapax legomenon, nonetheless remains marginal and isolated, scattered along with a few others of the same tone throughout Lévi-Strauss's book; never systematically examined, and in any case drowned in the vast sea of words of his other writings, they have escaped the notice not only of the general reader but also of the majority of scholars and commentators.

Why Lévi-Strauss's Criterion Remains Influential

If the sharp contrast between nature and culture nevertheless remains a popular theme, and if the weakness of the arguments advanced to justify it has gone either unnoticed or ignored, this evidently is not because of Lévi-Strauss's circumspection in reformulating it. It is because the thesis itself, and the reasons given in support of it, agree very closely with certain powerful tendencies of contemporary thought, which, though they surely benefit from having fresh and reputedly scientific guarantees, arise from much deeper and more remote causes. It is plausible to suppose that these causes are not only scientific in nature, but also political and religious, and that their convergent effects have ended up giving an air of obviousness to a particular view of the world, which ethnology has only served to strengthen in its turn.

"It is now accepted that man does not have a nature, but instead has—or, rather, *is*—a history" (Malson 1964, 7). These are the opening words of a work first published more than a half-century ago, and endlessly reprinted since, that describes the culmination of three centuries of Western thought in a phrase that can claim affinity with both Sartrean existentialism and

Lévi-Straussian structuralism. Nature is only a blank slate, imposing no norm on individual or collective conceptions of human freedom (in the existentialist version) or of the human mind (in the structuralist version), whether they are pure products of freedom and therefore virtually infinite (existentialist version) or, on the contrary, self-normed and finite in number (structuralist version).

If one were to try to trace the genealogy of this view of the world and to explain its success, it would be necessary first to go back to the Galilean revolution, which substituted for the closed and hierarchical world of Aristotelian cosmology an infinite and uniform universe. The world of classical physics is, in Pascal's phrase, a "mute universe," in which man unavoidably figures as a stranger. Kant, reckoning that Newton had once and for all legitimized the new physics, now seen to constitute the model of any possible science, sought to conceive in historical terms the singular condition of mankind in a world subject to natural necessity. His philosophy is the source of the opposition between nature and history, of which the opposition between nature and culture is an avatar, and, more generally, the source of all philosophies that treat history as something peculiar to mankind.

During the same era, interest in tales of travel to previously unknown parts of the world deepened the appeal of the new historicism. By contrast with the uniformity of laws of nature, the diversity of morals and customs suggested that social norms are arbitrary forms imposed on a homogeneous human nature. A taste for exoticism thus went hand in hand with political philosophy: in opposition to power and authority in their manifold forms, held to be contingent and therefore oppressive, there was now a belief in the natural equality of all men. Physics and history, the sciences of nature and of man, were thus harnessed in tandem to democratic passions.

The apparent alliance of science and politics is nonetheless illusory, for democracy and equality cannot be founded on a supposed uniformity of nature. On this point one must concur instead with both the Sophists, portrayed by Plato in his dialogues, and Nietzsche: nature presents at every moment the spectacle of inequality and relationships among forces; its laws alone are uniform, not the things they govern. Thus, for example, the respective forces that the earth and the sun exert upon each other do indeed obey the same law of gravitation, but they are not therefore equal. Science and egalitarian humanism, far from being identical, are fundamentally opposed to each other—yet the modern world, as Simone Weil observed (1949, 204–6), does not have the intellectual courage to notice the contradiction. Resting neither on nature nor on reason, the belief in the equality of all human beings can only have, as Schumpeter showed, a religious foundation, or perhaps merely a religious origin:

> Or take Equality. Its very meaning is in doubt, and there is hardly any ratio-
> nal warrant for exalting it into a postulate, so long as we move in the sphere
> of empirical analysis. But Christianity harbors a strong egalitarian element.
> The Redeemer died for all: He did not differentiate between individuals
> of different social status. In doing so, He testified to the intrinsic value of
> the individual soul, a value that admits of no gradations. Is not this a sanc-
> tion—and, so it seems to me, the only possible sanction—of "everyone to
> count for one, no one to count for more than one"—a sanction that pours
> super-mundane meaning into articles of the democratic creed for which it
> is not easy to find any other? (Schumpeter [1942] 1950, 265–66)

Modern egalitarianism, one might say, is what remains of Christianity when everything else has been forgotten. One thinks of feminists who conflate two religions, each of which has its own special character, when they ascribe to the Judeo-Christian tradition a will to enslave women, forgetting that in the Gospels all female figures are positive,[5] and seeming not to notice that it is, after all, in Christian lands that feminism first appeared and developed.

We know that Saint Paul, in his letter to the Galatians, tells Christians that their common condition as children of God permits them, not to abolish, but to transcend all differences—ethnic, statutory, even sexual: "There is neither Jew nor Greek, there is neither slave nor free person, there is not male and female: for you are all one in Christ Jesus" (Galatians 3:28). If human beings are thus declared equal before God, they are not thereby undifferentiated—they remain different and nevertheless they are one, since they come from the same creator. Modern egalitarianism is an avatar of this idea. It is a Christian value that, deprived of its theological mooring—so that all natural differences are erased, or rather denied—became a fertile soil for radical feminism, for same-sex marriage, for theories of gender, and so on;

that is, with all due respect to those who champion such causes, for extreme interpretations of this same value.

The probable origin of contemporary egalitarianism also makes it possible to elucidate a paradox. In principle, the radical opposition between nature and culture can only have the effect of depriving norms—all norms, whatever they may be—of any possible natural foundation, or, to put the matter another way, of reducing nature to a neutral and undifferentiated material capable of receiving innumerable differences and values from outside itself, since it is altogether devoid of determination and value. In practice, however, and as a vast literature concerned as much with politics as with science attests, this cardinal distinction serves to surreptitiously convey the idea that equality is a norm prescribed by nature—as if nature, supposed to be undifferentiated and without any axiological character, therefore takes over from the Christian God, whose values modern thought imagines can be preserved while dispensing with their guarantor. In this regard ethnology has not wished to be outdone: while believing that it has freed us from Western values, it tends on the whole to approve them and even to promote them.

The separation of nature and culture in Lévi-Strauss's work gives rise to a more specific difficulty. In reducing kinship to matrimonial exchange, an emblematic feature of culture, it abolishes the mother-child relationship and the fundamental difference between the sexes, both of which are regulated by nature. But since it is men who exchange women and not the other way around, this difference reappears at once in culture, setting male partners apart from female objects of exchange. This inequality of status between men and women is foreign to the principle of reciprocity, and thus obliges him either to recognize it as a brute and enigmatic fact (see Lévi-Strauss [1958a] 1963, 48–49) or to pretend that it can be deduced from "symbolic thought," the supposed foundation of all culture, while conceding that the woman, as an object of male exchange, is no less than the man "a generator of signs" (Lévi-Strauss [1949c] 1969, 496). Refusing to base the theory of kinship on an undeniable natural difference, he leaves himself no other choice than between confessing to utter powerlessness and defending an arbitrary inequality.

CHAPTER TEN

Reik, Guardian of Dogma

Couvade, Initiation Rites, and the Oedipus Complex

Theodor Reik is probably the most original and the most perceptive of the collaborators Freud enlisted to help him strengthen the hold of psychoanalysis over anthropology by pressing on further along the path cleared by *Totem and Taboo*. Reik's study on the ritual use of the shofar (see Reik [1919] 1931, 221–361), a ram's horn whose harsh, groaning noise on being sounded resembles the bellowing of a bull at the slaughter (259), is a small masterpiece and, unavoidably, a point of departure for any inquiry into the sacrificial origins of music. But it is distressing that someone so knowledgeable about biblical traditions, and so attentive to the originality and the richness of ethnographic materials, which he has a remarkable talent for selecting and assembling, should not only embrace Freudian dogma but also strive to validate it at any cost. When he analyzes couvade (27–89) and rites of initiation, he is often just inches away from exposing errors in the Oedipus theory, as well as ones that later were to become apparent in structural anthropology. All the more discouraging, then, is it to see so clear-sighted a thinker bewildered and led astray by the force of preconceived ideas that prevent him at the last moment from achieving his true purpose.

Couvade

The very structure of his essay on couvade is particularly telling. It consists of two successive and largely independent waves, so to speak, the one purely anthropological, the other psychoanalytic—a secondary contrapuntal wave that nonetheless overtakes and overwhelms the first, and in the end almost entirely submerges it.

Things begin rather promisingly. Notwithstanding a few allusions to Freudian theory here and there, the first two-thirds of the essay owe nothing whatever to it. The same is true of two subsequent passages, written in the same vein, which usefully extend the argument. Reik applies himself in these parts to the task of describing and analyzing the principal aspects of couvade and related rituals. He gives a coherent picture of them, as well as a plausible explanation, both of them self-contained.

Couvade is not a privilege that a king idly enjoys as his wife labors to bring their baby into the world before at once resuming her domestic duties. The obligation that falls on him to observe a period of complete repose, putting his weapons aside and respecting various dietary taboos until the child has been delivered, has the effect of keeping him apart from the mother while she gives birth, and thus of protecting both her and the child from the potential danger that he represents to them. It must be emphasized that this danger is by no means imaginary, nor are the measures taken to ward it off in any way irrational, even when the menace is imputed, as often happens, to demons or other evil spirits endowed with deadly powers. Lethal violence committed by the father is well attested, notably the custom of killing the first-born child, which, as Frazer showed, has been practiced virtually everywhere in the world. And it is precisely because the threat is a very real danger that the belief in demons and the rites that accompany it, far from being gratuitous superstitions,[1] make it possible for those who conduct such rituals to safeguard the life of the newborn and its mother by diverting the father's aggressive impulses toward supernatural beings. These impulses therefore find an outlet in the ritual combat, sometimes a very fierce one, that the father must wage against the demons that threaten his family. Reik gives many examples that leave no doubt as to the meaning and function of these rites. In one, the father aims gunshots in the immediate vicinity of the mother as she is giving birth; in another, again to chase away the evil spirits that are imagined to assail her, he stands next to her and thrashes about with a stick, though she ends up receiving a good many of the blows; in still another, he fires arrows that pass just above the hut in which the mother and baby are lying, and so on. Each time the hostile outburst is liable to harm the very persons it is meant to protect, as if they were the ones for which it was originally intended; at the last moment, however, it is redirected to an alternate target. Just as the God of the Old Testament spares the life of Isaac by deflecting Abraham's knife toward a ram, the battle against demons spares the life of the mother and child by turning against their supposed aggressors the very real violence that threatens them. Thus Reik can plausibly pass from pagan rites to the Old Testament custom of the redemption of the firstborn child, without even establishing an explicit link between them,[2] by recalling that the primary form of redemption is animal sacrifice, which the ancient Hebrews substituted for the killing of their own children, as had been their habit previously (see Reik [1919] 1931, 70–72).

For violence committed by the male parent, which these various customs aim at preventing or else causing to fall upon victims outside the community of human beings, he proposes a very simple explanation. Couvade and the puberty rites that he goes on to study in the essay immediately following, as well as certain clinical observations (see ibid., 47–58), reveal that men envy the ability of women to bring children into the world and even desire to dispossess them of it (see 88), and that this desire is accompanied by anger toward the mother and her offspring. For the man who becomes a father, the child appears as a "stranger" and "intruder." Thus the father is seized with an impulse that, in the absence of some institutional restraint, leads him to "kill and devour" the newborn, as we know from cultures in which such a thing has actually been observed (61). Couvade and related rites foresee this fatal outcome and seek to erect a barrier against the murderous and cannibalistic impulses of the male parent. All this emerges quite clearly from the examples presented by Reik. More recent ethnographic evidence corroborates his hypothesis. Among the Guayaki, for example, the father must not witness the birth of his child (see Clastres 1972, 21). When the time comes, he must instead go out to hunt, and this for two very different reasons. On the one hand, his wife's confinement provides him with an exceptional opportunity that day to bring back more game than ever before; on the other hand, it also forces him "to run a mortal risk that can be avoided only on one condition, that he kill animals [instead]" (23). In this example, one clearly sees the displacement of the danger to which the child is exposed onto the person of the father, and the transfer of the violence that threatens the child to the slain animal.[3]

Reik could have simply left it at that. "This paper," he himself acknowledges, "might have been concluded with the preceding attempts at explanation" (Reik [1919] 1931, 69). Indeed, he has just accounted for customs that appear strange at first sight, showing the motivations for them and their functionality. In doing so, however, he involuntarily but nonetheless unmistakably strayed from psychoanalytical orthodoxy: on the one hand, by suggesting that the hostile impulses of parents toward children may in fact have a primitive, and not a reactive character, as the standard Oedipal theory maintains; on the other, by giving an explanation for customs meant to contain these impulses that entails a theory of sacrifice and blood rituals in which such practices are no longer seen as the neurotic repetition of an antediluvian crime, but as a defense mechanism allowing men to protect themselves *hic et nunc* against their own violence by channeling it toward external victims. Evidently Reik could not advance heretical ideas of this kind without committing both sacrilege and parricide. As if overcome by remorse, and on the pretext that the dietary taboos imposed during couvade recall "primitive totemic laws," he therefore proposed to undertake an additional inquiry that would allow him to find a deeper motivation for the latent hostility shown by the father toward his child. In reality, what he needed to do was somehow or other reconcile his interpretation of the facts with psychoanalytic orthodoxy.

The challenge is so daunting that Reik advances no less than three different explanations of the paternal attitude, which I shall treat here in order of increasing complexity. Though they are claimed to be complementary, they recall Freud's famous comparison of a patient's inconsistent explanations with those of a man accused of having damaged a borrowed kettle who tries to exonerate himself by giving three mutually incompatible reasons: "The defendant asserted first, that he had given it back undamaged; secondly, that the kettle had a hole in it when he borrowed it; and thirdly, that he had never borrowed a kettle from his neighbour at all" (Freud [1900] 1953, 4:120).

The first attempt at explanation is derived directly from the Oedipus theory. Aware that he himself had wished for the death of his own father, the new father dreads being the object of the same murderous desire on the part of his son (see Reik [1919] 1931, 75–76). He therefore looks with grave mistrust upon the newborn, and indeed is tempted to kill it. To avoid the horrible fate that would then await him, he moves at once to prevent it from coming about. But as simple and as rational as this explanation may seem, it rests on a series of more or less problematic assumptions. Let us accept that every male child wishes to kill his father and that, once he has become an adult, he retains a more or less conscious memory of this infantile desire. Unless it is to be supposed that the new father had actually killed his own father—a fairly rare thing, after all—it is hard to imagine that what he knows to be an infantile fantasy, and nothing more, causes him to tremble with fear before his newborn son, and to seriously contemplate putting him to death.

But even before we are able to formulate this objection, Reik launches into another explanation, which he considers to be better founded, of the father's lethal feeling: the "fear of retaliation" (ibid., 76–77). For this he relies upon the rather widespread belief, which we have already met with, that the grandson is a reincarnation of his grandfather. On this view, the new father does not dread so much the hatred of his son as the vengeance of his own father, who has come back to avenge the violent injustice that his son had previously sought to visit upon him. It is this fear that impels the new father to seize the initiative, to kill his own son—the armed surrogate of the grandfather, in effect—before his son can carry out the dreaded reprisals against him.

It will immediately be apparent that this second gambit only compounds the difficulty of the first, since it makes a supposedly universal phenomenon rest on a principle of alternating generations—namely, that the father of the father is his son, and the son of the father his father—that is not itself universally accredited. Moreover, from a purely psychoanalytic point of view, the new hypothesis exhibits remarkable features that require scrutiny as well. In the preceding case, the feeling of hostility was directed at two quite distinct persons in succession: the father attacks his son after having wished to kill his own father; to two different potential victims there correspond two potential murders of differing character, the one spontaneous, the other reactive. In the present case, the target of hostility is unique, for it is his own father whom he tries to kill in the child (see Reik [1919] 1931, 78); in place of two different victims we have instead two occurrences of one and the same murderous desire. This second scenario calls to mind the indefinite repetition of the murder of the father of the primal horde, postulated by *Totem and Taboo* and then revived in *Moses and Monotheism*. The fate of the father reproduces, on a personal scale, the compulsive repetition of an original murder that is supposed to punctuate the collective history of humanity. This parallelism nonetheless also conceals an important difference. In the institution of sacrifice, which arose from the primordial murder, the collective repetition of the founding act imagined by Freud is generally attenuated, having been displaced onto an animal victim and ritualized to the point that it could be regarded as a purely symbolic event. In the individual counterpart imagined by Reik, by contrast, if the murder were actually to occur, it would have the effect of aggravating the impulse to violence, since in taking the life of his child the father would now have done something that previously he had desired but had not succeeded in doing. Moreover, since the retaliation that the son is ready to carry out in the name of the grandfather, whether real or imagined, will have been nipped in the bud, and therefore will remain merely potential, nothing more, in the end it is the father, and the father alone, who bears responsibility for having actually committed a murder.

Note that on this point Reik's two hypotheses have the same implication. In both cases there is more violence on the part of the father than of the son, which is to say of the adult than of the child. Whether the murderous impulses imputed to the son are spontaneous or whether the son is supposed to act by proxy, the attitude of the father is the same: he is prepared actually to take the life of his son in order to prevent a hypothetical, still unactualized attempt on his own life. Each time, the retaliatory response is more real than the violence that it is intended to forestall. The result is therefore the opposite of the one anticipated by Reik. Instead of restoring his own analysis of couvade to the bosom of Freudian theory, he has shown that it is in fact incompatible with this theory.

It remains to examine a third attempt at psychoanalytic interpretation. Unlike Reik himself, who begins with it, I have placed it last, because it depends on a still more complex version of the relationship between grandfather and grandson. It suggested itself to him when he came to consider the ritual murder of the firstborn male child, and this at a moment when he could no longer conceal the ever-widening gap that had opened up between anthropological data and psychoanalytic theory. Indeed, the theme of sacrifice and the redemption of the firstborn do not involve private, impulsive acts; they are organized practices—what may rightly be called institutions—that reveal the existence of murderous impulses emanating directly from adults and aimed specifically at children. They therefore constitute a genuine challenge for the classical theory of Oedipal impulses. To dispel them, Reik starts off from the idea that supernatural entities, whether the God of the Bible or pagan divinities, are generally supposed to have begotten humanity. It follows that when a god, who is himself the father of all human beings, demands that the father of a family offer up his child in sacrifice, in a sense he is ordering him to sacrifice the grandson to the grandfather. But then, Reik asks, taking for granted the expiatory value of such a sacrifice,[4] of what crime can primitive men be guilty that they should find themselves liable to so cruel a ritual exaction? (see Reik [1919] 1931, 73). Reik's response will not come as a surprise: they are punished for having collectively assassinated the father of the primal horde and then trying individually to reprise this murder, each killing his own father. Freudian theory thus allows him to suggest a possible religious interpretation of the sacrifice of the firstborn. But Reik himself does not seem to be satisfied with this option, since he does not stop there; though he does not rule out the possibility, he heads off at once in search of other, more attractive explanations, ending up finally with the two very doubtful proposals that I have already described.

He therefore presents three distinct solutions, resting on the quite different ideas of expiation, fear of retaliation,[5] and preventive action. These solutions in turn assume three different targets of the act of violence, whether real or desired, which themselves are now in need of explanation. Aware that the various motivations he imagines for the killing (actual or merely wished for) of children may seem to be little more than a jumble, Reik suggests that they have a common origin in the variety of conflicting emotions that every man feels toward his father, and correspond to different phases of human evolution that are associated in turn with this or that aspect of the relationship to the father. So it is that the father exchanges the status of victim for that of a god to whom a victim is offered (see ibid., 80), having passed through an intermediate phase in which he is both god and victim, the grandfather having been reincarnated in the grandson. But Reik fails to explain in any convincing fashion how these historical transitions might have occurred, or why they should have become stabilized in one form rather than another.

Through an excess of loyalty to Freud, his interpretation of the rites of couvade is no less confused than that of "totemic sacrifice" given by his master, in which once again one fails to see why it should be necessary to repeat the murder of the father of the primal horde if it is true that this act had left those who perpetrated it with an inexpiable feeling of guilt that could therefore only be reactivated indefinitely by memory, rather than appeased and eventually forgotten. Above all, there is a striking contrast in Reik between his anthropological analysis of factual matters and their psychoanalytical interpretation. Having cast light on what appear at first to be curious customs, he then proceeds, on the pretext of uncovering their deeper significance, to shroud them once more in mystery. This is due to a change of method. At the beginning of his essay he studies the belief in demons that torment the mother, and the rites to which they give rise, placing himself outside of both the rites themselves and the perceptions of those who perform them in order to try to extract a kernel of rationality that will make them amenable to explanation by appeal to external factors. At the end, he resorts to psychoanalysis. This is where things become muddled. He has a tendency to put on the same level not only elements of Freud's theory (such as the murder of the primal father) and of indigenous theories (such as the reincarnation of the grandfather in the grandson), but also various interpretive models, both vernacular and scientific, and the rites and practices to which they are applied, without it always being very clear which ones are supposed to account for which. He also gives the impression of confounding science with myth, and of exposing himself to the same objection that Lévi-Strauss was later to bring against Freud, namely, of inventing a myth in order to explain facts, instead of working back from facts and myths to structure in order to explain both facts and myths (see Lévi-Strauss [1949c] 1969, 492). Here Lévi-Strauss is undeniably right. But the remedy he proposes, of treating all the fascinating problems that formerly were associated with totemism as illusory, and so disposing of them altogether, is still worse than the disease. It is a sad thing to realize that Reik's overzealous pleading on behalf of psychoanalysis helped to encourage this disastrous reaction, from which anthropology has yet to recover.

Rites of Initiation

Appearing only a year after his study of couvade, in 1915, Reik's paper on
male rites of initiation aggravated the defects of the earlier one by adopting a
psychoanalytical perspective from the very outset. Everything is explained by
a concern to punish and to repress the twin Oedipal desires of incest and parricide. Reik's approach is consequently much clearer, though without being
any more persuasive for that, since into this Procrustean bed he must now try
to fit data that sometimes turn out to be more recalcitrant than he had anticipated. What is more, he himself seems aware of the difficulty. Despite the
assurances he gives of having the appropriate interpretive tools to hand, once
again he puts off drawing any conclusions, and ends up giving the impression
of having raised essential problems without managing to resolve them.

In most societies, young people are subjected to rites of initiation that
take place or else begin with the onset of puberty, and that may be thought of,
in Frazer's felicitous phrase, as a "drama of death and resurrection" (quoted
in Reik [1919] 1931, 92). Kept apart from women, the novices are supposed
to have been killed or devoured by spirits or monsters, then brought back to
life by their fathers, who conduct the rites and who cause them to be reborn,
without the help of their mothers, so as to make each of them a true and
complete man, guardian of the cardinal values of the community, capable of
killing and procreating, of hunting and going to war, as well as of marrying
and becoming the head of a family. Throughout this period of apprenticeship, they are made to undergo painful ordeals, and are subjected to more or
less grievous physical abuse that may on occasion actually be fatal, as well as
mutilations that leave indelible marks on the body: scarification, amputation
of a phalanx (sometimes of a whole finger), extraction of a tooth, and so on;
the most common of these is circumcision, still practiced by highly civilized
peoples.

Reik is confident that he can explain all this on the basis of a very simple
idea. Initiation rites were instituted to prevent new generations from committing the twin crimes committed by their distant ancestors of the primal
horde, for the seeds of these crimes remain latent within every family and
may generate violence again at any moment if nothing stands in the way.
Like the explanation given for couvade, the one given for initiation ceremonies seems curiously to attribute to all peoples a precise, albeit implicit,

knowledge of the repressed desires that Freudian theory nonetheless prides itself on having been the first to uncover. It could be argued, of course, that the genesis of these preventive rituals is every bit as unconscious as that of the Oedipal desires that they are supposed to hold in check. However this may be, it is enough for our purposes that we look to see whether or not the supposed existence of these fatal desires suffices to account for the most common features of such ceremonies.

The camp where the initiation ceremonies are performed is situated apart from residences and is occupied exclusively by male adults and youths. The initiates are thus totally cut off from the female world. The reason for this, according to Reik, is that these young men, who have now reached puberty, must be prevented at all costs from having incestuous relations with their mothers. But that does not explain why in this case it is women, and not the initiates, who are subject to a strict taboo; on pain of death, they are forbidden either to come near the camp or to try to find out what is going on there. That no incestuous relationship is possible under such circumstances is perfectly obvious; but this is a secondary effect of the prohibition, which bears primarily on a certain kind of knowledge, and not on sexuality, and is aimed at all women without exception, as well as their uninitiated male children.

Reik does not pretend not to see the harassment, physical abuse, mutilation, and other forms of violence inflicted by the adults on the young men. They reveal a very strong sense of hostility toward the new generation, he says, to judge from "the refined tortures which they impose on the youths" (Reik [1919] 1931, 103). Yet at the same time he declines to see in any of this the signs of gratuitous or spontaneous cruelty. The violence to which the initiates are subjected has a pedagogical character, and it is always reactive. "The circumcision is carried out for the purpose of punishing and preventing incest; the killing for the punishment and prevention of parricide" (116). The explanation is the same as for couvade. In the man who has now become a father himself, there lives the "unconscious memory of incestuous and hostile impulses of childhood which were turned upon his parents. . . . He fears the realisation of these wishes, in which he might be the object injured at the hands of his own child" (105).

What is new here is Reik's concern to dissociate circumcision and symbolic murder, so that the rite of initiation can be seen to contain the two main

principles of the Oedipus theory, especially the idea that castration provides
the most effective support for the prohibition against incest (see ibid.). Circumcision is therefore only a symbolic form of castration, independent of
the pretended murder of the novices. Reik insists upon this point at length,
for he sees quite clearly that if initiation, as he himself suggests, is an attenuated version of more ancient practices in which children actually were put
to death, circumcision could well be, like animal sacrifice, a form of blood
redemption, an attenuated version of sacrifice, in which the part stands for
the whole. Perhaps he recalls, too, that when Hubert and Mauss, at the end of
their famous essay, wished to illustrate their definition of sacrifice by means
of an example, they did not choose a classic sacrificial rite, but instead a case
of circumcision, borrowed from the Bible,⁶ that must in any case have been
well known to him by virtue of his Jewish heritage. Unalterably attached to
Freudian theory, however, he resolutely maintains that "circumcision does
not take the place of the human sacrifice; the killing and the circumcision
are two separate acts that are only associated unconsciously" (124). There is
only a symbolic association between the two rites, the two states of death and
resurrection representing nothing more, ultimately, than "the flaccidity and
erection of the penis" (125). Thanks to this detour through the unconscious
and the supposed omnipotence of the libido, murder, the thing that gives the
rite of initiation its distinctive character, is thus made to disappear, having
been reduced to an ordinary physiological phenomenon.

What is stranger still, Reik also believes that two phases must be distinguished in rites of pretended death. He holds that ethnologists have been
deceived by "the manifest content of the rites, and therefore only see a direct
continuation of the death rites in the ceremony of resurrection" (Reik [1919]
1931, 123). To his way of thinking, symbolic murder, with its train of cruelties,
presents no mystery: whether the fathers who supervise initiations act out
of fear of retaliation or in order to avoid submitting to misdeeds that they
themselves attempted to commit in the past, they are moved exclusively by
impulses of hostility and vengeance. By contrast, rites of pretended resurrection are more enigmatic, since now the adults show feelings of tenderness
toward the youths and take care not to mistreat them. Why, then, does tenderness follow upon cruelty? (see 119). Reik rapidly mentions the hypothesis of emotional ambivalence, cherished by psychoanalysis, but he is not
satisfied with what he considers to be too vague an explanation. In reality,

this tenderness is conditional: "The primitive fathers signify to their sons by means of these rites that they are ready to receive them into the company of men, but only on one condition, namely, the youths must renounce their incestuous and hostile impulses" (119–20). Once again we encounter the idea that averting incest is the main purpose of the institution.

It is only after he has developed this theme at length that Reik finally turns to a major aspect of the rite, one that has attracted the attention of all ethnographers. Initiation is a rebirth brought about by men, and the initiates are twice born. Having allowed the youths to narrowly escape death, the adults are not content with sparing their lives; acting as though the initiates had really been killed, they claim to bring them back to life and then to raise them without the help of women, sometimes actually behaving as foster fathers (see Jaulin 1971). All this is accompanied by numerous rites and the deployment of a transparent symbolism: the hut where the initiation ceremonies are conducted is often compared to a womb, the main entrance is called the clitoris, and so on. Reik scarcely mentions this point, though it clearly reveals a desire on the part of males, tinged with envy, to obtain from the initiation ritual a capacity for giving life equal to or greater than the one that nature has conferred upon women. It is nonetheless impossible for him to evade the matter altogether when he considers Australian rites. But he raises the question as though it were no more than a picturesque detail: "What does this absurd pretense signify—that the novice is born again from a totem that is certainly male?" (Reik [1919] 1931, 145). Remarking that this form of male pregnancy accentuates the semblance of childbirth contrived by couvade, he infers from it that in the initiation "the fiction of being born from the man is a nullification of birth from the woman" (146 n. 1).

We must pay close attention to the words Reik uses here. In speaking of nullification and implying that it is absolute, Reik emphasizes the negative aspect of the rite. The rite is not a means for men to compete with women, to seize the power of procreation from them, to show themselves capable in their turn of giving life by constructing between father and son a bond at least as strong as the one between mother and son. It is aimed solely at eliminating, at doing away with, at abolishing the bond between mother and son altogether, and this always for one and the same reason: the potentially incestuous character of this relationship. If we are to believe Reik, human beings are obsessed by incest; they consider it to be the greatest of all transgressions, the crime par excellence, the final cause of all evils. When Reik extends his analysis to the biblical religions, he claims to detect incestuous connotations even in the Christian conception of original sin (see ibid., 159 n. 3). I shall come back to this point.

Like Freud, Reik almost always contemplates the mother as sexual object rather than as progenitor. His study of puberty rites represents one more step in this direction. Whereas we saw him hesitate in connection with couvade, giving due weight to ethnographic findings, now he is sure of his case. Loath to admit a truth that leaps to the eye but that contradicts psychoanalytic dogma, he refuses to see that it is not women who envy the male attribute of virility, but men who envy the female prerogative of maternity. This is the secret of male initiation—the secret that men try to hide from women at all costs, and that, paradoxically, psychoanalysis seeks to conceal as well. Failing to grasp this key fact, the very thing that gives the rite its unity, Reik artificially distinguishes two phases of the rite, which in fact are interdependent: the killing of novices and their rebirth. Although the whole of ethnography testifies to it, it escapes him that killing, for a man, is the equivalent of giving birth for a woman. It is in symbolically killing the youths that men act as initiating fathers, and it is in teaching them to kill in their turn that men make the youths capable of having a wife and children and of succeeding them. It is everywhere in his capacity as a killer—as warrior or hunter, as avenger or sacrificer—that the man manifests his virility and certifies his power over life.

Reik quite rightly points out that initiation, in training warriors, teaches young men to control their violence by redirecting toward enemies a hostility that was originally aimed, or so he supposes, against the father (see Reik [1919] 1931, 112); more generally, it serves to protect the community against its own internal violence by reorienting it toward external victims (see Girard [1972b] 1977). Additionally, by instilling in novices the habit of washing away in blood any injuries and affronts they may suffer, it teaches them the value of maintaining an approximate equilibrium among various rival groups, through a system of proportional retaliation that not only permits each group to preserve its "life-capital" and its reputation (see Verdier 1980), but also allows each man to acquire and defend his own honor (see Iteanu 1980). In the course of preparing novices to exploit violence for social purposes, but only under certain specified conditions, initiation impresses upon them above all the idea that there is no other way to attain manhood than by shedding blood. Indeed, ritual murder is sometimes carried out even before a boy is physically capable of bearing arms and before he has learned to handle weapons effectively, which is to say at about the moment when girls of his age reach puberty.[7] It is through menstrual blood, which flows spontaneously from their bodies, that women manifest the power that is specifically theirs, of giving birth. Symmetrically, it is in deliberately making blood of others flow, in war, in hunting, or in rituals, that men acquire and manifest an equivalently specific power.[8] Hence the fact that the hunt, war, and sacrifice are everywhere, as we have seen, a male monopoly (see Testart 1986a).

Adam and Eve, or the Inversion of Hierarchy

In a late work that uses the myth of Adam and Eve to examine "the creation of woman" (Reik 1960), Reik's inability to free himself from the psychoanalytic straitjacket becomes clearer still. The case is exemplary. Adam is issued not from a woman, but from the dust of the earth; and it is from him, man (*ish*), that woman (*ishah*) is supposed to have been born. The natural process of procreation, in other words, is denied and inverted in the myth. On this point, no controversy is possible. But how are we to interpret the story itself? Reik, for his part, proposes a paradoxical reading: "The Genesis narrative does not present the story of Eve's birth, but a distorted tradition of Adam's rebirth" (83). This claim, which Reik himself concedes is "surprising," seems to me to mix the true with the false, enveloping a plausible conjecture about the content of the biblical myth in a mass of gratuitous and superfluous considerations.

Reik rightly notes that the structure of the Genesis narrative recalls that of initiation rites, which is to say an imaginary death followed by rebirth. Indeed, before creating Eve, God plunges Adam into torpor, a deep sleep similar to death (ibid., 96). Then he performs a mutilation ritual having the same effects as the circumcision of novices. In removing a part of Adam's body from him, God changes his status, which passes from that of human being in general to that of a man, a male human being. Whereas once he had been Adam—the Hebrew name is homologous with Latin *homo*, meaning "formed from the earth (*humus*)," terrestrial, as opposed to celestial—henceforth he is *ish*, equivalent to Latin *vir* (see 106). Here the universal effects of initiation are plain to see.

With all due respect to Reik, however, this by no means prevents the myth from being seen also as recounting the birth of woman. Neither the text in Genesis nor what we already know about rites of initiation tells against it. The text itself admits of no ambiguity. It clearly mentions two successive births separated by a rebirth. Created by God, Adam, the native man reborn as *ish*, is properly male, and he gives birth to woman, *ishah*, which means "issued from man"—thus the biblical account, which deliberately inverts the classic schema of childbirth. Nothing in this licenses the view of the creation of woman as an arbitrary or superfluous detail. And to the extent that the text describes an initiation rite, still less does it permit us to see the creation of woman as in any way incongruous, since initiation always leads on to procreation.

Reik is nevertheless not wrong to compare the biblical myth with the many accounts that, like the Vedic myth of Purusa, relate that all beings, notably man and woman, come from a dismembered sacrificial victim (see Reik 1960, 120–21). A comparative approach of this sort, if it were to be properly developed, would undoubtedly enrich our knowledge of the invariant structures and the ultimate sources of myths and rites.[9] But it is of no help to Reik in the present debate. Authors before him had thought that Adam might well represent the original sacrificial victim from whom all human beings are descended, and not only a generic ancestor common to both sexes.[10] If this hypothesis were shown to be true, the most that could be concluded is that the account in Genesis is incomplete, not that it deforms or distorts anything at all, as Reik imagines. It lays stress on the notion that woman was created from a male victim, and rightly so, because it is fundamental. The biblical story describes, in an exaggerated manner, what men have always tried to do in initiation rites: bring children into the world. And if they fail in this, it is with good reason.

In writing about the creation of woman, Reik could not avoid dealing with this theme. He mentions authors such as Bruno Bettelheim ([1954] 1962) and Margaret Mead (1949), who maintain that "during the initiation rituals men try to take over the functions of women, especially that of childbearing" (Reik 1960, 116), and seek to show that "men . . . can do as well as women in this area" (123). This in no way changes his own view of the matter. Competition between the sexes naturally holds little interest for him. While he recognizes that "it has sometimes been emphasized that men are envious of woman's ability to bear children" (123), his very manner of reporting the thing speaks for itself: at worst, it is a mere opinion; at best, a secondary aspect of the initiation ritual. He remains firmly attached to the thesis he had argued for earlier, namely, that the supposed rebirth of novices from their ancestors is a means of strengthening the prohibition against incest by detaching sons from their mothers (see 123–24). As for the account of Eve's birth from Adam, which throughout this work he calls absurd, ridiculous, grotesque, farcical, and so on, it is bound to spring from the same motivation: "The reversal of the birth can have no other meaning than to deny the origin of Adam. It is a determined negation of the fact that Adam was the son of the goddess whose husband he became. This refusal to acknowledge the mother-son relation has the obvious meaning of denying the incestuous nature of Adam and Eve affiliation" (117).

The story that we read in the Bible is therefore a necessarily reworked, if not actually falsified, version of an earlier tradition. But Reik advances no persuasive argument in support of this claim. Even supposing that he did, and that the earlier version were known, what would entitle us to say that one of these two versions is more important or more authentic than the other? Reik does not pose the question. What is more, he notes himself that this supposed reworking would not have abolished incest, only displaced it; incest would take place instead between a father and his daughter (see ibid., 131). But then why would the authors of the revised version not have made a point of forcefully condemning any possible form of incest? These elementary objections do not occur to him, or else do not trouble him. He pays them no mind in any case, apparently persuaded that he has Freud's warrant for doing so, for he quotes the master shortly before proposing his own interpretation of the myth: "The creation of Eve has something about it that is quite peculiar and singular. Rank recently suggested to me that a reversal could easily have been brought about in the myth. That would make the tale clear. Eve would be the mother from whom Adam was born, and we should then encounter the mother-incest so familiar to us, the punishment of which and so on . . ." (Freud, Letter to C. G. Jung, 7 December 1911, quoted in Reik 1960, 74).

This brief reference to the psychoanalytic literature could not be more revealing. Anything that does not agree with the dogma, itself held to be clear and lucid, is "peculiar and singular." It is inevitably the effect of a distortion aimed at obscuring a bothersome reality, of a defense mechanism intended to protect the self against perceptions that might feed unconscious impulses, and so on. It is obvious that under these circumstances anthropology could have nothing new to teach psychoanalysis, could do no more than furnish it with fresh illustrations of its main concepts. This is why Reik, through blind loyalty to orthodoxy, misses the chance to make a discovery that might have led him to give psychoanalysis a completely different foundation. It is tempting to turn against him the quote from Anatole France that he uses to chastise scholars who are uninterested in matters that fall outside their area of specialization: "Les savants ne sont pas curieux" (ibid., 137)—or, at least, not more interested than most people are in challenging preconceived notions.

Devereux and the Male Desire to Bear Children: Primal Envy or Later Fantasy?

Although his thinking is more sophisticated, one sometimes finds Georges Devereux adopting the same attitude. In a book on the subject of woman in Greek mythology, Devereux explicitly rejects the thesis that I am defending here. He dismisses it as an extreme argument, which in any case can hardly be considered indispensable,[11] saying: "One knows of no ethnic group that claims that a man can, *all alone*, make a child. Indeed it is exactly couvade that proves the contrary. This practice does *not* seek to usurp, if only symbolically, the role of the woman in procreation. The man imitates *the woman* giving birth, in the first place to deny parthenogenesis and to affirm the reality of his participation in procreation, and, secondly, to affirm in *this* manner that he *acknowledges* the *sociological* paternity of the child" (Devereux 1982, 174; emphasis in the original).

In reply to this one would like to say, after the fashion of Leibniz, that Devereux is right in what he affirms and wrong in what he denies. The fact that men recognize and imitate the power of women does not rule out the possibility that they may wish to seize it from them. Indeed, Devereux himself seems prepared to admit as much. "I even think," he writes, "that the few purely male procreation myths, far from being of very great antiquity, represent only a reaction of male envy to the visible role that woman plays in reproduction. . . . At the clinical level, these few myths reflect the fact that unconsciously men are often jealous of the female feats of becoming pregnant and giving birth, and, by way of compensation, develop fantasies of male childbirth" (ibid., 175).

Despite this concession, Devereux assumes what needs to be established: the secondary and marginal character of this male desire to give birth as women do, which he tends to reduce to a historically later pathological phenomenon, one that is therefore mostly, if not wholly, peculiar to modern societies. This claim also runs counter to one of his fundamental theoretical and methodological postulates, which I shall discuss later: the innate unity of the human race. According to this postulate, what manifests itself in a given society in the form of a simple fantasy exists, or once existed, in an institutional form, as in fact is the case for couvade as well as initiation rites and the myths related to them.

A Hierarchical Model of Initiation

It is quite true that, in the matter that occupies us here, renowned anthropologists have come to the aid of psychoanalysis, however critical of it they may be otherwise. One thinks of Lévi-Strauss in particular. He certainly did not have a phobia about procreation (unlike Simone de Beauvoir, as we saw earlier [see Lévi-Strauss and Éribon (1988) 1991, 48]), but, with a single exception (see Lévi-Strauss [2011] 2013, 47–59), he nonetheless had the greatest difficulty making room for it in his anthropology. Whether he is examining kinship or myth, procreation does not seem to fit into his analytical framework, or even to be worth thinking about. In *The Jealous Potter*, for example, he really does give the impression of beating about the bush.[12] Considering the feminine connotations of pottery, he remarks that in societies possessing ceramics, a pregnant woman is often compared to a large pot. Studying myths in which excrement is turned into clay pots, a transformation that causes it to pass from a state of being contained to one of containing, he devotes an entire chapter to tales in which beings are alternately contained and containing. In these accounts he discerns a topology analogous to that of a Klein bottle, the basis for his daring "canonical formula," which he proceeds at once to apply to mythology. Curiously, however, he seems not to see what connects the two facts from which he started out: the affinity of women for pottery and the cycle of transformations. He does not notice that every woman can go from the state of being contained, which she has known in the course of her own gestation, to that of containing by becoming a mother in her turn, whereas a man forever remains a being who was initially contained without ever becoming one who contains (see Scubla 1998, 105–8)—except, of course, in certain myths, not least that of Adam and Eve. The whole issue of procreation, and of the associated rivalry between the sexes,[13] is thus neglected.

Louis Dumont, for his part, explicitly uses the myth of Adam and Eve to illustrate his holistic conception of hierarchy (see [1979] 1980, 239–45). Indeed, he says that it is the "best example" (239) that he could give of it. A hierarchical structure is a structure in which not only are the parts subordinate to the whole; it is also the case that one part represents the whole and therefore encompasses an opposing part. In short, it is an "encompassing of the contrary" (240). Thus, in the beginning, Adam is man, undifferentiated, the prototype of the human species; then, in a second stage, he is its male representative, by contrast with its female representative; and finally, he is both things at once—the "representative" of the human species and the "prototype of the male individuals of this species" (240), opposed to its female prototype. By virtue of this second quality, Adam, as man, is the contrary of woman; by virtue of his first quality, as representative of the species as a whole, he encompasses his contrary.[14] "These two relations," Dumont says, "characterize the hierarchical relation, which cannot be better symbolized than by the material encompassing of the future Eve in the body of the first Adam" (240).

Fair enough. But why should it be the man who encompasses woman and not the other way round? In other words, what is it in the hierarchical model that qualifies one part rather than another to represent the whole? Oddly, in a work seeking to sketch a theory of hierarchy, the question is not addressed. And there is something disconcerting about the example Dumont gives as well. Having just emphasized that hierarchy is not a mere ordering relation, expressing the subordination of something lower to something higher, the domination of the lower by the higher, and so on, he seems nonetheless to approve the common bias in favor of male preeminence.

It is not enough to say that it is the relation to the whole that forms the basis for this preeminence[15] if one does not also show what renders one part or term more suitable than any other to support a privileged relation with the whole. In the event, this requirement is all the more reasonable as the biblical myth, disregarding the relation of containing to contained I mentioned earlier, expressly overturns the natural and primary relation of the encompassing of man by woman. Now, Dumont does not even mention this inversion. This is especially surprising since he calls attention, on the very next page, to another characteristic property of hierarchical systems, namely, inversion of hierarchy: if A is superior to B on a certain level, there necessarily exists another level on which B is superior to A. "The same hierarchical principle," he writes, "that in some way subjugates one level to another at the same time introduces a multiplicity of levels, letting the situation reverse itself. The mother of the family (an Indian family, for example), inferior though she may be made by her sex in some respects nonetheless dominates the relationships within the family" (Dumont [1979] 1980, 241).

Here Dumont takes the example of relations between the sexes in a society, but for no very obvious reason fails to apply his own principle of hierarchical inversion to the myth of Adam and Eve, though this would furnish undeniably powerful evidence in its favor: in nature, man is issued from a woman; in myth, it is the opposite.[16] Furthermore, Dumont does not say whether—and if so, how—the two fundamental principles of his theory (encompassing of the contrary and inversion of hierarchy) can be deduced from each other, or whether, by contrast, they are independent of each other. The biblical myth, however, has the virtue of associating these two principles in an elegant way, since it reverses the encompassing relation. It is therefore quite remarkable that Dumont should be utterly silent on this point.

The example most famously given by Dumont, a scholar of ancient India, is the relationship between the king and his priest. On the religious level, the Brahman has a higher status than the king, for he is the purer of the two; on the political level, he is inferior to him and subject to his power. But these levels are themselves structured hierarchically. Since religious values are superior to political values, the king is superior on the lower level but inferior on the higher level, whereas the Brahman is inferior on the lower level but superior on the higher level. This example nonetheless raises several questions. Are we dealing here with a local and particular form of hierarchy? Or is religion necessarily superior to politics? If it is, why? If it is not, what explains its preeminence in this case? Are we even sure that this preeminence is real? Could it be that the primacy of religion is nothing more than a priestly pretension, or else an illusion expressly cultivated by the king for the purpose of more readily imposing his authority? These questions go unanswered.

Whatever the answers may be, it cannot be disputed that Dumont's model of hierarchical reversal is very well suited to describing relations between the sexes and analyzing rites of initiation, without rehearsing once more the familiar platitudes about the universal subjugation of women by men. Proof of this is to be found in the work of Marika Moisseeff, trained as both an ethnologist and a psychotherapist.

From the very beginning she has stressed four essential points. First, the necessity of conceiving the difference between the sexes in terms of procreation—more precisely, of "the relational asymmetry instituted by maternity" (Moisseeff 1987, 126)—and not the sexual act, which "leads to a conception of the relation between the sexes as one of equal status" (Moisseeff 1997, 2). Not only is this relation not symmetrical, its natural asymmetry is expressed in the form of a dual hierarchy, between the sexes themselves and between generations; as a Tahitian proverb very nicely puts it, "The shell of man is woman, for it is through her that he comes into the world, and the shell of woman is woman, for she is born of woman" (Dumont, quoted in Moisseeff 1997, 1). Gestation immediately accords a primacy to the woman over the child she carries and contains within her, and over the man, who does not have this same capacity.

After having thus taken note of the paramount role of procreation and of the natural hierarchy of the sexes that is bound up with it, Moisseeff makes two important observations about their social treatment. In most human societies, procreating is less "an individual initiative" than a matter of "collective social participation," required of all; and this social function, whether it is cause or consequence, goes hand in hand with the fact that procreation is conceived "as emanating from a transcendent force" (Moisseeff 1987, 137). To this she adds another, no less far-reaching observation that she claims is deducible from the preceding one and from the primacy that is naturally enjoyed by women: "Since [the difference between the sexes] rests

on a natural asymmetry that confers upon women a superiority in relation
to men, there is superimposed on it a strictly inverse cultural asymmetry:
men are superior to women, by virtue of the fact that they are the privileged
mediators of the transcendent" (137).

Finally, Moisseeff emphasizes the singular character of Western individualistic and egalitarian thought, which not only rejects the idea of transcendent, or even merely social, regulation of procreation ("a child if I wish,
when I wish"), but tries to "demonstrate the absence of a foundation for the
difference between the sexes, which is to say the natural asymmetry favoring
women," with the joint assistance of biology and psychoanalysis. The one
discipline, in showing "the similarity of the embryonic structures of primary
sexual characteristics," provides what it takes to be "irrefutable proof that the
two sexes are not only equal, but potentially identical"; the other, extending
Freud's conjecture that bisexuality is at the root of every individual history
(see Freud [1905] 1953), denies childbearing any specific function and reduces
the child to an "organic appendage" that gives the woman her native duality
(Moisseeff 1987, 137–38).

In her search for evidence in support of these general propositions,
Moisseeff set out in two opposite directions: first, among the aboriginal
peoples of Australia, to whom she devoted an important book (Moisseeff
1995) and whom periodically she comes back to study; and more recently
into the realm of science fiction, which she takes to be the Western counterpart of Australian mythology, a magnifying glass on the ideology and the
fantasies of those whom she amusingly calls Dentcicos (see Moisseeff 2000,
478–89).[17] Rather than follow her exploration of the dark side and hidden
face of Western rationality, I shall look more specifically at how far her ideas
about sexual difference are borne out by research on the most famous indigenous Australian population, the Aranda (or Arrernte, as they are also called).

By comparison with Western habits of thought, or even with the view
of Australian societies promoted by a psychoanalyst such as Róheim, whom
we will encounter later, Moisseeff's approach is original: in order to examine
the nature of human society, she does not start from relations among adults
or sexual relations, but from relations among generations, or more exactly
the relationship between a child and its mother. In the aboriginal world,
"preeminence is accorded not to the sexual act as such, which is to say dissociated from its procreative function, but to the original fusional relationship

between mother and child" (Moisseeff 1997, 2). To construct a social world, the child must be able to extract itself from this primordial fusional relationship. Now, by virtue of the asymmetry of the sexes, the road that boys have to travel is much longer and more difficult than the one girls enter upon. A girl becomes autonomous once she acquires the capacity to have children, which is to say to pass from the condition of being encompassed to that of encompassing. But puberty does not give a boy a corresponding power to distance himself from his mother; instead it aggravates the risk that he will return to the original fusion—hence the necessity of undertaking a long journey that will lead him both to separate himself from his mother and to become a father. Among the Aranda it is believed that two conditions must be satisfied in order to have a child: first, sexual contact permitting the fluids of the two parents to form a shapeless and inert primary material; second, the action on this material of a "child-spirit," which emerges from the surrounding wilderness and which male initiates learn to control. For if the physical pole of procreation is feminine, its spiritual pole is exclusively masculine; the woman gives life in general, whereas the man, through his ritual powers, individualizes human beings and differentiates them into male and female. It follows that while the maternal function is individual, the paternal function, derived from ritual, is assumed by the community.

At the end of his ritual journey, the initiate receives the *tjurunga*,[18] a sacred object whose properties are responsible for having brought the spiritual part of his being into existence. This ritual contact undoes his original bond with his mother: it separates him once and for all from her, enabling him to make *tjurungas* in his turn and to manipulate them during fertility rites. In this way men become capable of reproducing all plant and animal life as well as human life. Like the heaven of one Aranda origin myth, they thus reverse to their advantage the hierarchical relationship of male and female:

> Just as heaven, originally encompassed by the earth, ended up encompassing it in the myth, each man, physically encompassed by a woman, his mother, during pregnancy, ends up through his ritual functions encompassing the female procreative function: it is men who are capable of bringing about the differentiation of the content of fertile wombs by prompting the male and female child-spirits to enter into them. . . . Like the heaven that hangs over the earth, the male procreative function governs the female

procreative function, for it is ultimately the child-spirits of boys and girls who allow women to bring into the world, to give life to children of both sexes. (Moisseeff 1997, 10)

We are therefore dealing with two opposed conceptions of the difference between the sexes. "In the first conception, the feminine encompasses the masculine, whereas in the second it is the masculine that encompasses the feminine." But these two conceptions are not reversible in the way that the terms of a structural opposition are. "Each one is ordered in terms of the other: a young man must first be born of a woman in order to be initiated. On this view, the second conception, the encompassing of the feminine by the masculine, presupposes the first, which is therefore asserted to be primitive" (ibid., 11).

The story does not end there, far from it. Initiates are taught that "physical begetting based on the feminine" ultimately derives from "spiritual begetting based on the masculine" (ibid). To be sure, *tjurungas*, which represent child-spirits, come in pairs: one female, in wood; the other male, in stone. But one origin myth relates that the founding hero of rites and *tjurungas*, Numbakulla, succeeded in begetting a ritual leader with the aid of a *tjurunga* made of a unique, and therefore male, stone. The myth recounts something that men may only dream of: a purely male begetting, without female mediation—for this unique and original *tjurunga*, from which ritual leaders and all male and female *tjurungas* are issued, is, as it were, the womb of society itself. The very fact that it gave birth to mixed *tjurunga* pairs testifies to an explicit recognition of the complementarity of the sexes.

Moisseeff therefore manages to extract from the Aranda mythico-ritual system three successive hierarchical figures, the third of which brings together all the elements, and which may be represented by the following schema:

$$1.\ M \subset F$$
$$2.\ M \subset F \rightarrow F \subset M$$
$$3.\ \frac{F \subset M}{M \subset F}$$

She began by describing the encompassing of the male by the female (1), which is to say by establishing the hierarchical relation $M \subset F$. Then she demonstrated the inversion of hierarchy (2), which is to say the transformation $M \subset F \to F \subset M$. Finally, she showed that these two inclusions are not symmetrical: the first occurs at a lower level, the second at a higher level (3). All the properties of the concept of hierarchy, in Dumont's sense, are thus clearly illustrated by a more complete and more persuasive example than the one of Adam and Eve given by Dumont himself.

Does this exotic case study do nothing more than settle a fine point of academic debate? Moisseeff does not think so. Owing to its relative complexity, she believes it allows us to see that the usual Western view of the relations between sexuality and procreation is simplistic by comparison, and probably harmful.[19]

CHAPTER ELEVEN

Hierarchy of the Sexes and Hierarchy of Knowledge, or Plato among the Baruya

L et us come back to the West. Men, we are told, have everywhere and always imposed their will on their mates; only the motives invoked to justify the subjection of women vary from one society to another. For in this struggle for supremacy no holds were barred. Nor did philosophy and science remain neutral: from Aristotle to Spinoza and then on to Freud,[1] it was in the very name of reason that, until recently, vast resources of intellect and ingenuity were deployed in order to perpetuate this subordination— with the result that Western societies were the first to denounce the violence committed against women for so many centuries and to call for an end finally to be put to it. But where did this change of mind, this sudden clear-sightedness come from? Was it all as straightforward a business as feminist orthodoxy imagines?

To show that in this case naiveté and perceptiveness are mixed together to a greater degree than is generally believed, that anthropologists are not necessarily more lucid than philosophers and the customs of savages not less subtle than the speculations of intellectuals, I propose that we undertake a modest but nonetheless instructive exercise. Let us look at the relations between men and women in, on the one hand, a classic work of the Western tradition, Plato's *Symposium*, and, on the other, in the initiation rites of exotic peoples in Africa and New Guinea. This comparison is all the more natural as Plato himself likens the learning of philosophy to a religious initiation. I shall come back to this comparison later. If we are to grasp its full import, however, it will be better to begin by once again visiting lands where initiation is still a living practice.

We have already seen that the most elaborate rites of initiation are reserved for boys and organized by men, whereas women and young children are deliberately kept apart from them. It is very commonly the case that the men make the women think that evil spirits kill the boys, who are then reborn with greater courage, and that only persons who have already been initiated, which is to say adult males, can participate in the ritual as assistants to these supernatural powers without fatal risk of injury. Not only are women disqualified from taking part; like children, they are taken in by the hoax. Why should this be so?

Initiation and Cooking among the Sara

The manner in which the Sara of Chad justify male privilege is not without interest in this regard. In their culture, initiation is for men what cooking is for women. The candidates for initiation (*koy*) are like uncooked foods, unfit for human consumption. Just as women make the animal and plant nourishment that their husbands bring back to them in its raw state edible, and in this sense more human, so men in their turn make the children that their wives likewise give them in a raw state sociable, and in this sense more human as well (see Jaulin 1971, 241–42, 274, 301).

The comparison is illuminating. In assigning culinary duties to women, the Sara entrust them with a responsibility that is in no way trivial or demeaning. Cooking is undeniably a mark of humanity; indeed, it is often thought to be the very symbol of culture itself. Lévi-Strauss popularized this idea, and it is altogether pertinent for our purposes here, since cooking may be regarded as a frame of reference and a model for defining ritual.

Nevertheless, among the Sara as elsewhere, ritual activities are judged to be superior to other activities. It is for just this reason that men, who are responsible for performing them, are thought to be superior to women, who are prohibited from taking part. But the hierarchy of the sexes is not less complex or more stable for all that. For it is not characterized by a unilateral subordination of the female order to the male order; to the contrary, it may be likened to a dance in which each of the two sexes takes the lead role in its turn. Through cooking and initiation, women and men contribute in different and complementary ways to the process of civilization, alternating in preeminence, so that the hierarchical relation between the sexes is reversed when one passes from one domain to the other.

If this exchange of services does not create an egalitarian relationship between them, it is because we are dealing here not only with distinct domains but also with different *levels*. The Sara present us with a fresh example of hierarchy in Louis Dumont's sense. In India, the Brahman has a religious status superior to that of the king, and the king a political power superior to that of the Brahman, but since religious status has a higher value than political power, the Brahman is superior to the king overall (see postface to Dumont [1979] 1980, 239–45). Similarly, among the Sara, the man is superior to the woman overall, since it is only at a lower level that the woman is superior to him, whereas she is inferior to him on a higher level. Indeed, since initiation alone confers on a human being his complete humanity, a woman is equivalent, in certain respects, to an uninitiated child, which is exactly how the Sara themselves see the situation.[2]

Although these relations are very clear and coherent within Sara culture itself, to anyone looking at this culture from the outside there appears to be something in need of explanation. If we grant that a certain equivalence does in fact obtain between ritual and cooking, the question nonetheless arises why cooking should from the very beginning have become a female duty. Dyed-in-the-wool structuralists obviously would consider the question improper. By virtue of the axiom that the meaning of symbols is primarily, indeed exclusively, positional,[3] they would reject as "substantialist" the idea that there may be intrinsically masculine or feminine activities and functions. To their way of thinking, masculine and feminine are not predetermined, they are mutually codetermining. Only the structural opposition of cooking and ritual matters, for it is this and nothing else that tells us how the difference between male and female operates among the Sara.

This objection in principle may seem to be all the more well-founded since cooking is apt to be a highly masculine activity, as the "great chefs" of French culinary tradition testify. But Hocart showed long ago that, where cooking is reserved for a corps of specialists, it was originally a ceremonial activity. In the caste system, cooks, barbers, and washermen are not mere technicians specializing in the preparation of foods, haircutting and shaving, and cleaning laundry; they are ritual assistants to the king on grand occasions (see Hocart [1936] 1970, 200; 1950 passim).[4] The incumbents of other ritual offices are men as well. It is exactly this male prerogative that needs to be elucidated. But here the structuralist perspective is of no help at all. Even in linguistics,[5] where it is supposed to have first achieved respectability, and more generally in the world of signs and symbols, which is its preferred domain, its usefulness is rather limited. The use of red and green lights to regulate vehicular traffic, for example, cannot easily be regarded as an arbitrary code. The two colors are not only different but complementary, each with its own connotations that make permutation difficult.

This is still clearer in the domain that concerns us at the moment, where male and female offices are not all interchangeable. The monopoly that men exercise, among the Sara and elsewhere, over rites of initiation must be seen as the counterpart of a strictly female function: whereas bringing children into the world is the province of women, initiation rites (and ritual in general) are to men what procreation is to women. Among the Sara, as in other cultures, initiation is an imaginary death, followed by a rebirth. The men pretend to kill the neophytes, then to revive them—as if they, the men, had the power to give life unaided, without the assistance of women. The ritual therefore not only endows the initiates with an additional measure of soul, as it were, but tries actually to recreate them ex nihilo. Consider that the initiation camp represents the belly of the woman; that the novices emerge from the bush as the fetus does from the mother's womb; that each one has an initiating "mother," impersonated by a man, who feeds him with pap as one would a baby, as well as a cultural "father" who gives him meat to chew so that he may attain adulthood, and so on. It is altogether as though the ritual were intended symbolically to rob women of their procreative and nutritive powers; as though men, implicitly recognizing a primary inequality favoring women, try to compensate for its effects by claiming for themselves the power, real or imagined, of conferring on boys a spiritual life, essentially masculine, superior to the natural life, essentially feminine, that they have received from their mothers—in short, as though the ritual were a male cultural prerogative meant to establish an equilibrium with the natural female privilege of bringing children into the world, on which the community's survival depends first and foremost.

Nevertheless I do not believe that men pretend to put initiates to death with the sole aim of creating for themselves the illusion of being able to (re) beget them without the help of women. I think that this idea comes from the confluence of two things that, though they are independent, are nonetheless mutually compatible and reinforcing: on the one hand, the intrinsic nature of the ritual, and on the other, the male desire to control procreation. The ritual is organized around the theme of death and rebirth (see Hocart 1927, 1954), and it is presented, rightly, as a source of life, for it does in fact assure the community's survival through a process of salutary death, of which sacrifice is the canonical form.[6] Men are therefore spontaneously inclined to claim the right of supervision for themselves in order to acquire a cultural (or what I also call symbolic) mastery of life that compensates for its natural mastery by women.

Initiation and Scarecrows among the Baruya: The Male Point of View

That the symbolic mastery of procreation by men is an essential trait of initiation was shown by Maurice Godelier in a memorable summary of the initiation cycle of the Baruya of New Guinea, delivered extemporaneously in response to a talk by Massimo Piattelli-Palmarini at a conference at Royaumont in 1972.[7] The cycle begins when the son, at the age of ten or eleven, leaves his mother and goes to the men's house. It does not really end until he has become not only a warrior but also the father of at least three children, for it is only then that the son can once more eat in the presence of his mother and speak to her directly—his mother being "the first person one leaves and the last one comes back to" (Piattelli-Palmarini et al. 1978, 3:145). This essential point could not be more clearly stated. If the male ritual allows its beneficiaries to meet their maternal progenitors on equal terms, it is because it gives men the equivalent of female procreative power.

What is more, the men of this patrilineal society seek not only to compete equally with women but also to dispossess them of their reproductive and nutritive functions, so as to become the exclusive holders of these functions.

In this regard, two customs are significant: the making of scarecrows, and the gift of sperm to young married women. The making of scarecrows is a ritualized activity, reserved for women and uninitiated boys, that forms part of the system of male initiation (see Alland 1985, 39–44). The scarecrows are invariably male figures. The women dress them in grass skirts similar to the ones worn by adult men and the ones boys are given to wear during the most important phase of their initiation. Despite its formal correspondence with the great male ritual, however, the making of scarecrows is a degraded rite that bears the mark of female inferiority. Whereas the men manage all by themselves—and notably through gifts of sperm, made by older boys to younger boys, during several years of the initiation cycle (see Godelier [1982] 1986, 54)—to create proud warriors, the women try to produce men on their own but succeed only in producing scarecrows, good for nothing more than frightening birds (see Alland 1985, 42). This failure is considered to justify excluding women from the most important ceremonies, for it shows the decay that could not help but fatally undermine Baruya society if ever men were to risk confiding all or part of ritual activities to their mates.

Since initiation is equivalent to procreation, denying women the ability to celebrate rites amounts, indirectly, to challenging their power to perpetuate life. With regard to reproductive capacity this male denial is only implicit, of course, but in connection with nutritive functions men entertain no doubt as to the facts of the matter. Women owe the ability to breastfeed to their husbands, whose sperm "develops their breasts, and makes them nursing mothers. Consequently, before making love to his wife for the first time, the young bridegroom must give her his sperm to drink, and he must go on doing so until she is sufficiently strong, until the soot has blackened the walls of their new home" (Godelier [1982] 1986, 52).

The Platonic Reversal

Let us now turn to the *Symposium*. Here we find ourselves in the presence of an oratorical ritual that once again is strictly reserved for men. It does not really start until the flute player is sent away, a girl who does not speak and whose departure (176e) and return (212c) symbolically mark the beginning and the end of the rite.[8] Moreover, although each participant delivers an original speech in praise of love, they are all agreed, except for a few minor differences of opinion, in placing "Celestial Aphrodite" above "Common Aphrodite," which is to say in putting male homosexuality above heterosexual love, and the male education of young boys above the female procreation of children of both sexes.

It is therefore as though Plato held exactly the same view of the difference between the sexes and of generation as the Sara and the Baruya. This is not surprising, even if it took a long while for anthropologists and historians to convince Hellenists themselves that the Greeks were a people like any other, and for Hegel to convince philosophers not only that no style of thought can be detached from its time, but also that considering it in its proper context may help to illuminate the whole of the civilization that produced it. The feast of Adonis in Athens, in the course of which women symbolically reproduce the agricultural cycle of growth and decay (see Vernant 1972), is functionally analogous to the making of scarecrows among the Baruya: in each case women show that, left to their own devices, they are condemned to be barren. As for the Platonic *logos*, it repeats, or renews with several variants, the myths it has done no more than supplant: all of them are meant to justify the precedence of men over women.

On closer examination, however, one finds a richer and more complex picture. Let us consider first the structure of the *Symposium*, which is constructed on the same principle as the *Republic* and the *Phaedo*. Together, these works furnish three complementary statements of the doctrine of Ideas in its basic form. In the famous equation *pulchrum = bonum = verum = unum*, the "erotic" ascension to the Beautiful, contemplation, and immortality that occurs in the *Symposium* is seen to pass through the same steps and lead to the same end as the "logical" ascension toward the Good, wisdom, and immortality that occurs in the *Republic* and the *Phaedo*. All this is too well known to warrant any further discussion here. But one other aspect deserves to be noticed, which Plato himself was at pains to emphasize (at 174a): the *Symposium* is not only a dialogue, or even, like the *Phaedo*, an account of a dialogue, but an account of an account. Apollodorus, the chief reporter, was not present at the symposium: he reports the testimony of Aristodemus, the authenticity of whose account he took care to check, he assures us (173b), with Socrates himself. And so when we are "coming up" with Apollodorus, from Phalerum to Athens (172a), we are starting out from the lowest forms of hearsay knowledge. Far from having direct access to the truth, we are subjected, like novices, to a lengthy course of initiation, and obliged to follow the tortuous path of a doubly indirect discourse.

But things turn out to be more complicated still. For in Aristodemus's telling, Socrates himself, after having listened to five speakers and questioned Agathon in particular, recalls a conversation he had had with Diotima. We are thus dealing in the *Symposium* with a whole series of nested discourses whose Russian-doll structure is this:

(Apollodorus	(Aristodemus	(Socrates	(Diotima))))
4	3	2	1

By numbering, from inside to outside, the parentheses corresponding to the various interlocking levels, it becomes possible, as one might have expected, to bring out the arithmetic emblems of the four levels of knowledge[9] that are explicitly distinguished in the *Republic* (509c–511e). And if now we shift our attention from the structure to the form of the text, we note with equally little surprise that speeches give way to dialogues, and that dialectic yields in the final instance to religious revelation, just as at the end of the *Phaedo*.

What is remarkable and even astonishing, by contrast, is that the higher truths are revealed to us here through the ministry of a woman, as if Plato had insidiously wished to subvert the cultural order that he is describing. For Socrates, in relating his conversation with Diotima, introduces a woman into the male society of drinkers, like a Trojan horse, whereas until now such care had been taken to keep women apart, even the flute girl having been sent away at the beginning. Still more remarkably, he saves for them the supreme place, since—the height of irony, this—it is not from a man but from a woman, and more precisely a priestess, that he claims to have received what he himself calls an *initiation* (210a).

Here it would seem we are very far not only from the Sara and the Baruya, but also from the oversimplifiers and the half-clever commentators of our own day. Plainly men did not have to wait for modern feminist manifestos, nor philosophers for modern anthropological research, in order to recognize the equality of the sexes, or indeed to admit the supremacy of the female sex. There is even good reason to suppose that if Western countries today are on the verge of militant feminism, it is due to the long shadow of Platonism, extended and deepened by Christianity, whose importance in this regard is no less unappreciated.

It will perhaps be objected that Diotima does not actually take part in the drinking party, and that her fictional presence is a device that permits Socrates, speaking through a woman (here as elsewhere),[10] to express his approval of the strictly male order that in spite of everything prevails in the *Symposium*. In pretending to give pride of place to a virtual representative of the female order, he reinforces the subordination of women to men as an actual fact of the real world.

Looking at the matter more carefully, however, one discovers no hint of a ruse on Socrates's part, nor any attempt at one-upmanship. No ruse, for in declaring that he himself is sterile (*Theaetetus* 150c) and regarding the philosopher as a sort of midwife, he clearly shows that philosophical initiation does not seek to rob women of the power to procreate, or even to compete with it.[11] Nor one-upmanship, for in yielding to Diotima, Socrates does not offer women an illusory revenge upon men through the substitution of an inverted replica of the male order. Putting philosophy on the same level as maieutics, he recommends a less aggressive attitude while at the same time giving a great lesson in modesty that is intended for both sexes. For if men seek in vain to seize for themselves the imaginary powers they attribute to women, and dream of giving life to other men without the intercession of their mates, women are liable for their part to forget that procreation, in the last analysis, has something "divine" about it (*Symposium* 206c); in other words, that children *are made* in them much more than women themselves *make* them. One might even suppose that Diotima owes her preeminent place as priestess and initiatrix to her knowledge of this fundamental truth, of which she is the repository and guardian. It would therefore become clear that in revealing it to Socrates she had determined his philosophical vocation as a midwife of minds, and not as a creator of knowledge or truth.[12]

Among the Baruya Again: The Female Point of View

Must we therefore grant the final word, if not to Diotima herself, or to Socrates, who did not write the *Symposium*, but to its author, who is supposed to have been the father of philosophy? It is tempting to do so. For it is as though Plato wished to tell the attentive reader that, while appearing to endorse a general opinion about the separateness of the sexes, he was in fact describing an external and higher point of view, namely, that of philosophy. And yet if we turn once again to the Baruya we shall find that, among them as well, there are several levels of "reading" their institutions, not only from the standpoint of the anthropologist but also, and especially, from the standpoint of the persons whose lives they govern, for this plurality of levels is inherent in institutions. All of this will lead us to doubt that philosophy has access to any privileged form of knowledge, much less occupies an unattainable and almost divine meta-level.

Let us look a bit more closely at the initiation rites themselves. In the course of the ceremonies, the men cause the youths to be reborn as warriors, having duped the women into believing that they had been put to death by evil spirits, and reinforce their own superiority by forcing the women to make scarecrows, visible proof that they are incapable of producing true men. This, at least, is what the adult males themselves are pleased to believe, and what they reveal to the young novices; the act of deception is the great secret that is shared and transmitted by those who preside over the initiation rites.

But the women are not fooled. Even if they pretend to believe that spirits are really present at the ceremonies from which they are excluded, like women in other societies they know the men's "secret." And in making scarecrows, far from being the helpless victims of yet another humiliation, the women heap scorn upon the male pretension to make children. They take a mischievous delight in giving grotesque forms to these marionettes, mocking the supposedly whole and complete men that their male partners imagine they produce, and in dressing them up in grass skirts, all this in a playful and jovial mood—an ironic rejoinder, in effect, to the grave seriousness with which the men dress up the initiates (see Alland 1985, 41–42). Whereas the men suppose they are taking advantage of their gullibility, the women seem to understand the nature of ritual activities better than the men who supervise these activities.[13]

Crossed Hierarchy and Avoidance of Transparency

Do Baruya women therefore enjoy the same superior lucidity as Diotima, and is theirs, like hers, the dominant point of view? This would probably be granting them too much. For the origin myths of initiation show that in New Guinea, as elsewhere in the world, men are not naive either. Even if they do not say so in as many words, they know that the ritual is intended to rob women of the power to give birth to children. This, in fact, is one of the great secrets that Baruya men reveal to their initiates. In earlier times, they relate, it was the women who had possession of the cultural emblems of the community, who guarded the sacred flutes and organized the grand ceremonies, from which the men were excluded. But they were so inept, and sowed so much confusion, that the men had to steal the ceremonial totems from them, taking their place in order to restore social order.[14] Of course, this inversion of the prerogatives of the two sexes, a commonplace of mythology,[15] never actually occurred. But it is not only a belated justification of male domination. In showing that men know they occupy a secondary position in relation to women, it reveals the real origin of their current dominance, even if it is still couched in the language of myth. One detail of the Baruya myth is exceptionally significant: the men frankly acknowledge that they stole the sacred objects from the menstrual huts, which amounts to saying that these objects represented women's reproductive power.[16]

The most remarkable aspect of all of this is perhaps the place that is granted to what is implicit and left unsaid, rather than to ignorance or a lack of information. Among neither the men nor the women is knowledge distributed unequally; to the contrary, the situation is one of shared knowledge, where each person knows what everyone else knows but without knowing whether everyone else knows it—and at the same time knowing that there is no need to try to know! It is as though everyone had spontaneously agreed to avoid what today is called "common knowledge"[17] and its consequences, the perfect symmetry of information and the undifferentiation of members of society; as though the lack of transparency—the relative and mutual mistrust of others' points of view, and the rivalry that accompanies it—were a lesser evil, or even a means of protection.

It would appear to be thus in every society in which initiation rites similar to the ones that I have described are found. And in Plato himself, the male exoteric discourse and its female esoteric counterpart, while intertwined, remain separate. But is this deliberate difference, and the contrast of light and shadow that it creates, the condition of a stable equilibrium and of a complementarity of the sexes that every institution should somehow seek to preserve? Or is it a mask designed to perpetuate an oppressive male order, which modern Western society, being more clear-sighted than others, will at last be able to destroy by bringing into existence an egalitarian and transparent world? We know in which direction the received wisdom points today. It is harder to say whether in this respect it is genuinely wisdom, or merely presumption.

CHAPTER TWELVE

Ethnology and Psychology in Róheim and Devereux

Identity, Homology, or Complementarity?

I n spite of a deep acquaintance with ethnography, Freud's disciples almost invariably aggravated the defects of their master—not only, as we have seen, through a dogmatic application of the Oedipus theory, but also on account of a psychologism that frequently was more pronounced than Freud's own. The work of Géza Róheim, in particular, often seems to verge on caricature.

This is all the more striking because his writings have undeniable virtues. A scholar of vast learning and sound training, Róheim had a huge capacity for work, attested by his extensive field research among a great variety of peoples, the source in turn of a great many publications over the course of a long career. Even if his primary interest was in establishing that Hungarian folklore convincingly illustrates the grand themes of psychoanalysis, his very first article, accepted by a major international journal, presented a case of ritual regicide that had escaped the notice of even so erudite a scholar as Frazer, in a sober style devoid of any reference to Freudian theory (see Róheim 1915). Later, turning his attention to the social organization of Australian aboriginal peoples and the agricultural calendar of the inhabitants of Normanby Island in New Guinea, he revealed his own gift for precise observation and technical analysis. But he chose not to dwell on such topics. Once he had rapidly sketched the natural environment and social institutions of a particular population, he concerned himself almost exclusively with the rearing of children, the sexual life of young people and adults, the dreams of his informants, and the myths that they recounted to him. Everywhere he found the same things; everywhere he gave the same type of interpretation. This, he would have said, was because human nature is everywhere the same. Perhaps so—but it is also because his analytical framework acts as a selective filter. Even when the explanation he proposes seems plausible, one remains a bit doubtful, for it could not be more plain that the ethnographic materials he assembles, like Rorschach's ink blots, are valued mainly as evidence in favor of his own theoretical presuppositions and personal obsessions. I shall limit myself to two examples of this tendency,[1] simple and persuasive, drawn from the introduction to a rather large book that Róheim ([1950b] 1968) published three years before his death.

The cavalier fashion in which he treats a famous tale of the Brothers Grimm, "Hansel and Gretel," is particularly instructive (see ibid., 4). It recalls, in an extreme way, the manner in which Freud himself truncates the Oedipus myth and inverts its dynamics. Róheim summarizes the principal phases, but he omits altogether the tale's point of departure: the abandonment of the two children, to which their father reluctantly agrees at his wife's insistence. After several days of wandering the two children arrive at the home of a wicked witch, manifestly a double of the evil mother, who offers them shelter and food in order to lure them inside and make a meal of them. But Gretel manages to push the witch into the very oven she intended to cook them in, and in the end the two children rejoin their father, now a widower, with whom they live happily ever after.

Two aspects of this tale are particularly noteworthy. The first is readily apparent. Although the witch is finally killed by the children, it is adults who initiate violence, not once but twice—the parents, by abandoning their offspring, then the witch, by trying to devour them. The second aspect cannot possibly escape the notice of anyone who is familiar with initiation rites.[2] At the end of the story, the children have been permanently separated from their mother and her evil twin—the one deceased, the other killed—and placed in the care of their father, who henceforth enjoys uncontested parental authority.[3]

Róheim, for his part, considers neither aspect. He ignores the plain content of the story, which he turns inside out like a glove, without even describing it beforehand. "The witch who wants to eat Haensel and Gretel in Grimm's tale," he writes at the very outset, "is but the child's body destruction phantasy in talio form." Since "it is the witch mother and not the child who is shoved into the oven 'like a loaf of bread,' it is clear that the witch mother eats the children (projection) because the child wanted to eat the witch mother" (Róheim [1950b] 1968, 4). Without any argument other than appeal to the authority of Melanie Klein and a belief that children are sorcerers and cannibals, attested in various regions of the world, he lays before the reader an interpretation whose obviousness he takes for granted, but that actually contradicts the tale itself as well as the practices, real and symbolic, that are associated with it. Far from enlightening us, he conceals behind cannibalistic impulses very real facts of abandonment and exposure of children, of infanticide and anthropophagy, of whose existence he is nonetheless aware (see 60–62), and misses an opportunity to inquire into the function of initiation rites, whose structure the tale discloses.

The second example has to do with the initiation rites of the Aranda, an Australian people among whom Róheim lived for a considerable time and with whom we have ourselves become acquainted in an earlier chapter. Recall that a *tjurunga* is a ritual object believed to allow men to exert control over the reproductive functions of women. Here is how Róheim presents the matter: "According to the belief of the Aranda and neighboring tribes, the child goes into a woman from a *tjurunga*, i.e., a bull-roarer swung by an ancestor. The child is identical with the ancestor. The analysis of a woman's conception dream shows that the mythical ancestor is really her own father. She still wants what all women want—a child made by her own father. The fully formed infant emanating from the phallic *tjurunga* is simply the child coming from the [paternal] penis" (Róheim [1950b] 1968, 29).

Let us suppose that this woman's dream has been correctly interpreted. Does anyone believe even for a moment that it can shed the least light on *tjurungas* and rites of initiation? For if one takes seriously the hypotheses of Freud and his disciple, it would be necessary to accept that not only the dream of this woman but the whole Aranda mythico-religious system derive wholly and "simply" from one and the same thing: the desire felt by this young Aranda girl, ever since discovering her "castration," to have a child by her father in order to compensate for the loss she imagines she has suffered. This is totally implausible, and yet it is exactly the sort of claim that

Róheim is habitually bent on making. From his earliest writings, as Roger Dadoun points out in his preface to the French translation of *Psychoanalysis and Anthropology*, Róheim reduces the first fruits rite "to the behavior of a mother who tastes food and chews it before giving it to the baby to eat" (in Róheim [1950a] 1967, 11).

That he was determined never to deviate from this approach may be seen from a short monograph, written in the later part of his career, in which he sketches a general theory of the origin and function of culture (see Róheim [1943] 1971). Although he does not pretend to give "an exhaustive interpretation of the cultural process" (vi), and indeed tries to make peace with his critics by admitting to a youthful error of judgment, he persists in spite of everything in working solely with the concepts of psychoanalysis, as if they sufficed by themselves to construct a complete theory of culture. He was mistaken, he says, in likening culture as a whole to a neurosis (see 29), as he came to see in trying to answer objections made by Margaret Mead and other ethnologists. Culture is a form of sublimation, he has now come to believe, by virtue of its social character: "A neurosis isolates; a sublimation unites. In a sublimation, something new is created—a house, or a community, or a tool—and it is created in a group or for the use of a group" (96).

These lines remind us of Freud at his best. Freud himself, it will be recalled, was sometimes tempted to admit the priority of culture over neurosis. But Róheim quickly repents. For scarcely has he made this concession than, taking back with one hand what he had given with the other, he hastens to drag society down to the level of the individual. Sublimation is a sort of internal reshaping of the subject, a search for impulsive and libidinal equilibrium that is analyzable in purely psychological terms. It proceeds by means of an operation carried out by the ego that transforms a libido focused on an external object into a narcissistic libido (see ibid., 97, 100, 102–3). Culture is no longer a pathological phenomenon, but it remains a purely psychological reality.

In spite of this retraction, his old demons have not really been exorcised. When one of his colleagues takes issue with Freud, objecting that religion is not a disease but a cure, Róheim replies that sickness is itself an attempt at healing, and that "fundamentally we find that the disease and the cure of the disease are successive phases" of a single reality, or even are "identical" (Róheim [1950b] 1968, 109). Ultimately, illness cannot be escaped, because one cannot free oneself from the old infantile fears and behaviors from which it arises. The newborn's spontaneous gestures and grasping reflexes are sometimes interpreted as a first attempt to master the various operations of seizure, capture, and predation that later will be necessary for it to survive. It is thus that Lucretius, for example, conceived of the first head movements of calves that do not yet have horns, and the first beating of wings by birds that do not yet have feathers, comparing these behaviors with the babbling of children who have not yet acquired language. But Róheim sees matters differently. For him, infantile grasping reflexes do not prepare a child for manual activities, such as hunting, gathering, or agriculture. These activities are only new ways for a person, on reaching maturity, to satisfy his earliest grasping impulses, which united him with objects he feared losing (see 41–42, where Róheim revives an argument originally due to Imre Hermann).

The same is true for all other activities, which to Róheim's way of thinking seem not to have any character of their own. It is not enough to assert that childhood has left indelible marks on every one of us, that as adults we are in many respects no more than grown-up children, and that dangerous situations and relationships may awaken infantile fears. To his mind, culture is—and can only be—a continuation of childhood, a manifestation of its anxieties and its defense mechanisms by other means. Civilization, he says, "is a huge network of more or less successful attempts to protect mankind against the danger of object-loss, the colossal efforts made by a baby who is afraid of being left alone in the dark" (ibid., 131). This is his final word on the subject.

Far from loosening the psychoanalytic straitjacket, then, Róheim is determined to protect and preserve dogma, never to amend it. Like Freud himself, he comes ever so close to making fine discoveries. He mentions sacred royalty, for example, and with it the theme of the incestuous scapegoat king developed by Frazer, but only at once to reduce the projection mechanism whose operation he detects in it (see Róheim [1950b] 1968, 96) to a self-defense mechanism, and so to drag the collective aspects of the institution down to the level of the subjective fantasies that it arouses. The divine king is no more than a sort of magnifying glass of the infantile self, an imaginary receptacle of the desires that the young are supposed to renounce in order to become adults, and from which they try to free themselves, at risk of their lives. "[He] lives in incest as his subjects would like to, and he represents, what they can no longer attain, infantile omnipotence" (107).

The sacred king is thus a prisoner of the canonical Oedipal schema, with the result that the strictly ritual character of royal incest and the social function of the scapegoat king,[4] although they are touched upon, are not really dealt with. By Róheim's own admission, clinical experience revealed to him the importance of scapegoat phenomena in the psychic economy of individuals. But he does not suspect that these phenomena may also be responsible for the formation of social bonds. He does not see that one might easily move from the individual mechanism that psychoanalysis calls "projection" to a social aggregation operator—what René Girard (see [1972b] 1977; Girard et al. [2004] 2008) was later to call the scapegoat mechanism. He relies instead on the notion of "introjection" (more precisely, "mutual introjection") in trying to describe society. In his view, society is not created through common and purely collective action under the influence of a supposedly transcendent third party; it is a consequence of each person having internalized, for his own purposes, the same type of more or less fantastic imago as his fellows (see Róheim [1943] 1971, 108). Social cohesiveness comes from a sort of harmony, preestablished through the laws of the unconscious, among monadic beings—each one grappling with his own internal demons, but all exhibiting the same type of neuroses and defense mechanisms.

One must nevertheless give Róheim credit for correcting Freud on one essential point. Rather than rummage through dreams, myths, and rites in search of the indelible traces of a distant past, rather than conceive of ritual regicide, for example, as a repetition of the inaugural murder of the father of the primal horde, he tries to explain them in terms of present causes, and therefore in terms of the invariant psychic structure of human beings. The principle is excellent, so long as one does not regard the past as a wholly fantastical construction. Now, it is precisely this pitfall that Róheim does not manage to avoid. In his ontogenetic perspective, there is nothing external to individuals. And yet these same individuals owe a good part of their humanity to the social heritage that has been bequeathed to them. A language, for example, can never be reduced to the universal grammar that underlies it. It is not reconstructed ex nihilo by individuals in each generation; instead it is received and transmitted with very slight modifications. It possesses singular and permanent traits that give it a thoroughly distinctive character. This is what explains the diversity of languages and cultures, which is to say the very identity, the flesh and blood of each one of them. A culture is a set of traditions, a collection of spiritual goods that is handed down and shared, transmitted in its turn, enriched and modified—and in this way endowed with its own peculiar temperament and quality. Róheim's great failing is his chronic tendency to ignore a basic fact of human existence.

It is true that the academic quarrels of his time, which are still those of our own time, partly explain the radical positions he embraces. He rightly objects to the sophistic opposition of nature and culture that attributes to the latter not only a sui generis reality but also an arbitrary content, said to be due to the plasticity of human beings and to the fact that they can be "conditioned" in an infinite number of ways. The culturalist school overlooks the fundamental unity of humanity: "They forget that those who condition are subject to the same biological laws as are the others whom they are conditioning" (Róheim [1950b] 1968, 489).

Culture is not external to nature, in other words, it is a modality of it. "If cultural phenomena were not natural, how could they exist? If I were inclined to indulge in paradoxical statements," Róheim adds, "I might claim that it is natural for man to behave in an unnatural manner." But this formula, as he is the first to recognize, is specious. One should say instead that *"human nature, which is culture, is based on a biological substratum"* (ibid., 438; emphasis in the original). Indeed, culture is the very nature or essence of humanity. But Róheim should have gone further. He should have made it clear that humans are by nature cultural beings in the same sense that Aristotle had in mind when he said that man is by nature a political animal, that is, a being whose natural capacities (for writing and doing mathematics, to name only two) can be developed only within a society equipped with institutions that themselves are sufficiently developed. It is this institutional dimension of human life that almost always escapes Róheim. To be sure, institutions, like technologies—for institutions are themselves techniques of collective organization—are products of human activity; but like technologies, too, they are subject to decisive internal constraints that are not, or not only, biological and psychological. Human beings do not determine the forms their familial and political institutions assume any more than they determine the forms of their tools and machines. On this point, culturalism, like Marx's "materialism," which is a particular variant of it, is impregnable.

The Unity of Man and the Diversity of Cultures

In the work of Georges Devereux, an orthodox Freudian and a disciple of
Róheim, albeit an independent-minded one with a very relaxed manner and
a baroque prose style, we encounter an apparently less doctrinaire and more
nuanced style of thought. Combining clinical data and field observations
with a fund of classical learning and original epistemological insight,[5] he
tried to reconcile two things that are generally supposed to be incompatible:
the ambition of giving a complete psychoanalytical explanation of human
behavior, on the one hand; on the other, the necessity of recognizing the
specific character of cultural facts and, as a result, the autonomy of ethnology. On behalf of this program he makes two principal arguments, one
drawn from research in anthropology and ethnopsychiatry, the other from
his early training in the physical sciences and his familiarity with the ideas of
Poincaré and Bohr.

The first argument has to do with a general correspondence principle
between psychoanalysis and ethnology, which he discovered by comparing
clinical data with reports collected by ethnologists concerning the practice
of abortion in four hundred different societies. Devereux conjectured that it
might be possible to extend to all human behaviors what he had learned from
the analytic study of this single cultural practice: "Were anthropologists to
draw up a complete list of all known types of cultural behavior, this list would
overlap, point by point, with a similarly complete list of impulses, wishes,
fantasies, etc., obtained by psychoanalysts in a clinical setting" (Devereux
[1972b] 1978, 63–64; see also 76–77).

This extrapolation, and the hypothesis that results from it, run counter
to the inclination of the human sciences today to confine their attention
to collections of particular facts, discouraging even the slightest interest
in generalization. Devereux traces the origins of this counter-tendency
to Durkheim and Freud. He agrees with Durkheim, to begin with, that
"when a law has been proved by a single well-made experiment, this proof
is universally valid" (Durkheim [1912] 1995, 418). As for Freud, Devereux
holds that his discoveries constitute just such a proof—in the event, of the
correspondence principle. Although Freud's adversaries were perfectly right
to say that the theoretical corpus of psychoanalysis was elaborated on the
basis of the clinical study of a group of neurotics belonging to the Viennese

middle class, the conclusion they drew from this was mistaken because "psychoanalytic theory is probably the most penetrating set of conclusions ever drawn from the intensive study of a single social class, living at a certain point in history, in a distinctive cultural milieu" (Devereux [1972b] 1978, 66). The intensive analysis of a single institution in a single tribe, or of a single type of disease in a single social group, is therefore claimed to make it possible to derive propositions that are valid for all people everywhere, without exception. Conversely, one could establish exactly the same propositions through an extensive analysis of the same institutional or cultural trait, or of the same type of illness in a great number of different societies (see 66).

Lévi-Strauss, in appealing to Durkheim as well, stated the correspondence principle in a more radical form: "It is not comparison that supports generalization, but the other way around" ([1958a] 1963, 21, and see passim). There is no symmetry or equivalence between generalization and comparison; the former is prior to the latter. Science therefore consists not in passing gradually from the particular to the general, but in rising directly from the singular to the universal. It is devoted, in other words, to detecting the universal law in the singular fact. Devereux's own work conforms to this precept. On the basis of an intensive study of abortion alone, he claims to be able to establish the fundamental unity, at both the individual and the social level, of the human species: "Each man is a complete specimen of Man and, if one studies him on all levels, his total behavior is a complete repertoire of human behavior. . . . Each society is a complete specimen of [S]ociety and its behavior, too, is a complete repertoire of social behavior" (Devereux [1972b] 1978, 178).

The existence of a single human nature, identical in all times and in all places, is not seen to pose any obstacle to asserting a diversity of cultures. It only excludes the relativistic thesis that there are as many different forms of humanity as there are different cultures. Nevertheless it admits, and even implies, the existence of a multiplicity of cultures by virtue of the distinction Devereux makes between a "repertoire," which is common to all cultures, and "structure," which is peculiar to each of them. "Contrary to structure, a repertoire does not and may not distinguish between a real behavior and a repressed fantasy, nor between an explicit and positive custom and a taboo or criminal act. Thus, for example, it does not distinguish between the sacred and obligatory marriage of a Pharaoh with his sister and the taboo on such a marriage in other societies; in both of these cases the basic notion is that of a 'marriage with a sister'" (ibid.).

More precisely, all societies have the same repertoire, because the sum of conscious and unconscious elements is the same for all cultures, but they do not all have the same structure, because the system created from the elements constituting a culture varies from one society to another. In other words, different cultures are able to take shape because there are different ways of organizing elements selected from a universal repertoire, and there are as many potential cultures as there are stable partitions between the conscious and unconscious elements of this repertoire.

Devereux nevertheless does not specify the principles of selection and organization that permit different cultures to be derived from one and the same repertoire, each one equipped with its own structure. He remains deliberately vague on this point, avoiding even the terms "selection" and "organization," which have seemed to me indispensable in setting forth his ideas. He limits himself to distinguishing between structure and repertoire and, on the strength of this distinction alone, claims that his point of view is not contrary to that of structural anthropology, but complementary. In Lévi-Strauss, however, only the child is able to draw, and then only temporarily, upon a universal repertoire (or 'repertory'). From this common resource, the repository in germinal form of all possible modes of thought and all cultures, each society must choose the elements that it will then set about organiz-ing (see Lévi-Strauss [1949c] 1969, 93). Not all possibilities are mutually compatible, however. Choice is constrained, in other words, by principles of consistency and stability. This is true not only of phonological systems (see Lévi-Strauss [1958a] 1963, 57–58), which make use of only a small number of available sounds, but also of kinship systems and, more generally, of all systems of rules, explicit or not, that likewise obey similar laws. Hence the hope of one day being able to establish, for all cultures, the equivalent of the periodic table of chemical elements, in which "all customs, whether real or merely possible, would be grouped by families, and all that would remain for us to do would be to recognize those which societies had, in point of fact, adopted" (Lévi-Strauss [1955] 1961, 160).

This analogy with a physicochemical model shows that the anthropolo-gist considers cultural boundaries to be much more clearly marked than the ethnopsychiatrist does: for Devereux, the structure of every culture is suffused with a sort of nimbus in which all other cultures are virtually present; for Lévi-Strauss, there are as many differences between two cultures as between a carbon atom and an iron atom, making it difficult, if not impossible, to imagine that each one virtually contains all the properties of the other. We are therefore dealing with two unmistakably opposed conceptions. The structuralist point of view has the advantage of honestly acknowledging the diversity of cultures, without prejudice to the unity of human nature. Indeed, a single law—the Pauli exclusion principle—allows us to derive the whole of Mendeleev's table, that is, to explain the diversity and stability of all atomic forms. The existence of universal laws therefore does not exclude laws describing the behavior of specific, relatively autonomous entities, and vice versa. On this view, it is possible to recognize the actual diversity of cultures without subscribing to the relativist thesis of their incommensurability; to admit that human nature is governed by universal laws without denying the originality and specificity of cultural forms.

Despite their differences, each of these two theories of culture has the defect of describing its object almost exclusively in psychological terms. Lévi-Strauss seeks to derive all cultures from the thinking of the child, which is supposed to contain, "in the form of adumbrated mental structures, . . . all the means ever available to mankind to define its relations to the world in general and its relations to others" (Lévi-Strauss [1949c] 1969, 93). Devereux tries to base cultures solely on the impulses, desires, perceptions, fantasies, and defense mechanisms common to all persons. Both of them, like Róheim (and notwithstanding the fact that Lévi-Strauss attaches great importance to cooking),[6] omit the essential part of culture represented by technology—that is, by all those things that human beings produce under conditions whose parameters they are able to control only to a small extent and that, once produced, enjoy their own reality and a considerable share of autonomy. This is true not only of technology in the narrow sense of the term, having to do with things and the activity of making them, but also of institutions, which can be thought of—I cannot stress this point often enough—as techniques of social organization. It is striking to note, by the way, that Lévi-Strauss and Devereux show themselves to be no less careless with regard to ritual. The one sees it as a sort of disease that is parasitic on the healthy operations of mythical thought (see Lévi-Strauss 1969–1981,

4:674–75, 679–80), the other simply as the "frosting on the [cultural] cake" (Devereux [1970b] 1980, 13); for both of them, then, it is an ideological superstructure, nothing more. That Durkheim ([1912] 1995) and Hocart (1954) had already shown that ritual forms the infrastructure of human societies, the base on which all other institutions rest, or from which they derive, is of no interest to either one.

In the case of Devereux, moreover, it is hard to see how he could incorporate technologies in the broad sense in the universal repertoire of conscious and unconscious elements—that is, of all those things that are acknowledged or repressed—which he considers to constitute the womb of culture. To be sure, it is possible that a given technology may be explicitly rejected—a particular form of matrimonial union, for example, or of any other custom—in keeping with the schema of "antagonistic acculturation" that he very well describes (see Devereux [1972b] 1978, 216–48). The fact remains, however, that in the majority of societies that do not possess writing, the blowpipe, weaving, and so on, these technologies are simply absent, not rejected or otherwise ignored. What is everywhere given to human beings is only a general aptitude for developing such technologies one day, if not only natural circumstances but also cultural circumstances (in particular, the technologies already invented by preceding generations) are favorable.

The principle of point-by-point correspondence between the cultural and mental elements of human life seems therefore to rest on an overly restrictive definition of culture, and carries with it the risk of reducing ethnology to psychology. Lévi-Strauss, of course, when he turned from kinship to mythology, chose to take this risk. He maintained, or at least pretended, that it was necessary to leave the study of the infrastructure of human societies to the other sciences, and to confine his attention to the superstructures, on the ground that "ethnology is first of all psychology" (Lévi-Strauss [1962b] 1966, 131). Devereux, for his part, always insisted on the autonomy of each of these disciplines and their mutual irreducibility. It may be wondered, however, whether his correspondence principle does not in fact amount to carrying out the same kind of reduction, except for this difference: that his psychology, nourished by affects and impulses, is much richer than the emaciated, purely intellectualist psychology of Lévi-Strauss.

Poincaré and Bohr: Equivalence or Complementarity?

The second argument advanced by Devereux to defend his correspondence principle, with a view to immunizing it against this type of objection, is somewhat more technical.[7] And since he appeals to the authority of both Henri Poincaré and Niels Bohr, it is also problematic, to say the least. Indeed, Devereux refers to two distinct notions by a single term, "complementarity." For most people today this term cannot help but call to mind quantum mechanics, but he associates it for the most part with an equivalence principle drawn from a work by Poincaré published in 1901 (see Devereux [1970b] 1980, 185; [1972b] 1978, 1, 38, 44, 87), which he states in the following manner: "If a phenomenon admits of one explanation, it will admit also a certain number of other explanations, all as capable as the first one [of elucidating] the nature of the phenomenon in question" (Devereux [1972b] 1978, 1). This statement, it should be noted, differs slightly from Poincaré's own formulation and alters its philosophical implication somewhat.[8] But this does not interfere with Devereux's attempt to extend Poincaré's equivalence principle, mutatis mutandis, to the human sciences.

It is reasonable to suppose that there exist general epistemic principles common to all branches of knowledge. If in fact this is the case, principles discovered in the natural sciences not only should be transposable to the human sciences, but taken together they should constitute a general criterion of scientific validity. And indeed this is how Devereux understands Poincaré's principle. It is, he says, "the possibility of a human phenomenon being explained 'completely' in at least two [complementary] ways which proves, on the one hand, that the phenomenon in question is both real and explainable and, on the other hand, that *each* of these two explanations is 'complete' (and therefore valid) within its own frame of reference" (ibid.; emphasis in the original). This is why there are several human sciences (psychology, sociology, ethnology, and so on), which is to say several possible theories of the human phenomenon and not only one. These theories are not reducible to one another, nor can their contents be combined. Nevertheless it may be more or less convenient, depending on the case, to use one rather than another in order to study a particular aspect of the human phenomenon.

So far, so good. It is a matter, in effect, of extending to the human sciences what is customarily called Poincaré's "conventionalism."[9] "Two

contradictory theories," the mathematician writes, "provided that they are
kept from overlapping, and that we do not look to find in them the explanation of things, may, in fact, be very useful instruments of research" (Poincaré
[1902] 1952, 216). Devereux echoes this idea when he notes that the "principle of the double discourse" he advocates is opposed to any form of inter-
disciplinarity of an "additive" type: "Authentic ethnopsychoanalysis is not
interdisciplinary but *pluri*disciplinary, since it performs a double analysis of
certain facts, within the framework of ethnology on the one hand and within
the framework of psychoanalysis on the other" (Devereux [1972b] 1978, 2).
Yet he distances himself from Poincaré—surreptitiously changing gears, as it
were—when he goes on to identify this "non-fusioning" pluridisciplinarity
with a "mandatory 'double discourse'" (2). How does one move from what
the mathematician regards as a *possible* form of discourse to what the ethnopsychiatrist regards as a *necessary* form of discourse?

   Devereux had engaged in this same logical sleight of hand earlier, in
fact, when he spoke of constructing two exhaustive explanations of the same
human phenomenon that are not only "different" but "complementary."
On Poincaré's view, this complementarity of explanations, if one wishes to
call it that, is merely heuristic. It amounts to saying that one theory may,
depending on the circumstances, be more suitable than another. It is more
convenient for a sailor, for example, to navigate on the assumption that the
earth is stationary, whereas an astronaut finds the opposite to be true. Two
distinct theories are used here in an alternative rather than a complementary
manner. Devereux himself often reasons in this fashion, particularly when
he develops two different theories of schizophrenia (see Devereux [1970b]
1980, 185–213 and 214–36), here explicitly—and correctly—appealing to
Poincaré's "criterion of *commodité* [convenience]" (213).

   But he is mistaken when he imagines that this complementarity (or
rather "equivalence") between two discourses suffices to render impossible,
or at least illegitimate, any sort of reductionist claim, which is to say any
claim by one or the other discourse to hold an explanatory advantage. "It is
hardly necessary to add," he feels justified in saying, "that it is precisely the
independence and complementarity of these two discourses which makes
[*sic*] all 'reductionism'—the one which seeks to reduce ethnology to psychoanalysis or vice versa—absolutely illusory" (Devereux [1972b] 1978, 3). Not
at all. For if each of the two discourses is complete, as Devereux has already

said, in the spirit of Poincaré, each one, by definition, is sufficient unto itself and has no need of the other. The psychoanalytic discourse can add nothing to the ethnological discourse, nor the latter to the former. They differ only with respect to idiom and style. Neither one can impose itself on the other, but each one can wholly ignore its counterpart. This being so, from two things one.

We therefore face a choice. Either we see in this very situation the proof (or at least the sign) that science, in its current form if not in an absolute sense, cannot get to the bottom of things, and the question of determining which of the discourses accords more closely with reality does not arise: it is undecidable and will forever remain so. This is the conventionalist solution preferred by Poincaré. Or we suppose that science does have the capacity to grasp reality (even if this cannot help but be in a halting and fragmentary manner), that it is possible to indefinitely improve this approximate knowledge of the real world, and, in the present case, that one cannot hold two theories to be equivalent on the sole ground that both can be successfully applied to the same class of phenomena: reality being unitary, one of the two theories necessarily gives a better picture of it than the other. This is the realist solution, urged by classical rationalism, which can be illustrated by a simple example, the propagation of light.

We know that the fundamental laws of geometrical optics (rectilinear propagation in an isotropic medium, reflection, refraction) are all deducible from Fermat's principle, which states that light always follows the path that can be traversed in the least time. It is as though, in order to go from point A to point B, a ray of light compares all the possible routes between A and B and chooses the one that allows it to reach B after the shortest journey. To determine the light's trajectory, the physicist therefore searches for the path that corresponds to this minimum time, with the aid of a mathematical tool whose foundations were laid by Fermat, the differential calculus, which makes it possible to solve the problem without having to examine every possible path. Experiment showed that light does in fact follow the trajectory determined by the calculus. But, of course, since it was difficult to imagine that light itself calculates this trajectory before traveling along it, and since science seeks also, and perhaps above all, to enlarge our understanding of the world, a theoretical explanation was sought. Although Descartes failed to find one, Huygens succeeded a few decades later by applying the principles of Cartesian mechanicalism, which is to say by conceiving of light as an undulatory motion of physical particles that is gradually and, so to speak, blindly propagated in the surrounding space, necessarily taking one path rather than another depending on whether or not it encounters a medium that would deflect its trajectory. In this fashion, Huygens managed to give a comprehensive geometrical account of the behavior of light. We therefore have two theories of geometrical optics, one due to Fermat, the other to Huygens, which yield exactly the same results but which are not therefore equivalent,[10] still less complementary in the strict sense of the term. Fermat's theory is appealing, and convenient to use, but Huygens's theory does a better job of explaining the phenomena in question and better satisfies our need to understand. The former is nothing more than a mathematically very elegant expression of the latter. Contrary to what Devereux maintains, then, the mere existence of several rival theories of the same phenomenon shows neither their equivalence nor their complementarity; it prohibits us neither from preferring nor reducing one to the other.

Devereux himself seems to have recognized this, for he often seeks to justify his conception of a complementary double discourse by appealing to quantum mechanics as well. If so, it would not come as a surprise, since both the term and the notion of complementarity evidently came to him from Bohr, who introduced, or at least popularized, them in the sciences (see Devereux [1970b] 1980, 71, 293; [1972b] 1978, 72). The strange thing is to see him assimilate quantum complementarity and Poincaré's pluralism, citing indiscriminately to the authority of one or the other, as though they were equivalent ways of expressing the same idea. The example of light shows that this is not at all the case, however. Is it by nature corpuscular or undulatory? The undulatory conception proposed by Huygens, having long been outdistanced by its rival, which benefited from Newton's prestige, regained the lead in the nineteenth century; with the discovery of the photon at the beginning of the twentieth century, however, physicists were obliged to associate particles with waves, and thus to regard the corpuscular and undulatory aspects of light as inseparable. Conversely, the necessity of associating waves with electrons, which until then had been thought of simply as particles, came to be recognized as well—hence the appearance of a new mechanics, first called undulatory, then quantum, which considered the corpuscular and undulatory properties of the fundamental elements of the physical world to be intrinsically linked and complementary. We are not dealing here with two complete theories—the one corpuscular, the other undulatory—each sufficient unto itself and capable of being applied either exclusively or alternatively, as in the examples Poincaré chose to illustrate his thesis; here each point of view is incomplete, appropriate in some cases, in others having to give way to another perspective." Here, in other words, there is a genuine complementarity of points of view. To use Devereux's terms, the double discourse is obligatory.

The Autonomy of Culture: Methodological Principle or Ontological Reality?

It is therefore by no means a matter of indifference whether one appeals to Bohr or Poincaré in thinking about the relationship between psychoanalysis and ethnology. In the first case, one is pleading on behalf of a strong irreducibility of the two disciplines, which is to say of the ontological autonomy of their respective objects, mental life on the one hand, culture on the other. In the second case, one is arguing only for their methodological irreducibility, which is to say their conceptual autonomy—the possibility of describing the same phenomena either in psychological terms, or in cultural terms (as one may describe the path of light in either the style of Fermat or that of Huygens). Now Devereux, who had started out studying physics, could not have been unaware of all this. How is it, then, that through a queer sort of Freudian slip he seems to forget what he once knew and conflate the two perspectives? The reason, it seems to me, has to do with an unresolved—and probably unresolvable—tension between his desire to distance himself from the reductionism of his predecessors, of which we have considered a number of examples above, and his reluctance to grant culture and institutions their own reality.

Devereux rightly speaks of complementarity when he seeks to show the mutual compatibility and irreducibility of a method that "permits Lévi-Strauss to discover the *structural (logical) invariants* of a group of variants of a given myth" and his own method, which enables him "to discover the *invariance of the affective content* in the variants of another myth" (Devereux [1972b] 1978, 12; emphasis in the French edition retained here). There is indeed a relationship of the figure/background type here, of form to content, but complementarity nonetheless obtains between the two components—intellectual and affective—of mental life. The very fact that Devereux refers to mythology is revelatory, since Lévi-Strauss is interested only in the intellectual operations that myths set in motion. Devereux does not manage to show the complementarity of psychology and ethnology, then, only the complementarity of two psychologies, one of the emotions, the other of the intellect.

Plainly Devereux has a hard time recognizing the distinctive character and the autonomy of culture. Like all the disciples of Freud whom we have met with so far, no sooner has he taken a step in this direction than he changes his mind and turns back. "It is an illusion," he writes, "that culture constricts behavior." In reality, "maximum individualization and maximum socialization go hand in hand" (Devereux [1970b] 1980, 290, 291). True enough. Theories of conditioning are, in fact, wrong to regard the individual personality and collective culture as two antagonistic realities. But it does not follow that neither one has a reality of its own, as he goes on to argue in a subsequent work (see Devereux [1972b] 1978, 87–88), in contradiction of his own complementarist premises. For here we are dealing with a single reality that may be described in different yet equivalent ways—with the consequence that psychoanalysis can dispense with ethnology. If this were a case of true complementarity, however, it would be necessary, for example, to conceive of culture as nourishing personality in the way that heat and water nourish a plant. But it is exactly this sort of relationship that Devereux, as an ethnopsychiatrist, has the greatest difficulty imagining.

The nearest he comes to doing this is when he considers the relations between the normal and the pathological. Criteria of normality and sickness, he maintains, not implausibly, are absolute and transcultural and apply to societies as well as individuals. And precisely because an entire society can be sick, individual adaptation to the group is not an admissible manner of defining normality (see Devereux [1970b] 1980, 4–5). Nevertheless, though a culture does not furnish its members with norms of health and sickness, it acts in three principal ways on the appearance and treatment of pathological phenomena.

First, a culture determines "the ethnic unconscious" of the individual: "Each culture permits certain impulses, fantasies, and the like to become and remain conscious, while requiring others to be repressed. Hence, all members of a given culture will have certain unconscious conflicts in common" (ibid., 6).

Second, it protects individuals by strengthening defense mechanisms that spontaneously guard against the return of "repressed material" through additional means of defense, such as "scapegoating," developed on the model of the innate defense mechanism of projection (Devereux [1970b] 1980, 5, 10), or else by redirecting psychotic tendencies and behaviors toward socially useful ends, such as shamanism. Like the scapegoat, the shaman is a sort of fixation abscess: "Its nearest clinical equivalent is the utility of the psychotic child who plays the role of 'deputy lunatic' for a latently neurotic family" (25). Myths, for their part, can also in certain respects be considered a means of defense, for they "may serve as a sort of impersonal 'cold storage' for a number of individual fantasies related to inner conflicts" (12).

Third, and especially in dealing with the most serious cases, the culture supplies "patterns of misconduct" that make it possible to control deviant behaviors to some extent, so that they assume traditionally sanctioned forms. It is as though the group said to the individual: "'Don't go crazy, but, if you do, you must behave as follows'" (ibid., 34). Devereux gives many examples of such directives for "how to act when crazy," with which every culture provides its members, ranging from the figure in Malay society who runs amok—going to meet a certain death by violently threatening those around him with a dagger while nonetheless warning them of danger through a ritual cry ("*Amok! Amok!*") (see 28–29)—to female juvenile sex delinquency in a puritanical society (see 155–84).

Two things in particular stand out in these writings, and indeed in Devereux's work as a whole. In the first place, there is the primacy accorded to the internal conflicts experienced by individuals (in this he follows his predecessors) and the small amount of interest, if not actually the lack of interest altogether, shown in conflicts that are liable to develop between individuals. The social function of the shaman, on which I have laid emphasis, seems to him secondary. Culture is regarded primarily as a sort of prosthesis serving to compensate for the weakness of the natural defense mechanisms of individuals. In the second place, Devereux gives no precise indications regarding the formation, status, or effectiveness of these auxiliary defense mechanisms, which jointly constitute culture. Culture seems only to enlarge innate unconscious structures, crowning them with a halo of consciousness, as it were, without really having any substance of its own (the technique of the scapegoat, for example, is nothing more, in effect, than a conscious usage of the unconscious mechanism of projection).

The ambiguities of Devereux's epistemological analysis reflect the tentative nature of his empirical research. On the one hand, he advances a theory of complementarity that supposes the incompleteness of each of the two disciplines he claims to practice, as well as a form of ontological autonomy of cultures; on the other, he almost invariably reasons as though psychoanalytic theory suffices by itself, in principle if not in fact, to account for the whole of human experience. Despite its professed dual allegiance, his ethnopsychoanalysis is by and large the work of a psychoanalyst. In a book published near the end of his life, he finds it both deplorable and astonishing, that a reviewer of his 1972 work *Ethnopsychanalyse complémentariste*—"whose title," he says, "as well as every page, affirms that psychology and sociology-ethnology are mutually irreducible"—should "sharply reprimand him for wishing to reduce ethnology to psychology" (Devereux 1982, 22 n. 11). But is there really anything in the least surprising about this? After all, he himself has just declared that "every ritual begins with an individual and spontaneous act that then, in one way or another, comes to be generalized, ceasing to be a merely obsessional and private act and becoming a social ritual" (12). With all due respect, it must be said that in regarding ritual as a mere generalization of private neurotic acts and showing no interest whatever in the process that "in one way or another" might explain their presumptive generalization, Devereux gives once more the impression of seeking to derive the whole of society from the individual, and culture itself from the psychological—if not actually from the psychopathological.

CHAPTER THIRTEEN

Should *Totem and Taboo* Simply Be Forgotten?

The appearance of *Totem and Taboo* in 1913 may have seemed to celebrate the marriage of psychoanalysis and anthropology. A century later, it is clear that their union was illusory and barren. Having set out to conquer ethnology, Freud's heirs failed to seize the many opportunities that were offered to them to revise the dogmatic Oedipalism and the fundamentalist individualism of psychoanalysis. Nor did they succeed in reorienting the work of anthropologists, some of them victims of the same blindness. The certainty that they were laying the foundations of a genuine science of humanity, and the confident expectations it created of soon making huge strides forward, so perceptible in the writings of authors in each field in the early twentieth century, very quickly came to nothing. Not only did the two disciplines fail to enrich each other, they seemed, like the two sexes in Vigny, determined to die—or perhaps only resigned to dying, each slumped over in its own corner, without giving even one last exasperated look at the other.

Indeed, there has long been a sort of tacit agreement between psychoanalysis and anthropology, each allowing the other to retreat into its own private world, accompanied by an explicit agreement to more or less unanimously condemn *Totem and Taboo*, as if Freud's clumsy attempt to throw a bridge between the worlds of mind and society, solely by reason of its failure, rendered any enterprise of this kind futile. Devereux unreservedly approves the very harsh verdict that Lévi-Strauss hands down against this work at the end of *The Elementary Structures of Kinship*: instead of going back "from experience to myths, and from myths to structure . . . a myth is invented to explain the facts" (Lévi-Strauss [1949c] 1969, 492; see Devereux 1965, 224–25; 1972a, 169–70). Lacan, even closer to structural anthropology than Devereux was, never pushed his "return to Freud" to the point of calling for the rehabilitation of *Totem and Taboo*. "This blessed story of the murder of the father of the horde, this Darwinian buffoonery" is absurd, he says, "a cock-and-bull story" (Lacan [1991b] 2007, 112, 114).

In fact, those who believe they still must refer to it in order to lend credence to the theory of the Oedipus complex succeed only, in spite of themselves, in confirming its mythical character. Like every myth, the hypothesis of the primal horde assumes the very thing that it is supposed to establish. In order to explain a present structure, it does no more than cite to an original precedent that is held to be foundational. Now, this citation is doubly useless. It is tautological in its form and superfluous in its relation to reality. The simple fact that every child necessarily has a father and a mother, Róheim and Devereux claim, suffices to reproduce the Oedipal triangle indefinitely. But it is the structure of this triangle that has to be identified and properly analyzed. To do this, there is no need whatever to see it as the reproduction of a prior triangle.

Unassailable though the premise of their argument may seem, it overlooks the fact that a child, while it necessarily has two progenitors, does not therefore necessarily have a mother or (still less) a father. In other words, Róheim and Devereux regard the nuclear family as something obvious, as a primary and autonomous datum rather than the minimal part of a vast totality on which it depends. Freud, by contrast, notwithstanding the undoubted weaknesses of *Totem and Taboo,* and in spite of its individualistic assumptions, had the great virtue of inquiring into the relationship between the individual and society, and, notwithstanding its mythical character, of trying to deduce the structure of the family from that of the social group as a whole. In abandoning this approach, psychoanalysis aggravated the defects of Freud's work and wrongfully demeaned the achievements of anthropology. Whereas Rousseau had long ago refused to consider the "social bond of the city" as an extension of family ties, psychoanalysis gave new life to political theories that treat the leader, the king, as the father of his people, and political power as an extension of paternal authority. But as Maurice Halbwachs noted in his commentary on the *Social Contract*, "far from the relationship of son to father being the origin of the relationship between subject and leader, it is the opposite. Granet showed that, in ancient China, the duties of the son toward the father are modeled on those of the vassal toward his lord" (in Rousseau [1762] 1943, 1.2, p. 64). Hocart, for his part, it will be recalled, developed the idea that almost all major social institutions derive from sacred royalty (see Hocart 1954). This is notably the case with marriage, a major element of the royal rite, but also with paternity: it is the authority of the king that explains that of the father, and not the power of the father that of the king. In 1793, the psychoanalysts say, the French "killed the father." This is not false, but only so long as the situation is correctly understood. In decapitating Louis XVI, the Convention not only decapitated the monarchy; in so doing, it also severed the roots of paternal power. The fall of the king entailed that of the father, despite all of Napoleon's efforts to slow the process by establishing a hereditary empire, attributing to the father unchallenged authority within the family (the "paternal power" of the civil code), and providing for the same punishment to be inflicted upon a parricide as upon the author of an attempt on the emperor's life.[1] In the long run, however, none of this mattered: paternal power was now diluted in parental authority, with the result that the figure of the father became more and more evanescent. His last prerogative, the automatic transmission of his name to his children, ended up being taken away from him, the patronymic having given way to the "family name," jointly chosen by the two parents. Just as the term "patronymic" was deleted from the French civil code, "parricide" no longer figures in the modern-day penal code.[2] The penal code recognizes only murder committed against an ascendant, which itself is placed in the same category and assigned the same penalty of life in prison as murder committed against a minor or a representative of the state, or murder inspired by racial hatred.

From Symbolism to Religion: Lacan between
Lévi-Strauss and Durkheim

The demotion of paternity in French law over the last two centuries shows
once again, if any further proof were needed, the weakness of the Oedipus
theory. Ordinary practitioners of psychoanalysis still cling to it, but the
more lucid Freudians, such as Devereux and above all Lacan, had ceased
to appeal to it, when they did not actually abandon it, not long after the
master's death. More than sixty years ago, in a lecture later published as
"The Neurotic's Individual Myth," Lacan frankly declared that "the whole
Oedipal schema needs to be reexamined" (Lacan [1953] 1979, 422). Observing that, in the modern conjugal family, "the father is the representative,
the incarnation, of a symbolic function which concentrates in itself those
things most essential in other cultural structures" (422–23), he proposed to
substitute for the Oedipal triangle a "quaternary system" that is manifestly
a sketch of his future "Schema L." This latter model, though inspired by
Lévi-Strauss, furnishes a much richer conception of social structure than
the one Lévi-Strauss devised.

In order to fully appreciate Lacan's innovation, one must first recall
the polemical dimension of structural anthropology and keep in mind the
vulnerabilities of the conceptual arsenal at its command. For Lévi-Strauss's
Elementary Structures of Kinship was in large part an engine of war directed
against Durkheim's *Elementary Forms of Religious Life*. In holding that the
incest taboo is only the flip side of a positive rule of exchange, and that the
principle of reciprocity underlying exchange is enough by itself to produce
and sustain a stable society, Lévi-Strauss sought to show that religion, considered by Durkheim to be the foundation of society, has no more reality
than the phlogiston of the old physics. It was therefore necessary to eliminate both Durkheim's cherished notion of the sacred and the *hau*, its Maori
avatar, on which Mauss had relied—in vain, because he divided exchange,
the principle responsible for the immediate synthesis of the self and others,
into three obligations that thus appear, falsely, to be independent. By separating myths from rites, by exposing ritual and sacrificial activities as a desperate attempt to undo the intricate workings and distinctions of totemic
and mythic thought, the very things that make societies cohesive and the
world intelligible, *The Savage Mind* and *Mythologiques* pursue the same

end. Religion, they maintain, far from being a generative principle of the social and symbolic order, constitutes a secondary and regressive enterprise, fortunately doomed to failure.

It is against this background that the enigmatic "canonical formula" for analyzing myths (see Lévi-Strauss [1958a] 1963, 228) can be seen to hold unexpected interest. For it conceals an implicit recognition—denied but quite real—that structuralism fails, ultimately, to repress religion. Indeed, paradoxically, it was not to mythology, but to the rites of headhunting and sacred royalty that Lévi-Strauss himself initially applied his canonical formula. Moreover, the very structure of the formula suggests the subordination of exchange and reciprocity, supposed to constitute the very essence of society, to an authority that encompasses and hangs over them (see Scubla 1998). As we will see shortly, another intellectual curiosity of the period, Lacan's Schema L, inspired in part by Lévi-Strauss's formula, illuminates this relationship of subordination, which in a way represents the return of the Durkheimian repressed in the structuralist sphere.

The crux of the matter is the relation between what Lévi-Strauss calls symbolism (*le symbolisme*) and what Lacan calls the symbolic (*le symbolique*—a term that Lévi-Strauss shuns, refusing to employ the adjectival form nominatively). I should like to show that this slight difference of vocabulary conceals a significant conceptual disagreement that we need to be clear about if we are to avoid misunderstanding. Lacan, who gladly acknowledges his indebtedness to Lévi-Strauss, seems eager to follow the path opened up by the structural model, but in fact he heads off in the opposite direction. Looking at the matter more closely, it will be seen that Lévi-Strauss begins with a sort of intellectual feat of strength. What is generally called symbolic function is the ability to use symbols or signs, which is to say things that make it possible to designate other things in the absence of these same things. This definition, particularly suited to language, turns out to be much richer than it appears at first, but Lévi-Strauss is not content to stop there. On the ground that language is never a neutral *medium*, but instead helps to forge the image of the very things it allows to be described, he defines symbolic function as the power of the human mind to impose structural laws, for the most part unconscious, on a shapeless material, and in particular on the affective and impulsive contents of mental life. Language being common to human beings, there follows at once a new definition of the unconscious (as the "mediating term between self and others" [Lévi-Strauss 1950, xxxi]), which Lacan was subsequently to adopt.

All this is well known, of course. Nevertheless, though most commentators pretended to ignore the fact, it is also extremely vague. For Lévi-Strauss, seldom inclined to go into much detail in his major theoretical works, presented no "structural law" in his 1949 article on the effectiveness of symbols; he claimed merely to postulate the existence of laws analogous to those of phonology. It was not until the mid-1960s that he gave the first precise instance of such a law, the "culinary triangle," constructed by analogy with the vocalic triangle (see Lévi-Strauss 1965).

Compounding this absence of empirical illustration is a large measure of theoretical fuzziness. When Lévi-Strauss does try to flesh out his conception of symbolism, particularly in his introduction to the works of Mauss, he begins by dragging the symbolic function down to the level of language, then reducing language to communication,[3] and finally identifying communication with exchange and reciprocity, as if all structural laws were reducible to laws of kinship and alliance. At bottom, "symbolic function" and "principle of reciprocity" appear to be two names for the same thing. To be sure, when he analyzes forms of dual organization he seems to recognize the existence of a vertical axis, having to do with religion, that is quite distinct from a horizontal axis of exchange, and that moreover is attested by ethnography (for example, among the Bororo); but in all other contexts he tends to interpret religion as a sort of secondary residue of exchange (see chapter 8 of Lévi-Strauss [1958a] 1963, 132–63). Even where it appears to land him in trouble, he is quite sure that the theory of reciprocity cannot possibly be in doubt. "In anthropology this theory continues to [be] as soundly based," he says, "as the gravity theory in astronomy" (162). The most that its author is prepared to concede is that dualist societies await their Einstein (see 162), which is to say a theorist of reciprocity who will give it its final expression, in the same way that the theory of relativity completed and crowned classical physics.

In Lacan, paradoxically, in view of his convoluted and affected style,[4] things are clearer in this regard. In his Schema L—the developed form of which I reproduce in figure 9 together with a simplified variant in the form of a Z—the symbolic, far from being conflated with reciprocity, is plainly opposed to it. In this schema one finds two orthogonal axes analogous to

FIGURE 9. Normal Form (*left*) and Simplified Form (*right*) of Lacan's Schema L

those exhibited by certain forms of dual organization. The *o-o'* axis represents the relation that Lacan calls "imaginary," because each of its terms is the mirror image of the other. This relation is one of symmetrical doubles: the relation of communication, exchange, and reciprocity. The *O-S* axis represents the symbolic. It crosses the preceding one, governs it, and frames it. In the detailed graph of Schema L, this transcendence of the symbolic is indicated by the fact that *O*, representing uppercase Other, is the only term of the quartet from which two arrows depart and where, as a consequence, no arrow arrives. In the simplified figure, by virtue of the simple fact that the *o-o'* axis is situated on the diagonal stroke of the Z, the imaginary finds itself at once encompassed by the symbolic; moreover, in this same graph, the positions of the symbols *o* and *o'* have been switched, an indication that the terms they designate are interchangeable.

In Lacan, in other words, the principle of reciprocity, far from being the alpha and omega of human relations, is subordinated to something more powerful.[5] His Schema L reveals and assumes the necessity of reintroducing a vertical axis of transcendence, which, in Lévi-Strauss, never enjoys the status of an independent variable. It is as if the psychoanalyst, while looking to structural anthropology for inspiration, noticed its inadequacies and, without quitting his own field of expertise, set about incorporating (or reincorporating) the elementary structures of kinship within the elementary forms of religious life; as if he tacitly undertook, and perhaps even without knowing it, or against his will, to rehabilitate a cardinal thesis of Durkheim and of Mauss, which Lévi-Strauss thought he had disposed of once and for all. In any case, although he approaches human reality in terms of the individual psyche, the analysis he gives of it allows us a glimpse of a conception of the symbolic, which is to say of the cultural order, that permits human beings to create a less reductive, and possibly a more just society than that of Lévi-Strauss.

It is true that, in its details, Schema L presents many obscurities that are often deepened, rather than dispelled, by the commentaries with which Lacan and his disciples later equipped it. I used to regard it—like Lévi-Strauss's canonical formula, from the same period—as a baroque monument to a kind of preciousness that was very fashionable in certain intellectual circles in the middle of the last century. It was only in studying Rousseau that I discovered the first convincing illustration of this schema, showing that it is not a gratuitous construct but a plausible representation of a set of relations that do in fact structure social life. In Rousseau's case it is all the more forceful as he was not only a social and political theorist, but also an analyst of the most private motivations of human behavior. His insight can therefore make the abstract considerations I have just reviewed more vivid, and help to corroborate, if not actually validate, them.

Rousseau, Judge of Lacan

It is well known that after having had to discontinue his public readings of the *Confessions*, Rousseau began writing another work meant to clear himself of the charges, real or imagined, that he believed had been leveled against him. Abandoning a first-person narrative, he composed three dialogues under the title *Rousseau, Judge of Jean-Jacques*, in which two characters, Rousseau and "the Frenchman," compare their respective opinions of Jean-Jacques. An insane work? A work written by a madman? Assuredly not. Even if they do mix the real and the imaginary in describing the persecutions for which the enemies of Jean-Jacques are held responsible, the *Dialogues*, as the work is commonly known, far from being demented, are essential for understanding the fundamental principles of Rousseau's political thought as well as the very nature of social bonds (see Scubla 1992a, 117, 124).

I shall limit myself here to the book's general architecture. Autobiography is never a simple relation of self to self, since it supposes the mediation both of the act of writing and of the public to which it is addressed. The *Dialogues* nonetheless rest on a more complex form of mediation than that of the *Confessions*. Rousseau, judge of Jean-Jacques, is evidently not

Jean-Jacques, judge of Jean-Jacques, nor Rousseau, judge of Rousseau, but neither is the writer the judge of the man, since Rousseau does not appear here as the author but as one of the characters of the book; in the text, Jean-Jacques is "the Author of books" (as opposed to "the Author of crimes" that his detractors claim him to be). The *Dialogues* differ from the *Confessions* in another respect as well. The *Confessions* are situated on the near side of publication, as it were, for Rousseau thought it advisable to give readings of the work himself, anticipating that in this way he could reach his public, in every sense of the term, more directly. The *Dialogues*, following upon the disappointment of this calculation, are situated on the far side of publication, in the sense that they are addressed not to men, but to God. There is a well-known anecdote, told by Rousseau himself. Despairing of ever being able to bring the true portrait of Jean-Jacques before his peers, he resolved to seek divine judgment and made plans to place a manuscript of his work on the high altar of Notre-Dame in Paris, in the hope that it might at least come to the attention of Our Lady's earthly lieutenant, the King. Alas, the day he arrived at the cathedral to perform this solemn act, he perceived that an iron grille, which he had never noticed before, denied him access to the choir—as if God himself had thus communicated His refusal to hear him, a sign of His invincible transcendence.

Now, in all of this we find four terms whose relations correspond perfectly to the configuration of Lacan's Schema L. Indeed, it is a very simple matter to display the basic structure of the *Dialogues* using the simplified Z-shaped figure. Rousseau and the Frenchman, whose conversation forms the content of the book, communicate along the imaginary axis o-o', being situated at opposite poles. Jean-Jacques, the subject of the book, is at S, and God, to whom it is addressed, at O. The religious character of the symbolic axis S-O is still more readily perceived in the diagram accompanying Michel Foucault's excellent introduction to *Rousseau juge de Jean Jaques* (see Foucault 1962). The underlying structure of this diagram is revealed by rotating the Schema L to the left,[6] which puts the imaginary relation in a horizontal position, so that the symbolic relation appears vertically. This arrangement exhibits a twofold symmetry: on the one hand, of the two terms of the imaginary relation corresponding to the interlocutors of the *Dialogues*; on the other, of the two terms of the symbolic relation corresponding respectively to God, situated above the iron grille, and Jean-Jacques, as he himself will in the end

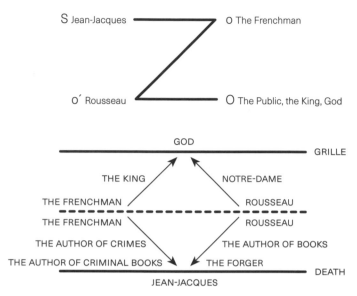

FIGURE 10. The *Dialogues* of Rousseau according to Lacan's Schema L (*top*) and Foucault's Diagram (*bottom*)

have been changed by death. The religious dimension of this symbolic relation could not be pictured more clearly.

At the same time, of course, one must not exaggerate the significance of these comparative formal exercises. While they do make it easier to grasp what Lacan and Lévi-Strauss were trying to get at, their properties obviously do not determine the nature of things. It is nonetheless not uninteresting to see how formidable the difficulties structuralism runs up against turn out to be when it attempts to replace religion with the symbolic. If two such powerful minds did not succeed in such an undertaking, it is perhaps because their mission was impossible.

One thing is sure. Lacan realized that Lévi-Strauss's "symbolism" was incapable of replacing religion: what he called "the symbolic," though it has the same function as its cognate, is not a variant of it; to the contrary, it is, strictly speaking, orthogonal to it. But the psychoanalyst was well aware—and this, again, is to his credit—that this terminological substitution is not wholly dispositive, and might even be regarded as a way of furtively reintroducing the sacred without going to the trouble of reformulating the concept. Lévi-Strauss, he says, "is afraid that the autonomy of the symbolic register will give rise to a masked transcendentalism once again, for which, as regards his affinities, his personal sensibility, he feels only fear and aversion. . . . He doesn't want the symbol, even in the extraordinarily purified form in which he offers us it, to be only a re-apparition, under a mask, of God" (Lacan [1978] 1988, 35).

While Lacan freely speculates about Lévi-Strauss's reasons for silence, his own feelings remain in the realm of the "half-said": he sees the limits of structural anthropology, and yet declines to invite ethnology to sponsor a return to Durkheim that would parallel his own return to Freud. Is it or is it not necessary to inquire anew into the nature of the sacred? He does not answer, or even explicitly raise the question. He seems to be aware, like the philosopher Vincent Descombes, that the question of religion trails structuralism like a shadow; unlike Descombes, however, he is not prepared to subject it to close scrutiny.[7]

Lacan stops along the way, in other words, before getting to where he seems to want to go. Like Lévi-Strauss, he is overly intellectual. He fails to see that, despite its missteps and its florid prose, *Totem and Taboo*, which like everyone else he ridicules, contains a theory of religion that could free his intuitions about the symbolic from the suffocating influence of structural linguistics. As we saw a moment ago, his reservations concerning the Oedipal schema lead him to speak very unfavorably of this work (see also Lacan [1991b] 2007, 102–17). Yet the two things must be dissociated. To the extent that it seeks to supply the Oedipus complex with a founding myth, *Totem and Taboo* is surely gratuitous and unnecessary. But as an original attempt to think about the relations between violence and the sacred in religious phenomena, sacrifice notably among them—which is to say in the rites that Durkheim and his successors placed at the origin of society—it is a step in the right direction. René Girard, not without a hint of provocation, and while expressing reservations of his own, was to go so far as to say that it represents Freud's soundest contribution to the scientific study of mankind.[8] Indeed, the truth of the matter is that the part of psychoanalysis that has been most roundly condemned by its critics constitutes nothing less than the cornerstone of anthropology.

Girard, Reader of Freud: Original Murder
or Universal Mechanism?

The author of *Totem and Taboo* shows himself to be still more clear-sighted than the scholars to whom he turns for support. With a very sure intuition, he perceives that the camel sacrifice practiced by the Bedouins of the Sinai desert,[9] which Robertson Smith takes to be exemplary, is the deliberate repetition of a spontaneous, more savage, and paradigmatic act of violence. And he infers from it—validly, Girard points out—that every ritual killing reproduces, in a more or less attenuated fashion, the same model.

Freud nonetheless has a hard time grasping the social function of sacrificial rites. Conceiving of the founding murder as a singular crime whose memory was to haunt the minds of men, while at the same time seeing it as the ultimate source of civilization, he depicts its ritual repetition as being above all a neurotic fixation on the past. His constant insistence on regarding religion as a pathological phenomenon prevents him from fully appreciating its cathartic and morphogenetic virtues. At least he has the merit of keeping religion at the heart of society and of not irrevocably consigning it to the realm of the imagination. Religions are rooted in reality: even if they harbor fantasies and irrational beliefs, they do not rest on them; they are real solutions—however partial, inadequate, and even calamitous they may turn out to be—to real problems. Behind the more or less muffled violence of sacrifice, there is the actual violence, often very brutal, that men are capable of inflicting upon one another and that rituals help to diminish and redirect.

In this regard Freud, whose dogmatism often had unfortunate consequences, was right to obstinately defend Robertson Smith, who had been the first to detect and clearly describe the kinship of sacrifice and collective murder. "A denial is not a refutation, an innovation is not necessarily an advance," Freud replied to those who thought his hypotheses had been made outmoded by the supposed or proclaimed progress of science (Freud [1939] 1964, 23:131). So sure was he of the correctness of his position that, far from giving up the idea that blood rituals reproduce a collective murder, he believed that it lent decisive support to Ernest Sellin's disputed conjecture that Moses was assassinated by his own people and only afterwards venerated as the repository of the Law. In other words, Freud came to consider that the violence on which human societies are founded, rather than having occurred only once, long ago in a prehistoric past, occurred over and over again in the recorded history of humanity.[10] In the event, Freud's perseverance paid off. As I indicated earlier, it led Alfred Kroeber to soften somewhat the severe judgment he had brought against *Totem and Taboo* when it first appeared. Lévi-Strauss very well summarized Kroeber's new attitude thus: "If Freud gave up the idea, as he seemed to have done, that the act of parricide was a historical event, it could be viewed as the symbolic expression of a recurrent virtuality, a generic and non-temporal model of psychological attitudes entailed by repetitive phenomena or institutions such as totemism and tabus" (Lévi-Strauss [1962a] 1964, 69). Nevertheless he felt obliged to add at once: "But this is not the real question. Contrary to what Freud maintained, social constraints, whether positive or negative, cannot be explained, either in their origin or in their persistence, as the effects of impulses or emotions which appear again and again, with the same characteristics and during the course of centuries and millennia, in different individuals" (69).

And yet they are so explained, with the slight qualification that these necessary conditions are still not sufficient: the free play of impulses and emotions is indeed the source and the primary cause of both the passions and conflicts that rend the social fabric, and the rites that foresee and hasten to repair their ravages; it remains to determine the conditions under which these opposed effects emerge and fluctuate, and under which they can be regulated.

To be persuasive, the central claim of *Totem and Taboo*—that there was a founding murder—has therefore not only to renounce the singular character of the original crime, by showing that a collective murder can be repeated indefinitely in analogous conditions, but also to explain how it actually operates, that is, to account for the effects it produces and the institutions it creates. Now, it is precisely this additional condition that Girard satisfies by associating not only sacrifice and blood rituals, but indeed the majority of social institutions with an instinctive regulatory mechanism: the scapegoat (or victim) mechanism, which rests on the possibility that thwarted violent impulses may readily find an alternative object.[11] It is a means of unleashing, and then limiting, more or less spontaneous phenomena of collective violence—such as the lynching of a real or imagined troublemaker, or the hunting and killing of a dangerous or dreaded animal—that allows a group to ensure its survival, not only by repelling a real or imaginary danger, but also by inducing its members to cooperate while at the same time providing an outlet for their lethal impulses.

Sacrifice and related rites can be seen as deliberately making use of this spontaneous mechanism, or, more exactly—for rites are the product, not of a utilitarian calculus, but of a sort of process of trial and error—as reproducing the conditions under which the mechanism is triggered, in the hope of prolonging and intensifying the civilizing effects of ritual. Such rites therefore constitute a crucial element of a process of social self-regulation that permitted human beings to domesticate themselves—that is, to curb their murderous instincts by ritualizing them. Expiatory, initiatory, and other rituals, through the mechanism they set in motion, gradually purged the human species of its natural savagery by channeling and redirecting the violence internal to every society, concentrating it on substitute victims who are selected almost always from outside the society but who, whenever possible, are considered equivalent to its own members, which is to say considered as belonging to the community but occupying a marginal place in it: foreigners, prisoners of war, domesticated animals, or tamed wild animals. Sacrifices and similar rites, however violent they may be, are thus a lesser kind of violence, well circumscribed, that protects human beings from the violence that they carry inside them by giving it a bone to gnaw on, as it were, and in this way holding it in check (see Girard [1972b] 1977).

Although Girard's theory was greeted in the anthropological community with something like contempt, almost as unanimous[12] as the disfavor in which *Totem and Taboo* continues to be held still today, it is interesting to note that, without knowing him or expressly subscribing to his ideas, a number of fine scholars whom we have already met, trained in psychoanalysis or ethnology, developed very similar views in their campaign against the intellectualist bias of structuralism and its cognitivist offspring. André Green delivered a very harsh indictment of Lévi-Strauss (see Green 1999, 37–38) in which he makes a point of citing Walter Burkert, whose thinking coincides with that of Girard on several essential points (see Burkert [1972] 1983; Hamerton-Kelly 1987), in support of Freud's thesis of a founding murder. Gillian Gillison likewise took structuralism to task for steering clear of violence and conflict, and for failing to integrate them in its models—whereas from "the psychoanalytic point of view, violence is neither aberrant nor inexplicable; it is to be expected when there are no rituals" (Gillison 1999, 49). She makes the same point more precisely, and in a way that Girard himself could endorse,[13] when she says that the "task of ritual is to desexualize maternity and to expel violence from the heart of the nuclear family to the periphery of society" (50).

Additionally, in the same issue of *L'Homme* in which the articles by Green and Gillison appeared, André Mahé, reviewing a work by Abdellah Hammoudi, regretted that the author did not strengthen his case by reference to Girard's writings (see Mahé 1999, 246). These three appeals, dating from the end of the last century, do not seem to have roused anthropology from its theoretical torpor in the years since. Still today, however, they invite a new generation of researchers to discover the intellectual tremors of a hundred years ago, to resume work in the years ahead on the great project inaugurated by Freud in *Totem and Taboo* and revived by Girard in *Violence and the Sacred*, and to inaugurate at long last the fruitful dialogue between psychoanalysis and anthropology that so far has not taken place.

I have shown elsewhere the great explanatory power of the scapegoat mechanism, on the one hand with regard to facts, on the other hand with regard to the interpretations of these facts that the best analysts, notably the founders of religious anthropology, have advanced, and which Girard's hypothesis makes it possible to unify, complete, and revise as necessary, producing a synthesis that will impart added clarity and force to all of them (see Scubla 1982, 1993a, 1999, 2003, 2005, 2008, 2009b). This is not the place to review these arguments in detail. It ought nevertheless to be emphasized that the victim mechanism gives us the key to an enigma that Girard's predecessors were powerless to solve, whether they had passed over it in silence to conceal their bafflement, or had discounted it as further evidence of the "irrationality of savages," or else had frankly confessed their perplexity, like Hocart, and so allowed it at least to be perceived: how did the ritual murder of a living being come to be regarded as a source of life, indeed the most important one of all?

Ritual, Hocart says, is a form of organization whose purpose is to "promote life, fertility, prosperity by transferring life from objects abounding in it to objects deficient in it" (Hocart [1936] 1970, 3). This definition does three things at once. It implicitly admits that sacrifice constitutes the heart of ritual; points out the singular character of the sacrificial mechanism, which, in order to favor the expansion of life, begins by taking away a life; and, finally, offers a rational solution to this paradox by likening ritual, as a method for equalizing life, to a system of communicating vessels. But does Hocart really believe in this solution? One may doubt it. For in rites of initiation, for example, the recipient and giver of life are one and the same person, as if death (or ritual mutilation, which is a substitute for it) had by itself the capacity to grant an increase in life. Hocart himself discusses another, no less disconcerting case where the sacrificial victim is divine. At first sight it seems strange, he writes, "that men should kill what they regard as a benefactor and a god; but we must get used to the idea, because it is fundamental" (53).

One could not more plainly confess one's failure to find an explanation, or more humbly acknowledge one's obligation to face up to the facts. Among the Koryak, for example, the domesticated reindeer is part of the family cult. It brings good luck and protects the family; to sell a live reindeer to someone else is a grave offense. But that does not prevent it from being sold or killed. If the animal is destined for slaughter, it is necessary to kill it oneself before selling it, for this killing is then considered to be a sacrifice. Knowing that "the reindeer is the protector of the family," Hocart adds, "we jump to the conclusion that it is treated with respect. That does not follow: it is lassoed, harnessed, whipped, and treated just as we treat animals that we need, or rather worse" (ibid.).

In short, the reindeer is a tutelary creature, a sort of secondary divinity; it is subject to certain taboos, and yet it is ritually sacrificed and even mistreated by those who themselves benefit from its protection. Must we content ourselves with simply taking notice of these undoubted facts, or can we unravel what appears to be a knot of contradictions? Girard's hypothesis—and this is its great strength—makes it possible to choose the second branch of the alternative. The divine character of the reindeer and its status as a sacrificial victim are but one and the same thing; it is this very status that makes it the guarantor of domestic harmony, for it is through its ritual killing, actual or in any case always possible, that it is a tutelary creature having the power to protect the family from the risks of internal dissension. The reindeer is not sacrificed in spite of the fact that it is divine; it is because it is sacrificed, or capable of being sacrificed, that it is divine. More generally, a god is nothing other, by its very nature, than the victim whose immolation, serving as an outlet for human violence, prevents societies from destroying themselves.

Thus the fundamental paradox noted by Hocart, the sacrifice of a god, is resolved. But the Koryak example calls our attention to another curiosity: if the reindeer is a sacred animal, doomed to undergo a ritual death, how are we to explain that it may nonetheless be the object of mistreatment as well? To answer this question, it will be necessary to consider the victim mechanism more closely, coming back to a point that remains undeveloped in the succinct exposition I have given above. The salutary effects of the victim mechanism are produced in two types of situations that it is important to distinguish.[14] The mechanism may be put into effect ritually, as we have just seen, but it may also be triggered spontaneously, as in the case of a lynching. In situations of crisis, when violence reaches the point that it tears a society apart and threatens to destroy it, it may happen that a collective murder, which is to say the spontaneous convergence of all individual impulses to violence on a single victim—the so-called emissary victim, or scapegoat—suffices, at least for a time, to reestablish peace by restoring the cohesion of the group, now united against the victim, whose killing serves as a common outlet for the aggressiveness of all its members. Now, Girard advances the hypothesis that human beings discovered the cathartic virtues of the victim mechanism in just such situations of crisis and spontaneous resolution, where, by turning violence against itself, as it were, and so putting an end to it, the members of a society can be reconciled with one another and work together again to reestablish their institutions.[15] It follows that the ritual victim is a substitute for the emissary victim of the spontaneous collective murder, which serves as a model for it. But this substitute is not a mere replica, and it may assume several forms; generally the sacrificial victim is holy and pure, but like the scapegoat, of which it is the avatar, it may also be more or less impure. Indeed, at the moment when he is killed, the scapegoat, if only by virtue of all the violence erupting around him, is considered to be demoniacal; but once peace has been restored, and without any apparent cause other than his own death, he is considered to be a divine being who caused human enmity to cease.[16] The emissary victim therefore presents two faces in succession, the one negative, the other positive. In general, rituals reproduce this duality by associating two opposed types of sacrifice (white sacrifice, at the center of the village, and black sacrifice, at the periphery; non-blood sacrifices to vegetarian gods, and blood sacrifices to carnivorous goddesses, and so on), or, like the ritual of the two rams in Leviticus, by associating a sacrifice in the strict sense with a rite that more directly recalls the death of the emissary victim: one of the two rams was offered to God, and the second, the "scapegoat," all the sins of the community having been laid upon its head, sent out into the desert, there to meet its death from the top of a cliff. Of course, the same ritual victim may also assume the two contrasting aspects of the emissary victim. This is evidently the case with the reindeer of the Koryak—sacrificed, the victim of mistreatment, it reunites in itself, one might say, the two rams of Leviticus. Thus the second paradox noted by Hocart comes to be resolved as well.

Girard's theory also sheds a new light on rites of passage (see Girard [1972b] 1977, 300–308). Symbolic death and rebirth can now be seen as the ritualistic image, or counterpart, of crisis and violent resolution. Initiation rites endow novices with greater vitality—an extra dose of life, as it were—by forcing each one to experience on a small scale the decomposition and recomposition of the entire social order; by forcing them individually to travel the road traveled collectively by the community. In this light, the rite can be seen to have the character of an ordeal: physically and mentally harassed, victims of violence of every kind and of ritual mutilation, the novices occupy, for the duration of the ceremonies, the place of the emissary victim;[17] and they emerge from it, having barely escaped death, as full members of the community, authorized to practice blood rituals such as headhunting, sacrifice, and circumcision, which in many societies mark the passage to adulthood, the coming of age.

The claims made for the theory should perhaps be qualified, since Girard himself gives no specific example in support of it. But there is some evidence from African societies that, without wholly corroborating his interpretation, does seem to lend credence to the idea that novices in these rites occupy a place analogous to the one that in his model is assigned to the emissary victim. Among the Mundang of Chad, for example, "in the circumcision camp, there was in each session a boy who died from the after-effects of the operation or from particularly severe bullying" (Adler 2007, 100). He was buried without ceremony, and his mother did not have the right to weep over him or to go into mourning; indeed, "the random death of a member of the cohort was considered by the masters of the initiatory institution as the price to be paid for the success of the session overall" (100). Evidently we are not dealing here with a sacrifice, since the victim is neither deliberately selected nor treated in any special way; nor does he die under the blows of a spontaneous act of collective violence as an emissary victim proper does. And yet we are not dealing here with a regrettable accident either; the death is welcome, occurring in a collective setting and considered to be a necessary element in assuring the effectiveness of an important ritual, and therefore of the normal functioning of society. The likening of the novice's death to that of Girard's scapegoat is all the more plausible as Alfred Adler, the French ethnologist whom I have just quoted in connection with the Mundang, himself compares it to that of their sacred king, whose body, he says, must be "'sacrificed,' expelled, removed from society, so that society may be as one, may go on living and perpetuating itself" (100). Moreover, Adler suggests an interesting parallel with another African society, in which a more conscious attempt is made to trigger an accident that is considered to be beneficent. The Chaga of Tanzania used to dig a very deep trench for the novices' excrement: "[The novices] were obliged to defecate in this trench every day, and if by chance a boy should fall in and sink to the bottom there was no question of lending a helping hand, and he was left to die in this cruel fashion. The Chaga . . . believed that at least one of the novices had to die, even if it meant pushing him into the trench" (102).

These examples would appear to suggest that all peoples reckon certain specific ways of administering death to be not only not criminal or in any way destructive, but, to the contrary, salubrious and actually life-giving. This opinion can scarcely be attributed to some sort of mental confusion, since all human beings, even if they practice human sacrifice, consider it to be a crime to kill a member of one's own community. What is more, they are no less careful to distinguish between sacrificer and murderer (and even warrior) than between a hunter who sheds blood and a woman who loses her blood; in many societies, a sacrificer who commits a homicide, even accidentally, is stripped of his office.[18]

For the moment, Girard is alone in proposing a plausible explanation of these beliefs and these practices. What is more, his explanation identifies a very particular, though almost universally recognized, link between taking life and giving life. And if ritual is indeed, for the reasons that he claims to have discovered, a source of life, it becomes all the clearer why, as we have seen many times up to now, ritual is for a man what childbirth is for a woman. These activities are analogous and complementary, for both ensure the continuity of the community: procreation perpetually renews the life of the group by bringing into the world children who replace the dead; ritual guarantees its survival by anticipating crises and, if not extinguishing them, limiting their effects before they can destroy the community from within. Both are therefore guardians of life—and since nature assigns responsibility for childbirth to women, it is now obvious why responsibility for ritual, and particularly sacrifice, should have fallen to men.

CHAPTER FOURTEEN

Freud, in Spite of Everything

W ith only a relatively modest therapeutics to recommend it, a narrow field of application, and limited effects, psychoanalysis nevertheless claims to have assembled a body of hypotheses that one day will give a complete explanation of human nature. It is in this light that we have considered it up until now. We have seen Freud and his disciples invite peoples and their ethnographers to lie down on the analyst's couch, as it were, and then proceed, more or less plausibly, to decipher their myths and their rites, their dreams and their practices, their free associations and their rationalizations. The results can hardly be regarded as dispositive, however. This may be an opportune moment, then, to reverse the perspective by installing the psychoanalyst in his turn on the couch of the anthropologist. I propose to regard Freud as an ethnographer in spite of himself—the ethnographer of a new continent that he purports to have discovered—and the materials that he has brought back from there as worthy of his analyst's respectful attention, which is to say useful in enlarging the evidentiary foundation of anthropology and also in better evaluating the adequacy of its hypotheses.

The idea is not new. Lévi-Strauss, for example, described analytic therapy as a form of shamanism, the recovery of Anna O. as the founding myth of its supposed effectiveness, and the theory of the unconscious as a new mythology. Psychoanalysis, though it is not itself a form of knowledge, may nonetheless be considered an object of scientific inquiry. To be sure, anthropologists must take into account Freud's "comments on the Oedipus complex," but they must keep in mind that these comments are themselves "a part of the Oedipus myth," of which they constitute only a new transformational variant, subject to the same structural laws as the others (Lévi-Strauss [1958a] 1963, 218). And while it is fruitful to compare analytic treatment to shamanic treatment, their relationship is not symmetric: shamanism is a help in understanding psychoanalysis, but psychoanalysis does not do much to illuminate shamanism (see 180–81, 198–205).

I shall therefore follow Lévi-Strauss's example, though without taking as severe a view of Freud as he does—not for the sake of politeness, but for good reason, because Freud accumulated an invaluable mass of data and hypotheses, no matter that the framework in which he tried to enclose them is wholly inadequate. To give some idea of the richness of his work, and in order to try to profit from it, I am going to examine a few of the examples that provided the basis for his interpretation of dreams and for his theory of parapraxis, and that will furnish us with an introduction to the studies he made of these things. Indeed, it was in working out their implications that Freud was led to formulate the pairs of basic concepts that together make up what is commonly known as the first Freudian topic: unconscious system and conscious/preconscious system; thing-presentation and word-presentation; primary process and secondary process; sexual impulses and ego impulses. But first I am going to make a detour through the theory of sexuality, one aspect of which, well known but often neglected, will serve us as a guiding thread.

Freud identified three initial stages in the development of the libido: oral, anal, and phallic (see Freud [1905] 1953). The priority of the anal stage (also called sadistic-anal) in relation to the phallic stage, characterized by the child's discovery of sexuality, is interesting for two reasons. First, because it reveals, or assumes, the priority of aggression in relation to sexuality to begin with, and subsequently the special character of aggression, which Freud did not notice until much later. At the time of the first topic, he considered aggression to be a secondary and reactive phenomenon triggered by a frustration of sexual and ego drives. It was only in the course of elaborating the second topic that he grouped these two latter drives under the head of "life drives" and opposed them to "death drives," now considered to constitute an autonomous category.

Second, corresponding to the anal stage is the fantasy of the "primal scene"—the coupling of adults, perceived or imagined as an act of violence and taking the place of the origin myth of procreation, since it is supposed to answer the question: where do children come from? (see Freud [1908] 1959). The priority of the anal stage over the phallic stage therefore implicitly postulates the primacy of procreation over sexuality, even if access to the genital stage proper comes after puberty. Note, too, that the close association of violence and procreation in the primal scene, its fantastic description as a sort of generative chaos, is consonant with the idea of an original act of violence, common to both Freud and Girard. Violence is already present in the oral stage as well, where it is associated with the fantasy of devouring, that is, with cannibalistic impulses, either in the child, as Freud and his disciples maintain, or in the parents, as Devereux proposes, more plausibly, and as both ethnography and the historical record testify. These bodies of evidence also suggest that infanticide, simulated or narrowly escaped during rites of initiation, may have been the most common form of human sacrifice, and thus expose an ambivalent feeling toward procreation: human desire vacillates between the satisfaction of having a descendant and that of being the surviving member of one's line of descent.[1]

In both the Freudian unconscious and societies with initiation rites, then, life and death, and birth and violence can be seen to be closely linked. Sexuality in the strict sense is manifested last, but violence is observed in all stages, from devouring to castration, not omitting the sadistic-anal interpretation of the procreative act.

The succession of stages displays yet another remarkable property. The oral stage is a period of identification, through the incorporation of the paternal and maternal imago; the anal stage, of the destructive violence and confused entanglement of love and hatred; the phallic stage, of the generative violence of the difference between the sexes. Identification, confusion, castration, differentiation—thus one finds in the Freudian model the principal moments of the Girardian model: imitation, crisis of undifferentiation, founding violence, reemergence of a differentiated world.[2] Is the primary process, despite its name, only an inferred effect of the mimetic process, and the avatars of the libido merely the image on an individual level of the avatars of collective violence? The suggestion is all the more attractive as castration, being a savage form of circumcision (itself, it will be recalled, an avatar of sacrifice), is the counterpart of the founding murder in mimetic theory, of which sacrifice is the ritualized form.

It should nevertheless be observed that Girard's theory, tempted in its turn to reduce every aspect of human life to a single cause, is marred by a very damaging error: the idea that human desire, like mimetic rivalry, which is supposed to be its sole source, is always, and by its very nature, "without object"—that is, aimed at nothing, groundless, unmotivated. It is quite true, as Hobbes saw very clearly, that human beings often contend with one another, and may even massacre one another, over mere trifles; and, equally, that nothing can be understood about the political troubles of humanity and, more generally, about its turbulent and tumultuous history, if this crucial observation is not borne in mind. But it by no means exhausts human reality, contrary to what Girard would have us believe in sketching an increasingly "apocalyptic" and "catastrophist" vision of the world, in which the forces of life count for little against the forces of death. Remarkably, like most of the psychoanalysts and anthropologists whom we have encountered so far, he does not notice the considerable place that procreation occupies in human affairs, notably in rites of initiation, where it is particularly striking. As we have seen from the beginning of the present work, the newborn child, or the child about to be born, is the object in every society of the covetous desires of the members of its immediate family, male and female. The convergence of desires on a single object is not a guarantee of peace, of course, and Girard is right to join with Hobbes in considering it to be a source of the most terrible strife: the father vies with the mother and, more generally, men with women; the father vies with the maternal uncle and, more generally, men with one another. But ethnography shows, beyond the several examples we have already considered, that most human communities faced with this problem have found balanced and stable solutions, making it possible to ritualize conflict and minimize violence. Overall, life tends to prevail over death, and the struggle for life over pure, groundless rivalry. Why should it be any different in the future?[3]

Let us come back to Freud. If we hope to reform psychoanalysis, it will not be enough to work our way back from the libidinal economy to mimetic theory and sacrificial logic; we must try to go still further back, to the sources of these things. We are already familiar with the path that connects the blood of the sacrifice and menstrual blood. By following in Freud's footsteps, it will be possible to clear a path alongside it that leads back not only from sexuality to mimetic and ritual violence, but also from violence to procreation.

The Dream of Irma's Injection and Mimetic Rivalry

It is well known that the author of *The Interpretation of Dreams* (Freud [1900] 1953) holds that every adult dream is the disguised fulfillment of a repressed desire. It is well known, too, that in this work he elaborates his theory of oneiric phenomena, beginning with analyses of his own dreams. Commentators have long pointed out that, if these dreams are to be believed, "the essential [thing] in Freud's hidden life seems to be not sexuality but desperate, unscrupulous ambition, the desire to succeed at all costs, to make a name for himself, to achieve immortality thanks to an epoch-making discovery" (Robert [1974] 1976, 66). This is particularly the case, as we shall see shortly, in the two dreams that I am going to consider here: "Irma's Injection" and "The Botanical Monograph."

Psychoanalysis, of course, has no difficulty resolving this paradox. Marthe Robert and other recognized authorities are agreed in saying that Freud concealed the sexual content of his dreams by shifting its center of gravity: "Sexual desire is replaced by the desire to be right, and amorous passion becomes the ambitious pursuit of an idea. Purified by censorship of its specific emotions and jealousies, sex, which is after all the main motif of the dream—for what otherwise would be the point in this story of a pregnant woman and of frustrated young widows—resolves itself into a purely scientific question, the crux of which is no longer an affair of the heart, but wounded vanity and self-esteem" (ibid., 89). Jacques Lacan, considering the same dream, likewise interprets Freud's "silences" in line with analytic orthodoxy: "At this point," Lacan imagines Freud excusing himself, "I can't tell you any more than this. I don't want to tell stories of bed and chamber pot" (Lacan [1978] 1988, 152).

But the official interpretation cannot help but appear naive. Surely it makes more sense to suppose that these "secrets" that Freud is imagined to hide from us, and whose contents he cleverly pretends to keep to himself,[4] serve on the contrary to divert our attention from feelings that are themselves shameful. For if sexual desire would really rather go unnoticed, it seems strangely talkative—as if it were seeking to cover up the disgracefulness of Freud's own envy, vanity, and amour-propre, to the point of concealing these things more and more artfully with each new edition of *The Interpretation of Dreams*. Robert herself admits as much, or at least she gives us every reason to think so. Present-day readers, she observes, may not see at once that "ambition is the central motive in those of his own dreams that Freud analyzes, because in the course of writing he included a large number of other people's dreams . . . and lost among them his own dreams lose much of their relief" (Robert [1974] 1976, 70).

In order to get to the bottom of the matter, we will need to closely examine the dream of Irma's injection and the dream of the botanical monograph, which by themselves take up a substantial part of the first version of the book. The two dreams are all the more important as Freud uses the first one to expound his method of interpretation, and therefore subjects it to very detailed analysis; and as the second one comes under the head of the same complex as the first, which is to say it involves the same "interdependent ideational elements cathected with affect" (Freud [1910] 1957, 11:31), while adding to it in one essential respect. I shall therefore read them in the order in which they are presented.

The first dream, which dates from 1895, may be summarized as follows. At a reception, Freud reproaches Irma, one of his patients, for not accepting his "solution." Since she complains of suffering from severe pains, he examines her carefully; several colleagues who are there then do the same, and give different diagnoses. The cause of her infection becomes clear: an injection of trimethylamine, administered by Dr. Otto with a dirty syringe (see Freud [1900] 1953, 4:107).

Does this dream have a sexual content? Yes, in the sense that the "solution" Freud mentions is that of the sexual etiology of neuroses from which, he maintains, hysterical young women who come to see him suffer. But while this etiology occupies a central place in the dream, it is as an object of controversy among the physicians present. Most of Freud's colleagues did not accept his solution, and he himself had begun to doubt it; when Irma, whose pale complexion worries him, describes her ailments, he wonders whether he may have missed some organic symptom. The subject of the dream is therefore not sexuality itself, but the scientific quarrel to which it gives rise, the rivalries and conflict among specialists that it arouses and feeds. The sexual life of Freud himself plays no role in this affair. If he is involved in the dream at all, it is because he is at the center of the dispute and the chief target of his colleagues' criticisms.

In the absence of any corroborating evidence whatever, it is therefore wholly gratuitous to suppose that some sexual motive on Freud's part will give us access to a "deeper" aspect of his dream and make it more intelligible. In assuming a decisive sexual motive one risks drawing a veil of modesty over the personal obsessions he hints at when he notes the ideas, memories, and feelings that spontaneously come to his mind in connection with each of the elements of his dream. One risks absolving him of responsibility for the failures of his research on the anaesthetizing properties of cocaine. One risks clearing him of suspicion for recklessly hastening the end of his friend Ernst von Fleischl-Marxow by prescribing a cocaine treatment, and for causing the death of a former patient by giving her sulfonal injections without paying due attention to possible side effects. One risks excusing him for giving free rein to his fantasies rather than working harder in order to be able to repay the money he owed Königstein and Breuer. And so on.

For it is indeed these accusations, these causes for remorse that torment him and that he seeks to free himself from. In the event, he succeeds. "Freud wins his case against himself: he is not the charlatan his friends and even his own family take him for" (Robert [1974] 1976, 88). But if this is so, what is to be gained from imagining that behind these very real fears and the oneiric satisfaction of triumphing over them, there exist impulses and desires of another kind that seek their own particular form of satisfaction? What benefit is to be had from postulating the operation of a mechanism that uses the manifest content of the dream to conceal a content of a wholly different nature—and from whom and by virtue of what? In believing that the deepest recesses of the human personality can be probed in this way, and the innermost divisions of the psyche exposed to view, do we not deny ourselves the opportunity to appreciate the lessons of interindividual ("interdividual," as Girard would say) psychology that the dream has to teach us?

However this may be, one thing is certain. There is no trace here of the Oedipal dynamic, which Freud in any case had not yet discovered or worked out. What is played out on the stage of the dream is not incest, but

the confusion of doubles; not the murder of the father, but fraternal or con-
fraternal rivalry. In real life, the three physicians whose competing diagnoses
bring them into conflict over Irma—called Otto, Leopold, and Doctor M.
in the dream—were Oscar Rie, Ludwig Rosenstein, and Josef Breuer, all of
them closely associated with Freud in various capacities. Leopold Königstein
and Karl Koller, who also haunt the dream of the botanical monograph,
overtook Freud for the lead in cocaine research. Rie, Rosenstein, and Freud
played cards once a week at Königstein's house. "With the exception of
Fleischl," Robert observes, "all the characters in the dream were members of
the same close-knit group, inhabiting the same moral and sentimental universe; all were connected by marriage, friendship, and professional ambition"
(ibid., 87). There can be no question that we are dealing here with a circle
of "mimetic rivals," of which Wilhelm Fliess, almost Freud's twin to judge
from their physical appearance[5] and omnipresent in both dreams, was also
a member.

It should not be thought that this way of talking, borrowed from Girard,
overstates the point. Indeed, it is all the more apt as Lacan had earlier, and
independently, proposed what might be called a pre-Girardian interpretation of the Irma dream, seventeen years before the appearance of *Violence and
the Sacred*, during the 9 March 1955 session of his seminar. Freud's account
of the dream, he observes, consists of two parts in which crisis gives way to
resolution. The point of crisis is reached at the end of the first part when the
patient opens her mouth and shows the doctor a hideous throat that leaves
him speechless with horror:

> Having got the patient to open her mouth . . . what [Freud] sees in there,
> these turbinate bones covered with a whitish membrane, is a horrendous
> sight. This mouth has all the equivalences in terms of significations, all the
> condensations you want. Everything blends in and becomes associated in
> this image, from the mouth to the female sexual organ, by way of the nose.
> . . . There's a horrendous discovery here, that of the flesh one never sees, the
> foundation of things, the other side of the head, of the face, the secretory
> glands *par excellence*, the flesh from which everything exudes, at the very
> heart of the mystery, the flesh in as much as it is suffering, is formless, in
> as much as its form in itself is something which provokes anxiety. (Lacan
> [1978] 1988, 154)

The reader familiar with Girard will recognize in this picture the figure of a "sacrificial crisis," characterized by the confusion of sacrifice and murder, of legitimate violence and illegitimate violence, and, more generally, by the obliteration of all differences in an unspeakable amalgamation.

The second part of the dream is a description of this crisis, of its development and its resolution, which grows out of the rivalry of enemy brothers: "Otto," Lacan says, "corresponds to the character who played a perennial role in Freud's life, the intimate, close friend who is both friend and enemy, who from one hour to the next changes from being a friend to being an enemy. And Leopold plays the role of the character who is always useful to counter the character of the friend-enemy, of the beloved enemy" (ibid., 156).

Then there is Doctor M., which is to say Breuer, of whom Freud is at once disciple and rival. Even though he stays in the background, in the end he too finds himself swallowed up by the mimetic vortex: "In the second part, the three characters together play a ridiculous game of passing the buck" (Lacan [1978] 1988, 157). Finally, amidst all the tumult, the threat of death appears. We have now reached the height of the crisis, with the naming of the scapegoat. In Lacan's reading of it, "At first, directly, *unmittelbar*, just as in a delirious conviction when all of a sudden you know that it is him who's got something against you, they know that Otto's the culprit. He'd given an injection" (157).

This moment of illumination is immediately succeeded by the statement of the formula for trimethylamine, which Lacan analyzes in two steps:

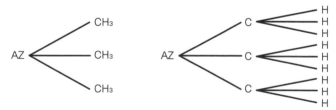

FIGURE 11. Condensed and Expanded Formulas for Trimethylamine

What we are looking at here is obviously, for Lacan, the appearance of the symbolic. He interprets it in terms of his so-called negative semiology, postulating the primacy of the signifier over the signified. "Like [an] oracle," he says, "the formula gives no reply whatsoever to anything." And yet it is "the answer to the question of the meaning of the dream," the meaning of the neurosis and of its cure. To such questions, which tormented Freud, the oracle responds: "There is no other word, no other solution to your problem, than the word" (ibid., 158).

Didier Anzieu proposes a less sibylline and more orthodox interpretation of this dream, according to which Freud's questions are in fact answered. Recalling that Irma is a young widow and that trimethylamine is associated with sexual metabolism (see Freud [1900] 1953, 4:116), he notes that the appearance of the formula, which also constitutes the culmination of the dream, settles the matter once and for all in favor of Freud's "solution": "A conclusive explanation is to be found in trimethylamin[e]. Irma's complaint has been caused by her frustrated sex life. It is Freud who is right, despite his detractors, when he advocates the sexual aetiology of neuroses. The merry-go-round of cocaine, sulphonal, amyl and propyl has jolted to a halt: Freud has found the formula he was looking for" (Anzieu [1975] 1986, 139). But this dream, to which Freud attached particular importance, is also the one that gave him the key to the interpretation of dreams and earned him a reputation as an exegete. "As the dream unfolds, Freud's mind understands how it operates: the dream's formal processes are, like its latent wishes, represented in its content. The Irma dream provides an answer to the question Freud has been asking himself for months (do dreams have a meaning?): yes, it says, not only do dreams express the meaning of our wishes, but that meaning derives from their symbolic structure" (150).

Anzieu thus makes a brilliant synthesis of the sexual and the symbolic, of classical psychoanalysis and Lacanian structuralism; unlike the actors in the dream, he reconciles the divergent points of view in advance—before they even come into conflict. But in so doing, he omits certain elements of this dream that caught Lacan's attention and that Girard's theory throws into still sharper relief. The appearance of the formula in its stereochemical form cannot be reduced to a voice that saves Freud from his torments and the birth of the dream's symbolic function. It also represents, Lacan says, the return of the "structured crowd" (Lacan [1978] 1988, 160)—in Girardian terms, the reemergence of the differences that had been erased by the mimetic crisis.

Furthermore, in Girard's theory, as Lacan seems already to have intuited, the resolution of the crisis is completed by the apotheosis of the emissary victim, who, once a source of evil, now becomes a source of good. For Lacan, this apotheosis is notable mainly for marking the birth of the symbolic, which, as we saw earlier, he takes to be an avatar of religion. But he does not leave it at that. He goes on to describe Freud's metamorphosis into the great shaman of psychoanalysis, at once exegete and therapist. But why Freud, one may ask, and not Otto, who in the dream embodies the emissary victim? Precisely because this is a dream, not real life. In reality, of course, the emissary victim would indeed be Freud, whom his colleagues consider to be a charlatan; in the dream, he deflects their accusations onto the person of Otto. Otto's guilt, recognized by all, exonerates Freud, and so from his point of view has the quality of an apotropaic sacrifice. The dream as a whole is thus a sacrificial crisis in miniature, from which Freud emerges transformed and invested with a religious office—having become not a god, but a prophet, which is to say the spokesman of the divine unconscious. This is how Lacan imagines Freud's sudden awareness of the change he has undergone:

> I am the one who wants to be forgiven for having dared to begin to cure these patients, who until now no one wanted to understand and whose cure was forbidden. I am the one who wants not to be guilty of it, for to transgress any limit imposed up to now on human activity is always to be guilty. I want not to be that. Instead of me, there are all the others. Here I am only the representative of this vast, vague movement, the quest for truth, in which I am obliterated. I am no longer anything. My ambition was greater than myself. No doubt the syringe was dirty. And precisely to the extent that I desired it too much, that I took part in this action, that I wanted to be, myself, the creator, I am not the creator. The creator is someone greater than I am. It is my unconscious, it is this voice which speaks in me, beyond me. (Lacan [1978] 1988, 170–71)[6]

This might be the end of our inquiry, and indeed Girard's theory would require that it be so. I said that it will be necessary to go one step further, however, for the dream we have just examined invites us to read it again. Even if mimetic desire is in fact more powerful than sexual desire, and "interdividual" psychology often more penetrating than psychoanalysis, it may be doubted, as I say, whether human desire can be absolutely groundless, without object. No matter how powerful it may be, mimetic desire seems less powerful than the desire, ascribed to Freud by Lacan, of being a creator—a longing that may even turn out to be the ultimate source of mimetic desire, and provide us with the key to it. For want of being able to satisfy the desire to be a creator, a person such as Freud would be prepared to enter into an interminable mimetic competition with those among his peers who made him believe that they had succeeded in satisfying this desire, or could do so if they wished. Thus the desire experienced by Freud as a young man, according to Lacan; or even a desire to be God, like the fisherman's wife who wishes to command the course of the sun in the Grimms' tale, which may well describe the sources of human motivation more profoundly than psychoanalysis and mimetic theory put together. The desire to create is typically manifested on the edges of the desire to procreate, but as an aberrant form,[7] "metaphysical" in Auguste Comte's sense of the term,[8] of this latter desire.

The Dream of the Botanical Monograph
and the Desire to Procreate

The dream of the botanical monograph will permit us to take this further step. It took place while Freud was writing *The Interpretation of Dreams*, whose outcome it in a sense anticipates. Freud summarizes it in these words: "I had written a monograph on a certain plant. The book lay before me and I was at the moment turning over a folded coloured plate. Bound up in each copy there was a dried specimen of the plant, as though it had been taken from a herbarium" (Freud [1900] 1953, 4:169).

This is plainly the dream of a man hoping to prove to his friends and colleagues, who reproach him for "being too much absorbed in my *favourite hobbies*" (ibid., 4:173; emphasis in the original), that he is capable of producing "a valuable and memorable paper" (ibid.; in Ignace Meyerson's French translation, the German phrase is more literally rendered as "un travail fécond," a fertile piece of work.—Trans.). This desire for justification and revenge is all the more plain as Freud had written a monograph early in his career on a plant, coca, from which he derived no immediate professional benefit. The article attracted the attention of his friend Koller, however, who then managed to announce the results of a new study on the anesthetizing properties of cocaine at a conference shortly afterward, thus depriving Freud of credit for a discovery that might have assured his reputation. As it happens, the day before he had his dream Freud went for a walk with Königstein, who had operated on his father for glaucoma, with Koller as the attending anesthesiologist. Despite the bonds of friendship that united the three men, the encounter with Königstein aroused unhappy memories, and the dreamer of the dream expresses his resolve not to allow himself once again to be robbed of credit for a new discovery, but instead to attain for himself the scientific recognition to which he aspires.

However pertinent and enlightening the hypothesis of mimetic rivalry may be here, I nonetheless do not believe that it exhausts the dream's significance or that it discloses its deepest motivations. For behind the rivalry and disagreements that set Freud against his colleagues, one detects a less apparent, though no less important, conflictual relationship between Freud and his wife. The author of *The Interpretation of Dreams* is evidently very discreet in this regard, but every commentator has remarked on his animosity toward Martha and the ambivalence of his feelings toward the child she is carrying inside her. By having prevented him from completing his work on cocaine as swiftly as he might otherwise have done,[9] she is, in his eyes, responsible for his failure to obtain the professional renown he covets; and whereas she is once again pregnant, he has not yet produced the work that might bring him immortality.

Here, then, in the small world that Sigmund and Martha inhabit, one finds the two forms of rivalry that we have already met with, on a larger scale, in many human societies: the one opposing men to other men, and in the first place the maternal uncle to the father, in kinship systems; and the other opposing men to women, and in the first place the father to the mother, in couvade and initiation rituals. For Freud, producing a work is the equivalent of giving birth; conceiving and composing a book is the equivalent of siring a child and bringing it into the world. The idea was hardly new. Long before, Lichtenberg had associated the pen with the reproductive organs. Moreover, the phenomenon it involves is very general. Culture is everywhere considered to be a male invention. In rites of passage, novices become "twice-born." Their second ("cultural") birth mimics their first ("natural") birth in giving men the illusion that they can conceive as well as women do, if not actually better, so that they attribute generative functions to themselves, in some cases even going so far as to "deny the mother's role in reproduction" (Bidou 1979).

The child is therefore not an accidental object of mimetic desire. The child is its preferred object, and this is what also no doubt makes it the sacrificial victim par excellence. This is why Lichtenberg, with a very sure intuition, connects the organs of generation not only with the pen but also with the rifle—hence the ambiguity, in the dream of Irma's injection, of the syringe of trimethylamine, at once giver of death and giver of life, filled with semen and filled with poison. But it is Otto who receives the poison. Freud has found the formula; he will be able to write *The Interpretation of Dreams*. The semen becomes ink, the syringe a pen, and the nightmare recedes. Anzieu very well grasps this transmutation: "Freud now feels fully responsible not only for his work but for the living being that Martha is about to bring into the world. This is not a case of a thoughtless trimethylamin[e] injection. The [F]uries who desire the death of that child as the price to be paid for the misdeeds of the father will not get the better of him. They have been warded off by the formula of life which Freud has discovered, and which he sees printed in bold type" (Anzieu [1975] 1986, 139).

But what is hidden behind the mythic figure of the Furies? Here again Lacan touches on the essential point, and can serve as our guide in going back beyond mimesis. He recalls that the Latin word *invidia* (envy) comes from *videre* (to see), and that the most exemplary instance of *invidia* was pointed out by Saint Augustine: the little child who sees his brother at his mother's breast: "Such is true envy—the envy that makes the subject pale before the image of a completeness closed upon itself, before the idea that the *petit a* [standing for lowercase *autre* ("other")], the separated *a* from which he is hanging, may be for another the possession that gives satisfaction" (Lacan [1973] 1977, 116).

The little other of Lacanian algebra therefore does not designate only the mimetic double of the dual relation, the "*o*" we have already encountered in the graph picturing the relationship between the imaginary and the symbolic. It is also the little child as seen by the male evil eye, the stopper it imagines to have plugged up the mother's desire, so to speak, by closing her gaping wound. And it is probably in this guise as well, which is to say as the object of an illusory and fantastical satisfaction supposed to have been obtained through an other, that it hurls the subject into an interminable spiral of mimetic violence that only death, received or delivered, can succeed in bringing to an end: Oedipus abandoned in the wilderness by Laius, Isaac under the knife of Abraham, the Gimi uterine nephew whose head is "eaten" by his maternal uncle.

Towards an Archeology of the Freudian Text

It now becomes possible, then, in the manner of an archeologist, to distinguish three successive layers in Freud's thinking. The first stratum, the outermost layer, is the elective domain of psychoanalysis, being composed of the libido and sexual impulses. It rests on a second stratum, the domain of mimetic desire and rivalry, theorized by René Girard, together with the violence that flows from them. This layer lies in its turn on top of a yet deeper one, where there emerges—more in Comte's than Girard's sense of the term—a "metaphysical" desire associated with procreation. In excavating Freud we therefore successively uncover sexuality, rivalry, and procreation.

An examination of the analysis of parapraxis in *The Psychopathology of Everyday Life* (1901) confirms this impression. The first two lapses that Freud studies, forgetting the name of the painter Signorelli and the Latin word *aliquis*, are treated in the same fashion as the first two dreams in *The Interpretation of Dreams*. Once again the author begins with a personal example. During a trip that took him from Dalmatia to Bosnia-Herzogovina, Freud fell into conversation with a fellow traveler about the customs of the Turkish peoples of the region, and began to relate two anecdotes that had been told to him by a physician practicing among them. The first concerned their resignation in the face of death. On being informed that a loved one is in a desperate state, they accept the news with fatalism: "*Herr* [Sir], what is there to be said? If he could be saved, I know you would have saved him." The second one had to do with the exceptional value that they attach to sexual pleasure. When they suffer from sexual disorders, they are filled with a despair that differs markedly from their calm acceptance of death. "*Herr*, you must know that if *that* comes to an end then life is of no value." But just as he was about to recount this second anecdote, Freud changed his mind: "I did not want to allude to the [delicate] topic in a conversation with a stranger" (Freud [1901] 1960, 6:3; the bracketed word in the final quoted passage appeared in all editions of this work before 1924.—Trans.). And so he abruptly changed the subject. Mentally crossing the Adriatic Sea and reaching the other side, so to speak, Freud thought to ask his companion whether he had visited the cathedral at Orvieto and seen the magnificent frescos there by Signorelli. To his great surprise and consternation, however, he was unable to complete his question because he could not recall the name of this Italian painter, familiar though it was to him. Two names came to mind instead, Botticelli and Boltraffio, and persisted in interfering even though he knew at once that they were incorrect. Someone else had to give him the name he was seeking, which then he recognized without a moment's hesitation.

What had happened? Freud wanted to change the subject of conversation, to leave the indecent land of sexuality and cross over to the nobler one of art, but he had been prevented from doing so—as though his mind were governed by a sort of inertia that made it impossible suddenly to change course. The forgetting of a name, Freud says, is "a case in which *a topic that has just been raised is disturbed by the preceding topic*" (ibid.; emphasis in the original). Here the previous subject, the relationship between sexuality and death, continued to be carried forward by its own impetus: the theme of the fresco of the Last Judgment in Orvieto, of which Freud began to speak, is exactly this, sexuality and death; the forgetting of the painter's name, in arresting this motion, acted as a defense mechanism, preventing him from once more meeting up with the taboo subject he had wished to sidestep in the first place. At the same time, however, in interrupting the conversation, the act of forgetting showed itself in reality to be an act of repressing, the working out of a compromise between the conscious and the unconscious.

It still remained to account for the substituted names and the insistence with which they presented themselves to Freud's mind so long as he could not retrieve from memory the name he had momentarily forgotten. Freud turns to this task at once, but his argument is rather cryptic and needs to be developed somewhat in order to be fully understood and properly appreciated. To begin with, one must be acquainted with the concepts of "condensation" and "displacement," on the one hand, which characterize the primary process and are regulated by the unconscious (what Freud was to call in the *Papers on Metapsychology* [1915–1917] the unconscious system [UCS]), and, on the other, of "rationalization," associated with the secondary process and belonging to conscious experience (more precisely, the conscious-preconscious system [CS-PCS]).[10] It is the successive operation of these two processes, acting on the term "Signorelli," that ends up replacing it by "Botticelli" and "Boltraffio."

Ever since structuralism made linguistics fashionable and gave a new lus-
ter to the categories of classical rhetoric, it has been thought necessary to illuminate the notions of condensation and displacement by those of metaphor
and metonymy; but it will be simpler to consult the tradition of association-
ist psychology from which they plainly derive. In this tradition, the human
mind is supposed to spontaneously associate ideas by means of resemblance
and contiguity. As Plato put it long ago in the *Phaedo*, a portrait of Simmias makes us think, through resemblance, of Simmias himself, and Simmias
himself makes us think, through contiguity, of Cebes, because the two form a
pair of inseparable friends, so much so that the portrait of one makes us think
of the other through a combination of the two operations. Freud maintained,
for his part, that unconscious mental processes make systematic use of such
combinations by using whatever is to hand and associating elements of all
kinds, without the concern for consistency and rationality that characterizes
the secondary process. This mechanism aims chiefly at preserving the unity
of mental life, for better or for worse, by trying to resolve the conflicts that
are inherent in it through operations of concealment and repression. It is this
functional dynamic that explains the apparently arbitrary, but in fact strictly
deterministic,[11] play of associations.

Let us now look at how "Signorelli" gives way to "Botticelli," the latter
being a disguised version of the former. "Signorelli," an Italian diminutive of
"Signor" ("Seigneur" or "Monsieur" in French, "Herr" in German), recalls
the two anecdotes about the Turks of Bosnia-Herzogovina that Freud wished
to banish from the conversation, and that came to be condensed somehow in
the word "Herr." This is why the Italian name is going to be repressed—or,
what comes to the same thing, disguised—by a series of unconscious operations. Through semantic resemblance, "Signor" is replaced by "Herr," thus
transforming "Signor-elli" into "Herr-elli," a mixture of German and Italian
in which the original word is barely recognizable. But the process does not
stop there. Through phonetic resemblance, "Herr" is replaced by "Her," the
first syllable of Herzegovina, where the Turks in question lived, yielding
"Her-elli"; then, through contiguity (since Herzegovina calls to mind Bos-
nia), one passes from "Her" to "Bo," respectively the first syllable of these two
names,[12] with the result that "Her-elli" becomes "Bo-elli." This concludes the
operations of the primary process. Through the mechanism of association
alone, without going beyond the bounds of the unconscious, one obtains the

desired concealment. Consciousness nevertheless goes on searching for the name of the painter, and proceeds to rework—via a "secondary elaboration," to use the analytical term—the material given to it by the unconscious. Thus "Bo-elli" becomes "Bo-ttic-elli" and "Bo-ltraffio."

But this is not the end of the story, for two reasons. First, if it is plausible to suppose that the passage from "Signorelli" to "Botticelli" occurs through a series of intermediate terms, or at least occurs gradually, the jump from "Bo-elli" to "Boltraffio" is abrupt by comparison. Freud does not expressly acknowledge the awkwardness of the transition, but one detail he mentions seems suspect: the name of Boltraffio spontaneously came to mind, he says, even though he knew nothing about Boltraffio other than that he belonged to the Milanese school. One is therefore led to seek in this painter's very name the unconscious reason for thinking of him. Freud is not slow to tell us: the last syllables of his name, "traffio," constitute a near anagram of Trafoi, an Italian village near the Austrian border where he had learned, during a brief stay, that "[a] patient over whom I had taken a great deal of trouble had put an end to his life on account of an incurable sexual disorder" (Freud [1901] 1960, 6:3).

Suddenly everything is clear. It is not merely an incidental detail that has been elucidated, but the entire meaning of the lapse itself—a revelation, Freud omits to say, that undermines the first interpretation he had given of the lapse. If he abruptly changed the subject of conversation with his traveling companion, it was not for fear of making inappropriate remarks, but of reawakening a bitter memory of yet another professional failure. To avoid this painful recollection, he tried to make a cultural escape, as it were, to Italy by mentioning one of its great masters, but his attempt to flee came to naught. Even in the course of analyzing this lapse, the long chain of associations that led from Signorelli to Botticelli was a sort of detour, a snare and a delusion. Boltraffio, representing the return of the repressed, reminded him of the cruel truth, poorly concealed by the forgetting of Signorelli's name.

The parallel with the dream of Irma's injection is striking. Once again, sexuality is neither the driving force nor the material that the mental processes exposed by the analyst act upon. Once again, the heart of the matter is Freud's fear of seeing his reputation ruined by therapeutic blunders. And once again Freud turns the situation to his advantage, since the analysis of the lapse, and the discovery of its mechanism, provides him with the opportunity to embark on a new scientific project and thus to take his revenge on both fate and his colleagues.

The interest of the second example studied by Freud is all the greater for our purposes as it corroborates the cases we have just looked at and no longer involves self-analysis. Here the author of the lapse is an intelligent and ambitious young Jewish man who blames anti-Semitism for the "atrophy" to which he believes his generation is "doomed," and expresses the desire that this injustice will one day be remedied. He wished to conclude his "speech of impassioned fervour," Freud reports, "with the well-known line of Virgil's in which the unhappy Dido commits to posterity her vengeance on Aeneas," but he could not recall the exact text: *Exoriare aliquis nostris ex ossibus ultor* (May someone arise from my bones as an avenger) (Freud [1901] 1960, 6:8–9). The young man forgets *aliquis*, the word that designates the nameless descendant to whom his ardent appeal is addressed.

Freud comes to the rescue, suggesting that it may be helpful in trying to determine the cause of his lapse if he will say whatever spontaneously comes to his mind in connection with the forgotten word. The subject begins by breaking it down into *a* and *liquis*, and immediately mentions relics, liquefying, fluidity, fluid. Then, "with a scornful laugh," he remembers the relics of Saint Simon, sacrificed while still a child, which he had seen in a church in Trent. Then he thinks of ritual blood sacrifice, which his fellow Jews still found themselves accused of performing in modern times. Then he recalls an article in an Italian newspaper about Saint Augustine's opinion of women, and goes on to recollect the names of several saints and fathers of the Church. Thus he comes to speak of Saint Januarius, a vial of whose dried blood, which miraculously liquefies once a year, is preserved in Naples. The people await this miracle with feverish anticipation; Garibaldi himself wished that it might take place in the presence of his soldiers. Finally, after a slight hesitation, he thinks of an Italian lady with whom he visited Naples, and from whom he fears receiving dismaying news. "That her periods have stopped?" Freud asks, confident of guessing correctly now that his attention has been drawn to thoughts of sacrificed children and the intense feeling aroused by the miracle of the saint's blood.

The young man forms the wish that some one of his descendants will come forward to cleanse his generation, to wash away the humiliation that it is presently suffering. But he himself wishes above all not to be the father of a child. Nothing is more significant than his first associations: relics (child), liquefying (suggesting liquidation, and so sacrifice), fluid (menstrual blood). If the lady from whom he fears learning that her periods have stopped turns out to be pregnant on his account, will he kill the child or will he acknowledge his paternity? Here one finds the ambivalence toward fatherhood that commentators on Freud detect in the dream of the botanical monograph, only this time explicitly—in suppressing *aliquis* from Virgil's verse, then decomposing it and depriving it, so to speak, of its head, he commits a symbolic murder and dismemberment. The word itself condenses a whole constellation of ideas: through its meaning, it points to both the man he wishes he were and the child he does not wish to have; through its sound, it evokes both the blood of murder and sacrifice, bearer of death, and the blood of menstruation and parturition, bearer of life. The associations that it arouses do not succeed one another by chance. They reach back from the blood of sacrifice to the blood of menstruation, from bloody murder to the signifier of procreation.

Whether one is dealing here with a lapse of memory or with a dream, the lesson is the same. The parallel is all the more striking as the mechanisms of origin and function are explained in each case as well. It is true that in the second example Freud chooses of forgetting a foreign word, the subject's sexuality seems to have a more important place than in cases where the psychoanalyst is personally involved. But this is an illusion. The driving force of forgetting is not sexual desire, but thwarted ambition and the desire for revenge, in conflict with a rejection of paternity accompanied by the fantasy of infanticide. There is no fundamental difference between the two lapses. In each case the analyst traverses the same stages and reveals the same graduated perspective. In the foreground is sexuality, the "delicate topic" that Freud, if he is to be believed, willfully avoided bringing up in a conversation with someone unknown to him, and the occasion of the young man's forgetting of the word *aliquis*. In the middle ground is the desire to succeed and to prevail over one's adversaries, darkened by the shadow of death in various forms: the suicide of a patient, representing yet another injury to Freud's amour-propre, is the source of the forgetting of "Signorelli"; charges of murder brought against the Jews, accused of performing bloody sacrifices on children, are the source of the forgetting of *aliquis*. In the background, finally, are procreation and its substitutes, as well as the ambivalence procreation inspires: Signorelli, no less than Irma, permits Freud to compensate for a personal failure by means of a new scientific discovery, and so of becoming, in his own way, as fertile as his wife; the young man who suppresses a word of Virgil's verse, while symbolically killing the child he longs to father, nonetheless gives voice to a desire to produce a progeny.

Oedipus Complex, Cain Complex, or Abraham Complex?

In all these great texts of Freud, passing from the most superficial level of interpretation to the most profound, the sequence is therefore always the same: first, sexuality; second, the violent offspring, murderous or sacrificial, of rivalry and conflict; third, survival and procreation. Nowhere does one find the Oedipus complex in its canonical form.[13] Neither murder of the father nor incest with the mother plays a privileged role. Elsewhere Freud reports the case (originally described by Ernest Jones) of a physician whose earliest childhood fantasy was associated with the birth of his youngest sister. He believed that "she was the child, firstly, of himself and his mother, and secondly, of the [family] doctor and himself" (Freud [1901] 1960, 6:196). To see in this example an incestuous desire diverted onto the doctor would be arbitrary. There is nothing to suggest that the small child perceives his mother as a sexual object, rather than quite simply as a progenitor, or that his interest in procreation does not precede the awakening of his strictly sexual impulses.

As Girard has argued, the Oedipus complex is a secondary effect of what Freud calls identification and what he himself calls mimeticism. The little boy identifies with the father and spontaneously imitates him, and the father, flattered, encourages him in this. He is thus led to do everything that his father does, even in the conjugal bed. The incestuous desire, or what the adult interprets to be such, is therefore in no way a spontaneous desire of the child. It is inferred through a mimetic relation (see Girard [1972b] 1977, 169–92). Girard's argument is altogether convincing,[14] and readily agrees with the findings of ethnology. Without having had the benefit of either ethnographic training or the experience of doing fieldwork, Girard is nonetheless, on this point at least, a better anthropologist than either Jones or Róheim.

If psychoanalysis has been loath to give up the standard scenario of the Oedipus complex, it is nonetheless not through mere blindness or obstinacy. It is because the child, boy or girl, independently of any incestuous desire, is supposed always to have a hard time cutting the umbilical cord that connects it to the mother. It is also because, in this regard, the fates of the girl and the boy are different, not for purely sexual reasons, but by virtue of the relation each one has with the power to procreate. The girl, like her mother, has the capacity to carry children and to bring them into the world, but not to engage in reproduction with her mother. In becoming a mother in her turn, she unavoidably detaches herself from her progenitor. The boy, by contrast, does not have the power to give birth, but he is indeed able to engage in reproduction with his mother, and so is not naturally led to detach himself from her. This is no doubt why certain social institutions exist for the purpose of bringing about a result that nature alone cannot achieve. In all societies, not only is the crime of mother-son incest the most severely punished of all, but male rites of initiation, which separate sons from their mothers (on this point Reik is partly right), are more developed than female rites (see Moisseeff 1987).

Let us now consider the aggressive component of the Oedipus complex and, more generally, the conflictual aspects of human relations. There can be no question that, on this point as well, Girard enlarges and enriches Freud's analysis. In mimetic theory, the dynamic of the father-son relationship is one example among others of the degenerate situation in which a model, having become an obstacle to the satisfaction of desires that he has himself aroused, turns into a potential rival. Although this situation cannot represent the essence of all conflict, it is a very important instance of it, because the father is the male adult to whom the child is closest; it is also the most familiar form of complex intergenerational relations, products of a mixture of constraint and seduction, of envy and admiration, of which the master-disciple relationship furnishes another remarkable illustration (see Girard [1972b] 1977, 183–85; [1978] 1987, 310–12). Moreover, Girard lays much greater stress than Freud does on intragenerational conflicts, where rivalry between enemy brothers and mimetic doubles is the prototypical form. In seeking the roots of psychoanalysis in Greek culture, Freud seems to him to give the impression of wishing to escape the biblical tradition and its propensity to see fraternal rivalry as the primary source of the violent episodes that have covered human history in blood since the earliest times; and yet this type of rivalry, denied though it may be, crops up almost everywhere in his work, and indeed has dominated the psychoanalytic movement from the very beginning of its history (see Roustang 1976). Cain must therefore be preferred to Oedipus.

In opposing certain of Freud's intuitions to analytic dogma, and in rehabilitating in an original manner his most contested work, Girard surely is more justified than anyone else[15] in claiming the right to hold psychoanalysis and its founder to account. But he is inclined to a dogmatism of his own that likewise must be guarded against. Rereading *Totem and Taboo*, he criticizes Freud, rightly, for placing emphasis on the father of the horde rather than on the collective murder, and thus of failing to grasp the universality of the victim mechanism. It is true that, in this respect, "we must put the father out of our minds" (Girard [1972b] 1977, 214). Nevertheless, and without necessarily detecting the presence of a symbolic parricide, it will be admitted that the injunction is ambiguous. Forgetting about the father in this instance is one thing; doing away at the same time with the whole issue of paternity and procreation is quite another.

Yet this is exactly what Girard seems determined to do. Once cast aside, the father never returns; he appears to have been dismissed once and for all. In this regard, mimetic theory resembles psychoanalysis, whose error it reproduces, only in an opposite way: whereas Freud neglects symmetry and rivalry among enemy brothers, Girard neglects difference and conflict among generations. In mimetic theory, all difference is transient and reduces in the end to an illusion. The more the disciple resembles the master, the more he tends to become a rival; the master, for his part, ceases to be a model and becomes an obstacle. Once the rivalry is established, however, it is without end or solution. The more the rivals clash, the more each one imagines he differs from the other—and the more each one resembles the other; they are twins of violence, as it were. The objects that they fight over have no value of their own; the individual quality of these objects is only apparent, an effect of the conflicts they arouse; deprived of this impetus, they would lose all their distinctiveness and power of attraction.

It is futile to object to this by pointing out that in every society there exist material possessions and marks of social status to which everyone accords an intrinsic value. In a Fang myth collected in Gabon, which by itself epitomizes vast tracts of ethnography, two brothers quarrel over their sister's periods.[16]

This is indeed a case of fraternal rivalry, but not of pure rivalry, since it bears upon a definite object, whether it is the power to give birth, as in this case, or the status of the maternal uncle of the children of a sister (in other words, the paternal function), that the two brothers simultaneously covet. No doubt Girard would say that this function and the child associated with it have, like anything else, a price solely by virtue of the very competition of which they are the object, and that, in accordance with a principle of negative enjoyment already described by Rousseau,[17] each of the rivals devotes himself to the business of robbing the other of something he possesses, rather than enjoying the same thing himself. There is some evidence, which we considered in an earlier chapter, suggesting that Girard is partly correct: among the Gimi, for example, when the maternal uncle "eats the head" of his nephew, he makes it clearly understood that he would have been justified in killing the nephew if he had not received the compensatory offerings that were his by right. The rivalry of father and uncle, were it not restrained by a rite of paternity and related rituals, would almost surely lead to the fatal result predicted by mimetic theory and by Rousseau's theory of amour-propre. Furthermore, Girard's theory of sacrifice[18] largely explains the existence and nature of these institutional firewalls, as they may be called, that prevent violence from spreading and spiraling out of control: thus, among the Gimi, the uncle's fury when the nephew dies is diverted onto a sacrificial victim. Nevertheless, as may be seen more clearly still in the myth I have just mentioned, in the background of this male rivalry there is a power, if not an object, that irresistibly overrules the two adversaries: the power of giving life, which, though it is the occasion of their conflict, eludes their grasp and in this way manifests its transcendence.

In fairness to Girard, then, it must be admitted that his work does help to illuminate this type of situation. But he allows himself to be carried away by the desire to prove too much. Like many others, to quote Leibniz again, he is generally right in what he affirms and wrong in what he denies. He affirms the destructive force of pure or mimetic rivalry; he denies the existence of all those things capable of curbing the spread of contagious violence that mimeticism cannot by itself create.

Girard's commentary on the Judgment of Solomon is instructive in this regard (see Girard [1978] 1987, 237–43). The symmetry of the charges brought against the two prostitutes, he says, makes this scene a version of the mimetic crisis in miniature. The symmetry is further emphasized by the threat to cut the child into two equal parts—a threat of violence that resolves the crisis by reconciling the adversaries to the need for arbitration by a third party. It also recalls the practice of child sacrifice among neighboring peoples, and among the Hebrews themselves until a rather late date, with the important difference, however, that in this case the child is not killed. The biblical account does indeed contemplate a sacrifice, but only in order to avoid going through with it.

All this is quite true, but there remains one essential point that Girard tries to minimize. What saves the child's life is not any moral condemnation of the sacrifice, nor even the wisdom shown by the king, at least not by itself; it is the love of the true mother for her child, which Solomon's decision succeeds in bringing to light. Maternal love acts here as a brake on mimetic rivalry, preventing it from taking its lethal course. But Girard does not believe he needs to dwell on this aspect of the matter. To the contrary, he invites us to disregard it: "The family setting... and the maternal character of the love that it reveals are only secondary elements" (ibid., 242)—elements, he says, that require no further consideration. Once again the verdict is implacable and irrevocable: like the father of the horde, the mother must be expelled for the sake of mimetic theory in order to bring out the universal value of Solomon's decision,[19] which is to say the condemnation and unconditional rejection of mimetic rivalry and its deleterious effects. But once again, this disregard for the particular, provisional though it may seem, turns out to be permanent; generally speaking, anything that might slow or hinder the course of mimetic rivalry is neglected or devalued—so much so that it is hard to know by what miracle human beings, reduced to such a state of destitution, could ever hope to escape mimetic hell.[20]

In the last analysis, then, neither psychoanalysis nor mimetic theory manages to achieve its purpose. The former, centered on the murder of the father, constructs epicycles in order to save the standard Oedipal model at all costs, as we saw earlier with Reik. The latter, founded on the murder of the brother, relentlessly develops the notion of pure rivalry, pushing aside anything that might check its unlimited expansion and the mutual extermination of enemy brothers. What is more, both theories ignore procreation: in the Oedipal triangle, the mother is indeed present, but only as a sexual object; in the mimetic model of fraternal rivalry, the sister, of whose importance we are fully reminded by the Gabonese myth, has no place, and even if, in the female version of the model, one mother is a party to the conflict, this fact is not considered to be of any significance. In neither Freud nor Girard is there a balance between the gifts of life and death; Oedipus is seen above all as the murderer of Laius, and Cain as the murderer of Abel. By contrast, in the figure of Abraham, sacrificer of Isaac, the contest is more equal: as Alain Besançon showed quite a while ago now, in the course of a journey along the "roads of the anti-Oedipus" (see Besançon 1973), Abraham represents the triumph of the gift of life over that of death. Though Besançon's aim was to shift the center of gravity of psychoanalysis, his endeavor may also prove to be helpful in reforming mimetic theory.

We have seen that reinterpreting the Oedipus complex requires it to be recentered on the attitude of the father, who in the myth, it will be recalled, attempts to take the life of his son by abandoning him after having pierced and bound his feet. This is what Besançon proposes to do, only substituting Abraham for Laius, since Freud's reliance on Greek myth seems to him to be misleadingly incomplete: the story of Abraham, he says, forms "the repressed and hidden negative of that of Oedipus" (ibid., 187). According to the index of the standard English edition of the complete works, the patriarch's name appears only twice in Freud's monumental oeuvre: once in the so-called Wolf Man case study, where the command that the father sacrifice the son is supposed to manifest God's cruelty toward his children (see Freud [1918] 1955, 17:65–66); and a second time in *Moses and Monotheism*, where Freud denies Abraham credit for introducing the custom of circumcision, ascribing it instead to Moses, whom he considers to have been an Egyptian (see Freud [1939] 1964, 23:26–28; also 23:44–45). These two passages have in common a determination to link a "denial of paternity" with a "denial of the Covenant," and exist solely for the purpose of testifying to the rejection of Jewish heritage: "Freud takes his models from outside the Bible. It is as though [the Bible] were framed and obscured by two great myths, the one prior to it, the other posterior. . . . *Totem and Taboo* forms a sort of new Genesis, and *Moses [and Monotheism]* a second Exodus, both built on Darwin's [notion of the] ruler of a primal horde. But the first myth, that of the Father of the Horde, is interpreted by the second, which is Greek. Darwin and Sophocles are each proved by the other. The Jewish heritage is rejected" (Besançon 1973, 189). Freud appropriated for his own purposes the idea that Moses had been murdered by his own people, and indeed thought of himself—the "father of psychoanalysis" and bearer of a "new doctrinal initiation"—as a new Moses, promised the same fate as his model, a fate to be delivered by his "children, the dissident disciples and all those who rejected the psychoanalytic message" (188).

Freud's insistence on the murder of the father is thus bound up with the rejection of his Jewish heritage. He turned toward the Greek world because he thought he had found in the story of Oedipus the theme of an irrepressible—and therefore indefinitely recurring—parricide. And this in turn led him to adopt a tragic view of the relations between generations, that conflicts can at most be identified, named, and recognized, but never resolved: "From the tragic *fatum* there is, by definition, no way out" (ibid., 193).

The story of Abraham, repressed by Freud though it is rich in tests of obedience, holds out the prospect of escaping this tragic circle. It is centered on the theme of sterility, but there is another theme as well, of a covenant with God, the source of all life and the cure for sterility. The biblical text is complex: it juxtaposes two different versions of the covenant and, as Besançon rightly points out, divides the covenant itself into two, or even three phases. Let us recall the main aspects of the story. Abraham, who is still called Abram, offers an animal sacrifice to God to seal a covenant with Him: he cuts the victims in two and God approves the sacrifice, passing between the victims in the form of a burning torch (Genesis 15). God had promised Abram a progeny as numerous as the stars in the heavens, but Sarai, his wife, was barren. Thus she proposes to her husband that her maidservant, Hagar, be substituted for her in order to give him a child; Hagar brings into the world Ishmael, destined himself to sire a numerous progeny (Genesis 16). Thirteen years later, God renews the covenant through a new ritual,[21] by which Abram institutes the practice of circumcision and becomes Abraham; in so doing he will be able to have his own line, endowed with its own land, with his wife Sarai, who will take the name Sarah (Genesis 17). Thus Abraham circumcises all the male members of his house (Genesis 17), and Sarah gives birth to Isaac (Genesis 21). A few years later, however, God demands that Abraham offer up Isaac as a burnt offering; Abraham submits to this command, binds his son, lays him on the wood atop the sacrificial altar, and takes his knife in hand—but just before he can kill Isaac, God substitutes for the child a ram (Genesis 22). Abraham thus becomes wholly the father of his son, from whom will come the nation destined to populate the land promised by God: the promise will finally be fulfilled.

Without making a detailed analysis of this whole sequence, Besançon extracts from it an essential theme that runs through the story from beginning to end and links all its events with one another. Life does not belong to man; it is a gift of God. Man is only the repository of it, not the owner, and still less the creator. He can only receive life and transmit the life that he has received. Thus the condition laid down by God when he demanded that Abraham offer up Isaac to him: man will be able to be the father of his progeny only if he renounces being the author and master of it. This condition is stated in a tragic context that arouses fear and trembling, but it is a promise of life, not of death. Unlike Laius, who desired the death of Oedipus, neither Abraham nor God wishes the death of Isaac. The scene of the sacrifice, or rather of the binding of Isaac, is connected with the institution of circumcision. Circumcision is a sacrificial rite, but it is a substitute for the sacrifice of the firstborn, which it replaces. To institute circumcision and to refuse to immolate Isaac therefore amount to one and the same thing. Life must not be destroyed; it must be received and transmitted, with only the ritual seal of its divine and provisional origin. This is the condition of founding a chain of generations. Their succession rests not on conflict, but on trust and a willingness to assume the responsibilities of fatherhood. "It is as if Abraham became capable of being a father only at the moment when he accepts being the son of the father whose gift he now at last accepts" (Besançon 1973, 191). This gift is not only the land that God offers to his servant; it is also, and above all, the son whom He has confided to him, and whose descendants are destined to populate this land.

Remarkably, Abraham's presence is altogether as discreet in Girard's work as it is in that of Freud. To my knowledge, his name appears only twice in Girard's major works,[22] once in *Violence and the Sacred*, in connection with the Muslim tradition that "God delivered to Abraham the ram previously sacrificed by Abel . . . to take the place of Abraham's son Isaac" (Girard [1972b] 1977, 4), and later in *Things Hidden since the Foundation of the World*, as one witness among others to ancient ritual practices subject to the victim mechanism, from which "Judeo-Christian scripture" gradually distances itself and which it ever more firmly condemns (see Girard [1978] 1987, 143). In all, then, there are only two allusions to this central episode of the Bible, though they illustrate in exemplary fashion the substitution of an animal victim for a human victim, which is supposed to constitute the very heart of the sacrificial economy. Like Freud, Girard seems to turn away from Abraham, and so from one of the most memorable moments of the Old Testament.[23] The story of Abraham does not really fit the mold of mimetic theory; those of Cain and Abel, of Esau and Jacob, and of Joseph and his brothers are much better suited to it (see 144–53), as well as those of other pairs of enemy brothers or mimetic rivals taken from the Greco-Roman world—such as Romulus and Remus, Eteocles and Polynices in Euripides's *Phoenician Women*, and Oedipus and Tiresias in Sophocles's *Oedipus the King* (see Girard [1972b] 1977, 44–48, 61–62, 68–73)—where mimetic rivalry is much more pronounced than in the biblical examples.[24]

In support of his signature hypothesis Girard is finally obliged, again like Freud, to search for what he needs outside the Jewish tradition, for which, unlike Freud, he sees himself as a spokesman. And yet, again unlike the father of psychoanalysis, he passes in complete silence over the question of paternity, which occupies no less important a place in Freud's thought than in the Bible. In this respect Freud remains faithful to Judaism, understood as a religion of the Father and filial submission, whereas Girard unreservedly appeals to the authority of Christianity, religion of the Son and of the union of brothers with one another. There is nothing accidental about Girard's omission of Abraham, for Abraham represents the non-mimetic loyalty and obedience of the son to the law of the father. Circumcision, which is the hallmark of these things, falls once again under the head of those sacrificial religions from which Judeo-Christian scripture, and Christianity most especially, have come to free humanity; but the categorical opposition he insists upon between "archaic religion" and "biblical religion" leads him to reduce the latter to a minute portion.

For all of these reasons Girard evidently cannot notice something that is essential to both the story of Abraham, which he avoids, and the Judgment of Solomon, which attracts his attention except, as we have seen, in one crucial aspect, which he pointedly neglects. In some ways the scenes of sacrifice and judgment seem to be opposites: in the story of Abraham, it is the father who is prepared to sacrifice his child, and it is God who stays his murderous hand at the last moment; whereas in the story of Solomon, it is the king who is prepared to cut the child in two, and the mother who prevents him from committing the act. And yet the lesson is the same in each case, for it is God who gives Abraham a progeny, not only in the flesh, by making his wife fertile, but above all through ritual, which confers the condition of paternity upon him; and it is the king, God's earthly vicar, who, by means of a decisive rite, identifies the woman who bore the child in her womb and confers the condition of maternity upon her. In both cases the person who is proclaimed worthy of receiving the child is the one who does not claim it as his own property, as a personal possession that would be exclusively his or hers to enjoy. The two scenes remind human beings of their finitude and enjoin them humbly to accept it. To beget is not to create: man must not claim to "make" children, any more than it is permissible for him to make idols; he can only receive life and transmit it. We find here, in connection with the transcendence of life, the formula that Lacan attributed to Freud—too generous a formula, perhaps, but surely a very wise one: "I am not the creator. The creator is someone greater than I am."

Girard, for his part, though he explicitly relies on Judeo-Christian scripture, rules out any form of transcendence. The paradox is due to an important modification of his understanding of human desire, often wrongly taken to be a mere change in terminology—the substitution of "mimetic desire" for "triangular desire"—when in fact it involves a genuine paradigm shift. The theory of triangular desire sought only to explain the origin of false transcendences; in substituting mimetic desire for triangular desire, Girard claims to have fully elucidated the genesis of all transcendence.

In *Deceit, Desire, and the Novel*, even if he does not expressly say so, Girard starts out not from imitation, but from admiration. This is because he was fascinated by the legendary exploits of Amadís de Gaule, whom Don Quixote takes as a model and tries to imitate. The point of departure for imitation is the existence of a prestigious model whom its admirer wishes to resemble. Far from being totally free—the master of his desires and his choices, arbiter of the beautiful and the ugly, of good and evil, that existentialism imagines him to be—man is in reality at the mercy of his impulses. He needs someone whose actions and choices can serve him as a guide; someone whose actions and choices will show him which ones are desirable. Between the desiring subject and the desired object there is always a kind of mediation, embodied by this model. Together they form a triangle of desire. Girard speaks of "external mediation" when the mediator is too remote to become a rival, and of "internal mediation" when the mediator is a potential rival.

Because the first form of mediation is prevalent in aristocratic societies and the second in egalitarian societies, there is a risk of underestimating the external variety, which rightly serves as the point of departure for Girard's first book. Its priority in relation to internal mediation is not due to historical reasons, but to the fact that since children are incapable of surviving without the help of adults, adults are the very first mediators they come into contact with. It is a pity that Girard himself neglects this fundamental point, on which Freud strongly insisted, of course, and rightly so; later, in resolving to forget about the father, Girard was prepared even to risk relegating external mediation to the periphery of mimetic theory, indeed of eliminating it altogether. By contrast, when Girard describes the fascination exerted by the mediator on the person who takes him as a guide, he dwells at length, with echoes of Pascal,[25] on a property of desire that could not be mimetic in origin: a craving for the absolute that leads the admirer to idolize his model, to confer a divine aura on it. In that case the model is an intermediary not only between the desiring subject and the desired object, but also between the subject and a transcendent God, from whom the model derives all his prestige and who is, ultimately, the true and obscure object of desire. Girard speaks in this connection of "deviated," rather than illusory, transcendence, which presupposes a genuine transcendence that he calls "vertical" (Girard [1961] 1966, 61).

By contrast with this aspect of triangular desire, described by Girard himself as "metaphysical" and present from the first pages of *Deceit, Desire, and the Novel*, the genesis of mimetic desire, introduced at the very beginning of *Things Hidden since the Foundation of the World*, is striking not least for its positivist spirit. This whole book, a treatise on anthropology and general psychology allied with a defense of the Christian religion, is founded on a single, empirically testable hypothesis: humans are somewhat more mimetic than other primates. From the moment that two people find themselves in each other's presence, they spontaneously seek to imitate each other—not only to have the same attitudes and make the same gestures ("representational mimesis"), but also to appropriate for themselves the same objects ("acquisitive mimesis"). It is on the basis of this unique and elementary axiom, and of the mimetic interactions of rivalry and conflict that immediately flow from it, that Girard attempts to reconstruct and broaden the results of his two previous works: his theory of the ritual regulation of human societies, laid out in *Violence and the Sacred*, and his conception of human desire and of psychopathology, presented in *Deceit, Desire, and the Novel*. Without entering into a detailed discussion here, I shall limit myself to indicating two awkward points that will suffice, I trust, to show the limits of his enterprise.

If human desire were solely mimetic, there would be no way, it seems to me, to make sense of human affairs. It would not be possible to explain why, the rival having been swept aside and the coveted object attained—though, by the same token, robbed of its illusory virtues—the disillusionment that accompanies this conquest does not make the conqueror any wiser in the ways of the world.[26] Instead, he sets out again in pursuit of a new lure, a fresh illusion. Pascal inferred from this that only an infinite object, inaccessible *hic et nunc*, could satisfy human beings. Thus he explained both idolatry and diversion (*divertissement*): idolatry consists in placing an infinite value on a finite thing or being; diversion in preferring "the search for things" to things themselves, this from a sense that nothing is commensurate with human desire. Girard's first book, inspired in large part by Max Scheler, was, as we have just seen, still very Pascalian in spirit; embedded in it is an apology for Christianity, which Girard conceived at this early stage of his intellectual development—and this is the point that interests me here—as a religion of transcendence, of which "metaphysical desire" appears as a degraded form. In *Things Hidden since the Foundation of the World*, by contrast, transcendence itself is nothing more than an illusion.[27] The accidental convergence of gazes on the person of some presumptively mimetic partner might momentarily confer upon him the semblance of a divine aura in the eyes of his admirers and, by inference, in his own eyes; but this apparent transcendence is all the more uncertain as it no longer has any support, either from above or from below: not from genuine transcendence, of which it is now seen to be merely a simulacrum, a sham and a mockery; nor from metaphysical desire, which Girard attempts to reconstitute on the basis solely of the natural mimesis of his new schema, and of which mimetic desire is but a highly implausible and pathological outgrowth.

Hocart had recognized long before the importance of imitation and snobbery in the formation, and above all the diffusion, of customs and institutions (see Hocart 1933, 33–34; 1952, 129–38). Whereas Girard seeks to derive all this from the mimetic interactions of human beings alone, with no reference to anything else, Hocart's purpose in insisting on the importance of imitation and on the weight of traditions was to incite human beings to greater modesty, and to make them see how little their behavior owes to their freedom and their wisdom. On the one hand, in holding that everything is a product of mimesis, Girard undermines still more completely the claim of individuals to autonomy; but on the other, in granting mimesis an immense morphogenetic capacity, he concedes to humanity truly demiurgic powers. In his own fashion, then, he unites contemporary constructivism and the aspiration to self-procreation. Like Sartrean existentialism, mimetic theory rejects Platonism in all its forms; like orthodox structuralism, it reduces human nature to an undifferentiated substrate (in effect, a set of initially indistinguishable mimetic automata) and leads it into the same dead-ends. At once all-powerful and powerless, human beings are doomed to a perpetual oscillation between these two abysses. They are all-powerful since God (or nature) has created only mimeticism; all the rest is the work of human beings. And yet they are powerless since once all false transcendences have been undermined or discredited, no task is left for them to undertake together that would not be wholly arbitrary. How could their egalitarian and purely mimetic dealings with one another lead to anything other than death if no other transcendence could take over from all those forms of transcendence that are now defunct? If human beings have neither a sacred repository nor a common heritage to protect and transmit to future generations?

These impasses are an invitation to revise mimetic theory, as I have already begun to try to do elsewhere;[28] an invitation, too, to reread the story of Abraham, which, in indissolubly combining the themes of procreation and ritual covenant-making—and thus in warding off death—suggests that the transcendence of life and of culture are related. While human beings can indeed give death, they cannot really give life; they can only receive it and transmit it—and this under circumstances that are in large part likewise beyond their control.

CHAPTER FIFTEEN

Conceiving and Transmitting

I n assessing the legacy of *Totem and Taboo* I have taken as my guide the relations between male and female, not only as they are manifested in various exotic societies but also as they are conceived in modern Western thought, of which psychoanalysts and anthropologists over the past one hundred years have been not merely observers and critics, but spokesmen and privileged representatives as well. In this sense the present work is, to a large extent, a description of the ambiguous—Auguste Comte probably would have said "aberrant"—relationship that the West has had for several decades now with differences between the sexes and with procreation.

This is why I have chosen to conclude by examining a book bearing just this title: *Aberrations*. Its author is Sarah Kofman, a feminist philosopher learned in psychoanalysis and enamored of deconstruction, and its subject is what Kofman calls "the becoming-woman of Auguste Comte." Published in 1978, it is emblematic of a style of thought born in France and Great Britain that became famous in the United States and then came back to Europe, where it has enjoyed enormous success in recent years, effortlessly triumphing not only in academia but also in the worlds of law, politics, and the media. The pages that make up the first part of this chapter were written in

1981. Apart from a few details, I have not thought it necessary to make any further revisions.

Auguste Comte's Lesson, or The School for Wives

To survey the monumental and much-discussed work of Auguste Comte from a fresh perspective, Kofman examines the webs of association woven by terms for which Comte has a particular fondness: "speculation," for example, very frequently used to denote the operations of the intellect and the interests to which they give rise; also "conception," almost always preferred to "idea" or "notion," to denote the fruits of speculation;[1] and, at the intersection of the paths opened up by these two words, the term "aberration" itself, which according to the publisher's description of Kofman's book is to be understood "in all its equivocacy: the optical, astronomical, biological senses [being] indissociable in it."

It is not entirely clear what this approach is intended to achieve. Is it meant to expose the blind spot of an entire system of ideas, or the unrecognized source of a particular work, or perhaps only the thought that unavoidably escapes the author just when he would have wished to express it? Or does it reveal instead the soundest part of his reasoning, the luminous point where all the rays of a fully developed argument converge? We know that Comte himself was exceedingly careful in his choice of words, and that he never failed to clarify or to justify their many shades of meaning. No philosopher is credited with greater thoroughness in the selection and arrangement of technical terms than Plato. Rémi Brague showed some years ago that a punctilious study of the vocabulary and dramatic construction of the *Meno* does not reveal a hidden significance that might have somehow eluded its author or that might have been deliberately hidden from the uninitiated. It reveals instead the most finely wrought aspect of the book—an esoteric aspect, perhaps, since apparent only to scholars, but in no way concealed from view, since it agrees at every point with the plain meaning that no reader will have failed to grasp, a meaning that it repeats and reinforces, as though to allow it to be seen from all possible angles (see Brague 1978).

It is Comte's insistence, so unlike Plato, on emphasizing the distinctive character of the words he uses that arouses suspicion. One cannot help but wonder if he is not avoiding something shameful[2]—and this at the very moment when he believes that he has openly stated his purpose; unless, of course, the naiveté is shared for the most part, and the inquirer no more reveals secrets about himself than about the object of his inquiry. However this may be, let us look at least at one of the arguments Kofman develops in this connection. Given that Comte "never speaks of his ideas or of his thoughts, but always of his *conceptions*"; given that his most constant interest was to "regenerate humanity"; given, finally, that he presents himself "as an organ of the history of the human mind that develops only from preexisting seeds"—given all these things, and taking this last expression literally, one is obliged to say that he is not "[the] father of positivism, but its mother" (Kofman 1978, 16; emphasis in the original). This is why barrenness is the principal vice of the metaphysical regime (see 90) and also the chief short-coming of Caroline Massin, Comte's wife, whom he eventually divorced; also why the spiritual reorganization of society, aimed at putting an end to the aberrations produced by this disastrous regime, consists in favoring the birth of "healthy positivist conceptions."

In so doing, Kofman claims, Comte places himself in a very dangerous position. For wishing to conceive is to wish one were fertile like a woman; it is therefore to come recklessly close to the worst of sexual aberrations, the very same one to which the metaphysical spirit led the Greeks, namely, homosexuality—hence Comte's "masculine protest," manifest in the very formulation of the law of three stages, and the force with which he proclaims that the age of positive maturity, the only normal age, is the *virile* age of the mind (see ibid., 41–42), whereas the theological stage and the metaphysical stages are "sexually neuter," the one representing the childhood, the other the adolescence of humanity.

Hence, too, Comte's "bad" philosophical style, his unsatisfactory expression of philosophical ideas. Comte never fails to contrast expression with conception. Flawed expression, Kofman says, is "the price that must be paid for having wished to *conceive*, [for having] wished to enjoy a forbidden pleasure. . . . This bad style, [a] scientific, masculine [style] according to Comte, is . . . a means of prohibiting access to this shameful secret. If Comte needs to display his virility, through and in his style, [needs] to exhibit such an *apotropaion*, it is because conceiving, for a man, is revelatory of an anomaly, of a *sexual aberration*, the worst of aberrations" (ibid., pp. 15–16; emphasis in the original). Hence, finally, the ambiguous, indeed contradictory, image that Comte proposes of woman, whom he exalts and humiliates at the same time, whom he idealizes in Clotilde de Vaux and despises in Caroline Massin—proclaiming at once "the worthy subordination of male reason to female sentiment" and "the indispensable subordination of the sexes," which is to say the necessary submission of the woman to the man.

Even so, is it fair to say that "Comte raises woman up, the better to pull her down" (ibid., 259)? For if he really desires to "become woman" and ward off the aberration that threatens him, would it not rather be the other way around, a question of pulling her down in order to avoid raising her up too high? More than this, what does he actually mean by "becoming woman"? Does he desire to conceive, which is to say be a mother in order to be able to be a woman, or does he aspire to be a woman in order to be able to be a mother? Kofman, though she never clearly poses this question, adopts the former hypothesis, whereas the latter seems to me to be the only admissible one.

Regeneration of Humanity and Delusion of Childbirth: Comte and President Schreber

The comparison between Comte and Daniel Paul Schreber, himself a constant presence in *Aberrations*, can only strengthen this feeling. Schreber, president of the appeals court of Saxony in the late nineteenth century, suffered a nervous breakdown marked by the delusion that he had to be transformed into a woman in order to give birth to a new race of men and so bring about the salvation of humanity (see Schreber [1903] 1955). Nothing could be more tempting than to elucidate Comte's delusion with reference to the analysis that Freud gave of the Schreber case (see Freud [1911] 1958). The surprising thing is that Comte's philosophy is nowhere consulted by Kofman in order to elucidate the Schreber case in its turn—all the more since, like Freud at his best, Kofman appears to see paranoia as a distorted form of philosophy rather than philosophy as a disguised form of paranoia. But if Comte's system takes the place of delirium for him, as she maintains, it is nonetheless clear that the system itself cannot be reduced to this condition. How, she asks, can Comte be taken seriously as a philosopher? This question goes unanswered, for to say that his system agrees marvelously well with the dominant phallocratic social order does no more than replace it with another. The question now becomes: Is philosophy the expression or the foundation of this order? Does it find refuge in this order or is it a constituent element of it? And what exactly does the phallocratic order itself amount to? Is it the aberrant fruit of a sort of collective delusion? Its nature is as enigmatic as that of religion in Freud, where one cannot really say whether it is an obsessional neurosis affecting mankind as a whole (per *The Future of an Illusion*) or whether it serves as a model for obsessional neurosis (per *Totem and Taboo*).

Yet one has only to pay close attention to Schreber's and Comte's own writings to be able to answer these questions. I shall limit myself here to comparing Freud's commentary on Schreber and Kofman's analysis of Comte. It will be obvious at once that Freud, even if one considers only the passage quoted by Kofman (1978, 91), himself hesitates between two possible interpretations of Schreber's delirium. On the one hand, the desire to produce offspring is seen as a secondary elaboration making it possible to put an acceptable face on the desire to experience female sexual pleasure and to satisfy homosexual fantasies. On the other, the impossibility of producing offspring is taken to be the primary cause of Schreber's madness: thus Freud compares Schreber to Napoleon, who divorced Josephine for being unable to bear children. Schreber had in fact never been able to be a father: six of his children were stillborn; after his illness had been brought under control, he adopted a thirteen-year-old girl. Freud, as one might expect, nonetheless prefers the first hypothesis, while conceding that Schreber's delusion may well have been "designed [also] to offer him an escape from his childlessness" (Freud [1911] 1958, 12:58; quoted in Kofman 1978, 91). And yet everything suggests that the impossibility of perpetuating his line was the principal reason for his psychosis, as Ida Macalpine and Richard Hunter (1955b) persuasively urged rather long ago now. It still remains, however, to tease out all the assumptions and implications of this argument.

As against Kofman, one may say that what differentiates man and woman is not so much sexuality as procreation. Both are sexed beings, but they are sexed in different ways: women can conceive and bring children into the world; men cannot. If one really insists, as Freud does, on asserting a symbolic equivalence between child and phallus, one should no longer see the child as a substitute for the phallus, but rather the phallus as a substitute for the child. It is not woman, then, but man who is marked by the minus sign.[3] Man is a mutilated, incomplete being, because he lacks the ability to bear children. And, as a consequence, the fundamental complex for Freud should no longer be associated with Oedipus, but—if one may be permitted to substitute for a hero as serious as the one imagined by Sophocles a figure as fantastic as the one imagined by Collodi—with Geppetto, who, longing for a child, decides to make one himself by sculpting from a piece of wood the famous Pinocchio.[4]

As innumerable myths and rites observed in all regions of the globe attest, and as initiation ceremonies, typically reserved for boys, show more especially, men envy women for possessing what (rightly or wrongly) they consider to be the extravagant privilege of bringing children into the world. Far from considering themselves superior to their mates, and although they are loath to acknowledge it, they feel—indeed, perhaps even know—themselves to be inferior to them in this respect, and possibly in other respects as well. This is why they seek to reserve for themselves a monopoly over cultural creation, in the hope of somehow compensating for women's natural prerogatives—hence the originally masculine character not only of the priesthood (whether "primitive," Catholic, or positivist), but also of political, artistic, scientific, and other offices, which, as Hocart showed, are almost always ritual in origin (see Hocart [1936] 1970; 1954).

Metaphysical Aberration and Positive Philosophy of Conception

Let us come back to Comte. It should be clear that in principle there is no contradiction between thinking about science and philosophy as exercises in conception and, at the same time, characterizing these activities as manly and unreservedly assigning them to men, for this is precisely the logic of what may, if one insists, be called the phallocratic order. Had Comte limited himself to "writing in capital letters and complete naiveté" what all philosophies say, only "in a more or less oblique fashion" (Kofman 1978, 41), he would have committed no offense and there would therefore be no reason to say anything more. If in fact the problem is the "virility" of positivism, it is because Comte, unlike his peers, was fully conscious of his desire to conceive, and because he neither could nor wished to repress this knowledge. Perceiving the feminine character of all human conception, he fully accepted all of its consequences—thus distancing himself from the masculine view of knowledge and action, and, by the same token, from a phallocratic order that, far from strengthening, he threatened to weaken instead.[5]

There are two possible ways of regarding women and the mother-child relationship. The one, imaginary and "metaphysical," might be called masculine; the other, real and "positive," might be called feminine. According to the one, women *make* children and *give* life; according to the other, women *have* children and *transmit* life. The one sees the mother-child unit as an indissociable whole, closed upon itself and sufficient unto itself; the other recognizes the otherness of the child and distinguishes the woman from the child that develops inside her—but also against her, with all the ambiguity that this expression contains.

Corresponding to these two conceptions of woman are two conceptions of philosophy and science, as well as two conceptions of politics and religion. The masculine conception of philosophy and science takes as its model an imaginary view of human generation and the mother-child relationship; the feminine conception is based on the reality of generation.[6] The former sees these disciplines as dedicated to the search for the productive causes of all things; it is encountered, for example, in Hobbes and Spinoza. Rational knowledge, Hobbes says in *Leviathan*, is "the Knowledge acquired by Reasoning, from the Manner of Generation of any thing, to the Properties" (Hobbes [1651] 2010, ch. 46, p. 399); to think, Spinoza says in the *Ethics*, is not to perceive but to *conceive*, that is, to form an idea ("a conception of the mind") from within oneself, rather than from outside (Spinoza [1677b] 2000, part 2, def. 3, p. 113). Furthermore, for these two philosophers, the genetic definition of a thing is also a complete definition of that thing, from which all its properties can be deduced (see Spinoza [1677a] 1995, letter 60 [to Tschirnhaus, January 1675], 290). Consequently, a true idea, which Spinoza calls an "adequate" or "complete" idea, is one of which we are completely the cause; a false ("inadequate" or "incomplete") idea is one of which we are not completely the cause. As for human reason, it is not reducible to the power to make valid inferences; it is neither more nor less than the power to form an adequate idea of any thing.[7]

Comte, for his part, proposes an altogether different conception of knowledge, which may rightly be called feminine if one accepts that women, "especially [those who are] uneducated" (Comte [1852] 1966, 43)—those who have no claim to masculine culture[8]—well know that they are not the adequate cause of the children that are formed inside them. In the sciences, our speculations about things must be limited "to analyzing with exactitude the circumstances of their production," without seeking to set forth their "generative causes" (First Lesson, *Course of Positive Philosophy*) or trying to "penetrate the mystery of their production" (*Discourse on the Positive Spirit*). Nor is the philosopher the first cause of a system or a sequence of ideas; he can only germinate these ideas and help to favor their systematic development.

Comte does not immediately reject his predecessors' ideal of completeness, however.[9] He emphasizes that the advent of sociology, which is to say the science of man, completes the series of sciences and loops back on itself, since the science of man is also the science of science. One thus ends up with "a single science" and a "full mental systematization"—man being at once its subject and its object, "its principle and its end" (*Discourse on the Positive Spirit*). "Even when science has become aware of the pointlessness of [searching for] causes and managed to gain acceptance for laws, it aspires, as much as theology and metaphysics do, to complete objectivity, dreaming of a universal explanation of the external world by means of a single law, not less absolute than gods and entities, in accordance with academic utopia." I have myself, Comte avows, momentarily yielded to this illusion, "from which the religious state alone has freed me," for "[science] is really as preliminary as theology and metaphysics, and, like them, must finally be expelled by the ultimate religion" (Letter to Doctor Audiffrent, quoted in Arnaud 1965, 30–31). Thus Comte escapes the mirage of absolute knowledge; the absolute preserves its transcendence, and masculine reason is made to submit to feminine sensibility.

Even if one is put in mind for a moment of Hegel, one cannot help but set him in opposition to Comte, since philosophy and religion occupy opposite places in their thinking, the former being the culmination of the latter in Hegel's *Encyclopedia* and the latter the culmination of the former in Comte's *Catechism*. To this it may be added that there are two conceptions of religion at work here—also of politics—as well as two conceptions of procreation and, consequently, of creation and human action in general: the one masculine, associated again with Hegel, which celebrates the "labor of the negative" and for which violence is the midwife of history, but also with Freud and the fantasy of the "primal scene"; the other feminine, associated not only with Comte but also with Nietzsche, the "thinker of pregnancy" (Derrida [1978] 1979, 65), which celebrates the labor of childbirth and denies any value to negative ("metaphysical" or "reactive") forces because one "destroys only what one replaces" (Comte [1852] 1966, 31). Masculine religion sanctifies violence, sacrifice, the impure blood that irrigates our furrows: it is a religion of rites of initiation, in which men play at conceiving children by subjecting them to ordeals of blood and death; a religion of warrior gods. Feminine religion sanctifies life, glorifies milk rather than blood: it is a religion of fertility cults and earth mothers, a religion of breastfeeding goddesses.

There are also, as I say, two conceptions of politics. The first is encountered in Hobbes, for whom, prior to the creation of laws and contracts, there was neither justice nor injustice among men, neither good nor evil. As men are the sole authors of laws and contracts, which is to say of the "causes of justice," politics and ethics can, like mathematics, be wholly deduced a priori from genetic definitions (see Hobbes [1651] 2010, ch. 15, pp. 88–98). The second conception is encountered in Comte, for whom "the natural order always constitutes a modifiable fatality" (Comte [1852] 1966, 67), consisting of immutable "fundamental laws," to which man must submit, and variable "secondary dispositions," which human intervention may modify; both of these, laws and dispositions, can be known only a posteriori. On the one hand, one concentrates all powers in a single hand, that of the Sovereign, not only in Hobbes (*Leviathan*) but also in Spinoza (*Tractatus Theologico-Politicus*), which legitimizes the complete subordination of religion to the political authorities; even if one refrains from going this far, advancing instead a purely naturalistic theory of society, wittingly or not one embraces the pretension of abstract intellectualism to produce a new humanity ex nihilo, to create new forms of society from nothing. On the other hand, one seeks to prevent a monolithic concentration of authority by advocating the formation of a spiritual power that will serve as the source of inspiration for the temporal power, while taking care to guard against granting political supremacy to the intellect—not, as Kofman wrongly puts it, to "intelligence" (1978, 209)—to the extent that the spiritual power is to the temporal power exactly what woman is to man.

The Madman, the Brahman, and the Philosopher

Let us now come back to the parallel Kofman draws between Comte and Schreber. If they both wish to become female, why does Comte escape madness and Schreber sink into delirium? The founder of positivism, we are told, avoids illness by producing a system, even if it means then having to record the details of his own derangement in it, whereas poor Schreber has to go mad first in order to conceive a work, the account of his own madness.[10] Perhaps so. But then why didn't Schreber compose the *Course of Positive Philosophy* and Comte the *Memoirs of My Nervous Illness*? And in what respect, then, does the *Course* differ from the *Memoirs*? How is it that Comte's philosophy is irreducible to a demented construct if it only expresses and strengthens a phallocratic order that Kofman tells us is aberrant? In reality, if Comte was able to become a philosopher, if he was able to escape Schreber's lamentable fate, it is because Comte—and without his having had to ask why—understood better than Schreber the true nature of his desire; because, far from experiencing it as fate, as a misfortune external to him, he was able to assume full responsibility for it.[11] It is not philosophy that saved him from delirium; it is his clear-mindedness that allowed him to philosophize—whereas in Schreber's case, delusion had the effect only of ensuring that he would remain the prisoner of madness, notwithstanding his heroic efforts to deliver himself from it. Consequently, with all due respect to feminists, we must do everything we can to rehabilitate the reputation of the august phallocrat. Women dread being "reduced" to the "animal" function of procreation because they well know that they do not make the children that form inside them. The task of bringing children into the world and raising them is apt to seem to them a rather trifling thing compared to the marvelous activities that men are intent on reserving to themselves. And yet, if Comte is right, this is an illusion: wisdom actually consists in *limiting oneself* to procreation, or at least to those activities that may be modeled on procreation; nothing is more absurd, by contrast, than the male claim that abstract reason is the source of all things. Thus the grand lesson, the moral of positivism.

Comte escaped madness because he knew how to allow himself to be impregnated by all the great men of the past whose tradition he carried on, and thus to rediscover the conditions under which society is possible, just as every woman rediscovers a universal way of bringing forth children. Schreber was no more able than Comte to create ex nihilo. But forced to rely on his own resources for the most part, and therefore in a way reduced to parthenogenesis, he produced a monstrous work that revitalized some of the major themes of the great mythologies by deforming them. Whether or

not a traditionally shamanistic society might have been able to accommodate Schreber's madness, no such question arises in Comte's case because he
brought over the dogmatic and institutional framework of Catholicism into
his Religion of Humanity. Instead of deliriously imagining that he could give
birth to a new human race through the power of his mind alone, he becomes
a woman by claiming a spiritual power whose preeminence over the temporal
power he affirms while at the same time acknowledging its subordination to
this power.

To be sure, the distance between Comte and Schreber is evidently very
slight—and all the less as Comte makes himself the pope of a positivist
church. Nevertheless, if it seems mad to found a spiritual power with only a
few disciples and then to proclaim oneself their leader, the very notion of a
spiritual power is perfectly coherent and sensible. Perhaps without realizing
it, Comte rediscovers certain features of the varna system in India, where the
Brahmans are likewise held to be higher than the king on whom they nonetheless depend. "In theory," Louis Dumont says, "[royal] power is ultimately
subordinate to priesthood, whereas in fact priesthood submits to power"
(Dumont [1979] 1980, 71–72). Furthermore, in India, as in Comte's work,
the same model serves to conceptualize the relationship between these two
authorities: "The *brahman*[,] being the source, or rather the womb, from
which the *kṣatra* springs, is superior; the *brahman* could exist without the
kṣatra, not conversely" (ibid., appendix C, p. 289).

Comte therefore does not invent. He describes the culture of a possible
society, or perhaps even a fundamental dimension of any society whatsoever,
neglected in *Homo aequalis* (Dumont 1976) but no less pertinent for the
argument of that work than for *Homo hierarchus* (Dumont [1979] 1980). As
Pierre Arnaud observes in his introduction to *Catéchisme positiviste* (Comte
[1852] 1966), it is in no way contradictory to assert the preeminence of the
spiritual power while at the same time holding that the spirit has no vocation
for governing, and that the direction of temporal affairs belongs unreservedly to the temporal power. It is contradictory only if one wholly miscon-
strues the nature and function of hierarchy, dreaming of a society that could
dispense with it altogether, and failing also to see that such a society is always
liable to degenerate into tyranny.

Comte holds that this hierarchical principle ought also to prevail within
the family. For, he says, "between two beings alone, spontaneously bound

together by a profound mutual affection, no harmony can endure unless one commands and the other obeys" (*System of Positive Polity* 2.3, quoted in Arnaud 1965, 137). Thus he proposes to temper "the worthy subordination of male reason to female feeling [by] the just practical domination of the man." In moving from the general to the particular, however, the implication is not preserved: society forms a whole having no normative principle external to it, whereas the family is part of a larger totality that is well suited to govern it. What is more, the complementarity imagined by Comte is illusory: it amounts to subordinating woman to man. Yet the fact remains that perfect equality in a couple is a source of instability, and inevitably has the effect of multiplying the number of marriage counselors and other psychotherapists, holders of a sort of spiritual power whose contours are indistinct. Plainly, too, love ("mutual affection") cannot be the foundation of the family, because the family cannot be reduced to a husband and wife and their *desire* to have offspring.[12] Comte raises a problem that modern societies have by no means yet fully resolved.

Rituals of Transmission and Male Violence

Throughout this work, we have seen that giving death—as the idea of taking a life can also be expressed in French—under socially and ritually determined conditions is a male responsibility in most societies, the equivalent of the female responsibility of giving life by means of childbirth. This is particularly true in the case of rites of initiation. In bringing forth daughters, women transmit reproductive power to them; in causing novices to be "reborn," men transmit to them the power of ritually administering death. Additionally, it is in making them submit first to violence that men transmit to their sons the power of using violence, so much so that to be initiated is ipso facto to be able to initiate other novices in violence. Does this mean that we are dealing here with a circular relation, which perpetuates itself indefinitely but which in principle one could get out from, or at least not enter into? Or would it be more accurate to say that a certain form of violence is the inevitable counterpart of any effective transmission of knowledge and technology—the price to be paid for any lasting appropriation of values and norms? In other words, must not the transmission and reproduction of culture necessarily include learning how to ritualize human violence, which is liable to have lethal consequences if it cannot be contained? This, it will be recalled, is what the story of Abraham in Besançon's interpretation suggests. I have adopted this reading myself, while at the same time trying to bring out its dark side, which Besançon tends to gloss over. Without pretending to settle these difficult questions once and for all, I believe it will be illuminating to consider three very different examples that nonetheless have enough in common to make one suspect that they are of something more than passing interest, at least insofar as they involve aspects of human behavior that seem to be found in all societies.

Quranic Education, or the Rule of the Teacher

A very faithful evocation of the religious education of young Muslim boys is to be found in the opening chapters of Cheikh Hamidou Kane's fine memoir, *Ambiguous Adventure*, first published in French in 1961 and still in print today. Kane describes not only his own personal experience but also that of many of his coreligionists in the region of Fouta on the Senegal River, and, more generally, of the Islamic populations of Senegal and Mauritania.

The traditional Quranic system of apprenticeship exhibits all the features of a rite of initiation. When a boy reaches the age of seven years, his parents entrust him to the care of a teacher (*Thierno*). Once the teacher has accepted the child as a pupil, he takes total possession of him—"body and soul" (Kane [1961] 1963, 12)—until his training is complete. For several years, the pupil lives under the teacher's exclusive and absolute authority; together with his fellow pupils, he must take up residence with the teacher and follow his austere way of life. He is given very little to eat. Whether his family is rich or poor, he is sent out each morning to beg for his food, usually coming back with unappetizing and sometimes putrid leftovers from meals of the day before. The rest of the day is taken up learning the Quran under very trying conditions. The pupil must learn to read and write the holy scripture on tablets, and most important of all, he must memorize it perfectly. He must be able to recite it by heart, to chant fluently without the least error or flaw, and this in its original version, which is to say classical Arabic—an idiom that is wholly foreign to the blacks of Fouta, and that even for the Arabic-speaking Moors of the region contains all the mystery of a language both sacred and secret.

Apprenticeship is therefore all the more difficult as the pupil cannot look to the meaning of the Quranic text for guidance, and all the more painful as distorting the divine word is a sacrilege, subject to corporal punishments administered with unrelenting severity. The first pages of *Ambiguous Adventure* testify to the harshness with which the pupil is reprimanded for the slightest lapse: ears pinched until they bleed, burns inflicted with blazing faggots, and, from time to time, extreme physical brutality: "One day, in the throes of a mad rage, the teacher had thrown him to the ground and had furiously trampled on him, as certain wild beasts do to their prey" (ibid., 7).

There can be no doubt, however, that instruction of this kind achieved its purpose. When the child returns to his family, he will be able—and proud of being able—to chant sacred scripture for an entire night in honor of his family. Despite the cruel abuse he has endured, he will continue to regard his teacher with respect and affection, and be grateful to him for having led him to the end of a long and difficult journey. Far from being alienated from religious tradition, he will regard the Quran with the veneration that is required if he is to succeed later in fully absorbing its significance through translation and commentary, one day perhaps becoming a teacher of the holy writ in his turn.

By its very nature, this sort of apprenticeship leaves no place for initiative on the part of the pupil, who has no other guide than the voice of the teacher in order to correctly reproduce the sacred verses. In this respect one might say that it is mimetic in the strictest sense, since reciting the Quran and faithfully repeating the words uttered by the teacher are one and the same thing. Regardless of a boy's native talent, this form of mimeticism carries with it no risk of rivalry. In repeating the text word for word in response to the teacher's dictation, it is not really the words of the teacher himself that the pupil reproduces, but words that the teacher received and learned to say from another teacher, who received and learned to say them from yet another, and so on—words constituting something impersonal, something of unsurpassable value, that can be passed down from generation to generation.

Cheikh Hamidou Kane describes this kind of transcendence very well. Because sacred tradition is external to both teacher and pupil, far from arousing feelings of rivalry or rebellion it leads to harmony and faithful obedience. "This sentence—which he did not understand, for which he was suffering martyrdom—he loved for its mystery and its somber beauty. This word was not like other words. It was a word which demanded suffering, it was a word come from God, it was a miracle, it was as God Himself had uttered it. The teacher was right. The Word which comes from God must be spoken exactly as it has pleased Him to fashion it. Whoever defaces it deserves to die" (Kane [1961] 1963, 4).

One has the impression, Girard remarks, "that if it were possible some cultures would dispense with individual choice altogether and so entirely eliminate the possibility of mimetic rivalry" (Girard [1978] 1987, 291). The Quranic school aims at such an ideal in its way, only by prohibiting individual choice while permitting mimeticism—and so bringing about the convergence that the sacred text makes possible. Nevertheless it does not rule out violence altogether, since it permits the teacher to resort to corporal punishment. But it does not grant him a purely discretionary power over the pupil; the teacher's authority, and indeed the very violence he practices, are placed in the service of a transcendent Word that both renders them legitimate and assigns limits to them. "In contemporary society," Girard continues,

> the exact opposite increasingly takes place. No more taboos forbid one person to take what is reserved for another, and no more initiation rites prepare individuals in common, for the necessary trials of life. Modern education does not warn the child that the same type of imitative behaviour will be applauded and encouraged on one occasion, and discouraged on another, or that there is no way of telling what will happen by simply paying attention to the models themselves or to the objects to which desire is directed. Instead, modern education thinks it is able to resolve every problem by glorifying the natural spontaneity of desire, which is a purely mythological notion. (291)

This is true of both secular and religious instruction in the West: not only the new "catechism" of post-conciliar Catholicism but also the cult of individual potential and fulfillment promoted by the modern "science" of education are diametrically opposed to the teaching of the Quran, not least in placing the greatest emphasis on the personal interests of students and the spontaneity of their motivations. However liberating this pedagogy is imagined to be, it is bound up with a crisis of values in both school and church, whose representatives no longer know to which transcendent order they ought to pledge their allegiance. "Tortured by our deficiency," Lévi-Strauss observed, "we anxiously await the coming of the creative man. And since we cannot glimpse him anywhere, in despair we turn to our children" (Lévi-Strauss [1983] 1985, 278). One may well fear that in freeing pupils from the burden of tradition, the reigning orthodoxy risks imposing on them a still heavier yoke by delivering them to the anxiety of the void and the agonies of mimetic desire.

The School of Painting of the Tin Dama and the Ritualization of Conflict

My second example concerns the Tin Dama, a matrilineal people of New Guinea whose livelihood depends chiefly on fishing, supplemented by hunting and horticulture, and among whom the mastery of painting is as prized as knowledge of the Quran among Muslim peoples. Indeed, the Tin Dama consider the painter to be the "teacher of the oral interpretation of tradition." He is not merely an artist in the usual sense of the term. Not only does he protect and preserve the pictorial traditions of his community, which he must also know how to enrich through borrowings and judicious innovation, he plays an essential role in the collective life of the Tin Dama.

All of our information about the Tin Dama comes from three lectures given by the ethnographer François Lupu, in different places and under different circumstances, on 7 May 1986, 13 February 1987, and 11 February 1991 (unfortunately no published version exists). The function of painting in their culture rests on a conception of life that may be compared to Stoic philosophy in view of the importance accorded to the idea of tension and the belief that a structural correspondence obtains between macrocosm and microcosm:

> For them, the world, the body, and society are organized on the same model. More exactly, the body is the referential model of everything that can exist (so that, for example, the different parts of the village are designated by the names of different organs); the human body is conceived of as something essentially precarious, a federation of organs that are held together through the will of the "subject" to be a properly human being; should this will weaken, should this federative tension diminish for one

reason or another, then the body begins to disintegrate . . . ; the whole conception of human life and of social life among the Tin Dama turns around this notion of voluntary tension opposed to a world of precarious aggregates. (Lupu, manuscript of 13 February 1987 lecture shared privately with the author)

On this view, the activity of the painter is similar in a sense to the "hegemonic" part of the soul in Stoic doctrine: it ensures the cohesiveness of Tin Dama society and culture in something like the way that a central authority in the Stoic conception is responsible for the unity of the human body.

It should be noted first of all that in the egalitarian and undifferentiated society of the Tin Dama—a society without hierarchy or professional specialization in which each person, according to his needs, catches fish, tends his garden, builds his pirogue, and so on—the painter is alone in having a specific activity, what we would think of as a trade. He lives exclusively from his paintings, which he sells to the other villagers; he is also the only member of the community who manages to accumulate a surplus of wealth (in the form of shells, services, modern money, and so on). And yet Lupu maintains that this way of describing his situation, solely in economic terms, is inadequate. The division of labor in a society is ritual in origin, as Hocart showed, and here we have another proof of it: if one examines the conditions under which the painter's services are sought and how his works are appreciated, it will be seen that he is the central figure of all the great rituals that punctuate the collective and individual life of the adult population.

The most highly esteemed public commission that can be entrusted to a painter involves the external decoration of the men's house, a very large building some forty meters long, twenty wide, and fifteen high that must be rebuilt every four or five years. It takes the form of an immense painting that depicts the blazon and the history of the clans residing in this imposing edifice. Other assignments are privately negotiated, the result of very lively competition among the male villagers, who seek to collect the greatest possible number of pieces of painted tree bark, which they hang from the roof of the men's house above the place they occupy in it. It is probable that these bark paintings are considered to be not only objects of prestige, or works of art in our sense of the term, but also, more importantly, life-giving totems that permit the men to maintain within themselves a vital tension that must always be preserved, on pain of death; for even if the birth of a human being marks the victorious outcome of a merciless intrauterine struggle, survival beyond birth remains forever uncertain, and ritual precautions against fatal misfortune need to be taken as long as one lives.

The value of such works is determined with reference to three criteria. First, a work fetches a higher price the more bitterly it is argued over, by virtue of the fact that it lends itself to a variety of interpretations. On showing the Tin Dama a sample of paintings from the Western tradition, Lupu discovered that everything done prior to the twentieth century seemed to them insignificant. *Mona Lisa* is obviously the picture of a woman and nothing else. Beginning with Miró, however, Western painting becomes more interesting to the extent that it is capable of provoking rival and complementary interpretations, and in this way reuniting the antagonistic forces of attraction and repulsion. Thus a picture by Miró represents at once a myth of origin and a map of the village; another by Pollock arouses the same contrasting emotions as the particularly treacherous zone (*iule*) that lies between the Tin Dama and their neighbors, and so on. In short, if no more than one interpretation is possible, a work is worthless ("unspeakable"); but if it inspires endless debate, opposing equally plausible interpretations, it is excellent. The main thing is the quality of the discussion. There is no attempt to arrive at a consensus, at a uniquely correct judgment; what matters is the richness of the debate itself, and generally it is only the weariness of the participants, not the reaching of any agreement among them, that puts an end to the conflict of opinions. Whether it is a question of acquiring works or of evaluating them, the painter's productions have the effect of polarizing, channeling, and ritualizing the rivalries that set people against one another, and so of reducing the threat of violence.

Next, the value of a work is a function of the intensity of the tensions that its various motifs portray. The most prized work will therefore be a sort of microcosm, a dynamic reflection of the whole of Tin Dama culture. A bark painting, for example, will command a high price if it represents at once the two cerebral hemispheres and the fetus and the placenta in the mother's womb, as well as two groups of men facing each other—and a still higher price if it expressively renders the fratricidal conflict in which the placenta and the fetus (which the Tin Dama see as twins) engage prior to birth, as well as the ritual struggle between two rival groups that precedes the founding of a new unit within the village.

Finally, the value of a work depends on the artist's talent in locating new motifs outside his village, or even his society, and then, having obtained permission to use them, on his ability to find a place for them in the traditional corpus of pictorial themes—all of which makes the artist a high-ranking diplomat and economic ambassador to neighboring peoples. Among the Tin Dama, in other words, the painter is not only a specialized producer; he is also a creator of social bonds and a guardian of cultural identity, someone who brings people together, individuals and groups alike, by directing and channeling their conflicts into peaceable outlets. Through his works of art, he maintains the living unity of his culture by guaranteeing the isomorphic representation of the human body, society, and the universe.

Considering the significance of the painter's function, it will now be clear why the Tin Dama attach such importance to the training his vocation requires. To see one's child become a painter is every parent's fondest hope. This qualification can only be obtained by attending an art school, which is to say by being accepted to study with an acknowledged master. Sixty to seventy percent of the boys in the village apply, but admission is very selective. Instruction is given in complete silence, for it is believed that a teacher who speaks loses the ability to paint. In the three or four years of apprenticeship, not a single word is exchanged between teacher and pupil during all the many hours devoted to painting. Learning is therefore entirely mimetic. The teacher breaks down his strokes into a series of movements. The pupils look not at the work itself, but at the teacher's body, and in this way come to acquire a command of basic physical techniques, beginning with breathing. Whenever the teacher thinks it opportune, he repeats a movement in excruciatingly slow motion—so slow that it actually produces a spasmodic trembling of the arm. It is by means of such painstaking repetition that every aspect of his mastery is passed on, and the very spirit of painting itself communicated to his pupils.

Now and then, while imitating the movements of the teacher, a pupil may fall into a trance, a cataleptic state that is taken to be a favorable sign for the rest of his studies, which is to say the course of his initiation. The pupil is then made to undergo a trial. Hiding himself in a corner of the village, he paints a piece of bark from a sago palm and then deposits it somewhere along the route taken every day by the painter. If the painter judges it to be a poor piece of work, he simply steps on it: he has seen nothing, heard nothing. Even in the case of repeated failure he does not sever relations with the pupil. He neither summons him nor sends him away; instead the parents come and withdraw their child from his class. The end of instruction is no less ritualized in the event of success, though here it is marked by the sudden separation of teacher and pupil. The teacher vehemently complains of having been rewarded for his efforts with an ungrateful rival: he browbeats him, spits on him, shoves him into the water or the mud. The pupil, for his part, having become his own master,[13] maligns his old teacher and refuses to have anything to do with him; it is only much later that he will speak of him with pride and gratitude.

It is well known how Girard describes the spontaneous and almost irrepressible process that gradually alters the master-disciple relationship by transforming the model into a rival, which is to say by converting a hierarchical relation into a symmetrical relation:

> The master is delighted to see more and more disciples around him, and delighted to see that he is being taken as a model. Yet if the imitation is too perfect, and the imitator threatens to surpass the model, the master will completely change his attitude and begin to display jealousy, mistrust and hostility. He will be tempted to do everything he can to discredit and discourage his disciple.
>
> The disciple can only be blamed for being the best of all disciples. . . . He does not recognize the signs of rivalry in the behaviour of the model. It is all the more difficult for the disciple to do so because the model tries very hard to reinforce this blindness. The model tries his best to hide the real reasons for his hostility. (Girard [1978] 1987, 290)

In effect, then, the Tin Dama try to contain this potential conflict between master and disciple by ritualizing it. The method is at once preventive and curative; one does not expect evil to show its face, but one takes precautions to neutralize its effects in case it does, treating the disease by prescribing the symptom, as it were. To control conflict, one deliberately raises it to its highest point in a public form that is at once spectacular and cathartic.

The Shaman's Initiation, or the Killing of the Teacher

My third example is taken from the Pawnee Indians of North America. Here we find the theme of rivalry between a venerable master of the healing arts and a potential successor, only this time in the form of a myth:

> An ignorant young boy becomes aware that he possesses magical powers that enable him to cure the sick. Jealous of the boy's increasing reputation, an old medicine man of established position visits him on several different occasions, accompanied by his wife. Enraged because he obtains no secret in exchange for his own teachings, the medicine man offers the boy a pipe filled with magical herbs. Thus bewitched, the boy discovers that he is pregnant. Full of shame, he leaves his village and seeks death among wild animals. The animals, moved to pity by his misfortune, decide to cure him. They extract the fetus from his body. They teach him their magical powers, by means of which the boy, on returning to his home, kills the evil medicine man and becomes himself a famous and respected healer. (Lévi-Strauss [1958a] 1963, 234)

This myth naturally lends itself to a Girardian interpretation as well, for it describes a situation of crisis and its violent resolution by the murder of the old shaman, now reviled as a wicked sorcerer. Using the language of Lévi-Strauss, one might describe this crisis as a confusion of culture and nature: shamanism, a cultural power requiring a period of apprenticeship, is initially presented as a natural power capable of developing spontaneously with age, like the capacity to produce children.

Nevertheless we are not dealing here merely with a blurring of categories, but rather, in miniature, with a sacrificial crisis in Girard's sense, which is to say a social crisis that undermines existing institutions and inverts the differences that make up a culture: the difference between generations, first of all, since the boy not only avoids apprenticeship to a master but inspires a feeling of jealousy in the old medicine man, who has gone to visit him as though he himself wished to become a disciple; next, the difference between sexes, since the boy becomes pregnant; finally, the difference between species, since responsibility for his education is ultimately assumed by animals and not by human beings. Here again the crisis is resolved by means of a founding murder. By permitting the boy to become a respected shaman in his turn, the killing of the emissary sorcerer (as he might be styled in Girardian terms) restores the cultural order and assures the survival of the society.

Not only does this myth confirm the implication of the preceding examples, it deepens our sense that the rupture of the master-disciple relationship is inevitable. In following a path that would seem to make it possible for him to avoid conflict, the aspiring shaman instead arouses the enmity of the old medicine man and sets in motion a process of escalation that intensifies the conflict to its highest degree. As with the priesthood of Nemi, limned by Ovid and commented on by Frazer, access to the office can only be attained through the murder of the incumbent.

The Failure of the Relationship

For want of a conclusion, I should like to complete these three ethnographic examples with a tale told in a work of modern fiction, "The Rose of Paracelsus," a very short piece by Jorge Luis Borges ([1983] 1998) that has both the restraint and the power of a great myth. It describes the crisis of a pedagogical relationship, the moment when the encounter between master and disciple, while still bearing the marks of courtesy and respect, gives way to hostile and ultimately irreversible confrontation.

The athanor is extinguished; the alembics are covered with dust. Paracelsus, wearied by age, asks a vague and indeterminate God, in whom he himself seems not to believe, to send him a disciple. A young man knocks at the door and offers him all his gold, declaring his desire to learn from Paracelsus, but he sets one condition. "'You are famed,' the young man says, 'for being able to burn a rose to ashes and make it emerge again, by the magic of your art. Let me witness that prodigy. I ask that of you, and in return I will offer up my entire life.'"

The two men size each other up. They argue. In the end, no master-disciple relationship has come into being—the longed-for passing of the baton does not take place. But was there still a baton to be passed? Could anything have overcome the sterile rivalry that was there from the beginning, between the fierce determination of a potential disciple who tests the master with relentless obstinacy and the imperturbable serenity of a master resolved to overrule the disciple's arrogance?

In a last gesture of despair and defiance, the young man throws the rose he held in his hand into the hearth. Paracelsus watches as the flower is consumed by the flames, saying nothing, doing nothing. He remains unmoved, as though robbed of his powers by the destruction taking place before his very eyes; the young man takes back his gold coins and goes away, filled with shame and disappointment. The failure is mutual and irremediable: for the young visitor, whose illusions have been dispelled once and for all; for Paracelsus, who will never have a disciple.

After the young man's departure, the old alchemist takes a few of the ashes in his hand, whispers a single word, and the rose reappears. Is the scene real or imagined? It hardly matters. For Paracelsus will die without a successor. His art, unable to be reborn in a disciple, will not survive him. Or will it one day reappear somewhere else?

Notes

Chapter 1. Freud and the Oedipus Legend

1. "It should not be forgotten," he writes in the middle of a note in *Totem and Taboo*, "that primitive races are not young races but are in fact as old as civilized races. There is no reason to suppose that, for the benefit of our information, they have retained their original ideas and institutions undeveloped and undistorted" (Freud [1913] 1955, 13:102 n. 1).

2. Freud, in private, was still more explicit. While he was writing *Totem and Taboo*, he wrote to Sándor Ferenczi: "The work connected with *Totem* is really useless. I read fat books that are devoid of any true interest, for I already know the conclusions. I trust my instincts." Quoted by Maurice Godelier [2004] 2011, 536).

3. See "Psycho-Analysis and Anthropology," paper delivered at a meeting of the Royal Anthropological Institute, 19 February 1924 (Jones 1951, 114–44).

4. See "Mother-Right and the Sexual Ignorance of Savages," paper delivered at a meeting of the British Psychoanalytical Society, 19 November 1924 (Jones 1951, 145–73).

5. On the works of these authors, see the old—but, to my way of thinking, still unsurpassed—study by Mikel Dufrenne (1953).

6. This point has been emphasized by the so-called Palo Alto school in connection with the notion of a "secondary gain" associated with illness. "On the whole, classical psychoanalysis remained primarily a theory of intrapsychic processes, so even where interaction with outside forces was evident, it was considered secondary" (Watzlawick, Beavin, and Jackson 1967, 28). At most, and by virtue of the ever greater place assigned by the theory to the notion of fantasy, the Freudian subject, paradoxically, is a world closed in upon itself, as it were, having neither a cultural nor even an interrelational component. Its internal relations wholly determine its external relations. On the relationship between the mental and the social, see the fine analysis of Roger Bastide ([1950]

1972), who distinguishes in Freud a "social psychology" and a "psychological sociology," and compares psychoanalysis to Durkheimian sociology, Marxism, and structural anthropology.

7. See chapter 7 in Lévi-Strauss [1949c] 1969, especially 93–94 and 96–97.

8. It is well known that to each basic fantasy (primal scene, seduction, castration) Freud assigns a theory of infantile sexuality that is presented as a myth of origin: the origin of children, for the fantasy of the primal scene; of sexuality, for the fantasy of seduction; of the difference between the sexes, for the fantasy of castration. The supposed universality of these individual myths is taken to explain not only the features common to many dreams and nightmares, but also the recurrent themes of many collective myths.

9. "The bypassing of parental cannibalistic impulses in psychoanalytic literature suggests the presence of massive resistances against this insight—even more massive, perhaps, than those that account for the fact that the child's Oedipus complex was discovered long before the so-called *counteroedipal* complex of the parents, and this *despite* the fact that one of Freud's first discoveries was the role of (real or imaginary) parental seduction" (Devereux [1970b] 1980, 136; emphasis in the original). This passage follows a note at the bottom of the previous page in the French edition that nonetheless attributes to Freud an "unerring sureness of touch and acuity of observation."

10. At one point in this lecture, which seems to border on self-parody, Freud justifies the greater modesty generally ascribed to women by postulating a desire to mask the defectiveness of their sex organ (what he calls "concealment of genital deficiency"). Although women have played a marginal role in the technological progress and the great discoveries that mark the history of civilization, he adds, their concern to hide the lack of a penis suggests that the invention of plaiting and weaving may have been due to them. "Nature herself would seem to have given the model which this achievement imitates by causing the growth at maturity of the pubic hair that conceals the genitals. The step that remained to be taken lay in making the threads adhere to one another, while on the body they stick into the skin and are only matted together" (Freud [1932] 1964, 22:132).

11. One finds many examples, taken from the most diverse civilizations and eras, in a work by Françoise Héritier (1996) that is almost entirely devoted to this question. I shall consider the importance and limits of her work in a later chapter.

12. See Evelyn Reed (1975), for example; also Nancy Jay (1992) and Marika Moisseeff (1987, 2000).

Chapter 2. Procreation and Headhunting: Fatherhood among the Marind

1. Breton's article rests on two sources: a very thick monograph by Jan van Baal devoted to the Marind-anim, published in 1966, and Breton's own more recent observations among the Wodani, another people of New Guinea. Shell money is supposed to play the same role among the Wodani as trophy heads among the Marind. Readers may easily satisfy themselves that the much less complex state of affairs observed among the Wodani corroborates my analysis of the ethnography of the Marind.

2. Here, of course, I am alluding to the title of Cai Hua's famous monograph about the Na people of China, *Une société sans père ni mari*, originally published in 1997. Such a society is not only possible and viable, but revelatory. In reducing its system of kinship to uterine relations alone, it presents us with a naked state, as it were; that is—and this is a crucial point, to which I shall return in a later chapter—with *the basis of the entire system of kinship*, and not one possible form among all others. Even an author as determined as Laurent Barry to exhaustively survey all conceivable structures and to show, for example, the symmetry obtaining between the "agnatic"

principle of the system found elsewhere in China and the "uterine" principle of the Na system and other societies practicing so-called Arab marriage, finds himself obliged to admit that, although "logically possible," a system assuming "an absolute negation of the mother-child link" is "apparently untenable sociologically" (Barry 2008, 820 n. 18). The fact remains that every society contrives to incorporate the primordial and irreducible matrilineal nucleus in a larger network, or otherwise to compensate by means of other relationships. Even among the Na, the aristocracy marries in the "classic" manner, as Emmanuel Todd notes (2011, 128–29), marked not only by the cohabitation of spouses but also by patrilocal residence.

3. While the men were occupied decapitating their victims, the women who accompanied them on these expeditions "seized whatever children they could find, sparing them and then raising them normally" (Breton 1999, 84). This female behavior plainly reveals the logic at work in the Marind system, which pushes to its farthest possible extent, as much on the real as on the symbolic plane, the substitution of ritual predation, organized by men, for the natural ability to give birth with which women are endowed. But it also calls attention to the unavoidable limits of the system. Even if men were to totally deprive the women of their community of the fruit of their wombs, they would still have to accept children borne by other women in order to assure the survival of their group. The Sobra myth is a way of recognizing this undeniable truth without actually stating it. More generally, the whole cosmology of the Marind shows the necessity of collaboration between a male principle and a female principle if human beings are to be brought into the world (see 90–91). Another significant detail points in the same direction. Male rites of initiation among the Marind, like those of other peoples whom I will discuss later, include a quite singular gift: to become fertile, the new generation must receive the sperm of its elders. Tellingly, however, "the novices were sodomized by the brother of their mother" (87). In other words, whereas the name, the spiritual (or "symbolic") principle, is given to a child by the paternal clan, sperm, the vital principle, is given to it by the maternal clan, and more precisely by the male relative closest to the mother. It is indeed a man who transmits life to it, but he belongs to the maternal line—a new way of expressing both the male desire to exert complete and exclusive control over procreation and the impossibility of doing this.

4. In developing his theoretical conclusions (see the very densely argued section in Breton 1999, 103–11), Breton expressly appeals to Durkheim. I am unable to comment here on this important aspect of his work, which merits an extended discussion.

5. In the Marind myth of origin, Breton says, "castration occurs in the context of the search for an object. It therefore does not constitute the central motif, which has to do instead with the symbolized loss of the object, with its original absence. Castration appears as the narrative consequence of a lack, not as its precondition; it is the illustration of it, but certainly not its explanatory principle. One must not confuse the penis, which may be cut off at any time, and the object that by definition is *lacking*, and in pursuit of which the myth sets out, believing that it can find [the object] *elsewhere*, in an *other*—hence its unreality. The masculine and paternal 'essence,' sought and then given, is not a natural organ, a positive object, but *the sign of an absence that must be transmitted*. It is a purely symbolic aspect whose resemblance to the notion of a 'name true,' designated among the Marind by the female genital organs, cannot be ignored. [Breton translates the Marind term *pa-igiz* by the French phrase "nom vrai," a deliberate inversion of the usual form "vrai nom" (or "nom véritable") translated in English by "true name."—Trans.] Obscured by the reification of the penis, and of the mythological substitutes that are forever being severed, is a dread of the apparently neutered genitalia of the woman. This is why an essential distinction can be made between the penis and the phallus—which designates something that is conspicuous by its absence, that is erected in place of a void, but that every man must give proof of possessing if he wishes to be a father. According to the Marind, man is defined by a *missing part*. This part can

complete the subject, if such a thing is possible, only on the condition that its purely symbolic character is doubly attested: it cannot be kept to oneself, it must be transmitted" (Breton 1999, 92; emphasis in the original).

6. It is undeniable that the flow of menstrual blood gives the female genitalia the aspect of a wound, and that this analogy has been not only perceived, but held to be significant since time immemorial. André Leroi-Gourhan notes that in prehistoric cave paintings one finds a sign that "may be identified either as a vulva or as a wound." More generally, the signs for female and for wound seem to have been, he says, "interchangeable symbols" (Leroi-Gourhan [1964] 1976, 105). But that does not suffice to justify the Freudian thesis. What I shall call in a later chapter "Testart's law" seems to me to be much better suited to illuminating the symbolic value of this analogy.

7. The Lacanian version of the phallic theory should not be rejected out of hand. The idea of an original (or inherent) lack, of an initial incompleteness that neither the child, in the case of the woman, nor its symbolic substitutes, in the case of the man, manage to fill, could be, after all, an ultimate reality of human affairs. It would provide an explanation for what Girard calls "metaphysical desire" (see Girard [1961] 1966), of which he gives many examples, and what is otherwise known as a quest, which may or may not be "mimetic," but which is never satisfied and forever renewed (one thinks of Pascal's description in *Pensées* [1963, frag. 425, pp. 518–20], and the Grimms' tale "The Fisherman and His Wife," a particularly striking example). One nevertheless expects an anthropologist to begin by identifying those fundamental aspects of human nature that are most directly accessible to observation, especially when, as in this case, their reality and their importance have not yet been either clearly recognized or well established. One can always appeal to a "scientific" theory of the lack later on, should the need make itself felt. But it will still be necessary to satisfy oneself first that this theory does in fact express a fundamental truth of Pascal's negative "theology," rather than some variant of it. I shall have occasion in the course of the present work to argue on behalf of some of Lacan's hypotheses.

8. Among the Marind, the father has to give a "head name" to each one of his children, without regard for sex [see Breton 1999, p. 85]. Without this name, Breton tells us, the child would be incomplete. But even though this is implicit, every analysis that has been made of the transmission of names privileges the male line of descent. Since the assignment of a name is a male monopoly, only a male child is able himself to give a name in return for the one that he has received. Though it is not expressly recognized, the fact that a woman gives life to children excuses her from having to give them names. The subject who would be incomplete without a name to give and transmit is indeed the male subject.

9. By "Lacanian theory" I mean here the few rudiments of this theory that Breton makes use of in his article and that he believes to be sufficiently well known to his readers to relieve him of any obligation to identify specific sources, or even once to mention Lacan's name.

10. In Lacan's own writings, if I am not mistaken, the mother-child relationship belongs to the realm of the imaginary, whereas the father-child relationship comes under the head of the symbolic. But women themselves, as far as I am aware, are not defined by their status as potential mothers. Breton, for his part, is silent on this point. One of Lacan's disciples, discussing "formulas of sexuation" in a work on the status of the father that appeared some years before, advances the following proposition: "We well know that, for every man, primary castration is the basic rule, the foundation: man is based on exactly this renunciation, of ever having a child in his belly" (This 1980, 273). This definition of castration, though it is couched in Freudian language, puts things right again; indeed, it could be approved by the Marind themselves, except that their ritual is not meant to acquiesce in the face of an impossibility, the presence of a child in a man's belly, but to make up for it.

11. One is put in mind of the anecdote Lévi-Strauss tells about Simone de Beauvoir, whom he had invited to have lunch at his apartment: "I remember it very well—my son had just been born—she looked at the crib with such revulsion! A baby was not the thing to show her!" (Lévi-Strauss and Éribon [1988] 1991, 48).

12. Feminists who do not repudiate the condition of motherhood sometimes interpret this ambition as a renewed male attempt to exercise complete control over procreation and to dispossess women of their unique power once and for all.

Chapter 3. The Guardians of Dogma: Jones, Malinowski, and the Maternal Uncle

1. This attitude can still be found in an article published much later by Bernard Pulman about the psychoanalytically inspired work of the British anthropologist W.H.R. Rivers. While acknowledging that relations between anthropology and psychoanalysis were, from the very beginning, characterized by "mutual incomprehension and mistrust" (Pulman 1986, 135), he imputes responsibility for this state of affairs to Rivers. Furthermore, what Pulman most revealingly calls Rivers's "reactions to the Freudian text" (135) is due, he says, to a series of grave misunderstandings concerning the nature of sexuality and, not least, to Rivers's own puritanism. None of Rivers's criticisms is accepted as legitimate. The "Freudian text" seems to be untouchable, not to say sacred. Nothing can be subtracted from it, or, it would appear, added to it.

2. Jones cites a newspaper of the day that, inveighing against the right of women to vote, assumes their inferiority as a sex to be demonstrated by the fact that the salt content of their blood is lower than that of men (see Jones 1951, 104–5). Underlying this result of modern science (the calculation of the relative proportions of sodium chloride is attributed to two French savants) there is, he says, the old idea that salt represents "the male, active, fertilizing principle." True enough. But he leaves it at that, whereas one would have expected a psychoanalyst to try to trace the sources of the recurrent concern that men seem to have of justifying their various prerogatives by arguments of this sort. Indeed, like the newspaper whose editorial opinion he reports, as well as ordinary mortals (psychoanalysts and anthropologists included), Jones reasons implicitly as though there were no alternative to the supposed inferiority of women than equality of the sexes—whereas obviously there is a third possibility, the innate superiority of women.

   On this point, the great classical thinkers have proved to be shrewder judges. Thus Hobbes, in seeking to justify paternal authority, begins by recognizing that in a state of nature, which is to say in the absence of established rules, "a *new-born child* is in the power of his *mother* before anyone else, so that she can raise him or expose him at her own discretion and by her own right" (Hobbes [1642] 1998, 2.9.2, p. 108; emphasis in the original). Although Rousseau does not explicitly endorse this thesis, the way in which he justifies the primacy of the father over the mother in the family is no less interesting. As in all groups composed of an even number of members, there must be, he says, in the family, a preponderant voice in order for it to be possible to reach a decision in case of disagreement: "However slight the incapacitations peculiar to the wife are thought to be, since they are always an inactive period for her, this is sufficient reason to exclude her from primacy, because when the balance is perfectly equal, the smallest thing is enough to tip it. Furthermore, the Husband should oversee his wife's conduct, because it is important to him that the children he is forced to recognize do not belong to anyone other than himself. The wife, who has no such thing to fear, does not have the same right over her husband" (Rousseau [1760] 1994, 90). The two arguments, each of which depends on the ability of women to give birth, may seem at first sight to reinforce each other. On closer examination, however, they can be seen to point in opposite directions. For while it may be admitted that during menstrual periods women are apt to find themselves in a position of relative weakness, to the extent that they are the primary guardians of children it is in fact they who, at the beginning, have an advantage over men. The husband's authority compensates for this initial disequilibrium. More generally, it may therefore be conjectured that if men have everywhere reserved for themselves a monopoly on the great political, military, and ritual functions, it is not in order to strengthen a supposed original superiority but rather to correct an asymmetry inherent in the difference between the sexes, by compensating through cultural prerogatives for the privilege that is naturally granted to women of bringing children into the world. This is what the rituals of the Marind suggest. It is intriguing to see the same idea subsequently reappear, if only in a minor way, in the work of the great Western political theorists.

3. In the modern American and British family, Malinowski notes, "the father is in process of losing his patriarchal position. . . . Psycho-analysis cannot hope, I think, to preserve its 'Oedipus complex' for future generations, who will know only a weak and henpecked father. For him the children will feel indulgent pity rather than hatred and fear!" (Malinowski 1927, 27).

4. The few well-documented cases available to us seem to show the accidental or exceptional character of these unions, generally held to be incestuous (for an overview, see Godelier [2004] 2011, 319–89). Among the Na of China, where there is neither marriage nor paternity, only private, and very free, sexual relations between members of distinct matrilineal groups, a very strict taboo is observed within each uterine group. Women may receive lovers only from other groups, and men may only visit mistresses belonging to groups distinct from their own. No union therefore is possible between a mother and son or between a brother and sister. It can only happen that a girl has relations with her father. In Persia, it is chiefly in the royal family that one finds marriages in the closest degree, not only between brother and sister but also between father and daughter, and even mother and son. To interpret this custom, it must be kept in mind that the king—as theorists of the sacred monarchy have shown, beginning with Frazer—is always a figure outside the system. He is not part of the social order, either at the top or the bottom; instead he moves back and forth between these two complementary positions, whose close association has been firmly established by René Girard (see [1972b] 1977, 89–118). The king is first and foremost a transgressor, and by virtue of this, a potential scapegoat. The Oedipal crimes of parricide and incest are almost always imputed to him, and their symbolic enactment is often part of an enthronement ritual (see Heusch 1958 [reprinted in Heusch 1987]).

   But the king is also a god, not only a higher being but also a virtually self-sufficient being. In this regard, incestuous relations, which place him outside the circle of exchange, are patently a sign of transcendence. The marriages of Persian kings reproduced the creative acts of the world and of humanity, which, according to Zoroastrian cosmology, issued from the three most intimate unions imaginable, between father and daughter, mother and son, and twins. Once the king had been endowed with divine attributes, his marriage could serve as a model for the nobility and high-ranking dignitaries. Yet it is unlikely to have spread throughout the larger population (on this point see the corroborative remarks of Godelier [(2004) 2011, 463], who, while acknowledging that brother-sister marriage was common, emphasizes its sacred character and the particular conditions of its celebration; and of François Héran [2009, 236], who notes the late character of the sources alleged to favor broad diffusion). My own feeling is that the same thing may be said with regard to the Egyptian custom of brother-sister marriage. It used to be supposed that it was reserved for the royal family, but since the middle of the twentieth century, this view has begun to be challenged (see Lévi-Strauss [1949c] 1969, 9–10; more recent research has convinced kinship theorists that this type of marriage was widespread; see Godelier [2004] 2011, 460–62; Héran 2009, 236–37). Nonetheless, as Emmanuel Todd observes, these works are concerned only with the Hellenistic period and therefore can assert nothing more than that it was a late phenomenon. It was with the Greek dynasty of the Ptolemies that this kind of marriage became commonplace in the royal family and in a certain segment of the population. The study of genealogies over a longer term makes it clear that such unions were relatively rare in the time of the ancient pharaohs. The Greek colonists of Egypt seem to have adopted and systematized a vestigial royal custom as a way of affirming their superiority over the native population (see Todd 2011, 582–84).

5. Georges Devereux emphasizes the hostility latent in what is conventionally referred to as the exchange of women. "The central purpose of the marriage rite," he says, "is not the creation of a bond between *husband* and *wife*, nor even an alliance between *two families*; its function is to mask hostility by proclaiming the creation of an alliance, to affirm an understanding so as to avoid a brawl, to substitute peace for war" (Devereux 1965, 237; reprinted in Devereux [1972b] 1978, 197 [emphasis in original]). Devereux illustrates this thesis with reference to the marriage pact between Jacob and Shechem, described in chapter 34 of Genesis. The pact was concluded in principle for the mutual purpose of giving and taking the daughters of their respective tribes, but in fact in order to wash out an insult in blood without having to respect the restrictions of the *lex talionis*, the injured party taking advantage of the occasion to exterminate the whole opposing group. More generally he argues, here with reference to another example, taken from the Mohave of Colorado, that matrimonial ritual is less concerned with creating a bond of marriage than with severing a bond of kinship.

6. The functionalist and structuralist schools discredited once and for all the theory of survival propounded by the older evolutionist school. No matter whether an institution, custom, or cultural trait is of ancient or recent origin, the decisive thing is the place it occupies in the structure of a society and the function it fulfills in it. If at a given moment it survives or subsists, its very vitality is proof that we are not dealing solely with traces or echoes of a bygone age, but with something that is wholly a part of the ambient culture.

Chapter 4. The Atom of Kinship, or the Absent Mother

1. There is no contradiction in principle, of course, between the concepts of structure and morphogenesis. And yet Lévi-Strauss, although he more or less openly acknowledges his debt to the work of Roman Jakobson, never really exploits, not even in his article on the "culinary triangle" (1965), Jakobson's insight that all phonological systems can be derived from a primary triangle (joining the phonemes /a/, /p/, /t/), which constitutes their generative principle.

2. Lévi-Strauss explicitly refers to "the structural conception of the atom developed in modern physics" (Lévi-Strauss [1958a] 1963, 54 n. 49). In spite of the title of his paper ("Structural Analysis in Linguistics and in Anthropology"), and a long preamble concerning what he takes to be the contribution of phonology to the human sciences (see 31–37), the strictly anthropological part of his argument owes absolutely nothing to linguistics. Moreover, Lévi-Strauss himself recognized, a few years later, that it would be futile to search for correlations between the structure of attitudes and the system of phonemes, or the syntax of a language of a given society; and, more generally, "perfectly hopeless" to imagine that formalizations regarding the atom of kinship are in any way transposable to the linguistic level (83).

3. One might say, using a structuralist term, that the proverb cited by Mauss recommends a form of "generalized exchange," only one that occurs between generations and not between lineages, and without any chance of reaching a conclusion except in an ideal sense (since an infinite chain is isomorphic to a circle). In reality, however, one is dealing here not with a logic of exchange, but with one of unilateral gifts and indebtedness.

4. In a few matrilineal societies, with matrilocal or uxorilocal residence, it may nevertheless rightly be said that it is women who give men (see Godelier [2004] 2011, 125–26). But this does not mean that, in systems of matrimonial exchange, men and women occupy interchangeable places.

The case of the Tetum in central Timor, who practice "brother-exchange" between female houses, shows this particularly well. "The houses consider themselves as possessors of a human capital that must not only be preserved, but made to grow. . . . The house as household, as a unit of production, thus expects to receive for every man given, not a man in return, but a woman" (Francillon 1989, 31). Here again, the scarce and coveted goods were women, capable of giving birth. The case of the Minangkabau of Sumatra (see Pak 1993) is somewhat different. Lévi-Strauss (see 2000, 718) reminds his critics (see, for example, Collard 2000) that he had already mentioned it in his magnum opus, noting that the husband in that society is considered to be a "borrowed man" (Lévi-Strauss [1949c] 1969, 116). The society is matrilineal and matrilocal, but because the men are polygamous they appear to belong to no allied house, moving between the residences of their various wives, the house of their sister, and the men's house, which they consider their real home (see Pak 1993, 113 n. 21).

5. Benoist makes a good point, but the reason he gives for recentering the Oedipus complex on the maternal uncle is ambiguous. In describing this complex as "the operator by means of which a break with the naturalistic conception of the family is made, the site where culture is freed from the natural order" (quoted in Green [1977] 1983, 102), he implies that the uncle, *as such*, represents the cultural order more completely than the father. Now, this is inaccurate. In the structuralist model being considered, it is the relation (of giver to taker) between the two men (the future uncle and the future father) that is the source of culture. And in this relation, as we shall see later, it is in fact the uncle, the mother's brother, who, as such, represents natural kinship, and the father, the sister's husband (who owes this aspect of his social status to marriage), cultural kinship. In a second stage, under certain conditions, the uncle can become a canonical representation of "culture," but then only by the very reason of his prior "natural" relationship with his nephew. René Girard, for his part, has much more clearly seen what psychoanalysis and anthropology can learn from matrilineal societies. As against the simplistic image we are apt to form of "primitive" societies, Trobriand society, Girard notes, is more differentiated than ours because it divides between the uncle and the father functions that we assign solely to the father. Unlike the Western father, the uncle in Trobriand society cannot become a rival; throughout his entire life he remains an "external mediator." For the child, the uncle is a model to be imitated, a bearer of culture (see Girard [1972b] 1977, 185–90).

6. Earlier, in note 4 of chapter 3, I indicated how the transgression of these fundamental prohibitions may plausibly be interpreted.

7. Even if genetic tests make it possible today to remove all doubt regarding paternity, the asymmetry pointed out by Martens, or, more precisely, the precedence of the feminine over the masculine, remains undiminished. One could well imagine a society of Amazons having, as some insect societies do, only a few reproductive males. The opposite situation is impossible, however. A male society having only a few women would not be viable.

8. As I have noted elsewhere (see Scubla 1982, 156–57), Robin Fox was one of the first kinship theorists to consider this elementary uterine structure as the true atom of kinship (see Fox 1975a, 30–31).

9. On these types of marriage, see the classic works of Lévi-Strauss ([1949c] 1969) and Fox (1967). Robin Fox's account has the advantage of adopting and reformulating the main part of Lévi-Strauss's theory of marriage in a much broader perspective, and assigning to descent the important place it deserves.

10. If "wife-givers" are in reality children-givers, it is understood that there are only three possible wife-givers: the brother of a woman, her mother, and the woman herself, as Lévi-Strauss says— without, however, giving any explanation for it. Likewise, while marriage is often an exchange of

women performed by men, it is never, strictly speaking, exclusively an exchange of men performed by women (see the example mentioned above at n. 4 of the present chapter).

11. Gillison argues very persuasively that the primary purpose of marriage ceremonies is not to establish a social tie, as Lévi-Strauss maintains, but, to the contrary, to institute a clear distinction between brothers-in-law (see Gillison 1986, 67; 1987, 198)—even to the point, as sometimes happens, of bringing about the "expulsion" (1986, 42) or elimination (1987, 168) of the mother's brother. She is less convincing when she says that the ultimate reason for the claims of the maternal uncle is to be sought in the mythology of the Gimi. The uncle's right to be considered the father of his sister's children arises, she maintains, from the primordial incest that in myth originally unites him with her (see 1987, 169). But in fact, the mythical account does no more than remind the members of this patrilineal society of the logical priority of matrilineal descent, and thus justify the right of the maternal line.

12. "The aim of sacrifice is to send things back, especially the most sacred things: to say goodbye to the Gods who, without the sacrifice, would exert endless pressure on the [sacrifier]; to turn away the gods by doing one's duty to them. Here is the whole notion of the Greek *apotropaion*, also found in Sanskrit: the individual is discharging an obligation, is sacrificing so that the god will go away" (Mauss [1947] 2007, 186).

Chapter 5. Incest of the Second Type: Impasses and Issues

1. This original and ineffable asymmetry does not remove the possibility that the parties concerned may nevertheless enjoy symmetrical relationships, such as so-called joking relationships (see Radcliffe-Brown 1952, 96–97). Similarly, the symmetry that obtains in principle between affines is often accompanied by asymmetrical relationships, for example, the one between givers and takers of wives, where the status of the males is generally unequal (see Lévi-Strauss [1949c] 1969, 233–54).

2. From a purely formal point of view, there is no fundamental difference between a succession of generations and a chain of alliances. Each person gives his descendants the life that he has received from his ancestors, as each one gives, in his capacity as giver, the wife he acquired in his capacity as taker. The fact that a succession of generations does not close back on itself, as a cycle of alliances does, is no obstacle to their equivalence: an infinite series of generations is formally equivalent to a circle. Hence the fascination exerted on superior minds by Australian systems of kinship and alliance, which, being steeped in symmetry, are apt to give the impression of assuring the permanence of a society by eliminating the arrow of time (see Lévi-Strauss [1949c] 1969, 146–67; Testart 2000; Héran 2009, 572). In this type of society, the initiation of young people by adults, or the distinction between senior and junior, nonetheless plays a role of primary importance (see Testart 1995). Generally it is a dual asymmetry, between sexes and generations, that assures the long duration, if not the permanence, of societies. Here we are faced with a natural fact, to which every system of kinship and alliance is subject. There would be no reason to repeat the point over and over again were it not for the many theories that are determined to erase this primordial and irreducible asymmetry.

3. Lévi-Strauss relies in this connection on an article by Murdock dating from 1937. The data that Lévi-Strauss cites diverge considerably from the results that Murdock was to publish later, on the basis of a larger sample (see Murdock 1949, 59, table 9). The fact remains that the four possible combinations have quite different frequencies.

4. Lévi-Strauss had already intuited that the Aranda structure might be the limiting case of a Crow or Omaha system reduced to four lines (see Lévi-Strauss [1949c] 1969, 422–37). Héritier's

great achievement was to have refined this conjecture and given a rigorous proof of it. But in restoring Crow and Omaha systems to the category of elementary structures, she indirectly showed that they probably do not form the link needed to unite elementary with complex systems that Lévi-Strauss was hoping to find. Certain Dravidian systems, common among Amerindian peoples, seem better suited to extending the structural theory of kinship in the direction of complex systems (see Hamberger 2010, 464–66). Like elementary systems of the Aranda type, they distinguish between parallel and cross relatives; like complex systems, however, they have an egocentric, rather than classificatory, terminology (on the meaning, often misunderstood since Kroeber, of the term "classificatory," see Jorion 1984, 87–88) and they contain a cognatic descent.

5. See Heinich (1995, 948–49), Godelier ([2004] 2011, 356), and Héran (2009, 563).

6. By contrast, all other proscriptions of the second type, notably the one of "uncover[ing] the nakedness of a woman and of her daughter" (Leviticus 18:17), are stated without any attempt at justification.

7. See Lévi-Strauss ([1949c] 1969, 71), Evans-Pritchard (1951, 31, 42), and Devereux (1965, 238).

8. Evidently this is a specious supposition. By definition, science cannot postulate a priori the ultimate nature of reality. Its results may well have ontological implications, of course, but these do not constitute a criterion of scientific validity (see Scubla 1992b). Moreover, it is difficult to regard as materialist an explanation that lays such emphasis on the perceptions of actors (ideologies, as Marxists would say) and, in the last analysis, on the opposition of "categories of sameness and difference" that are their common denominator and of which bodily substances are no more than tangible manifestations. Like the materialism of Lévi-Strauss ([1962b] 1966), from which it seeks to distance itself, this version is a form of intellectualism (see Godelier [2004] 2011, 355).

9. Far from clarifying matters, it obscures them. For why would indirect contact between relatives of the same sex, through the intermediation of a common partner, expose them to danger if no taboo forbids direct contact between them in the first place? Generally speaking, neither a father and his son nor two sisters are subject to such a taboo.

10. Some of the criticisms made by these influential authors nonetheless seem to me doubtful. Godelier ([2004] 2011, 354–57) and Héran (2009, 552–65) both fault Héritier for explaining prohibitions too often by omitting or dismissing the explicit perceptions and motivations of actors, concentrating instead on what she takes to be more decisive factors that it is the anthropologist's duty to bring to light. On balance, I believe, this reproach is unwarranted. Fustel de Coulanges noted long ago ([1864] 1980) that a ritual may remain very stable even though the beliefs supposed to justify it have varied considerably over time. And yet it will be admitted that the explicit beliefs, perceptions, and motivations of actors must be counted, no less than their actual behavior, among the phenomena that anthropologists must explain. On this point it seems reasonable to follow authors as different as Marx, Freud, and Pareto, whose respective concepts of ideology, rationalization, and derivation are functionally equivalent. In the presence of an action A, accompanied by a perception P that motivates it, one must systematically search for a cause C capable of accounting for both A and P. Héritier can be reproached only for failing to rigorously adhere to this program, that is, for taking certain perceptions as the final cause of the phenomena that she studies while dismissing others as secondary or illusory, without giving a persuasive reason for choosing some and rejecting others. Her critics, though they are right to point out this weakness, do not seem to have advanced any very explicit criterion of their own.

11. It does not follow from this that we must look at things the other way around and see exogamy as a mere consequence of the prohibition of incest. Just as the prohibition concerning the mother

cannot be reduced to a particular case of a prohibition falling on all the women of an exogamous clan, this general prohibition cannot be regarded simply as an extension of a prohibition concerning the mother.

12. French law, for example, punishes sexual relations between an adult and a minor, and ipso facto between an adult and his or her own child if the child is a minor; but it does not proscribe incestuous relations as such. By contrast, the same law forbids, without regard for age, marriage between a mother and her son or between a father and his daughter.

13. Fine discusses two such examples. The first concerns Baule sisters having the same sexual partner. Without furnishing any new argument, she endorses Héritier's opinion that fear of a possible rivalry between the two sisters, although expressed by the very persons who would be affected by the consequences of such a rivalry, is a secondary factor.

The second example is more interesting. It was noted by Vernier among the Jere of Nigeria, who justify the prohibition against a man sleeping with his brother's wife by the fear that the woman's genitalia would be contaminated through the mixing of the sperm of the two men. This would make the men sick and cause them to become rivals, each one seeking to kill the other. The same thing is thought to occur in the case of two male friends who share the same woman: they become enemies and can no longer cooperate (see Fine 2013, 105). No matter that the Jere justify the prohibition by reference to a theory of humors, the justification cannot be regarded as the basis for the prohibition. It is striking, moreover, to observe that the Jere, like the Baule, fear that transgressing the prohibition will unleash a murderous rivalry. Among both peoples this is the expected effect, but only the Jere believe that they are able to discern the cause of the rivalry. This is the one notable difference between them and the Baule. Does it therefore follow that we should look to the Jere for a better understanding of the nature of the prohibition in question? If we were concerned solely with people's perceptions, the question would be undecidable. We could only point to the justifications advanced by each side. But from experience, we know that two persons who covet the same object or the favors of the same person can easily become enemies. Whatever their beliefs may be, and unless all prohibitions are held to be arbitrary, we have a sufficient reason for the existence of prohibitions in this case: they have been imposed, and they have endured, because they help bring about order and peace.

14. "A work which embraces so much time and space is bound to contain many errors," Hocart observed. "But they have not begun to have a glimmering what science is who think it consists in never being wrong. Science is not infallibility; it is power over facts. Mere learning is dominance by facts. The clumsiest lever which helps us move the masses of facts that have now accumulated today is better than none, for it makes us masters of facts, not their slaves" (Hocart 1933, viii).

Chapter 6. The Brother-Sister Relationship and the Principle of Male Dominance

1. This symmetry between pairs of same-sex siblings seems obvious in egalitarian societies, which are accustomed to disregard birth order. It is much less obvious in societies in which the older-younger relationship plays a decisive role. Most societies find it natural to differentiate and discriminate. In Nepal and India, even twin brothers are thought to be dissimilar, since one is necessarily older than the other. They are associated with a pair of mythical heroes, Ram and Laksman, who in fact are not twins, but half-brothers born of the same father and different mothers, though Laksman himself has a true twin brother of whose existence we are aware from traditional accounts, but of whom we know nothing more—perhaps a way of emphasizing how different they are from each other in spite of being twins, as Marie Lecomte-Tilouine (personal communication) has suggested. Modern Western societies, by contrast, tend not to discriminate

in this fashion, as may be seen not only from their customs and rules of law, but also from the research to which these have given rise. One of the main purposes of the present chapter, and indeed of the book as a whole, is to measure the distance separating these two kinds of society.

2. This is particularly true of unilineal-descent systems. Whether the rule is matrilineal or patrilineal, it entails a parallel- and cross-cousin dichotomy.

3. For a somewhat more precise statement of the criterion, see Héritier (1981, 19–20); and for a detailed analysis of the various possibilities, Murdock (1949).

4. This point has been contested by Érik Guignard, in an oral communication to the author dating from 1990; whether his objection was ever published, I cannot say. It is described and discussed in Scubla 1991 and Jorion 1991.

5. Héritier frankly disclaims any intention to examine the question of male dominance. She contents herself with the observation that Lévi-Strauss's theory notices the fact, without trying to explain it, that women are objects, and not partners, in the exchanges arranged by men, and then mentions having herself tried a couple of years earlier to analyze the reasons "that are supposed to justify the appropriation of women and their reproductive capacities by men," in her entry "Maschile/ Femminile" in the *Enciclopedia Einaudi* (1979). But she says no more than that (see Héritier 1981, 70 n. 18). A few lines further on, in another note, she recalls that Harold Scheffler defined a kinship system as "a local theory elaborated to account for the fact that women bring children into the world" (70 n. 20). A more elliptical remark could scarcely be imagined.

6. The same thing may be said of Lévi-Strauss, who, despite a strong intellectual tropism, nonetheless wavers between a variant of Kantian idealism (Kantianism without a transcendental subject) and straightforward realism. More often than not, he thinks of culture as a product of the symbolic function, and describes it as an activity of the human mind that consists in giving form to unstructured content. The mind is thus seen as a reservoir of forms and schemas on which an order has previously been imposed that structural analysis is able to discover by scrutinizing institutions, rites, and myths. But Lévi-Strauss adopts an entirely different point of view when he refers to the "structural conception" of modern physics (Lévi-Strauss [1958a] 1963, 54 n. 49); or when, alluding to the intrinsically "left-handed" character of the neutrino, he reminds Sartre that the opposition between right and left, like the oppositions between positive and negative, and male and female, inheres in the natural world and, unlike grammatical gender, is a product neither of human thought nor of language (see Lévi-Strauss 1969–1981, 4:689). In that case, forms have been imposed on everything, including the human mind, which therefore can in no way be interpreted as exerting mastery over structures or dominion over forms. My own view is that this neglected aspect of structuralism is what accounts for its real interest.

7. Lévi-Strauss was to come back a half-century later to this brutal alternative between alliance and extermination, placing Tylor's "myth" on a par with Freud's "myth" in *Totem and Taboo* (Lévi-Strauss 2000, 717). Even if the term is not meant pejoratively here, it is a matter less of myths than of thought experiments. As in the case of the philosophers' state of nature, and as Hobbes and Rousseau knew perfectly well, pushing real or possible experiences to their logical extreme is an indispensable method in all the sciences. Furthermore, the two myths in question are not opposed to each other but complementary, the one helping to explain the morphogenesis of relations between distinct groups, the other of their internal relations.

8. Men, in their rites of initiation, attempt to create male lineages that replicate female lineages, and in some cases may even be meant to supplant them (see Scubla 1982; 1985b, 366–67). I shall come back to this point in subsequent chapters. In focusing attention on the masculine pole of society to the detriment of its feminine pole, men implicitly recognize the natural priority of this

feminine pole while trying to compensate for it through cultural prerogatives. Héritier is obviously not unaware of this (see 1996, 203–35, reprinting an article first published in 1985), but she will not grant it anything more than secondary importance. In her later works she increasingly lays emphasis on the mysterious production of the masculine by the feminine, with the result that she substitutes an intellectual problem for a social problem, and rather than try to think more deeply about rites of initiation, tends to turn attention away from them. These rituals are nonetheless essential, for in claiming to show that men are capable of bringing children into the world as well as, or even better than, women are able to do they reveal the inherent inferiority of the masculine in relation to the feminine; and, by the place they occupy in the cultural reproduction of the group, these rituals suggest that this fundamental difference of status is at the very root of the social order. By contrast, the idea that male initiation ceremonies seek to explain how a woman's body can give birth to that of a man contributes little or nothing to our understanding of them.

9. The diagrams in figure 7 adopt a uterine point of view, but their mutual relationships remain unchanged in kinship systems governed by an agnatic principle, that is, in systems where membership in a kinship group passes through the male line and is therefore transmitted through the father rather than the mother. Nevertheless, although they may have similar or even identical structural effects, I do not think that the uterine principle and the agnatic principle are equivalent. We can explain more by supposing that the latter is a replica, or copy, of the former, for it is easier to explain why this copy should be imperfect: no society has been able to push the logic of agnatic descent to the point that others have developed the logic of uterine descent.

10. In our system of cognatic kinship, which recognizes no difference in principle between kinship through the maternal (uterine) line and kinship through the paternal (agnatic) line, first cousins are thereby equidistant and of the same degree.

11. Under the uterine principle, marriage is preferentially with a female patrilateral parallel cousin; under the agnatic principle, with a matrilateral parallel cousin; under the principle of parallel kinship, with the cross cousins of classical structural theory. The cognatic principle, which makes no distinction between first cousins, generally excludes any union among them or else considers them all to be marriageable.

12. To the extent that it shows that all matrimonial systems are exogamous (see Barry 2008, 755), this theory of kinship groups could pass for a generalization of the structural theory involving degrees of consanguineal proximity between individuals rather than equivalence classes of close or distant relatives (see Héran 2009, 249). In a review of Héran's book, Klaus Hamberger contests this interpretation, noting that Barry's whole work amounts to an argument against the structural theory of exchange (see Hamberger 2010, 465). Hamberger himself has given an excellent critical appraisal of Barry's arguments, with due regard for their originality, force, and limits, in an article posted online (see Hamberger 2009). See also the very good essay by Dominique Casajus (2008) in the electronic edition of *La Vie des idées*.

13. The Baule case discussed in the previous chapter may in fact be seen as an extension of the prohibition against a man having sexual relations with his brother's wife. Even if a man shared by two sisters is married to neither one of them, as their common partner he is, in effect, for each of them, a relative by marriage by virtue of his relationship with the other.

14. Barry himself concludes his work by suggesting that the variability of forms that may be assumed by human kinship reveals the capacity of our species to "subvert" the world around it, "through the exercise of reason and understanding," and continues still today to "remodel" it, the better to "humanize" it (Barry 2008, 762). In spite of this profession of Promethean faith, some critics nonetheless find his description of kinship overly "essentialist." One reviewer, who raises

important questions, contrasts it with a "deliberately existentialist" conception of modes of alliance (see Berger 2009, 266–67).

Chapter 7. Conceptualizing Difference or Dissolving Hierarchy?: From Asymmetry to Parity

1. Héritier devotes only a few lines to the vital question of the demographic importance of women [see 2002 (2012), pp. 20–21]—and this in a paragraph where, remarkably enough, she does not describe so much the specific properties of women as male perceptions of these properties. "Women," she writes, "were held to be the most necessary possession for the survival of the group" [ibid., p. 20]. The use of the past tense and passive voice is significant; it would have been simpler, and more accurate, to say that women are, and remain, the most necessary possession for the survival of the group. Plainly a fear of naturalizing, indeed of animalizing, the feminine condition [see ibid., p. 387] restrains Héritier here from straightforwardly expressing an elementary truth that, in and of itself, implies no reductionism.

2. See Verdier (1980, 28–29, and 18ff.) on the notion of "life-capital." The idea that human beings can be used as a compensatory payment for harm or injury sustained is considered today to be an obvious proof of barbarism, a manifest assault on the dignity of the human person, in this case the female person—and so additional evidence of the immemorial subservience of women in a male world. Raymond Verdier and his colleagues, through a meticulous study of the "vindicatory systems" of stateless societies that attempts to think critically about vengeance, instead of merely abhorring it, and to identify its principles and function, have helped us to better understand this kind of phenomenon and at the same time to take a closer look at norms that seem to require no comment, because they have become familiar to us as members of state societies. To a modern moral sensibility, things alone can have a price, never persons; to attach a market value to another human being would amount to treating him as a thing as well, as a means for realizing our own ends and not as an end in himself.

    Kant, who first formulated these notions, also made more rigorous use of them. Morality requires only that human beings be treated (individually and without exception, in keeping with Kant's famous formula of universality) *never simply* as a means, but *always at the same time* as an end (see Kant [1785] 1998, 4:438, p. 45; my emphasis). For a sick person, however, a physician is a means to regain his health; for the physician, his patient is a means to feed his family. The service rendered to the patient and, more generally, "skill and diligence in work," though these are not physical things, nonetheless have a "market price" (4:435, p. 42). As Alfred Sauvy pointed out, it is not ethics that prohibits calculating the "economic value of a man" or the "cost price" of professional training; moreover, reckoning the "cost of a man" is not only of interest to slaveholding societies, it may in fact serve the most noble ends (see Sauvy [1952–1954] 1963–1966, 1:310ff.). Nevertheless, in addressing both the demographic and the economic aspects of the problem, Sauvy managed already a half-century ago to offend certain delicate sensibilities who nonetheless described themselves as Marxists (see 1:viii)—a sign of how strongly, and how bizarrely, the *doxa* of the modern age associates materialism and angelism. One has a right to expect more detachment from historians and anthropologists. Indignation and accusation cannot take the place of reasoned argument; in the worst case they may actually prove to be harmful (on accusation, see the fundamental work by François Tricaud [1977]).

3. The thing that really matters, Héritier says at the very beginning of her book, is "not relating and counting the nature, the variations, the degrees of difference, and the social hierarchies established between the sexes, but trying to understand, in anthropological terms, the reasons for them" (Héritier 1996, 9).

4. "It is a question of flushing out," Héritier says, "within the perceptions peculiar to each society, those invariant elements whose arrangement, though it assumes various forms depending on the human group in question, always appears as an unremarkable and natural inequality" (Héritier 1996, 9).

5. "Thus, *it is not sex, but fertility, that makes the real difference between masculine and feminine*" (Héritier 1996, 230; emphasis in the original). "The exchange of women between groups is an exchange of life since women produce children and give their power of fertility to others than their close relatives" (232).

6. "Male domination . . . is fundamentally the control, the appropriation of the woman's fertility, at the moment when she is fertile" (Héritier 1996, 230). "The exogamy rule on which every society is based must be understood as a rule governing the exchange of women and their power of fertility among men" (232).

7. "Thus is constituted in return a private male domain, [just] as there is a private, inaccessible domain of women, [the domain] of biological reproduction" (Héritier 1996, 233). "Among the Ona of Tierra del Fuego, the bow hunt is the man's province. . . . He learns at a very young age how to shoot a bow and arrow, and this apprenticeship is reserved exclusively for [boys]. A. Chapman shows that, without suitable training, adult women are no more able to use these things, in the physical sense of the term, than a man who has not learned how to do so as a child" (233).

8. The title and subtitle of the chapter in question ("The Blood of the Warrior and the Blood of Women: Control and Appropriation of Fertility") nicely links these two aspects of the matter.

9. Masculine responsibilities, Héritier says, are generally regarded as superior to feminine responsibilities, but not for any intrinsic reason. "It is not because hunting is 'noble' that men hunt, but because men are 'noble' that hunting becomes [noble] as well" (Héritier [2002] 2012, 372). Yet it does not follow that the allocation of responsibilities between the sexes is wholly arbitrary, as Héritier too hastily concludes (see 373); hunting and war might well be as peculiarly masculine as parturition is peculiarly feminine. Moreover, with regard to "female labor," it is strange to see the second term of this phrase interpreted to refer exclusively to professional activities as though they alone were worthy, whereas domestic activities are servile tasks, not real labor (see Héritier [2009] 2013, passim and esp. 99).

10. On the importance of the distinction between symbolic sacrifice and efficacious sacrifice, see Herrenschmidt (1979).

11. To the extent that the Catholic Mass now increasingly resembles the Protestant service (see Scubla 2009c, §§31–46), it is by no means unimaginable that the priesthood may one day be opened up to women. But that would only mean that the priest has ceased to be a sacrificer and has become a pastor instead.

12. "The principle of cultural relativism," she writes, "was invented in the middle [of the last century] by social anthropology in an attempt to instill a respect for differences, a recognition of variability, and to legitimize the defense of small societies, not to erect them into citadels of absolute incommunicability. All human societies are constructed on the basis of particular responses given to universal questions and problems" (Héritier [2002] 2012, 157).

13. At the end of an article analyzing the relationship of the masculine and feminine in African rites, Alfred Adler (2007, 107–13) points out this difficulty very nicely. In a long aside, he deplores the fact that ethnologists taking part in contemporary debates about the difference between the sexes, parity, descent, and so on, whether Maurice Godelier or Françoise Héritier (both mentioned by

name) or someone else, seem powerless to make a specifically and properly anthropological voice heard.

14. To start off by baldly asserting that "maternity is not a natural phenomenon" would not only be an affront to our moral sense, it would seem to contradict common sense as well; to maintain that it is not "in itself" a natural phenomenon, however, appears to say that it is indeed a natural phenomenon, but not solely a natural phenomenon. To claim that "maternity is not in itself a natural phenomenon" amounts to saying that it is not one by its essence, but by accident; and in that case it is not only the object of social construction, but in fact is itself the result of social construction as well.

15. The title of one of the book's chapters, "Privilege of Maternity and Male Domination," lays stress on this relationship.

16. See Héritier [1994] 1999, 257–64; 1996, 191–200; 2000, 35; [2002] 2012, 22, 49–50.

17. Aristotle expressly declares that "the female is, as it were, a mutilated male" (*On the Generation of Animals*, 737ᵃ 27–28). This formula seems not to have attracted Héritier's attention. More surprising in this regard, however, is the absence of any criticism of Freud and even of any reference to psychoanalysis in the two volumes of *Masculin/féminin*.

18. See Héritier [1994] 1999, 261, 263; 1996, 195–96; [2002] 2012, 22.

19. It is on this point, needless to say, but on this point only, that the feminist critique is pertinent: why the male rather than the female?

20. She rightly notes that this lack of masculinity "does not by any means imply a triumph of the feminine" (Héritier [1994] 1999, 260; see also 1996 passim), but she does not see that the birth of monsters is not a triumph or excess of femininity either.

21. Héritier refers to passages in *On the Generation of Animals* mentioning these two types of necessity (see [1994] 1999, 260, 263; 1996, 193, 198), but without quite grasping what is at issue in them, since she fails to see the importance of finality in Aristotle's theory of causality.

22. "Some [children], though resembling none of their relations, yet do at any rate resemble a human being, but others are not even like a human being but a monstrosity. For even he who does not resemble his parents is already in a certain sense a monstrosity; for in these cases nature has in a way departed from the type. The first departure indeed is that the offspring should become female instead of male; this, however, is a natural necessity. (For the class of animals divided into sexes must be preserved ... [and] it is necessary that animals should produce female young.) And the monstrosity, though not necessary in regard of a final cause and an end, yet is necessary accidentally" (Aristotle, *On the Generation of Animals*, 767ᵇ 4–15).

23. Aristotle, of course, while claiming to follow Plato, criticizes him above all for having separated ideal Forms from their material substrate.

24. I take up this question in the following chapter.

25. Héritier is nevertheless well aware, for example, that all of us recognize a man or a woman by the sound of the voice alone (see Héritier [2009] 2013, 99), but she draws no conclusion from this fact. Bent on deconstructing and denouncing the artificial images of masculine and feminine that have accumulated in the Western mind like a sediment over the centuries, she does not see that the man and woman she seeks to uncover, stripped of the secondary characteristics with which they are now encrusted, are pure abstractions. Paradoxically, she devotes not a single word to describing and analyzing the most obviously artificial of all such images: the human person enshrined in modern political constitutions, having neither sex nor age nor condition nor nationality—a

legalistic fiction making it possible to attribute the same rights to individuals who are perfectly equal because they are undifferentiated and interchangeable.

26. See Héritier [2002] 2012, 18, 28, 77, 118–19, 144, 201, 392.

27. "Women reproduce themselves identically, but they also have the extravagant ability to produce bodies different from theirs" (Héritier [2002] 2012, 18). It is curious to note that she sometimes refers the reader in this connection to her critique of Aristotle (see, for example, Héritier 2000, 35), although for Aristotle himself it is a woman's ability to conceive a daughter that needs to be explained, whereas the conception of a boy goes without saying.

28. "In order to reproduce himself identically, the man is *obliged to go through a woman's body*. He cannot do it by himself. . . . Women make their daughters whereas men cannot make their sons" (Héritier [2002] 2012, 23; emphasis in the original).

29. "It is this inability [of men to reproduce themselves by their own means] that fixes the destiny of womankind. . . . [It] is not penis envy that gives rise to female humiliation, but the mystery that women make their daughters whereas men cannot make their sons. This scandal, and this injustice, are at the root of all the rest, which has occurred in similar ways in human groups since the origins of humanity and which I call 'male domination'" (Héritier [2002] 2012, 23).

30. "It is not because they make children that women are kept in [a state of] dependence as an exploitable material; it is not because they are fertile like the earth, it is because men must have a woman to make sons for themselves" (Héritier [2002] 2012, 118–19).

31. Héritier quotes in this connection a representative of the Islamic Salvation Front in Algeria, who declared in 1989: "A woman is a breeder of men. She does not produce material bonds, but instead something essential, the *male* Muslim" (Héritier [2002] 2012, 24; emphasis in the original). Her commentary is as follows: "Obliterated here is the fact that a woman gives birth also to girls and to female Muslims. This does not really count. Girls are necessary, of course, but the body of the woman (a generic feminine like Aristotelian matter) is the necessary evil through which one must pass in order to make men and, incidentally, other women, who have intrinsic reality only insofar as they are future breeders of men" (24). This reading is a bit forced. It attributes a latent sense to the quoted statement that, true or false, does not exhaust its full meaning. The statement itself explicitly acknowledges the principle of uterine kinship that obtains in societies practicing so-called Arab marriage. Far from reducing the birth of girls to an incidental phenomenon or a necessary evil, this principle accords it an eminent place: the woman is no less essential than the "something essential" that she is supposed to produce. To be sure, the woman is not contemplated here as an individual, only as a potential mother; but the same is true for "the male Muslim," who is first and foremost the servant of Allah. More than anything else, it is this "holistic" point of view that offends the modern mind, accustomed as it is to recognize only individuals, which is to say persons whose sex and religious attachment (the latter often reduced to a mere opinion) are only secondary and incidental characteristics.

32. Héritier pauses here to expand upon this technological detail. In the case of female cloning, she says, once the sperm bank has been funded, the elimination of men would be carried out peaceably, so to speak, without any need for violent extermination or oppression. In the case of male cloning, however, she fears that the "violent enslavement" of women might follow, indeed their "complete subjugation" (Héritier [2002] 2012, 152, 228)—male domination in its extreme form, in other words. Generally speaking, this theme tends to crowd out all other aspects of the difference between the sexes in her work. Even if the campaigns she wages are legitimate, the obsession with domination has the effect of impoverishing her analytical insight and undermining the very positions she defends. In a world as saturated with male domination as the one she

imagines ours to have been historically, it is hard to see how powerful women such as Cleopatra, Valeria Messalina, Brunehild, Marie de' Medici, Christina of Sweden, and Catherine of Russia could ever have existed.

33. Except for a passage in *Mythologiques* in which Lévi-Strauss, making a virtue of necessity, claims to have shown in passing that dualist societies are characterized by "a relationship of reciprocity [that] does not exclude, but on the contrary implies, a constitutive dissymmetry" (Lévi-Strauss 1969–1981, 4:642).

34. See Scubla 1985a, 92–93, 110–13, 156–59, 224–27.

35. Associated with the moieties of Bororo society are two strikingly different ritual mediators whom Lévi-Strauss designates by the terms "sorcerer" and "priest," respectively. The model proposed by René Girard to account for the origin of myths and rites makes it possible to fully explain their characteristic traits and complementary offices: they correspond to two aspects, the first negative and the second positive, successively displayed by the "emissary victim"—symbol of crisis before he is put to death, and symbol of peace restored once the crisis has been resolved by his violent expulsion (see Girard [1972b] 1977). It is interesting to observe that, among the Samo, the pair consisting of the master of the rain (*tyiri*) and the master of the earth (*tudana*) is analogous to the one formed by the sorcerer and the priest of the Bororo: the *tyiri*, likened to a "rubbish heap," is a "scapegoat" (Héritier 1973, 127, 129). Significantly, too, the two sacred figures resemble the two sides of a coin: they are so indissociable that their complementary offices can be assumed by the same person (see 123).

36. On this ritual, see Crocker [1977] 1983, 162–63.

37. This opposition between the fixity of the feminine and the mobility of the masculine, already present in Aristotle's definition of male and female, and which differentiates the ovum from the spermatozoon, may hold the key to the difference between the sexes, not because "culture" is a mere reflection of "nature," or the symbolic a mere extension of the biological, but rather because each of these two orders structures its own domain on the basis of the same fundamental schema. We will encounter this problem in the next chapter.

38. One hardly does justice to Robert Hertz by describing him as a "precursor of structural anthropology" (see Tcherkézoff [1991] 2000, 324), who borrows a phrase employed earlier by Izard and Lenclud in the first part of their entry on Hertz in the *Dictionnaire de l'ethnologie et de l'anthropologie*). Because of its intellectualism, the structural conception developed by Lévi-Strauss constitutes a step backward by comparison with the approach sketched by his predecessor. Cut down on the field of battle at the age of thirty-three, in 1915, Hertz unfortunately did not have the time needed to work out his ideas and to construct a theory of the depth and power that his genius seemed to promise.

39. Structuralism not only insists on recognizing the priority of the whole to its parts and, more generally, the primacy of a relation over its terms (for example, of exchange itself over the partners to the exchange and the objects exchanged); it supposes the existence of a properly structural causality, and therefore the rehabilitation of the Aristotelian concept of formal cause.

   Aristotle, it will be recalled, gave the name "cause" to everything that in one way or another explains the existence and properties of an object or of a natural or artificial process: matter (or material cause), form (or formal cause), agent (or efficient cause), which "informs" matter, and the end (or final cause) pursued by an agent. The complete explanation of any thing or process requires reference to these four distinct types of causality, but it does not follow that they always and necessarily correspond to distinct and independent entities. When a carpenter (efficient cause) uses wood (material cause) to construct a boat (formal cause) to be used for fishing (final cause), the four terms are clearly differentiated, even if the end, which is to say the function of the boat, determines its form, that is, its structure. When, in the course of its germination, a seed (efficient cause) draws from the soil and the air the necessary elements (material cause) for reproducing (final cause) the adult form of the plant (formal cause) from which it is issued, the formal, final, and efficient causes are bound up with one another: the adult form acts as an attractor that guides the whole process of reproduction. The form par excellence is that of a living being; the form of an artificial object, such as a fisherman's boat or a bird's nest, has existence and stability only as a consequence of the activity of the living beings who preserve a memory of it and who take it as a model in fashioning their environment. Accordingly, when Aristotle defines the soul as the form of the body, he obviously is not referring to a mere material configuration, to an individual or generic silhouette, but to an active principle that makes it a living being, unified and stable, by contrast with the mere aggregate of matter that it will once again become once it is deprived of life and reduced to the condition of a corpse.

This conception of form as an active principle was abandoned by Galileo-Cartesian science, which, based on the principle of inertia, also rejected the notion of a final cause. With the advent of classical mechanics, a causal explanation came to be understood as an explanation of the transformations undergone by matter solely through the action of efficient causes. The form—or rather the "figure," to use the Cartesian term—no longer had any efficacy of its own; it was only the more or less stable result of more or less permanent efficient causes. On this view, the germinating seed does not reproduce a predetermined form that guides its development; its development is wholly determined by various external causes (heat, dampness, and so on) acting on it. It is nonetheless remarkable that quantum mechanics should have reintroduced, for better or for worse, the ancient formal and final causes that were thought to have been banished from science, and that scientific orthodoxy moreover still considers illegitimate. Think, for example, of a "structural law" such as Pauli's exclusion principle, which explains the stability of atoms and makes it possible to reconstruct Mendeleev's table by determining a priori the diversity of possible atomic forms; or else of the necessity of recognizing a sort of "micro-finality" to account for the tunnel effect, which is to say certain paths of elementary particles that are incompatible with the principles of classical mechanics (a billiard ball in motion goes nowhere—it preserves only the direction and the speed that it has received insofar as it is not prevented from doing so by obstacles or external forces; in the tunnel effect, a particle passes through a potential energy barrier that would be impassible if the particle behaved like a billiard ball) (see Auger 1966, 76–79, 176–95; Ruyer [1954] 1967, 142–43). It is also notable that biologists, though they are more inclined to materialism than physicists, cannot help but have resort to the concepts of structure and function, even of "teleonomy."

Lévi-Strauss, ever attentive to the most original results of the natural sciences, sensitive to the spirit that animates them, and determined not to make the sciences of man either an empire within an empire or the fiefdom of an outmoded scientism, wrote near the end of his life a massive work in four volumes called *Mythologiques*, an impassioned plea for a neo-Aristotelian conception of science—of which, if he is to be believed, structuralism was the precursor, indeed the vanguard. "Structuralism," he says, "is resolutely teleological; finality, after being long banned by a form of scientific thought still dominated by mechanism and empiricism, has been restored to its true place and again made respectable by structuralism" (Lévi-Strauss 1969–1981, 4:687). In rehabilitating the intuitions of the savage mind, structuralism anticipated the discoveries of contemporary science, which drew an image of the world very remote from the silent universe of Galileo-Cartesian physics, while at the same time providing "a glimpse of the natural order as a huge semantic field" (4:689). It is a pity that these admirably luminous last pages should have been obscured at the very end by a sort of twilight of the gods, an embittered rumination on the darkening fate of humanity with which Lévi-Strauss insisted on closing his tetralogy (see 4:693–95). Many readers have remarked upon the nihilistic tone of this coda, without seeing it as an aesthetic affectation that permitted Lévi-Strauss to distract attention from the offense against the materialist *doxa* that he had just committed; indeed the transgression of orthodoxy was so well hidden that his neofinalism ended up being virtually invisible.

It should be noted, too, that in spite of the materialism to which she typically appeals, Françoise Héritier has sought in her own way to rehabilitate the reputation of formal, or structural, causality by suggesting that alliance systems, and more generally, social systems, are governed by a principle of non-combination of identical things that immediately puts one in mind of Pauli's exclusion principle, which prevents two electrons from occurring in the same atom if all four of their respective "quantum numbers" are identical. If this principle should prove to be fertile, it can be counted on to make a decisive contribution to structural anthropology (see Scubla 2000a).

40. In a lecture titled "Structuralism and Ecology" dating from the same period as the final chapter of *Naked Man* ("Finale"), mentioned in the preceding note, Lévi-Strauss somewhat disingenuously maintains that he has wrongly been charged with what "my Anglo-Saxon colleagues" call "mentalism" (or "idealism")—a characterization of his approach to anthropology in which, he says, he fails to recognize himself (see Lévi-Strauss [1983] 1985, 102–3). It would have been more accurate to say that he no longer recognized himself, at least not at this point in his career. The truth of the matter is that his thought swung between a neo-Kantian idealism, dominant in the 1950s but never really repudiated thereafter, on the one hand; and, on the other, a realism that sometimes was materialist, making a first appearance in *The Savage Mind* and prefiguring the realism of the cognitive sciences, and sometimes neo-Aristotelian, particularly evident in the final volume of the *Mythologiques* and in the article just cited, which to my mind expresses what is true about structuralism.

41. Like Lévi-Strauss, Héritier tends to neglect ritual and to isolate kinship relations from other aspects of social life. This is all the more regrettable as her study of the brother-sister relationship, the importance of which she well demonstrated, might have been enriched particularly by attention to works that take its ritual dimension into account (see, for example, Jamous 1991). As Hocart (1933, 260–61) had shown much earlier, each kinship relationship must be reincorporated in the whole of which it is a part, and this whole itself in the network of ritual obligations for which it supplies the skeleton. A recent study of the Omaha system of the Mossi shows the pertinence and the fecundity of this point of view (see Laurent 2013, 62); it is to be regretted that its author, like the majority of French anthropologists, seems to be unaware of Hocart.

42. See Hocart 1927; 1933; [1936] 1970; 1950; 1952.

43. Hocart showed that royal rituals are everywhere formed from the same elements (see Hocart 1927) and that the majority of known institutions are issued from them (see Hocart [1936] 1970; 1952). Thus marriage, which had its origin as an element of the enthronement ceremony, was initially a royal privilege. Later, when the great lords took a wife, they wished to have a ceremony of their own imitating the royal rite, but with less pomp; next the other dignitaries followed suit, and finally marriage reached the people as a whole—all this in accordance with a law that applies to the majority of customs (see Hocart 1952, 118–24). This is why newlyweds are often called kings and queens for a day, and sometimes crowned in the course of the ceremony, a truncated version of the monarchical original. When Hocart first established this result, more than fifty years ago, one might have thought that the institution of marriage, having at last become universal, had achieved its final form. But the union of couples of the same sex, which has recently come into fashion in certain Western countries, shows that the process by which it has become increasingly common has perhaps not yet reached its end and may hold in store further surprises.

In view of the ongoing extension of rights to animals, the Vedic custom of sacred matrimony with a horse may point the way to yet another stage in its development in generations to come.

44. In the case of the feminization of vocabulary, one is dealing only with the foolish misjudgment of politicians claiming a right to regulate the language. It is odder, and more worrying, to see judges in France publicly protest (on 7 May 2013) against what they call the "abstract and outdated conception of the impartiality of the judge that underlies the code of ethics for magistrates published in 2010 by the [Conseil supérieur de la magistrature]: the judge must be transparent, without sex, opinion, or political commitment." Do these same people, whose duty is to say what the law is, have to have the distinction between their office and their person explained to them, so that they may avoid confusing the exercise of this office and the expression of their personal opinions?

45. See "Françoise Héritier: 'Oui au mariage homosexuel, non à la gestation pour autrui,'" interview with Philippe Petit, *Marianne* (4 February 2013), available online via www.marianne.net/ Francoise-Heritier-oui-au-mariage-homosexuel-non-a-la-gestation-pour-autrui_a226327.html.

46. See the conclusion of the interview mentioned in the preceding note:

> MARIANNE: What might you find shocking about the proposed law if it were to be approved one day?
>
> HÉRITIER: Nothing, to be honest. A law obeys the requirements of its time. It is binding because it corresponds to a majority conscience and will. Its influence is therefore beneficial in that it helps to construct and consolidate mental adaptations that one day become obvious to everyone. It must nonetheless be subject to fundamental and internally consistent ethical requirements: [it must] satisfy as far as possible individuals and their needs, taking into account all possibilities, cognitive as well as technological, but never to the detriment of others, however distant they may seem to us.

47. After the Second World War, Japan undertook to reduce its population by means of a campaign to encourage abortion that proved to be highly effective. In the space of a few decades this policy produced a considerably older population, inverting the pyramid of ages to the point that the government found itself obliged once more to encourage women to have more children and to contemplate banning abortion.

48. Fifty years ago in France, supporters of "family planning" maintained—this was one of their principal arguments, in fact—that the widespread availability of contraception would cause illegal abortions, which they estimated to number in the hundreds of thousands each year, to disappear. A few years later they lobbied, again successfully, on behalf of legalizing voluntary terminations of pregnancy, with all incidental expenses being covered by medical insurance. As far as one can tell, comparing recent statistics for legal abortions with the most reliable estimates of illegal abortions in the past, the abortion rate seems to have remained about the same as it was prior to legalization. In this case it seems clear that demographic constraints were not responsible for the changes that took place. The objective constraints weighing upon human societies are one thing; the subjective factors underlying human behavior are another. For the same reason it is highly probable that the French and Japanese lawmakers who legalized abortion, the former in 1975, the latter in 1948, did not act from the same motives, whether consciously or unconsciously. When Héritier mentions abortion, it is always as a way for women to free themselves from male domination by taking control of procreation (see, for example, Héritier [2009] 2013, 286). To my knowledge she has never addressed the question from the demographic point of view; with regard to contraception, she seems actually surprised to discover that the members of parliament who voted in favor of

legalization saw it "primarily [as] a means for regulating the birth rate, not a lever for attaining autonomy and freedom" (118).

This remark and, more generally, the reluctance to consider the demographic constraints of social life are typical of contemporary individualism. One encounters the same tendency in the very heart of the human and social sciences. In the spring of 2013, for example, one heard an economist call for the elimination in France not only of the dependents' allowance but also of the practice of calculating tax liability by family rather than on a per capita basis, all in the name of liberty and justice. On this view, those who choose to have children ought to assume the consequences alone, without benefiting from the reduction in taxes that a system in which those who make the opposite choice are penalized would entail. Alfred Sauvy remarked a half-century ago that while one could imagine a demography that analyzes population data independently of their causes and consequences, an economics having nothing to do with demography and sociology is inconceivable; thus he deplored the fact that, despite the enduring lessons of history, the separation of economics from these disciplines nonetheless persisted (see Sauvy [1952–1954] 1963–1966, 1:vii). In the meantime nothing has changed. It is as though the fragmentation of academic research reflects the condition of exactly the "society of individuals" that modern society dreams of being.

49. "Undoubtedly, in the centuries to come, other possibilities will become thinkable and possibilities that have not yet been formulated will become formulable and, in the more or less long term, realizable" (*Marianne*, 4 February 2013).

50. "Marriage," Héritier says, "now no longer unites two families and their common purposes but two individuals, and it is founded typically on love and on free choice. Yet we still are left with, from archaic times, the prohibition against incest that made exogamy necessary" (*Marianne*, 4 February 2013).

51. See Schumpeter ([1942] 1950, 235–302) and Rousseau ([1762] 1943), who famously distinguishes the "general will," which is "always right," from the "will of all," which is merely the "sum of particular wills"; on these problems, see Scubla (1992a, 2001b).

52. In one of its formulations: "Act in such a way that you always treat humanity, whether in your own person or in the person of any other, never simply as a means, but always at the same time as an end" (Kant, *Critique of Practical Reason*, 4:429).

53. Recent research shows that many people born as a result of medically assisted procreation have a dread of contracting incestuous unions. No doubt it is too early to draw definitive conclusions. Preliminary data nonetheless seem to confirm the idea that the prohibition of incest is not a consequence of the exogamy rule, as Lévi-Strauss maintained, but on the contrary implies it.

54. Nietzsche well expressed this point of view in fragment 39 of *The Gay Science* ([1886] 1974, 106):

> The change in general taste is more powerful than that of opinions. Opinions, along with all proofs, refutations, and the whole intellectual masquerade, are merely symptoms of the change in taste and most certainly not what they are still often supposed to be, its causes. What changes the general taste? The fact that some individuals who are powerful and influential announce without any shame, *hoc est ridiculum, hoc est absurdum*, in short, the judgment of their taste and nausea; and then they enforce it tyrannically. Thus they coerce many, and gradually more develop a new habit, and eventually *all* have a new *need*.

55. The unexpected, and sometimes denied, magnitude of the reaction against same-sex marriage seems to have forced politicians and the media in France to enter, with great reluctance, into

a contradictory debate that they formerly considered unnecessary and that they would have preferred in any case to avoid.

56. The preamble to the Constitution of 1791 reads as follows:

> The National Assembly, wishing to establish the French Constitution upon the principles it has just recognized and declared, abolishes irrevocably the institutions which were injurious to liberty and equality of rights.
>
> Neither nobility, nor peerage, nor hereditary distinctions, nor distinctions of orders, nor feudal regime, nor patrimonial courts, nor any titles, denominations, or prerogatives derived therefrom, nor any order of knighthood, nor any corporations or decorations requiring proofs of nobility or implying distinctions of birth, nor any superiority other than that of public functionaries in the performance of their duties any longer exists.
>
> Neither venality nor inheritance of any public office any longer exists.
>
> Neither privilege nor exception to the law common to all Frenchmen any longer exists for any part of the nation or for any individual.
>
> Neither *jurandes* nor corporations of professions, arts, and crafts any longer exist.
>
> The law no longer recognizes religious vows or any other obligation contrary to natural rights or the Constitution.

(French text reproduced in Godechot 1979, 35.) The English version given here, archived at https://web.duke.edu, is no longer available; a similar version may be found at https://archive.org/details/frenchconstituti00franrich.

57. In reality, the Constitution of 1791, like the Declaration of 1789, also recognizes the existence of a sui generis entity, the nation, as the depository of the sovereignty formerly held by the king, endowed, like the king, with a transcendent character; it is reducible neither to the citizenry as a whole (being eternal France, in contradistinction to the French) nor to the apparatus of the state, which is only a juridical structure characterized by the monopoly on legitimate violence (for a detailed analysis, see Scubla 2000b, 2004). As the holistic and religious complement of the state, the nation may well claim to be the cement that holds modern individualist societies together. Rousseau, it will be recalled, thought that a people had to have a "national character" in order to constitute a stable political entity. In our own day, however, in old Europe, after several centuries of national wars, the very ideas of nation and national identity are often considered to be almost as "dangerous" as the idea of race. In the eyes of a globalized elite, the only permissible attachment, as a matter of fact and settled law, is that enjoyed by all men and women as members of a common humanity. For many historians and ethnologists, determined to prolong the movement inaugurated by the drafters of the Constitution of 1791, there are no peoples, only populations: nations and ethnic groups are illusory political fictions, without any content of their own, sources of artificial division that therefore should be abolished in their turn. Several things nonetheless counsel caution, for they suggest that the illusion may lie elsewhere than one imagines it to be. Rousseau deplored the fact, or what he took to be a fact, that already in his own time there were no longer French or Germans or Spaniards or English, only Europeans, all of them resembling one another (see Rousseau [1771–1772] 2005, 11:179–80). Today his misjudgment is plain for all to see. Anyone who still doubts it may consult Emmanuel Todd ([1990] 1996), where the heterogeneity of Europe is conclusively demonstrated. Moreover, the number of national states has grown substantially since the end of the Second World War, and we may be sure that this process is not yet finished.

58. Leibniz, who had a complete mastery of the two disciplines, often compared law to mathematics. He observed that both have the same type of formal architecture, each one proceeding by means

of deduction from principles. In axiomatizing a logical or a mathematical theory, one judges the validity of a system of axioms by its consequences: if the chosen axioms imply undesirable statements, one removes an axiom or adds a new one. Faced with the petition for same-sex marriage entered in the name of equal rights, lawmakers could have proceeded in the same fashion by adding to the civil code an article providing that marriage is the union of a man and a woman, in keeping with the whole of historical practice. To the contrary, they chose to reason on the basis of the silence of the civil code on this point, and above all as if the Declaration of Rights were, like the Mosaic law, a text of divine origin and not an axiomatic system cobbled together by human beings during the summer of 1789. This mechanical application of a principle of equality, resulting as it does from a political choice, can in no way be considered logically necessary. And it surely would not have been possible in the first place if its sacred character had not been insisted upon in the founding document itself.

Chapter 8. Testart's Law: Division of Labor and Sexual Identity

1. "Tragedy is not a matter of differing opinions. . . . If the art of tragedy is to be defined in a single phrase, we might do worse than call attention to one of its most characteristic traits: the opposition of symmetrical elements" (Girard [1972b] 1977, 70 and 44). The second and third chapters of *Violence and the Sacred* develop this theme at length, particularly with reference to Euripides's *Phoenician Women* and Sophocles's *Oedipus the King*.

2. On this neologism, see Girard [1978] 1987, 35 and 299–305.

3. Girard nonetheless sketches (see 1978, 105–25) a dynamic and morphogenetic structuralism that is explicitly opposed to the static structuralism of Lévi-Strauss. On this point, see also Scubla 1993b.

4. Lévi-Strauss himself says more cautiously that the value of a term, in the event a symbol, is "primarily *positional*" (Lévi-Strauss 1969–1981, 1:56; emphasis in the original).

5. Saussure carefully distinguishes the "value" of a word from its "signification" (see Saussure [1916] 1983, 112–16). Contrary to the structuralist vulgate, he does not reduce the nature of a term to its contrastive value alone. Even in the case of phonemes, his analysis is qualified: they "are first and foremost," he says, "entities which are contrastive, relative and negative" (117)—primarily, but not only, contrastive entities.

6. This adjustment of the range of requisite functions to the range of available possibilities offered is always approximate and imperfect. Certain functions may remain unexercised, certain possibilities may turn out not to find expression. In modern society, where tasks are highly specialized, it is the second eventuality that is more common: the typical work day requires only a few particular aptitudes on the part of the individual, leaving the others unemployed. "That," Hocart says, "is the tragedy of our civilization: our men and women have not yet been narrowed down by nature to fit the narrowness of their tasks" (Hocart [1936] 1970, 298).

7. The usual assumptions of ecology, for example, are a mixture of incompatible ideas and beliefs. Ecologists postulate the existence of spontaneous and beneficial natural equilibria for which they profess a respect that is all the more religious in spirit as they consider the human technologies capable of destroying them to be given—as if, therefore, from the point of view of ecology, human beings were intruders upon nature and not themselves natural beings—quite specific ones, to be sure, but nonetheless ontologically similar to all other beings. The Aristotelian philosophy of nature is much more coherent. It regards mankind as consisting of natural beings, which is to say beings endowed with a spontaneous and purposeful capacity to act; and the natural world as a

whole as the result of the interaction of all the beings that compose it, a tangled web of natural processes that are joined together with one another or opposed to one another, and that combine in various ways without necessarily arriving at a general equilibrium. When a horticulturist prunes or trains a tree, he gives it, for his own ends, a shape and dimensions that it does not spontaneously assume on its own. But the same thing happens when a plant draws from the soil and the air the natural elements necessary to its own development; far from being in any way exceptional, it is a technique that is connatural with life. There is no difference in principle between the house built by a man and the nest built by a bird: in either case it is a question of natural beings providing themselves with artificial objects, by forcing other natural beings to take a form they do not themselves spontaneously assume. The world is thus a kind of fabric, or living tissue, in which "natural movements" and "forced movements"—natural entities and artificial entities—are closely woven together, where human art represents only a particular case. It would be absurd to denigrate the place of technology in such a world, and there is no need to fall into zoolatry to recognize the distinctive character of the living things in it.

8. It has not been sufficiently appreciated that Jakobson was totally opposed to the idea that each language constructs its phonological system on the basis of materials taken ad libitum from the set of sounds available to the human voice (see Jakobson 1963); his work is a much-needed corrective to the Saussurian dogma of the arbitrariness of the sign, that is, the absence of any correlation between signifier and signified (see Jakobson 1960). As for the idea that each language cuts up the light spectrum in its own way, it has come in for harsh criticism ever since the first attempts to verify it empirically (see Berlin and Kay 1969). It is now clear that, notwithstanding their diversity, both phonological systems and color classifications are constructed in accordance with universal principles.

9. I say "at a minimum" since to predict an event does not suffice to explain it: it was possible to predict eclipses long before it was possible to explain them. Leibniz compared scientific explanation to the discovery of a cipher in cryptography that by itself makes it possible to make sense of a series of terms that, though they display regularities, seem meaningless.

10. On the neglect of these fundamental rules, which mars much work in the human and social sciences, see Popper ([1944–1945] 1961).

11. Though the corpus analyzed by Testart does not contain these specific cases, he does contemplate their possibility in connection with certain Aeta (or Agta) groups in the Philippines, where women take part in bow hunting. This particular case, he quite rightly notes, would be compatible with the principle of separation "if women could hunt with the bow only outside their menstrual periods," a point he himself had been unable to decide (Testart 1986a, 48). Caution is therefore indicated. But in the absence of any further evidence, it is reasonable to suppose that we are dealing here with an ethnographic lacuna rather than a counterexample. The Eskimo case points in the same direction: Testart's research provides confirmation only of the rule, observed in most Eskimo societies, that use of the harpoon is reserved for men and that women are allowed only to bludgeon seals with a club (see 13 and 48). As we have just seen, however, this rule is not absolute, and when women are permitted to use the harpoon it is indeed subject to the condition stipulated by Testart.

12. This conjunction of bloody acts, of murder with blood ritual, is noteworthy because it is atypical. As a general rule, a murderer cannot become a sacrificer, and a sacrificer who commits homicide is deprived of his office. Sacrifice is a sui generis form of killing: like murder, it destroys life; but unlike murder it is a source of life, as procreation also is (see Hocart [1936] 1970; Girard [1972b] 1977; Scubla 1999). In making Chen Jinggu die following an abortion, the myth very elegantly

describes the impossibility of combining these three things: murder, sacrifice, and procreation, which taken pairwise are incompatible.

13. This silence is significant. As often happens in the absence of a theory to be tested, the ethnographer, no matter how scrupulous he or she may be, gives an incomplete description of the facts observed, whereas a general hypothesis such as Testart's naturally invites—and even requires, if it is to be confirmed or disconfirmed—much more precise observations. It is theory, as Auguste Comte insisted, that makes observation possible; but this precept is still too often ignored in anthropology (see Scubla 2009c).

14. The primary function of war was probably to capture human victims for sacrifices (see Hocart 1933, 269–70), as the famous case of the Aztecs attests. War, in other words, is a form of human hunting, one of whose variants is called, very tellingly, headhunting (see Hocart 1954, 143–45). Moreover, hunting itself is at bottom as much a ritual as an economic activity (see Burkert [1972] 1983, 12–48), and not least a means of procuring sacrificial victims, as the bear festival of the Ainu in Japan attests. Butchery derives from the ritual preparation and cutting up of the sacrificial victim. It is well known, for example, that in antiquity, in both Athens and Jerusalem, the slaughterhouse was an annex of the temple. Finally, the ritual origin of medicine and surgery can scarcely be doubted (see Hocart 1933, 213–22; 1954, 123–28); in particular, it is highly probable that animal dissection and the inspection of entrails for purposes of divination gave rise to both surgery and the diagnosis of illness.

15. "We are hardly in need of proof," Bettelheim now remarks, "that men stand in awe of the procreative power of women, that they wish to participate in it, and that both emotions are found readily in Western society" (Bettelheim [1954] 1962, 10).

16. See Héritier (1979) and Testart (1985, 364; 1987a; 1988; 1991, 48). Note that, even though it was published in 1986, Testart's essay on the sexual division of labor actually dates from 1982, and is therefore prior to Testart 1985 (finished 1984)—which explains why this essay could be mentioned in the bibliography of an apparently earlier work.

17. Recall that Leroi-Gourhan, having given the name "percussion" to the elementary action of a technological object on a material to be transformed (or gathered, or extracted, etc.), proposed classifying all such objects principally as a function of two criteria: the mode of percussion, whereby an object may be hurled (as with a pick or an arrow), or pushed (as with a plane or a needle), or driven with the aid of a striking tool (as with a chisel or mallet), which combines the two previous modes; and the type of percussion, which, depending whether it occurs at a point, or along a line, or over a surface, is called pointed (as with a pickaxe or a needle), linear (as with an axe or plane), or diffuse (as with a pestle or a millstone). The reader will readily see that these two criteria are independent, and by themselves make it possible to define nine broad classes of technological objects.

18. See the passage (Thom [1972] 1977, 97), cited earlier in chapter 3, where the author draws conclusions that are far from trivial. From the fact that the male sex exhibits "a more elliptical nature" than the female sex, Thom thinks it possible to explain two properties that are, he says, roughly verified from the bacterium *E. coli* to humans: that males are "more hairy (in a general sense) than their mates, and also biologically more fragile" (97). In the same spirit, one of Thom's disciples has tried to formalize the disjunction and conjunction of the sexes on the basis of two orthogonal figures defined within the framework of matroid theory (see Bruter 1973, 96–119).

19. "Natural" does not mean universal and necessary, nor legitimate, but first and foremost spontaneous. As I have already stressed, each society represents a choice of civilization; but this choice does not consist in shaping a neutral material ad libitum, in constructing a "culture" on the

ground of a "nature" that is totally external, indifferent, and foreign to it. Just as a horticulturist may prune an apple tree in various ways, to form a cordon or a fan-shaped espalier or a double-U shape, so each culture arranges and fashions irreducible natural tendencies in an original manner. Horticulture, and technology in general, represent a scale model of culture that is more instructive for our purposes than language and symbolism, which structuralism is so fond of and which open the way to every sort of constructivist illusion.

20. In speaking of a general neglect, evidently I do not mean that the facts falling under the jurisdiction of Testart's law have not been observed or collected by ethnologists, but that they continue to be without order or method, at the mercy of circumstances, incomplete and erratic, as most of the phenomena of our physical environment were before the advent of rational mechanics.

21. In 1986 the journal *L'Homme* noticed the appearance of Testart's monograph in its list of books received, but never published a review. Testart's article "La femme et la chasse," which appeared the same year in *La Recherche* (Testart 1986b), provoked an acerbic reaction from Michel Perrin (see Perrin 1987; Testart 1987c).

22. Considering certain recent aspects of this crisis, Jean-Pierre Digard (2012) has gone so far as to speak of an "obscurantist turn in anthropology."

23. The new version, slightly revised, of Tabet's seminal article (Tabet 1998) fails to mention Testart's work either in its text or its bibliography.

24. While it is true that a scientific hypothesis must have the form of a refutable proposition and that a single counterexample suffices to refute it, the mechanical application of "Popperian" principles can lead to catastrophic results (which has led wags, parodying the title of a famous book by the philosopher, to speak of the "poverty of Popperism"). It is in fact very difficult, if not impossible, to isolate from the whole of our knowledge, which is to say from the set of all surviving hypotheses, a particular proposition and to test its validity separately from the rest; when an observation is contrary to what we expect, we know only that at least one of our hypotheses is false, without necessarily being able to say which one (or ones): this is what is called the Duhem-Quine thesis. Moreover, a general hypothesis, or law, is always preferable to a collection of particular facts. This is why, as the whole of the history of science testifies, one never abandons a law so long as it cannot be replaced by a more powerful law, which is to say one that preserves the explanatory power of the original hypothesis while also accounting for the facts that it is incapable of explaining. Finally, when a general hypothesis, corroborated by many experiments or observations, encounters a phenomenon that seems to cast it in doubt, it often happens that the phenomenon arises from an unknown factor, which is to say one that is subsumed under another law whose existence was not suspected and that interferes with the original hypothesis. Thus the law of inertia, a pillar of classical mechanics, is not refuted because it is unobservable in the majority of our experiments and observations; to the contrary, the law makes it possible to detect the very forces (gravitational forces, for example) that seem to invalidate it, and even to determine their value.

      By virtue of the order that it introduces among a multitude of otherwise apparently disparate observations, Testart's law, even when restricted to hunter-gatherer societies, and a fortiori when extended to all activities involving bloodshed, seems to have the character of these great classical laws. One must be all the more circumspect with regard to facts that seem to tell against it since relations such as those associating men with the spear and women with the pestle, or men with the bow and women with the basket (see Clastres 1966), while they are universal, may sometimes be systematically reversed in certain well-determined ritual contexts. Serge Tcherkézoff, in a fine book (1983) inspired by the theoretical perspective of Louis Dumont, gives many such examples. It was on the basis of inversions of this kind, detached from their context, that Lévi-Strauss sometimes tried to deny the existence of a universal sexual symbolism. It is a simple matter to correct this error, however; see in this connection Scubla (1983, 807–8) on a curious passage in the second volume of *Mythologiques* (Lévi-Strauss 1969–1981, 2:349–50), which has also been discussed by Alain Caillé (1986).

25. One might even add, to lend credence to this reversibility, that if hunting implies the taking of life, it is also a source of food and, by virtue of this, a gift of life; and, conversely, that if menstrual blood is, by its very nature, from the onset of menstruation to menopause, the sign of potential fertility, and therefore of the gift of life, its flow, sometimes interpreted as a sign of miscarriage (see Hocart 1954, 108), itself marks the absence of pregnancy and therefore a want of life, and may even be seen as a gift of death.

26. A significant detail: when a man has killed an enemy, he must drink for five days a bitter beverage "identical to the one that women drink during their periods and expectant fathers in couvade" (Viveiros de Castro 1996, 82). I shall discuss the practice of couvade in a later chapter. The article by Viveiros de Castro appeared in a journal issue entitled "Destinies of Murderers" that contains a wealth of ethnographic observations that are instructive for our purposes here.

27. One must nevertheless mention a relatively recent work by Maurice Godelier, belatedly recognizing that "at the foundation of human societies" neither the economy nor kinship is to be found, as had previously been believed, but instead the sacred (Godelier 2007). Let us hope that Godelier's farewell to Marx and Lévi-Strauss, having made no mention either of Durkheim or Hocart, will be followed by a more systematic work than the last—a work of which the anthropological community is sorely in need.

28. The system for assigning names is, in reality, often more complex. I limit myself here to what the reader needs to know in order to follow the argument.

29. This equivalence of shedding these two kinds of blood, attested by Saladin d'Anglure himself, nonetheless does not prevent him a few lines earlier from reproaching both Paola Tabet and Alain Testart for being committed to what he calls an inappropriate dualistic framework, and for interpreting the cases of female hunters observed among the Inuit as exceptional—although this is just what they are.

30. The very existence of the pangolin, Mary Douglas notes, "contradicts all the most obvious animal categories. It is scaly like a fish, but it climbs trees. It is more like an egg-laying lizard than a mammal, yet it suckles its young. And most significant of all, unlike other small mammals its young are born singly" (Douglas 1966, 168).

31. It is clear that for the Inuit, as for all other peoples, the child has no difficulty recognizing his or her true sex. This observation would be superfluous were it not for the fact that some commentators on Saladin d'Anglure's work call the sex determined by biology (or, more exactly, by nature) the "apparent sex," and the one determined by the naming ceremony the "real sex" (see, for example, Héritier 1996, 202–3).

32. This freedom is a well-known property of so-called intuitionist logic, which attempts to show that the principle of excluded middle (p or not-p) is independent of the principle of non-contradiction (not [p and not-p]), traditionally supposed to be the foundation of rational thought. The "logic of fuzzy sets" that Saladin d'Anglure (2012, 156) seems bent on opposing to classical logic is in fact only an extension of it.

33. On the interpolation theorem see, for example, Kleene 1967, 349–61. Kleene's exposition of the principles of mathematical logic is unavoidably rather dense, owing to his desire to provide an exhaustive treatment of the subject, but not the least of its virtues is the comparison of classical and intuitionist points of view throughout.

Chapter 9. Nature and Culture: The Return of the Sophists
in Western Thought

1. See, for example, the altogether caricatural first chapter of a famous (and quite detailed) work on "wild children" (Malson 1964).

2. The Sophists could be said to have been the first relativist anthropologists. Impressed by the variability of customs and institutions, in contrast to the stability of natural phenomena, they concluded that these are all artificial and arbitrary constructions—hence the opposition of human laws, diverse and contingent, to natural regularities, uniform and necessary. But from this they did not all draw the same conclusions: some, holding that men are all equal by nature, called for the abolition of slavery; others, observing that some are stronger or more intelligent than their fellows, argued that nothing except an arbitrary decree could prevent the most powerful from enslaving the weakest (see Schuhl [1934] 1949, 356–64).

3. Today the term "anthropology," used in a general sense, refers to social anthropology. The shift in denotation is not trivial. Anthropologists used to study both race and civilization—"nature" and "culture." As late as the 1960s, the training of an ethnologist in France, at the Musée de l'Homme, still included an initiation into physical anthropology, which, like other disciplines, was differentialist; in other words, students were expected to have a broad acquaintance with not only the cultural and social differences between human populations, but also the natural differences. By its tendency to reduce ethnology to social anthropology—a stronger field than it once was, but still cut off from both physical anthropology and cultural technology—the academic reforms instituted after 1968 had the perverse effect of widening the gap between nature and culture, and leading by way of reaction to attempts at naturalization—the reduction of any kind of phenomenon to the physical laws of mechanics—that represent yet another symptom of the disease rather than an effective way of curing it.

4. The introduction to *The Elementary Structures of Kinship* respects the canons of philosophical composition. There is a delightful moment in *Tristes tropiques* when Lévi-Strauss makes a mockery of the verbal maneuvers and rhetorical ingenuity whose command constitutes a large part of what serves as training for "philosophers" (see Lévi-Strauss [1955] 1961, 54–55); alas, both before and after this memorable passage, he does not hesitate to avail himself of the very expedients that he himself so scathingly describes.

5. The matter appears still more clearly in medieval literature, notably in the writings of Robert de Boron, who seems to have been the first to give a Christian interpretation of the quest for the Holy Grail, identifying the precious vessel with the one that Jesus used for his final meal and imagining that later it contained his blood. The outstanding sensory quality of the Grail is the delightful fragrance that emanates from it. Robert implicitly associates this holy scent less with the Virgin Mary, who "has the lovely smell of wild rose" (Robert de Boron [ca. 1200] 1995, 17) than with Mary Magdalene, and more precisely with the perfume with which she anointed Jesus—a scene that, taking liberties with the canonical text, he set on the day of the Last Supper: "She found Jesus seated at the table, with his disciples: Judas ate in front of Jesus. She crouched beneath the table and knelt down at Jesus's feet, began to weep and to wash the feet of Our Lord with her tears and she wiped them dry with her beautiful hair. Then she rubbed them, as well as the head of Jesus, with a precious ointment that she had brought. The dwelling place was filled with the fragrance and good odor of this ointment, to the amazement of all" (20). All except Judas, who flew into a rage—thus throwing into still starker relief the unity of the Christian community, symbolized by the perfume applied by Mary Magdalene.

Chapter 10. Reik, Guardian of Dogma: Couvade, Initiation Rites, and the Oedipus Complex

1. It is quite true, of course, that demons also represent the many diseases that, in the absence of proper hygiene, likewise pose a genuine threat to the life of the child and the woman who delivers it. But this classic explanation of superstitions is insufficient. It is incapable of giving a complete account of the facts analyzed by Reik. The dangers faced by human beings do not come solely from external factors whose existence and mode of action they are unaware of. Additionally, and perhaps primarily, they come from human impulses themselves. Without this further assumption, one cannot explain why many forms of infanticide, ritual or otherwise, coexist with the idea, itself also very widespread, that a child is a very precious and fragile thing. The purpose of rites and "superstitions," as Reik sees and shows, is one way or another to control these dangerous impulses.

2. The redemption of the firstborn is discussed in the third part of his essay on couvade (see Reik [1919] 1931, 70–76), where the facts are weighed down with psychoanalytical considerations that help neither to illuminate nor to explain them.

3. We find also in this example a very general principle, already encountered at the outset of our inquiry: killing is equivalent, for a man, to bringing a child into the world for a woman. Among the Guayaki, this principle has an important corollary. When a hunter dies in the prime of life, a little girl is killed, generally one of his own children, to avenge his death and to accompany him in the hereafter (see Clastres 1972, 202). In sum, when a woman gives birth to a child, a man must kill an animal, and when the killer of an animal dies, a person capable of giving birth must also die. Hunting, gift of death, is never found but in the company of procreation, gift of life.

4. Reik is no doubt right on this point. Robertson Smith showed the belated character of the notion of a sacrificial gift, and Hubert and Mauss showed that the notion of expiation—"expulsion of an [evil] quality"—is, to the contrary, an irreducible element of sacrifice (Hubert and Mauss [1898] 1964, 17). The notion of a gift works to obscure the aspect of sacrificial violence, with the result that such violence is left wholly unexplained. Even if expiation is probably not the ultimate explanation, as Reik himself seems to suspect, it holds greater promise than either an offering or a gift for unraveling the enigma of sacrifice, that strange alliance of violence and the sacred, of crime and the religious obligation that characterizes it. Despite its defects, the great merit of *Totem and Taboo* is to confront this enigma.

5. On the crucial distinction between the expiation of a transgression, under the head of which come penalties and punishments, and compensation for an injury, under the head of which come vengeance and reprisals, see the invaluable commentaries of François Tricaud (1977) and Raymond Verdier (1980).

6. Hubert and Mauss rely on the story of the son of Moses, an exemplary case of circumcision, to illustrate the capacity of sacrifice to protect the sacrifier from deadly contact with the divine: "[The victim] alone penetrates into the perilous domain of sacrifice. . . . The sacrifier remains protected: the gods take the victim instead of him. *The victim redeems him.* Moses had not circumcised his son, and Yahweh came to 'wrestle' with him in a hostelry. Moses was on the point of death when his wife savagely cut off the child's foreskin and, casting it at Yahweh's feet, said to him: 'Thou art for me a husband of blood.' The destruction of the foreskin satisfied the god; he did not destroy Moses, who was redeemed" (Hubert and Mauss [1898] 1964, 98–99).

7. Among the Iatmul, for example, the father presents his young son with a captured man from a neighboring community for him to kill with a spear thrust. Since he is not yet strong enough to do this by himself, his maternal uncle holds the spear and guides the child's attempt (see Bateson [1936] 1958, 38).

8. See, for example, the equation "skull = womb" (Maranda and Maranda 1970), which summarizes the structure of Lau society described in chapter 8.

9. Van Gennep ([1909] 1960) and Hocart (1927) independently elucidated a structure common to the majority of rites, the former in terms of separation followed by aggregation, the latter in terms of death followed by rebirth. Having shown that the most common rites are avatars or survivals of royal consecration ceremonies, Hocart went on (in a posthumously published work) to suggest that the first kings were dead kings, which is to say sacrificial victims, and that human sacrifice is therefore the prototype of all rites (see Hocart 1954, 74–85). More recently, Girard has taken another step in the same direction, arguing in favor of "the unity of all rites" (see Girard [1972b] 1977, 274–308) and tracing their common source to a collective, spontaneous act of violence, the "scapegoat mechanism," which operates in all times and in all places. The murder of the primal father in *Totem and Taboo*, with which it is often confused, is neither the original form of rites nor, a fortiori, their foundation, but only a particular occurrence, and more likely a mythical than a real one. Girard's theory is thus more systematic than those of his predecessors. Even so, whereas Hocart made sacred marriage a key element of the paradigmatic ceremony of the installation of the king, Girard's theory has the defect of totally neglecting the relations between the coronation rite and procreation. In this respect it resembles both psychoanalysis and structural anthropology.

10. See, for example, Hocart (1954, 81–83).

11. Indeed, Devereux's aims here are at least as much normative as descriptive. He reproves the pretension to create ex nihilo, which Auguste Comte called metaphysical, and implicitly contrasts it with "feminine" wisdom, which we will encounter later in considering the founder of positivism.

12. The reference here to Lévi-Strauss's 1985 book, *La potière jalouse*, conceals a pun: in French, to beat about the bush is to go around in circles; literally, to go around the pot (*tourner autour du pot*).—Trans.

13. In the first chapter of his book, Lévi-Strauss mentions a myth in which Auju ("the Goatsucker"), in a jealous rage, shattered in pieces a child whom Moon had made out of clay ([1985] 1988, 17–18). Even though the motives of jealousy and greed occupy a very large place in the rest of this work, the myth itself is never analyzed or even mentioned again. An interesting detail: in this Jivaro myth, Moon has been created in virtually the same fashion as Adam. Lévi-Strauss interprets this as a manifest borrowing from the Bible, the Jivaro having been in contact with missionaries from the sixteenth century onward (see 17).

14. I take the liberty of very slightly reformulating Dumont's insight. Immediately before the sentence from which I have just quoted, he writes: "On a first level, man and woman are identical; on a second level, woman is opposite or the contrary of man" (Dumont [1979] 1980, 240). In reality, on the first level, man and woman are not identical, but still undifferentiated and indiscernible. The relation of encompassing, or inclusion, is already present in it, though only potentially, in the person of Adam. The second level is indeed, as Dumont says, one of opposition, of the mutual exteriority of man and woman. It is thus this level, this opposition, that makes manifest the relation of encompassing, which obviously is not constituted by it, but which results from the relation between the two levels.

15. Dumont does not make this relation to the whole explicit, and the manner in which he mentions it, in connection with the case we are now considering, is fairly obscure: "Only by reference to the first level can there be unity at the second. . . . You may well declare the two sexes equal, but the more you manage to make them equal, the more you will destroy the unity between them (in the couple or the family), because *the principle of this unity is outside them and because, as such, it necessarily hierarchizes with respect to one another*" (Dumont [1979] 1980, 240–41; italics in the original).

16. Useful illustrations of the principle of hierarchical reversal are found in a work by one of Dumont's disciples, Serge Tcherkézoff (1983), who recasts the whole catalog of dualist classifications in light of this idea. He seeks to go beyond both Lévi-Strauss's binarism, discussed explicitly and at length, and Girard's theory of violence and the sacred, implicitly acknowledged but summarily dismissed: "A universal theory of sacrifice (or of exchange) such as this," he says, "would distract our attention from the essential point" (146). Nevertheless, if it is easy enough to see how Dumont's hierarchical theory develops and completes Lévi-Strauss's structural theory, the rejection of Girard's is all the more surprising as it identifies sacrifice as the mechanism for passing from one level to another and for inverting hierarchy (see 146 n. 19; also 146).

17. "Dentcico," it will be recalled, is an anagram of the French word for "West."—Trans.

18. This object is sometimes referred to in its French spelling, *churinga*.—Trans.

19. See the final pages of Moisseeff 1997, subsequently published under the same title in *Sexe et guérison*, ed. André Durandeau, Jean-Marie Sztalryd, and Charlyne Vasseur-Fauconnet (Paris: L'Harmattan, 1998), 45–74.

Chapter 11. Hierarchy of the Sexes and Hierarchy of Knowledge, or Plato among the Baruya

1. See Aristotle, *On the Generation of Animals*, 737ᵃ 25–30, 766ᵃ 30–35; Spinoza, *Political Treatise*, 11.4; and the lecture on femininity in Freud [1932] 1964, 22:112–35.

2. The distance between woman and man among the Sara is nonetheless greater than that between king and Brahman. Like initiates, the latter two are both "twice-born"; each holds a preeminent position in the great rituals, the king in his royal capacity as "sacrifier," the Brahman in his priestly role as "sacrificer."

3. "The symbols have no intrinsic and invariable significance; they are not independent in relation to context. Their significance is primarily *positional*" (Lévi-Strauss 1969–1981, 1:56; emphasis in the original).

4. For Dumont, who separates political power from religious status, the king is principally, indeed exclusively, a political leader. In Hocart's view he is the principal figure of ritual, and the Brahman himself one of his assistants, or rather the one who occupies the highest rank. But even if the Brahman is the king's chaplain, "he is so high that he becomes higher than the king" (Hocart 1950, 68). Dumont's model has been a subject of debate in this regard, and some Indologists prefer Hocart's formulation (see Quigley 1993). I myself am inclined to side with them. Nevertheless, whatever the outcome of this debate may be, Dumont's hierarchical model itself will not have been invalidated, because it is independent of the caste system and attested elsewhere (see Jamous 1981; Tcherkézoff 1983).

5. Though structuralist orthodoxy appealed to the authority of Saussure, it confused the contrastive and semantic values of a sign—two quite distinct properties, as Kurt Goldstein's work on aphasia established almost a century ago (see Jakobson 1963, 60–61). Phonological systems are not constructed on the basis of just any sounds, arbitrarily selected from the whole of the phonatory possibilities of the human voice. All languages issue from a single fundamental triangle, which itself has two parts, a vocalic triangle and a corresponding consonantal triangle (see 137ff.). All languages possess the same vocalic triangle (a, i, u), constituted not only by the same relations but by the same elements. All instances of the vowel *a* are variants of the same sound (they have neighboring spectra and different Fourier coefficients). The thesis of the "arbitrariness of the sign," which goes back to the Greeks, turns out to be no more than very roughly true. Far from

confirming it, linguistics tends instead to show its limitations (see Jakobson 1960; Guiraud 1969; Leach 1971), if not actually to rehabilitate a certain form of "Cratylism" (see Nef 1979).

6. See Girard [1972b] 1977, to which I shall return later.

7. See the intervention by Godelier in Piatelli-Palmarini et al. 1978, 3:144–45. For a detailed presentation of the initiation rites of the Baruya, see Godelier [1982] 1986.

8. Hence the traditional practice of dividing the text into three parts. Léon Robin, in his introduction to the Belles Lettres edition published more than eighty years ago (see Plato 1929, vii–cxxi), observes that "the banquet is only a prologue" (xiii) to a "program," of which Socrates's speech constitutes the "closing number," whereas the final episode with Alcibiades forms a third part that falls "outside the program" (xcviii). Robin notes also that "the transition to the main part is accompanied by libations, prayers, and hymns" that make it "an almost religious act . . . , governed by traditional rites" (xiii).

9. A magisterial example of this type of structural analysis of Platonic texts is found in Brague 1978.

10. Ethnologists long ago showed that women were the best guardians of the male order. See, for example, Tillion (1966, 14, 204, 207).

11. A well-known detail of the *Symposium* brings out another characteristic of the ideal philosophical initiation. Whereas among the Baruya initiation includes an actual homosexual relationship between adolescents and adults, Alcibiades's confessions reveal that Socrates considers the pedagogical and pedophiliac relationship to be exclusively spiritual.

12. In the last chapter I shall discuss a related conception of philosophical activity, and of knowledge in general, in the writings of Auguste Comte.

13. Contrary to Alland, I believe that primacy must be accorded to the female interpretation of the making of scarecrows.

14. See Alland 1985, 42–43; Héritier 1996, 217; Godelier [1982] 1986, 70–71.

15. See Alland 1985, 45–51; Héritier 1996, 216–18.

16. Certain myths are very explicit on this point. In one Australian case, cited by Alland (1985, 46), a woman tells her sister: "The men have stolen the power of our totems and will never give it back. But not all is lost: we have the greatest of all powers, which cannot be taken from us. For children can come only from our womb."

17. A proposition *p* is said technically to be a matter of common knowledge if not only everyone knows *p*, but everyone knows that everyone knows *p*, everyone knows that everyone knows that everyone knows *p*, and so on indefinitely.

Chapter 12. Ethnology and Psychology in Róheim and Devereux: Identity, Homology, or Complementarity?

1. I examine only Róheim's theoretical views in what follows. For a critical appraisal of his empirical work, by an Australian specialist, see Barbara Glowczewski (1991).

2. The tale unfolds in keeping with the tripartite sequence of rites of passage identified by van Gennep. Separation rite: abandonment of the children in the forest, where a bird guides them to the witch's house. Liminal (or threshold) rite: a stay of several weeks in the witch's house, where they are nearly killed. Incorporation rite: return to the paternal home, thanks to a duck (according

to some versions, a white swan) who ferries them across the body of water separating the world of initiation from the world of ordinary experience.

3. It will be remarked that while the opposition of the sexes is pronounced among the adults (more precisely, between husband and wife), the contrary is true between brother and sister, where complementarity and reciprocity prevail. In the first part of the story, Hansel reassures his sister and demonstrates ingenuity in foiling their parents' plans; in the second part, Gretel does away with the witch and frees her brother, and then proves herself to be the more prudent of the two in considering how best to cross the water.

4. On these aspects of the royal institution, see Frazer ([1891] 1994); de Heusch (1987); Muller (1975); Scubla (2003).

5. Devereux's casual tone, his interest in structural anthropology, and his habit of referring to the hard sciences are apt to put one in mind of Lacan. The resemblance is merely superficial. For Devereux, Lacan was neither a model nor a rival, but a foil. Heaping scorn on the "nutty remarks that pass in some quarters today for psychoanalysis" (Devereux 1982, 165), Devereux refused to evade the difficulties that arise from substituting, in the manner of ancient oracles, for "a meaningful, though as yet incomprehensible, reality a purely verbal rebus inherently devoid of sense" ([1970b] 1980, ix). Notwithstanding the impression he gave of being an unruly disciple, Devereux remained unfailingly faithful to Freud's main ideas, and, despite an abiding concern to make Freud's arguments agree with those of Lévi-Strauss, allergic to Lévi-Strauss's intellectualism. Lacan, by contrast, while calling for a "return to Freud," assimilated the Freudian unconscious to the formal and empty unconscious of Lévi-Strauss, and undertook to reconstruct psychoanalysis on new foundations—philosophical, linguistic, topological, all of them totally foreign to its founder—which he felt at liberty to arrange and rearrange as the spirit moved him. Without seeking to reconcile Devereux and Lacan, Roger Bastide, an ethnologist close to Devereux who wrote a very fine preface to his *Essais d'ethnopsychiatrie générale*, also wrote a few pages on Lacan, subtle and profound, that are well worth a look (see Bastide [1950] 1972, 200–205).

6. For Lévi-Strauss, cooking is essentially—and for the same reason as matrimonial exchange—a paradigmatic symbol of the transition from nature to culture. As he famously says in connection with the function of animals in totemism, "natural species are chosen not because they are 'good to eat' but because they are 'good to think'" (Lévi-Strauss [1962a] 1964, 89).

7. Readers who have no interest in epistemological questions should feel free to skip this section and proceed directly to the next.

8. Poincaré expounded this principle in *Science and Hypothesis* (see [1902] 1952, 217–24). There he is concerned with phenomena satisfying the principle of least action, which applies in a great many areas of physics: "If the principle of least action cannot be satisfied, no mechanical explanation is possible; if it can be satisfied, there is not only one explanation, but an unlimited number, whence it follows that since there is one there must be an unlimited number. . . . If therefore a phenomenon allows of a complete mechanical explanation, it allows of an unlimited number of others, which will equally take into account all the particulars revealed by experiment" (221–22). It is essential to note that these explanations can only account for "all the particulars revealed by experiment," and not elucidate "the nature of the phenomenon," as Devereux claims. The existence of a plurality of different explanations, with equivalent interpretive or predictive power, reveals to the contrary the difficulty of getting to the bottom of things.

9. Conventionalism proposes a modest conception of scientific truth. Not being able to get to the bottom of things, to say how things really are, science cannot establish absolute truths; it can only construct more or less convenient models of reality. Since it is impossible to establish the existence

of absolute space, for example, it follows that "these two propositions, 'the earth turns round,' and, 'it is more convenient to suppose that the earth turns round,' have one and the same meaning. There is nothing more in one than in the other" (Poincaré [1902] 1952, 117; see also Poincaré [1905] 1958, 140–41, aimed at dispelling the misunderstandings to which this assertion gave rise).

10. Leibniz often described the possibility of explaining the same phenomenon through efficient causes (Huygens) and through final causes (Fermat) as a way of reconciling the mechanicalism of modern physics with the finalism of Aristotelian physics. But this example can hardly be considered dispositive, for the "finality" that is at issue here is merely apparent; it is an illusory finality, a pseudo-finality (see Ruyer 1946, 226). Moreover, Leibniz himself recognized that proceeding by means of final causes is, everything considered, "easier," whereas proceeding by means of efficient causes is "deeper" and, for this reason, to be preferred, though "rather difficult when one comes to the detail of it" (*Discours de métaphysique* [1686], §22). If, like Leibniz, one really wishes to reintroduce finalism into the sciences, one must do more than he himself did to rehabilitate the general principles of Aristotelian physics, and show how the mechanicalism of classical physics can be deduced from them (see Ruyer 1946, passim).

11. The topic of wave-particle duality in quantum mechanics is presented in a very accessible manner by Richard Feynman ([1965] 1967, 127–48), a transcription of the sixth in a series of seven lectures delivered at Cornell University. It is all the more interesting as, in a previous lecture, Feynman had illustrated Poincaré's thesis with examples of his own that amount to three different but equivalent ways of stating the law of universal gravitation (see 50–55). In the quantum case, there is no choice but to rely on two complementary theories; in the other case, any one of the three theories suffices to encompass the entire domain subsumed under the law.

Chapter 13. Should *Totem and Taboo* Simply Be Forgotten?

1. The provisions of the penal code of 1810 (Evans translation [London, 1819]) are as follows:

> Art. 13. The person condemned to death for parricide shall be conducted to the place of execution in a shirt, barefooted, and with his head covered by a black veil. He shall be exposed on the scaffold, whilst a sergent shall read to the people the sentence of condemnation; he shall then have his right hand cut off, and immediately be put to death.

> Art. 86. An attempt or plot against the life or person of the emperor is a crime of high treason; this crime is punished as parricide; and, moreover, infers the confiscation of property.

Just as the civil code, which Napoleon considered to be his finest achievement, dating from 1804, preceded the penal code, the punishment inflicted upon the parricide is defined before the punishment of the crime of lèse-majesté and serves as a model for it. It is as though Napoleon, heir to the Revolution and fascinated, like all its actors, by ancient Rome, had felt justified after the abolition of the monarchy in "resacralizing" the father of antiquity, for want of any other transcendent mooring, in the hope of founding imperial authority itself on this new rock. But in so doing he overlooked the fact that the responsibilities of the Roman *paterfamilias*, as Fustel de Coulanges was to recall a few decades later, were chiefly religious in character, whereas the father of the civil code was merely a bourgeois property owner.

2. So-called crimes against humanity seem to have replaced parricide in the hierarchy of transgressions.

3. "The ethnological problem is therefore, in the last analysis, a problem of communication" (Lévi-Strauss 1950, xxxii). Lévi-Strauss shared with many of his contemporaries in the middle of the last century a naive faith that they were witnessing the advent of "a vast science of communication," encompassing linguistics and ethnology—this on the basis mainly of Claude Shannon's theorems (see xxxvi–xxxvii), the nature of which he misunderstood, as did most social scientists without mathematical training, and the scope of which he overestimated. He himself even wrote a brief paper at the time entitled "Toward a General Theory of Communication" (Lévi-Strauss [1952] 1965).

4. The Schema L is supposed to describe the structure of the subject as it is manifested in the analytic relation, which is not a dual relation but a quaternary relation comparable to a game of bridge (see Lacan 1966a, 589). Here is how Lacan himself presents the simplified version of his Schema L: "This schema signifies that the condition of the subject S (neurosis or psychosis) is dependent on what is being unfolded [sic] in the Other O. What is being unfolded there is articulated like a discourse (the unconscious is the discourse of the Other). . . . Why would the subject be interested in this discourse, if he were not taking part in it? He is, indeed, a participator, in that he is stretched over the four corners of the schema: namely, S, his ineffable, stupid existence[;] o, his objects[;] o', his ego, that is, that which is reflected of his form in his objects[;] and O, the locus from which the question of his existence may be presented to him" (Lacan [1966b] 1977, 193–94).

5. Jacques-Alain Miller notes that, in the Schema L, "the symmetry or reciprocity belongs to the imaginary register, and the position of the [third term] implies that of the fourth, which is given according to the levels of the analysis, the name of 'barred subject,' or dummy [*mort*]" (in Lacan [1966b] 1977, 333). My brief summary of the quaternary structure here is not meant only to reintroduce the sacred in the form of the transcendent third party and of death. It also brings together all the elements involved in Girard's theory of the sacred: the mimetic rivals o and o', who generate the sacrificial crisis, and the complementary figures of death (S) and of God (O), products of its violent resolution. Only the victim mechanism is missing for everything to be connected from a dynamic point of view.

6. I do not know whether Foucault, writing in 1962, was inspired by Lacan's schema or whether, as seems plausible, he independently conceived of the same configuration while reading Rousseau.

7. "It is very true to say," Descombes remarks, "that the symbol is the origin of humanity. But what is the origin of the symbolic? In exchanging the *sacred*, unquestionably a disturbing notion, for *the symbolic*, apparently a concept purged of all mystery, French sociology imagines it has made progress in understanding its object. But [French sociology] asks the symbolic to do something that it is incapable of doing. It must be at once on the side of algebra, which is to say the manipulation of symbols, and on the side of the 'effectiveness of symbols,' as Lévi-Strauss put it, which is to say sacraments. The effect of sacrifices and sacraments is to produce society, from which the algebraists rush forth: one finds oneself dreaming of a kind of auto-production, of an algebra that would make it possible to manipulate society. Thus the theory of the symbolic has always fallen between two stools, half algebraic algebra and half religious algebra. It is therefore indispensable to renounce this prestigious "symbolic" in order to be able to reimagine, beyond structuralism, the enigmatic reality of the sacred" (Descombes 1979, 674).

8. "Nevertheless, Freud made an important discovery. He was the first to maintain that all ritual practices, all mythical implications, have their origins in an actual murder. . . . On the basis of secondary considerations *Totem and Taboo* was written off as misleading or trivial. . . . Freud's momentous discovery, the only one of which it may be said with certainty that it is destined to write down his name in the register of *science*, has always been held to be worthless, and ignored as

if it had never taken place" (Girard [1972b] 1977, 201). [The final sentence in the passage quoted has been translated with reference to the original French, having for the most part been omitted in the English version; see Girard 1972a, 276.—Trans.]

9. "The victim of the sacrifice, a camel, 'is bound upon a rude altar of stones piled together, and when the leader of the band has thrice led the worshippers round the altar in a solemn procession accompanied with chants, he inflicts the first wound . . . and in all haste drinks the blood that gushes forth. Forthwith the whole company fall on the victim with their swords, hacking off pieces of the quivering flesh and devouring them raw with such wild haste, that in the short interval between the rise of the day star [to which the sacrifice was offered] . . . and the disappearance of its rays before the rising sun, the entire camel, body and bones, skin, blood and entrails, is wholly devoured'" (Freud [1913] 1955, 13:138). The description of the rite follows an account by St. Nilus, dating from the late fourth century and cited by Robertson Smith, whom Freud quotes here.

10. Sellin's work, which relies chiefly on the word of the prophet Hosea, was judged more intriguing than convincing by specialists (see the talk given in April 1970 by André Caquot at Lacan's seminar [(1991b) 2007, appendix B, 209–13). A passage in book 17 of Exodus, relating the revolt of the people against its leader at Massah and Meribah (so called for being the site of an ordeal and an altercation), has always seemed to me to lend support to the idea that Moses died a violent death. The people and their livestock are dying of thirst, and the people begin to complain about their leader in menacing tones. Moses cries out to God for help, saying: "They are almost ready to stone me!" God enjoins him to go on before his people and, armed with his rod, to strike a rock, from which will come forth the water they long to drink. This extraordinary way of obtaining water, by striking a rock rather than digging a well, suggests that the reported scene was the object of a mythical transformation consistent with Girard's model of the violent resolution of crisis. Moses is not put to death by his people under a rain of stones; instead, he gives back life to his people by splitting open a rock with his rod. His spilled blood has therefore been transformed into wholesome water. One will find in Reik's excellent essay on the shofar, which I mentioned earlier, a fine analysis of other chapters of Exodus shrewdly describing the atmosphere of collective violence in which the Jewish people received the Tables of the Law. The sound of the shofar—a wind instrument made from a ram's horn—which punctuates the great Hebrew rituals and resounds when Moses meets God on Sinai, itself recalls, as he goes on to show, the cry of a beast whose throat has been slit (see Reik [1919] 1931, 221–361).

11. In giving this very cursory presentation of Girard's theory, it has seemed to me preferable to directly link the victim mechanism with the capacity for substitution, already present in the animal world, as Girard himself does in *Violence and the Sacred* (see [1972b] 1977, 4–8), rather than to deduce it from a mimetic faculty that is supposed to account for all aspects of human individual and collective life, as Girard ([1978] 1987) was to do later. From this point of view, mimeticism acts instead as a reinforcing factor and, ultimately, a generator of crisis, which is then resolved by the mechanism's operation.

12. Girard's ideas have been more calmly examined since, and systematically compared with those of some of the great theorists of religion and society, in Camille Tarot 2008.

13. See his interpretation of the incest prohibition (Girard [1972b] 1977, 219–20).

14. Most errors in the interpretation of Girard's theory arise from the confusion of these two things: the spontaneous collective murder of the scapegoat and the ritual killing of the sacrificial victim. Girard postulates that all societies have experienced, and may experience again at any moment, violent reconciliation around a collective victim (the scapegoat), and that they possess rites preserving the trace of this experience. Contrary to what many of his critics imagine, however,

he does not hold that they all possess properly sacrificial rites (that is, rites involving sacrificial victims); what he holds to be universal is not sacrifice or any other such rite in particular, but the victim mechanism, from which, directly or indirectly, they all proceed.

15. This, according to Girard, is part of the truth that *Totem and Taboo* contains. The notion of a founding murder must be retained, but with the clear understanding that it is neither an original murder nor a murder of the father: not an original murder since, the same causes producing the same effects, the collective murder can take place again at any moment; nor a murder of the father, for the identity of the victim is of no importance—the only thing that matters is the unanimity that is formed against it. "The 'murdered father' theory of *Totem and Taboo* is clearly indefensible, but the vulnerable element is not the 'murder' but the 'father.' . . . The error lies in the concept of the father and the application of psychoanalysis; the truth lies in the concept of the collective murder and, strange as it may seem, in Freud's ethnology" (Girard [1972b] 1977, 216).

16. On this hypothesis, the gods to whom sacrifice is made are identical with human violence itself, only now reified, externalized, and kept at a distance by the victim mechanism, which is to say by a collective act of murder and by the rites that proceed from it and prolong its effects. This is the central thesis of *Violence and the Sacred* and the justification for its title.

17. If the novices, for their part, find themselves placed in the position of the emissary victim, whose fate they actually risk suffering, as we will soon see, in the eyes of the adults who pretend to put them to death and subject them to ritual surgeries, the most common of which is circumcision, they have rather the status of sacrificial victims. Following Hubert and Mauss, circumcision may well be regarded as a form of sacrifice; indeed, in certain Australian societies, this practice has the same effect as sacrifice in Mediterranean societies, namely, of putting an end to a cycle of vengeance.

18. This is another aspect of Testart's law concerning the prohibition against combining different kinds of blood. But here it is not a question, as Testart would have it, of one occurrence among many of a general prohibition against "putting S with S." Given that blood sacrifice materially resembles a murder, it is crucial to distinguish carefully between the two, for one represents legitimate violence, the other illegitimate violence, and the confusion of these two kinds is the root of what Girard calls the sacrificial crisis, a state of generalized violence of which the only possible outcomes are destruction of the society and collective murder of an emissary victim— hence the fact that most sacrifices bear the caption, as it were, "This is not a murder" (see Scubla 1999). The incompatibility of the blood of a sacrifice and the blood of a murder is therefore of a quite different character than that of its incompatibility with menstrual blood. On this particular point, it should be noted, Girard himself commits the same type of error as Testart when he considers the taboo concerning menstrual blood, whose link with procreation he passes over in silence (see Girard [1972b] 1977, 33–36; Scubla, 1982, 1985b).

Chapter 14. Freud, in Spite of Everything

1. On the desire to be the surviving member of one's group, see the fine chapter in Elias Canetti ([1960] 1962, 227–78).

2. On these aspects of Girard's mimetic theory, which were not developed in the preceding chapter, see Girard [1972b] 1977, chapters 2–8; [1978] 1987, part 1.

3. Girard could obviously object that all the societies I have mentioned have disappeared or else are now in the process of disappearing; and there can be no doubt that his analysis is corroborated by certain tendencies that undermine the stability of contemporary societies. But one must reason

over the long term. We know more or less well the last one hundred centuries of human history. What will become of the world we know today in the next one hundred centuries?

4. "It will be understood that I have not reported everything that occurred to me during the process of interpretation," he writes in a note added in 1909 (Freud [1900] 1953, 4:118 n. 2), which by itself opens the door to a whole range of possible interpretations.

5. See the photograph of the two friends seated side by side, reproduced in and commented on by Octave Mannoni (1968, 52–55).

6. Tomaselli's unidiomatic, and sometimes misleading, translation has been slightly modified. The entire passage is italicized in the original.—Trans.

7. According to Otto Rank, Jung conjectured that alchemy "sets out ultimately to beget children without a mother" (Rank [1924] 1929, 169 n. 3). On the fantasy of the self-constructed man, see Rey (2006).

8. In Comte the metaphysical claim consists, in the field of physics, in wanting to go back to the first causes of all things; in politics, in wanting to build new forms of society ex nihilo; in biology, in wanting to create new forms of life rather than transmit received life, indeed to be capable of self-generation.

9. More charitably, one might say that Freud had gone away on vacation with her rather than finish writing his article, thus inadvertently allowing his rival the time he needed to publish first.

10. These terminological subtleties serve to sharply distinguish two types of representation that escape the control of consciousness: concepts belonging to the UCS come under the head of the primary process; ones belonging to the CS-PCS come under the head of the secondary process. The distinction between these two processes is in fact more important than the one between consciousness and the unconscious.

11. The last chapter of *The Psychopathology of Everyday Life* (Freud [1901] 1960, 6:239–79) is devoted to the principle of psychical determinism.

12. At first sight this explanation may seem arbitrary. But in its defense, one could argue that the beginning of a word is the crucial part; thus in French, for example, from *cinématographe* we have *cinéma*, then *ciné*; from *stylographe*, *stylo*; from *télévision*, *télé*, and so on. Two syllables seem to be necessary to avoid confusion; but the primary process, which has no interest in such fine points, performs the reduction by conserving only the head syllable.

13. The Oedipus complex, which first appears in a letter to Fliess dated 15 October 1897, was held to be universal in *The Interpretation of Dreams* (1900) and then considered as the touchstone of psychoanalysis from *The Three Essays on the Theory of Sexuality* (1905) onward. No trace of it is found in the analysis of the dream of Irma's injection, which was prior to 1897, or in the subsequent cases that I have just discussed and that were chosen by Freud himself to describe his theory—unless, of course, one were to join Reik in interpreting the refusal to assume responsibility for fathering a child, manifested by the forgetting of the word *aliquis*, as a refusal to transmit the life received from one's own father, and therefore as a symbolic murder of the person who is thus deprived of a progeny. But nothing tells in favor of such a conjecture.

14. Girard, in the chapter just cited, clearly shows that Freud proposed two incompatible theories of incestuous desire. In the classic version of the Oedipus theory, which, it will be recalled, reverses the scenario of the myth from which it purports to draw inspiration, this desire is supposed to be spontaneous and, for this reason, able to be repressed only through the threat or fear of castration. In Freud's later theory of identification, it appears as a necessary but nonetheless secondary

consequence of the process of identification. The desire is both induced and inhibited by the father, who, on the one hand, encourages the child to imitate him in everything, and, on the other hand, prohibits the child from imitating him in anything. Freud wished to retain the Oedipus complex, which in the meantime had become the central pillar of psychoanalysis; and though he became increasingly aware of the contradiction between the two theories, he never chose between them—as if he still hoped to be able one day to bring about their impossible reconciliation.

15. In this connection see Girard's article "Système du délire," *Critique*, no. 306 (November 1972), 957–96, an ironic and shrewd discussion of *L'Anti-Œdipe* by Deleuze and Guattari, published the same year as *La violence et le sacré*.

16. Some years ago I referred to this myth in discussing disputed aspects of mimetic theory at a conference on Girard's work (see Scubla 1985b, 363); in the discussion that followed (see Dumouchel 1985, 387–81), Girard hastened to reaffirm the ambition of mimetic theory to furnish an exhaustive explanation of anthropological reality.

17. "The primitive passions, which all tend directly toward our happiness, focus only on objects that relate to it, and having only *amour de soi* as a principle, are all loving and gentle in their essence. But when, being deflected from their object by obstacles, they focus on removing the obstacle rather than on reaching the object, then their nature changes and they become irascible and hateful. And that is how *amour de soi*, which is a good and absolute feeling, becomes *amour-propre*, which is to say a relative feeling by which one makes comparisons; the latter feeling demands preferences, and its enjoyment is purely negative, as it no longer seeks satisfaction in our own benefit but solely in the harm of another" (Rousseau [1772–1774b] 1990, 1:9; translation slightly modified.—Trans.].

18. I say "theory of sacrifice" here, rather than "mimetic theory," for it is my view that the former (or, more generally, the theory of the victim mechanism) is in large part independent of the latter. For arguments in favor of this opinion see Scubla 2013.

19. Girard himself says that the significance of this decision consists in the fact that it is "a prefiguration of the mission of Christ" (Girard [1978] 1987, 242). Solomon, in other words, anticipated Jesus, who was the first to reveal, through his very death, the violent foundations of human societies, and to exhort men and women, through his words and deeds, to settle their differences peaceably, so as to avoid the snares of mimetic rivalry and the lethal consequences to which it leads.

20. Since Christian revelation, which, according to Girard, is nothing other than the revelation of mimetic rivalry and the victim mechanism, is supposed to rob this mechanism of its effectiveness and thus take away from humanity its "last sacrificial crutches" (Girard [1978] 1987, 428), man's only hope can be the imitation of Jesus Christ, which is to say the imitation of a model that can never become a rival, so that "reconciliation with God can take place unreservedly and with no sacrificial intermediary" (183). But Girard is very laconic on this point. The Kingdom of God, he says, is "the substitution of love for prohibitions and rituals—for the whole apparatus of the sacrificial religions" (196). But can human beings really do without the prohibitions and rites whose protective and salutary character he had so well demonstrated in *Violence and the Sacred*? Would the Revelation change human nature, or does he too believe, along with other intellectuals of his time, that there is no human nature? Moreover, how could love by itself assure the stability and the survival of humanity? How could human beings simultaneously escape from the hell of mimeticism and gain entry to the Kingdom of God? "Mankind," Girard says, "can cross this abyss: [for this it suffices that] all men adopt the single rule of the Kingdom of God. The decision to do so must come from each individual *separately*, however; for once, others are not involved" (199; emphasis in the original; translation slightly modified, literally reproducing within brackets a

part of the original French text to which Scubla's commentary immediately following explicitly refers.—Trans.). The "it suffices" is surprising, to say the least—and all the more if one recalls that Girard constantly disparages social contract theories, and if one notices that the conditions he sets for entering the Kingdom are virtually indistinguishable from the ones laid down by Rousseau for guaranteeing the ideal but undiscoverable general will (on Rousseau's theory of contract, see Scubla 1992a).

21. It will be noted that the text tightly intertwines, as though they were indissociable, the themes of sterility (expressly opposed to fertility) and sacrifice, whose principal modalities are enumerated in a cyclical manner: animal sacrifice, circumcision, human sacrifice, and animal sacrifice once again.

22. Girard's works having originally been published without an index for the most part, one cannot be as sure of this calculation as in the case of the Freudian corpus.

23. In a later book of interviews, he affirms only that the sacrifice of Isaac, replaced in extremis by a ram, is "extraordinary, and one of the most significant points in the whole of the Bible" for illustrating the passage from human to animal sacrifice (Girard et al. [2004] 2008, 203). Unlike Kierkegaard, paradoxically, he does not consider it worth his while to devote a book, a chapter, or even a whole page to this "great scene."

24. The story of Joseph, for which Girard (see [1999] 2001, 107–15) has a particular fondness, is not a story of mimetic rivalry; in recounting to his brothers his dreams of greatness, Joseph deliberately provokes their animosity. Nor is there anything mimetic about the story of Cain and Abel; it shows the cathartic power of sacrifice, quite apart from any other consideration. Girard himself had made the essential point earlier, in a passage of admirable concision: "The Bible offers us no background on the two brothers except the bare fact that Cain is a tiller of the soil who gives the fruits of his labor to God, whereas Abel is a shepherd who regularly sacrifices the first-born of his herds. One of the brothers kills the other, and the murderer is the one who does not have the violence-outlet of animal sacrifice at his disposal. This difference between sacrificial and nonsacrificial cults determines, in effect, God's judgement in favor of Abel. To say that God [approves] Abel's sacrificial offerings but rejects the offerings of Cain is simply another way of saying—from the viewpoint of the divinity—that Cain is a murderer, whereas his brother is not" (Girard [1972b] 1977, 4).

25. "Men who cannot look freedom in the face are exposed to anguish. They look for a banner on which they can fix their eyes. There is no longer God, king, or lord to link them to the universal. To escape the feeling of particularity they imitate *another's* desires; they choose substitute gods because they are not able to give up infinity" (Girard [1961] 1966, 65; emphasis in original). The whole second chapter of *Deceit, Desire, and the Novel* is marked by this Pascalian tone.

26. Girard's theory is no more capable of explaining the abiding force of certain emotions, images, and inclinations that do not seem to be mimetic in origin. Descartes relates that as a child he loved a little girl his own age who was slightly cross-eyed, and for a long time afterward felt a particular fondness for women suffering from strabismus (see Letter to Chanut, 6 June 1647). He adds, somewhat less plausibly, that in searching for the reason for his first love he was later cured of this tendency. We know that Freud, psychoanalyst though he was, remained all his life under the influence of his youthful love for Gisela Fluss and of the yellow color of the dress she wore when they met. The same theme runs through the work of Gérard de Nerval, who admirably describes, in *Sylvie* and in *Aurélia*, the force of such obsessions and the impossibility of putting them out of one's mind. Yet no mimeticism is either apparent or even likely as the source of these indelible traces of the choice of a first love—an example of "imprinting," a phenomenon that Konrad Lorenz showed is also found in the animal world.

27. At the time of its publication in France, *Violence and the Sacred* was considered to be an atheistic (or, at the least, a radically agnostic) theory of religion, which indeed it is. Later, in claiming to be able to deduce from it a defense of Christianity, Girard was criticized for having tried to pass off a theological proposition as a scientific program, and since then he has had the reputation of a theologian disguised as an anthropologist. And yet his theory of revelation is no less atheistic than his theory of sacrifice; they are two sides of the same coin, describing human beings—the one before, the other after the discovery of their true condition—solely in terms of mimetic confrontation. "The really important apocalyptic writings," he says—and here it must be kept in mind that, etymologically, apocalypse signifies revelation—"say nothing except that man is responsible for his history. You wish for your dwelling to be given up to you; *well then, it is given up to you*" (Girard [1978] 1987, 195; emphasis in the original). This passage confirms the lesson of *Violence and the Sacred*: violence is human; it does not express God's anger. But a God who is supposed to be good, stripped of all violence but also of all power, turns out to be just as remote as the Epicurean gods—a God who has deserted the human condition altogether, who has gone away and left human beings behind as orphans, having destroyed their religious illusions and deprived them of all ritual assistance. Without either God or master, but also without any compass or norm to guide him, man in Girard's conception is thus perfectly free, but every bit as helpless as Sartrean man, and destined, like him, if the theory is true, forever to endure a hell of mimetic others.

28. For some paths that may be worthwhile exploring see Scubla 2013, where I try to show that Girard's theory is not monolithic, and that its soundest part does not depend on the mimetic hypothesis. The victim mechanism, for example, rests primarily on the capacity of thwarted violent impulses to readily find alternate outlets.

Chapter 15. Conceiving and Transmitting

1. Kofman furnishes no statistics, but a quick glance at three of Comte's major works yields the following tally: in *Course of Positive Philosophy* (First and Second Lessons), speculation (5 occurrences), conception (31), idea (14); in *Discourse on the Positive Spirit*, speculation (42), conception (30), idea (16), notion (14); in *Positive Catechism* (preface and parts 1–3), speculation (7), conception (34), idea (2), notion (3). Unless I am mistaken, the word "concept" is never encountered.

2. Thus the title of the introductory chapter of Kofman's book, "L'inavouable" (That Which Cannot Be Acknowledged).

3. It is surprising that Kofman, who reproaches Freud for being a phallocrat (notably, and curiously, in connection with a letter to his fiancée where he declares that woman is different from man, but not inferior, "for it is rather the reverse" [quoted in Kofman 1978, 219–20]), and who devoted an entire work to the "enigma of woman" in Freud's writings, should not have managed to discover and clearly state this elementary truth, even though she cites to the relevant texts (see Kofman 1980, esp. 236). The same thing might be said with regard to a book by Geneviève Delaisi de Parseval (1981, 288), which adduces a great deal of evidence favorable to the conjecture I am advancing here, but nonetheless argues for the total equality of the sexes in respect of procreation. By contrast, a book by Bernard This (1980) seems to me much nearer the mark. Am I therefore obliged to repeat Nietzsche's famous injunction, which Kofman hurls at poor Clotilde: "*Mulier taceat de muliere*"?

4. Note that the Pinocchio theme is encountered in the mythology of the Indians of South America (see Lévi-Strauss 1969–1981, 1:55–57; [1985] 1988, 20–21); and also that, in conjunction with the Schreber case, the case of Christiane Hegel, to which Kofman alludes (see 1978, 28 n. 29),

shows that it is much easier to conceive of a female Geppetto complex than a female Oedipus complex.

5. It is far more probable that a fear of destroying this order before it could be replaced, rather than any "horror of homosexuality," was the main reason for Comte's "virile protest."

6. In this sense, and this sense only, one may agree with Kofman that "philosophical discourse . . . cannot be sexually neutral" (Kofman 1978, 42). It would nevertheless be better to say that every conception of philosophy involves a philosophy of conception.

7. On the nature and role of genetic definitions in Hobbes and Spinoza, see Guéroult (1961–1974, 2:467–87). See also Spinoza's correspondence with Tschirnhaus, which must be reread in the light of the completeness and incompleteness theorems of mathematical logic proved three centuries later, and of the different interpretations these can be given depending on the status accorded to mathematical symbols ("beings of reason" [*entia rationis*]) and geometrical figures ("auxiliaries of the imagination").

8. One might say that feminism consists in women mimicking the behavior of men who have themselves constructed their personality on the basis of an imaginary conception of women. As Jacques Derrida puts it, "Feminism is nothing but the operation of a woman who aspires to be like a man. And in order to resemble the masculine dogmatic philosopher this woman lays claim—just as much as he—to truth, science and objectivity in all their castrated delusions of virility. Feminism too seeks to castrate. It wants a castrated woman" (Derrida [1978] 1979, 65).

9. This may perhaps explain Comte's "bad style." One may wonder whether Comte in this work is not trying to reflect an imaginary unity of mother and child—as though he had not managed to wholly detach himself from the male point of view. Indeed, what is Comte's "bad style" if not a propensity to write sentences without a hole, so to speak, without the least space left over inside; to saturate them with adjectives and adverbs to the point that no complement whatever can be added to them; to endow them, in other words, with maximum "completeness"?

10. Schreber began writing in 1900, during the course of his second hospitalization (November 1893—December 1902); see the chronology in Macalpine and Hunter 1955a, 3–4.

11. Schreber's own condition improved once he accepted the idea of being transformed into a woman. On the symptomatology of his illness, see Macalpine and Hunter 1955a, 7–8; also the account of his recovery in Macalpine and Hunter 1955b, 403–4).

12. There must be something other than desire that constitutes the objective basis of the family. As Godelier puts it, "a family is founded not on the union between the sexes but on the *birth and care of the children the women will bear over their lifetime*" (Godelier [2004] 2011, 455; emphasis in the original).

13. The pupil sets himself up in a studio of his own constructed by his matriclan on land belonging to his patriclan—strengthening still further the unifying role of painting among the Tin Dama.

Bibliography

Adler, Alfred. 2007. "Initiation, royauté et féminité en Afrique noire: En deçà ou au-delà de la différence de sexes?" *L'Homme* 47, no. 183: 77–116.

Alland, Alexander, Jr. 1985. "Rituel masculin de procréation et symbolisme phallique." *L'Homme* 25, no. 94: 37–55.

Andler, Daniel, ed. 1992. *Introduction aux sciences cognitives*. Paris: Gallimard.

Anzieu, Didier. (1975) 1986. *Freud's Self-Analysis*. Translated by Peter Graham. London: Hogarth Press.

Aristotle. (1910) 1984. *On the Generation of Animals*. Translated by Arthur Platt. In *Complete Works*, 1:1111–218.

———. *Metaphysics*. (1958) 1984. Translated by W. D. Ross. In *Complete Works*, 2:1552–728.

———. 1984. *The Complete Works of Aristotle: The Revised Oxford Translation*. Edited by Jonathan Barnes. 2 vols. Princeton, N.J.: Princeton University Press.

Arnaud, Pierre. 1965. *Politique d'Auguste Comte*. Paris: Armand Colin.

Auger, Pierre. 1966. *L'homme microscopique*. 2nd ed. Paris: Flammarion.

Baal, Jan van, with the collaboration of Father J. Verschueren, MSC. 1966. *Dema: Description and Analysis of Marind-anim Culture (South New Guinea)*. The Hague: Martinus Nijhoff.

Barberi, Maria Stella, ed. 2001. *La spirale mimétique: Dix-huit leçons sur René Girard*. Paris: Desclée de Brouwer.

Barry, Laurent. 2008. *La parenté*. Paris: Gallimard.

Bastide, Roger. (1950) 1972. *Sociologie et psychanalyse*. Rev. ed. Paris: Presses Universitaires de France.

Bateson, Gregory. (1936) 1958. *Naven: A Survey of the Problems Suggested by a Composite Picture of a*

New Guinea Tribe Drawn from Three Points of View. 2nd ed. Stanford, Calif.: Stanford University Press.

Benoist, Jean-Marie, ed. (1977) 1983. *L'Identité: Séminaire interdisciplinaire.* Papers delivered at 1974–1975 Collège de France seminar sponsored by Claude Lévi-Strauss. Paris: Presses Universitaires de France.

Benveniste, Émile. 1969. *Le vocabulaire des institutions indo-européennes.* 2 vols. Paris: Minuit.

Berger, Laurent. 2009. "La parenté, entre taxinomie intuitive et réseau relationnel égocentré." *L'Homme* 49, no. 191: 249–70.

Berlin, Brent, and Paul Kay. 1969. *Basic Color Terms: Their Universality and Evolution.* Berkeley: University of California Press.

Berthier, Brigitte. 1988. *La Dame-du-bord-de-l'eau.* Nanterre: Société d'ethnologie.

Besançon, Alain. 1973. "Freud, Abraham, Laïos." *Contrepoint* 12.

Bettelheim, Bruno. (1954) 1962. *Symbolic Wounds: Puberty Rites and the Envious Male.* Rev. ed. New York: Collier Books.

Bidou, Patrice. 1979. "A propos de l'inceste et de la mort: Un mythe des Indiens Tatuyo du nord-ouest de l'Amazonie." In Izard and Smith, eds., *La fonction symbolique,* 107–38.

Bonte, Pierre, and Michel Izard, eds. (1991) 2000. *Dictionnaire de l'ethnologie et de l'anthropologie.* Paris: Presses Universitaires de France.

Borges, Jorge Luis. (1983) 1998. "The Rose of Paracelsus." In *Collected Fictions,* trans. Andrew Hurley, 504–7. New York: Penguin.

Brague, Rémi. 1978. *Le restant: Supplément aux commentaires du* Ménon *de Platon.* Paris: Vrin.

Breton, Stéphane. 1999. "Le spectacle des choses: Considérations mélanésiennes sur la personne." *L'Homme* 39, no. 149: 83–112.

Bruter, Claude-Paul. 1973. *Sur la nature des mathématiques.* Paris: Gauthier-Villars.

Burkert, Walter. (1966) 2001. "Greek Tragedy and Sacrificial Ritual." Reprinted in *Savage Energies,* 1–36.

———. (1972) 1983. *Homo necans: The Anthropology of Ancient Greek Sacrificial Ritual and Myth.* Translated by Peter Bing. Berkeley: University of California Press.

———. (1990) 2001. *Savage Energies: Lessons of Myth and Ritual in Ancient Greece.* Translated by Peter Bing. Chicago: University of Chicago Press.

Caillé, Alain. 1986. "Le mythe du mythe." *Bulletin du MAUSS* 17.

Canetti, Elias. (1960) 1962. *Crowds and Power.* Translated by Carol Stewart. London: Gollancz.

Capdeville-Zeng, Catherine. 2010. "Réflexions sur la parenté chinoise." *L'Homme* 50, no. 195/196: 431–50.

Cartry, Michel, ed. 1987. *Sous le masque de l'animal: Essais sur le sacrifice en Afrique noire.* Paris: Presses Universitaires de France.

Casajus, Dominique. 2008. "Du nouveau sur la parenté." At www.laviedesidees.fr/Du-nouveau-sur-la-parente.html.

Clastres, Pierre. 1966. "L'arc et le panier." *L'Homme* 6, no. 2: 13–31.

———. 1972. *Chronique des Indiens Guayaki*. Paris: Plon.

———. (1977) 1994. "Sorrows of the Savage Warrior." In *Archeology of Violence*, 169–200.

———. (1980) 1994. *Archeology of Violence*. Translated by Jeanine Herman. New York: Semiotext(e).

Collard, Chantal. 1987. Review of Alain Testart, *Essai sur les fondements de la division sexuelle du travail chez les chasseurs-cueilleurs* (1986). *Anthropologie et sociétés* 11, no. 1: 170–71.

———. 2000. "Femmes échangées, femmes échangistes: A propos de la théorie de l'alliance de Claude Lévi-Strauss." *L'Homme* 46, no. 154/155: 101–16.

Collard, Chantal, and Françoise Zonabend. 2013. "Parenté sans sexualité: Le paradigme occidental en question." *L'Homme* 53, no. 206: 29–58.

Comte, Auguste. (1844) 1963. *Discours sur l'esprit positif*. Paris: Union Générale d'Édition.

———. (1852) 1966. *Cathéchisme positiviste*. Paris: Garnier-Flammarion.

Crocker, Jon C. (1977) 1983. "Les réflexions du Soi." In Benoist, ed., *L'Identité*, 157–84.

Debray, Régis. (1981) 1987. *Critique de la raison politique; ou, L'inconscient religieux*. Paris: Gallimard.

Deguy, Michel, and Jean-Pierre Dupuy, eds. 1982. *René Girard et le problème du mal*. Paris: Grasset.

Delaisi de Parseval, Geneviève. 1981. *La part du père*. Paris: Seuil.

Delcourt, Marie. (1944) 1981. *Œdipe; ou, La légende du conquérant*. Paris: Les Belles Lettres.

Derrida, Jacques. (1978) 1979. *Spurs: Nietzsche's Styles*. Translated by Barbara Harlow. Chicago: University of Chicago Press.

Descartes, René. (1637) 1999. *Discourse on Method and Other Writings*. Edited and translated by Desmond M. Clarke. Harmondsworth: Penguin.

Descombes, Vincent. 1979. "L'équivoque du symbolique." *MLN* 94, no. 4: 655–75.

Detienne, Marcel. 1972. *Les jardins d'Adonis*. Introduction by Jean-Pierre Vernant. Paris: Gallimard.

Detienne, Marcel, and Jean-Pierre Vernant. 1979. *La cuisine du sacrifice en pays grec*. Paris: Gallimard.

Devereux, Georges. 1965. "Considérations ethnopsychanalytiques sur la notion de parenté." *L'Homme* 5, no. 3/4: 224–47.

———. 1968. *From Anxiety to Method in the Behavioral Sciences*. The Hague: Mouton.

———. 1970a. *Essais d'ethnopsychiatrie générale*. Foreword by Roger Bastide. Paris: Gallimard.

———. (1970b) 1980. *Basic Problems of Ethnopsychiatry*. Translated by Basia Miller Gulati and George Devereux. Chicago: University of Chicago Press.

———. 1972a. *Ethnopsychanalyse complémentariste*. Paris: Flammarion.

———. (1972b) 1978. *Ethnopsychoanalysis: Psychoanalysis and Anthropology as Complementary Frames of Reference*. Berkeley: University of California Press.

———. 1982. *Femme et mythe*. Paris: Flammarion.

Digard, Jean-Pierre. 2012. "Le tournant obscurantiste en anthropologie: De la zoomanie à l'animalisme occidentaux." *L'Homme* 52, no. 203/204: 555–78.

Douglas, Mary. 1966. *Purity and Danger: An Analysis of the Concepts of Pollution and Taboo*. London: Routledge & Kegan Paul.

Dufrenne, Mikel. 1953. *La personnalité de base.* Paris: Presses Universitaires de France.

Dumont, Louis. 1976. *Homo aequalis.* Paris: Gallimard. (Translated in English as *From Mandeville to Marx: The Genesis and Triumph of Economic Ideology* [Chicago: University of Chicago Press, 1977]).

———. (1979) 1980. *Homo hierarchicus: The Caste System and Its Implications.* Translated by Mark Sainsbury, Louis Dumont, and Basia Gulati. Complete rev. ed. Chicago: University of Chicago Press.

Dumouchel, Paul, ed. 1985. *Violence et vérité: Autour de René Girard.* Paris: Grasset.

Dupuy, Jean-Pierre, ed. 1992. *Introduction aux sciences sociales: Logique des phénomènes collectifs.* Paris: Ellipses.

Durkheim, Émile. (1897) 1951. *Suicide: A Study in Sociology.* Edited by George Simpson, translated by John A. Spaulding and George Simpson. New York: Free Press.

———. (1912) 1995. *The Elementary Forms of Religious Life.* Translated by Karen E. Fields. New York: Free Press.

Eibl-Eibesfeldt, Irenäus. (1973) 1976. *L'homme programmé: L'inné, facteur déterminant du comportement humain.* Translated by Anneliese Plank. Paris: Flammarion.

———. (1976) 1979. *Par-delà nos différences.* Translated by Trudi Strub. Paris: Flammarion.

Étienne, Pierre. 1975. "Les interdictions de mariage chez les Baoulé." *L'Homme* 15, no. 3/4: 5–29.

Evans-Pritchard, Edward Evan. 1951. *Kinship and Marriage among the Nuer.* Oxford: Oxford University Press.

Febvre, Lucien. (1922) 1970. *La terre et l'évolution humaine.* Paris: Albin Michel.

Feynman, Richard P. (1965) 1967. *The Character of Physical Law.* Cambridge, Mass.: MIT Press.

Fine, Agnès. 1998. Review of Françoise Héritier, *Masculin, Féminin: La pensée de la différence* (1996). *Clio: Histoire, femmes et société* 8: 249–52.

———. 2013. "Retour critique sur l'inceste de deuxième type." *L'Homme* 53, no. 205: 99–114.

Flaubert, Gustave. (1881) 2005. *Bouvard and Pécuchet.* Translated by Mark Polizotti. Normal, Ill.: Dalkey Archive Press.

Foucault, Michel. 1962. "Introduction." In Rousseau, *Rousseau juge de Jean Jaques*, vi–xxiv.

Fox, Robin. 1967. *Kinship and Marriage: An Anthropological Perspective.* London: Penguin.

———. 1975a. "Primate Kin and Human Kinship." In Fox, ed., *Biosocial Anthropology*, 9–35.

———, ed. 1975b. *Biosocial Anthropology.* London: Malaby Press.

Francillon, Gérard. 1989. "Un profitable échange de frères chez les Tetun du Sud, Timor central." *L'Homme* 29, no. 109: 26–43.

Frazer, James G. (1891) 1994. *The Golden Bough.* Vols. 1 and 2 of *The Collected Works of J. G. Frazer.* 28 vols. Richmond, Surrey: Curzon Press.

Freud, Sigmund. (1893–1895) 1955. *Studies on Hysteria.* Translated by James and Alix Strachey. Vol. 2 in *Standard Edition of the Complete Psychological Works.*

———. (1900) 1953. *The Interpretation of Dreams*. Translated by James Strachey. Vols. 4 (first part) and 5 (second part) in *Standard Edition of the Complete Psychological Works*.

———. (1901) 1960. *The Psychopathology of Everyday Life*. Translated by Alan Tyson. Vol. 6 in *Standard Edition of the Complete Psychological Works*.

———. (1905) 1953. *Three Essays on the Theory of Sexuality*. Translated by James Strachey. In *Standard Edition of the Complete Psychological Works*, 7:123–243.

———. (1908) 1959. "On the Sexual Theories of Children." Translated by D. Bryan, revised by James Strachey. In *Standard Edition of the Complete Psychological Works*, 9:205–26.

———. (1910) 1957. *Five Lectures on Psycho-Analysis*. Translated by James Strachey. In *Standard Edition of the Complete Psychological Works*, 11:1–55.

———. (1911) 1958. "The Case of Schreber" (Psycho-Analytic Notes on an Autobiographical Account of a Case of Paranoia [*Dementia Paranoides*]). Translated by Alix and James Strachey. In *Standard Edition of the Complete Psychological Works*, 12:1–82.

———. (1913) 1955. *Totem and Taboo: Resemblances between the Psychic Lives of Savages and Neurotics*. Translated by James Strachey. In *Standard Edition of the Complete Psychological Works*, 13:vii–xv, 1–161.

———. (1915–1917) 1957. *Papers on Metapsychology*. Translated by James Strachey. In *Standard Edition of the Complete Psychological Works*, 14:105–215.

———. (1915–1916) 1963. *Introductory Lectures on Psycho-Analysis* (Parts 1 and 2). Translated by James Strachey. Vol. 15 in *Standard Edition of the Complete Psychological Works*.

———. (1918) 1955. "From the History of an Infantile Neurosis." Translated by Alix and James Strachey. In *Standard Edition of the Complete Psychological Works*, 17:3–122.

———. (1925) 1959. *An Autobiographical Study*. Translated by James Strachey. In *Standard Edition of the Complete Psychological Works*, 20:1–74.

———. (1927) 1961. *The Future of an Illusion*. Translated by W. D. Robson-Scott, revised by James Strachey. In *Standard Edition of the Complete Psychological Works*, 21:1–56.

———. (1932) 1964. *New Introductory Lectures on Psycho-Analysis*. Translated by James Strachey. In *Standard Edition of the Complete Psychological Works*, 22:1–182.

———. (1939) 1964. *Moses and Monotheism*. Translated by James Strachey. In *Standard Edition of the Complete Psychological Works*, 23:1–137.

———. 1953–1974. *Standard Edition of the Complete Psychological Works of Sigmund Freud*. Edited by James Strachey, in collaboration with Anna Freud, assisted by Alix Strachey and Alan Tyson. 24 vols. London: Hogarth Press.

Fustel de Coulanges, Numa Denis. (1864) 1980. *The Ancient City: A Study on the Religion, Laws, and Institutions of Greece and Rome*. Translated by Willard Small. Baltimore: Johns Hopkins University Press.

Garine, Igor de. 1980. "Les étrangers, la vengeance et les parents chez les Massa et les Moussy." In Verdier and Poly, eds., *La Vengeance*, 1:91–124.

Gauchet, Marcel. 1989. *La révolution des droits de l'homme*. Paris: Gallimard.

Gennep, Arnold van. (1909) 1960. *The Rites of Passage*. Translated by Monika B. Vizedom and Gabrielle L. Caffee. Chicago: University of Chicago Press.

Gillison, Gillian. 1986. "Le pénis géant: Le frère de la mère dans les hautes terres de Nouvelle-Guinée." *L'Homme* 26, no. 99: 41–69.

———. 1987. "Incest and the Atom of Kinship: The Role of the Mother's Brother in a New Guinea Highlands Society." *Ethos* 15: 166–202.

———. 1999. "L'anthropologie psychanalytique: Un paradigme marginal." *L'Homme* 39, no. 149: 43–52.

Girard, René. (1961) 1966. *Deceit, Desire, and the Novel.* Translated by Yvonne Freccero. Baltimore: Johns Hopkins University Press.

———. 1972a. *La violence et le sacré.* Paris: Grasset.

———. (1972b) 1977. *Violence and the Sacred.* Translated by Patrick Gregory. Baltimore: Johns Hopkins University Press.

———. (1978) 1987. *Things Hidden since the Foundation of the World.* Translated by Stephen Bann and Michael Metteer. Stanford, Calif.: Stanford University Press.

———. (1999) 2001. *I See Satan Fall Like Lightning.* Translated by James G. Williams. Maryknoll, N.Y.: Orbis Books.

Girard, René, with Pierpaolo Antonello and João Cezar de Castro Rocha. (2004) 2008. *Evolution and Conversion: Dialogues on the Origins of Culture.* London: Continuum.

Glowczewski, Barbara. 1991. "Entre rêve et mythe: Róheim et les Australiens." *L'Homme* 31, no. 118: 125–32.

Godechot, Jacques. 1979. *Les Constitutions de la France depuis 1791.* Paris: Garnier-Flammarion.

Godelier, Maurice. (1982) 1986. *The Making of Great Men: Male Domination and Power among the New Guinea Baruya.* Translated by Rupert Swyer. Cambridge and Paris: Cambridge University Press/Éditions de la Maison des Sciences de l'Homme.

———. (2004) 2011. *The Metamorphoses of Kinship.* Translated by Nora Scott. London: Verso Books.

———. 2007. *Au fondement des sociétés humaines: Ce que nous apprend l'anthropologie.* Paris: Albin Michel.

Green, André. (1977) 1983. "Atome de parenté et relations œdipiennes." In Benoist, ed., *L'Identité,* 81–107.

———. 1999. "Le psychisme entre anthropologues et psychanalystes: Une différence d'interprétation." *L'Homme* 39, no. 149: 25–42.

Grimm, Jacob, and Wilhelm Grimm. 1972. *The Complete Grimm's Fairy Tales.* Trans. Margaret Hunt. New York: Pantheon Books.

Gualde, Norbert. 2004. *Ce que l'humanité doit à la femme.* Lormont, France: Éditions Le Bord de l'eau.

Guéroult, Martial. 1961–1974. *Spinoza.* Vol. 1, *Dieu*; vol. 2, *L'Âme.* Paris: Aubier.

Guiraud, Pierre. 1969. "Distribution et transformation de la notion de 'coup.'" *Langue française* 4: 67–74.

Hamberger, Klaus. 2009. "Un nouveau modèle de parenté: A propos de *La parenté* de Laurent Barry." Posted 17 December 2009 at www.ethnographiques.org/2009/hamberger.

———. 2010. "Espaces de parenté." *L'Homme* 50, no. 195/196: 451–68.

Hamerton-Kelly, Robert G., ed. 1987. *Violent Origins: Walter Burkert, René Girard, and Jonathan Z. Smith on Ritual Killing and Cultural Formation.* Stanford, Calif.: Stanford University Press.

Heinich, Nathalie. 1995. "L'inceste du deuxième type et les avatars du symbolique." *Critique* 583: 940–52.

Héran, François. 1987. Review of Alain Testart, *Essai sur les fondements de la division sexuelle du travail chez les chasseurs-cueilleurs* (1986). *Revue française de sociologie* 28, no. 4: 713–16.

——. 1996. "Figures et légendes de la parenté." Doctoral thesis, Université de Paris-V.

——. 2009. *Figures de la parenté: Une histoire critique de la raison structurelle.* Presses Universitaires de France.

Héritier, Françoise. 1973. "La paix et la pluie: Rapports d'autorité et rapport au sacré chez les Samo." *L'Homme* 13, no. 3: 121–38.

——. 1979. "Symbolique de l'inceste et de sa prohibition." In Izard and Smith, eds., *La fonction symbolique,* 209–43.

——. 1981. *L'exercice de la parenté.* Paris: Seuil.

——. (1994) 1999. *Two Sisters and Their Mother: The Anthropology of Incest.* Translated by Jeanine Herman. New York: Zone Books.

——. 1996. *Masculin/féminin: La pensée de la différence.* Paris: Odile Jacob.

——, ed. 1999. *Séminaire de Françoise Héritier: De la violence II.* Paris: Odile Jacob.

——. 2000. "Articulations et substances." *L'Homme* 40, no. 154/155: 21–38.

——. (2002) 2012. *Masculin/féminin II: Dissoudre la hiérarchie.* Paris: Odile Jacob.

——. (2009) 2013. *Une pensée en mouvement.* Edited by Salvatore D'Onofrio. Paris: Odile Jacob.

Herrenschmidt, Olivier. 1979. "Sacrifice symbolique et sacrifice efficace." In Izard and Smith, eds., *La fonction symbolique,* 171–92.

Heusch, Luc de. 1958. *Essais sur le symbolisme de l'inceste royal en Afrique.* Brussels: Institut de Sociologie Solvay, Université Libre de Bruxelles.

——. 1987. *Écrits sur la royauté sacrée.* Brussels: Éditions de l'Université de Bruxelles.

Hobbes, Thomas. (1642) 1998. *On the Citizen.* Edited and translated by Richard Tuck and Michael Silverthorne. Cambridge: Cambridge University Press.

——. (1651) 2010. *Leviathan, or the Matter, Forme & Power of a Common-Wealth Ecclesiasticall and Civill.* Edited by Ian Shapiro. New Haven, Conn.: Yale University Press.

Hocart, Arthur Maurice. 1927. *Kingship.* Oxford: Oxford University Press.

——. 1933. *The Progress of Man: A Short Survey of His Evolution, His Customs, and His Works.* London: Methuen.

——. (1936) 1970. *Kings and Councillors: An Essay in the Comparative Anatomy of Human Society.* Edited by Rodney Needham. Chicago: University of Chicago Press.

——. 1950. *Caste: A Comparative Study.* London: Methuen.

——. 1952. *The Life-Giving Myth, and Other Essays.* Edited by Lord Raglan. London: Methuen.

——. 1954. *Social Origins.* London: Watts.

Hua, Cai. (1997) 2000. *Une société sans père ni mari: Les Na de Chine.* 4th rev. ed. Paris: Presses Universitaires de France. [An English version based on the French edition was subsequently published as *A Society without Fathers or Husbands: The Na of China,* trans. Asti Hustvedt (New York: Zone Books, 2001).]

Hubert, Henri, and Marcel Mauss. (1898) 1964. *Sacrifice: Its Nature and Functions.* Translated by W. D. Halls. Chicago: University of Chicago Press.

Iteanu, André. 1980. "Qui as-tu tué pour demander la main de ma fille? Violence et mariage chez les Ossètes." In Verdier and Poly, eds., *La Vengeance*, 2:61–81.

Izard, Michel, and Pierre Smith, eds. 1979. *La fonction symbolique: Essais d'anthropologie.* Paris: Gallimard.

Jakobson, Roman. 1960. "Why 'Mama' and 'Papa'?" In *Perspectives in Psychological Theory: Essays in Honor of Heinz Werner*, ed. Bernard Kaplan and Seymour Wapner, 124–34. New York: International Universities Press.

———. 1963. *Essais sur linguistique générale.* Translated by Nicolas Ruwet. Paris: Minuit.

Jamard, Jean-Luc, Emmanuel Terray, and Margarita Xanthakou, eds. 2000. *En substances: Textes pour Françoise Héritier.* Paris: Fayard.

Jamous, Raymond. 1981. *Honneur et* baraka: *Les structures traditionnelles dans le Rif.* Paris and Cambridge: Éditions de la Maison des Sciences de l'Homme/Cambridge University Press.

———. 1991. *La relation frère-soeur: Parenté et rites chez les Meo de l'Inde du Nord.* Paris: Éditions de l'École des Hautes Études en Sciences Sociales.

Jaulin, Robert. 1971. *La mort sara.* Paris: Plon.

Jay, Nancy. 1992. *Throughout Your Generations Forever: Sacrifice, Religion, and Paternity.* Chicago: University of Chicago Press.

Jones, Ernest. 1951. *Essays in Applied Psychoanalysis.* Vol. 2, *Essays in Folklore, Anthropology, and Religion.* London: Hogarth Press.

Jorion, Paul. 1984. "L'inscription dans la structure de parenté." *Ornicar?* 31: 56–97.

———. 1991. "Le frère de ma mère sera toujours mon oncle." *Revue du MAUSS* 14: 117–25.

Journet, Odile. 1987. "Le sang des femmes et le sacrifice: L'exemple joola." In Cartry, ed., *Sous le masque de l'animal*, 241–65.

Juillerat, Bernard. 1995. "Du roman familial à la honte d'engendrer." *L'Homme* 35, no. 135: 87–108.

Kane, Hamidou. (1961) 1963. *Ambiguous Adventure.* Translated by Katherine Woods. New York: Walker.

Kant, Immanuel. (1785) 1998. *Groundwork of the Metaphysics of Morals.* Edited and translated by Mary Gregor. Cambridge: Cambridge University Press.

Kleene, Stephen Cole. 1967. *Mathematical Logic.* New York: John Wiley & Sons.

Kofman, Sarah. 1978. *Aberrations: Le devenir-femme d'Auguste Comte.* Paris: Aubier-Flammarion.

———. 1980. *L'énigme de la femme.* Paris: Galilée.

Krige, E. Jensen, and Jack D. Krige. 1947. *The Realm of a Rain Queen: A Study of the Pattern of Lovedu Society.* London: Oxford University Press.

Kroeber, Alfred L. 1920. "Totem and Taboo: An Ethnologic Psychoanalysis." *American Anthropologist* 22, no. 1: 48–55.

———. 1939. "Totem and Taboo in Retrospect." *American Journal of Sociology* 45, no. 3: 446–51.

Lacan, Jacques. (1953) 1979. "The Neurotic's Individual Myth." Edited by Jacques-Alain Miller, translated by Martha Noel Evans. *Psychoanalytic Quarterly* 48 (1979): 405–25.

———. 1966a. *Écrits*. With commentary by Jacques-Alain Miller. Paris: Seuil.

———. (1966b) 1977. *Écrits: A Selection*. Abridged edition, translated by Alan Sheridan. New York: W.W. Norton.

———. (1973) 1977. *The Four Fundamental Concepts of Psycho-analysis*. The Seminar of Jacques Lacan, Book 11. Edited by Jacques-Alain Miller, translated by Alan Sheridan. London: Hogarth Press.

———. (1978) 1988. *The Ego in Freud's Theory and in the Technique of Psychoanalysis, 1954–1955*. The Seminar of Jacques Lacan, Book 2. Edited by Jacques-Alain Miller, translated by Sylvana Tomaselli. Cambridge: Cambridge University Press.

———. 1991a. *L'envers de la psychanalyse: Le Séminaire*. Book 17. Paris: Seuil.

———. (1991b) 2007. *The Other Side of Psychoanalysis*. The Seminar of Jacques Lacan, Book 17. Edited by Jacques-Alain Miller, translated by Russell Grigg. New York: W.W. Norton.

Laurent, Pierre-Joseph. 2013. "Système de mariages et terminologie de parenté chez les Mossi (Burkina Faso): Contribution à l'approche de la terminologie omaha." *L'Homme* 53, no. 206: 59–87.

Leach, Edmund. 1971. "More about 'Mama' and 'Papa.'" In Needham, ed., *Rethinking Kinship and Marriage*, 75–98.

Leroi-Gourhan, André. 1943. *L'homme et la matière*. Paris: Albin Michel.

———. (1964) 1976. *Les religions de la préhistoire*. 3rd rev. ed. Paris: Presses Universitaires de France.

Lévi-Strauss, Claude. 1944. "Reciprocity and Hierarchy." *American Anthropologist* 46, no. 2: 266–68.

———. 1949a. "L'efficacité symbolique." *Revue de l'Histoire des Religions* 135, no. 1: 5–27; reprinted as chapter 10 of Lévi-Strauss, *Structural Anthropology*.

———. (1949b) 1967. *Les structures élémentaires de la parenté*. Rev. ed. Paris and The Hague: Mouton.

———. (1949c) 1969. *The Elementary Structures of Kinship*. Rev. ed. Edited by Rodney Needham; translated by James Harle Bell, John Richard von Sturmer, and Rodney Needham. Boston: Beacon Press.

———. 1950. "Introduction à l'oeuvre de Marcel Mauss." In Mauss, *Sociologie et anthropologie*, ix–lii.

———. 1952. "Toward a General Theory of Communication." Unpublished paper prepared for the Conference of Anthropologists and Linguists, Indiana University, 21–31 July.

———. (1955) 1961. *Tristes Tropiques*. Abridged ed., translated by John Russell. London: Hutchinson & Co.

———. (1958a) 1963. *Structural Anthropology*. Translated by Claire Jacobson and Brooke Grundfest Schoepf. New York: Basic Books.

———. (1958b) 1973. "La Geste d'Asdiwal." In *Anthropologie structurale II*, 175–233. Paris: Plon.

———. (1962a) 1964. *Totemism*. Translated by Rodney Needham. London: Merlin Press.

————. (1962b) 1966. *The Savage Mind.* Chicago: University of Chicago Press.

————. 1964–1971. *Mythologiques.* 4 vols. Paris: Plon.

————. (1964) 1969. *The Raw and the Cooked.* Vol. 1 of *Mythologiques* (1969–1981).

————. 1965. "Le triangle culinaire." *L'Arc,* no. 26: 19–29.

————. (1966) 1973. *From Honey to Ashes.* Vol. 2 of *Mythologiques* (1969–1981).

————. 1969–1981. *Mythologiques.* 4 vols. Translated by John Weightman and Doris Weightman. New York: Harper and Row.

————. (1971) 1981. *The Naked Man.* Vol. 4 of *Mythologiques* (1969–1981).

————. (1983) 1985. *The View from Afar.* Translated by Joachim Neugroschel and Phoebe Hoss. New York: Basic Books.

————. 1984. *Paroles données.* Paris: Plon.

————. (1985) 1988. *The Jealous Potter.* Translated by Bénédicte Chorier. Chicago: University of Chicago Press.

————. 2000. "Postface" to special issue on kinship, *L'Homme* 40, no. 154/155: 713–20.

————. (2011) 2013. *Anthropology Confronts the Problems of the Modern World.* Translated by Jane-Marie Todd. Cambridge, Mass.: Belknap Press of Harvard University Press.

Lévi-Strauss, Claude, and Didier Éribon. (1988) 1991. *Conversations with Claude Lévi-Strauss.* Translated by Paula Wissing. Chicago: University of Chicago Press.

Macalpine, Ida, and Richard A. Hunter. 1955a. "Translators' Introduction." In Schreber, *Memoirs of My Nervous Illness,* 1–28.

————. 1955b. "Translators' Analysis of the Case." In Schreber, *Memoirs of My Nervous Illness,* 369–416.

Mahé, Alain. 1999. Review of Abdellah Hammoudi, *Master and Disciple: The Cultural Foundations of Moroccan Authoritarianism* (1997). *L'Homme* 39, no. 149: 245–46.

Malinowski, Bronislaw. 1927. *Sex and Repression in Savage Society.* London: Kegan Paul, Trench, Trubner & Co.

Mannoni, Octave. 1968. *Freud.* Paris: Seuil.

Malson, Lucien. 1964. *Les enfants sauvages: Mythes et réalités.* Paris: Union Générale d'Édition.

Maranda, Elli Köngäs, and Pierre Maranda. 1970. "Le crâne et l'utérus: Deux théorèmes nord-malaitins." In Maranda and Pouillon, eds., *Échanges et communications,* 2:829–61.

Maranda, Pierre. 1963. "Note sur l'"élément de parenté."" *Anthropos* 58: 810–28.

Maranda, Pierre, and Jean Pouillon, eds. 1970. *Échanges et communications: Mélanges offerts à Claude Lévi-Strauss à l'occasion de son 60ème anniversaire.* 2 vols. The Hague: Mouton.

Martens, Francis. 1975. "A propos de l'oncle maternel, ou modeste proposition pour repenser le mariage des cousins croisés." *L'Homme* 15, no. 3/4: 155–75.

Mauss, Marcel. 1906. "Essai sur les variations saisonnières des sociétés eskimos: Étude de morphologie sociale." *L'Année sociologique* 9: 39–132.

————. (1936a) 1950. *Sociologie et anthropologie.* Paris: Presses Universitaires de France.

———. (1936b) 1950. "Les techniques du corps." In *Sociologie et anthropologie*, 365–86.

———. (1947) 2007. *Manual of Ethnography*. Edited by N. J. Allen, translated by Dominique Lussier. New York and London: Durkheim Press/Berghahn Books.

Mead, Margaret. 1949. *Male and Female: A Study of the Sexes in a Changing World*. New York: William Morrow.

Moisseeff, Marika. 1987. "Entre maternité et procréation: L'inceste." *Patio* 7: 121–45.

———. 1995. *Un long chemin semé d'objets cultuels: Le cycle initiatique aranda*. Paris: Éditions de l'École des Hautes Études en Sciences Sociales.

———. 1997. "Rêver la différence de sexes: Quelques applications du traitement aborigène de la sexualité." Paper presented on 14 March 1997 at the conference "Sex and Healing" sponsored by the Department of Psychopathology of Université Paris-Nord.

———. 2000. "Une figure de l'altérité chez les Dentcico, ou la maternité maléfique." In Jamard, Terray, and Xanthakou, eds., *En substances*, 471–89.

Muller, Jean-Claude. 1975. "La royauté divine chez les Rukuba." *L'Homme* 15, no. 1: 5–27.

———. 1997. "Circoncision et régicide: Thème et variations chez les Dii, les Chamba et les Moundang des confins de la Bénoué et du Tchad." *L'Homme* 37, no. 141: 7–24.

Murdock, George P. 1949. *Social Structure*. New York: Macmillan.

Needham, Rodney, ed. 1971. *Rethinking Kinship and Marriage*. London: Tavistock.

Nef, Frédéric. 1979. "La langue universelle et les langues: Leibniz biface?" *Critique* 387/388: 736–51.

Nietzsche, Friedrich. (1886) 1974. *The Gay Science*. Translated by Walter Kaufmann. New York: Vintage Books.

Olsen, Jan Kyrre, Stig Andur Pedersen, and Vincent F. Hendricks, eds. 2009. *A Companion to the Philosophy of Technology*. Chichester, U.K.: Wiley-Blackwell.

Pak, Ok-Kyung. 1993. "Royauté et parenté chez les Minangkabau de Sumatra." *L'Homme* 33, no. 125: 89–116.

Pascal, Blaise. 1963. *Pensées et opuscules*. Edited by Léon Brunschvicg. Paris: Classiques Hachette.

Perrin, Michel. 1987. "Correspondance: La femme et la chasse." *La Recherche* 18, no. 184: 88.

Piattelli-Palmarini, Massimo, Edgar Morin, and André Béjin, eds. 1978. *L'unité de l'homme: Essais et discussions*. 3 vols. Paris: Seuil.

Plato. 1929. *Le Banquet*. Edited by Léon Robin. Paris: Les Belles Lettres.

Poincaré, Henri. (1902) 1952. *Science and Hypothesis*. Translated by George Bruce Halsted. New York: Dover.

———. (1905) 1958. *The Value of Science*. Translated by George Bruce Halsted. New York: Dover.

Popper, Karl R. (1944–1945) 1961. *The Poverty of Historicism*. 3rd ed. New York: Harper and Row.

Pulman, Bernard. 1986. "Aux origines du débat ethnologie/psychanalyse: W.H.R. Rivers (1864–1922)." *L'Homme* 26, no. 100: 119–42.

Quigley, Declan. 1993. *The Interpretation of Caste*. Oxford: Clarendon Press.

Radcliffe-Brown, Alfred R. 1952. *Structure and Function in Primitive Society: Essays and Addresses.* London: Cohen and West.

Rank, Otto. (1909) 2004. *The Myth of the Birth of the Hero: A Psychological Exploration of Myth.* Translated by Gregory C. Richter and E. James Lieberman. Rev. and aug. ed. Baltimore: Johns Hopkins University Press.

———. 1911. *Die Lohengrinsage: Ein Beitrag zu ihrer Motivgestaltung und Deutung.* Leipzig: F. Deuticke.

———. (1924) 1929. *The Trauma of Birth.* New York: Harcourt, Brace.

Reed, Evelyn. 1975. *Woman's Evolution: From Matriarchal Clan to Patriarchal Family.* New York: Pathfinder Press.

Reik, Theodor. (1919) 1931. *Ritual: Psycho-Analytic Studies.* Translated by Douglas Bryan (from 2nd ed. [1928]). London: Hogarth Press.

———. 1960. *The Creation of Woman: A Psychoanalytic Inquiry into the Myth of Eve.* New York: George Braziller.

Rey, Olivier. 2006. *Une folle solitude: Le fantasme de l'homme auto-construit.* Paris: Seuil.

Robert, Marthe. (1974) 1976. *From Oedipus to Moses: Freud's Jewish Identity.* Translated by Ralph Manheim. Garden City, N.Y.: Anchor Books.

Robert de Boron. (ca. 1200) 1995. *Le roman de l'histoire du Graal.* Translated by Alexandre Micha. Paris: Honoré Champion.

Rogers, Susan Carol. 1975. "Female Forms of Power and the Myth of Dominance: A Model of Male/Female Interaction in Peasant Society." *American Ethnologist* 2: 727–56.

———. 1979. "Espace masculin, espace féminin: Essai sur la différence." *Études rurales* 74: 87–110.

Róheim, Géza. 1915. "Killing the Divine King." *Man* 15: 26–28.

———. (1943) 1971. *The Origin and Function of Culture.* Garden City, N.Y.: Doubleday.

———. (1950a) 1967. *Psychanalyse et anthropologie: Culture, personnalité, inconscient.* Translated by Marie Moscovici. Paris: Gallimard.

———. (1950b) 1968. *Psychoanalysis and Anthropology: Culture, Personality, and the Unconscious.* New York: International Universities Press.

Rousseau, Jean-Jacques. (1760) 1994. *Geneva Manuscript* (First Version of *On the Social Contract*). Translated by Christopher Kelly. In *Collected Writings*, 4:76–125.

———. (1762) 1943. *Du contrat social.* Edited by Maurice Halbwachs. Paris: Aubier-Montaigne.

———. (1771–1772) 2005. *Considerations on the Government of Poland and Its Planned Reformation.* Translated by Christopher Kelly. In *Collected Writings*, 11:167–240.

———. (1772–1774a) 1962. *Rousseau juge de Jean Jaques: Dialogues.* Introduction by Michel Foucault. Paris: Armand Colin.

———. (1772–1774b) 1990. *Rousseau, Judge of Jean-Jacques: Dialogues.* Translated by Judith R. Bush, Christopher Kelly, Roger D. Masters. Vol. 1 of *Collected Writings*.

———. 1990–2013. *Collected Writings.* Edited by Roger D. Masters and Christopher Kelly. 13 vols. Hanover, N.H.: University Press of New England.

Roustang, François. 1976. *Un destin si funeste*. Paris: Minuit.

Ruyer, Raymond. 1946. *Éléments de psycho-biologie*. Paris: Presses Universitaires de France.

———. 1952. *Néo-finalisme*. Paris: Presses Universitaires de France.

———. (1954) 1967. *La cybernétique et l'origine de l'information*. Paris: Flammarion.

———. 1964. *L'animal, l'homme, la fonction symbolique*. Paris: Gallimard.

Saladin d'Anglure, Bernard. 2012. "Le 'troisième genre.'" *Revue du MAUSS*, no. 39: 141–61.

Saussure, Ferdinand de. (1916) 1983. *Course in General Linguistics*. Edited by Charles Bally and Albert Sechehaye, translated and annotated by Roy Harris. La Salle, Ill.: Open Court.

Sauvy, Alfred. (1952–1954) 1963–1966. *Théorie générale de la population*. 2 vols. 3rd rev. ed. Paris: Presses Universitaires de France.

Schipper, Kristofer. 1982. *Le corps taoïste*. Paris: Fayard.

Schreber, Daniel Paul. (1903) 1955. *Memoirs of My Nervous Illness*. Edited and translated by Ida Macalpine and Richard A. Hunter. London: Wm. Dawson & Sons.

Schuhl, Pierre-Maxime. (1934) 1949. *Essai sur la formation de la pensée grecque*. 2nd ed. Paris: Presses Universitaires de France.

Schumpeter, Joseph. (1942) 1950. *Capitalism, Socialism, and Democracy*. 3rd ed. New York: Harper & Brothers.

Scubla, Lucien. 1981. "Philosophie, procréation, religion." *Le Temps de la Réflexion*, no. 2: 506–16.

———. 1982. "Contribution à la théorie du sacrifice." In Deguy and Dupuy, eds., *René Girard et le problème du mal*, 103–67.

———. 1983. "Diversité culturelle et unité de l'homme." *Critique* 437: 796–818.

———. 1985a. "Logiques de la réciprocité." *Cahiers du CREA* 6: 7–273.

———. 1985b. "Théorie du sacrifice et théorie du désir chez René Girard." In Dumouchel, ed., *Violence et vérité*, 359–74.

———. 1988. "Diversité des cultures et invariants transculturels." *Revue du MAUSS*, no. 1: 96–121, and no. 2: 55–107.

———. 1991. "Diversité des cultures et invariants transculturels: Une mise au point (retour sur la loi du sang et les nomenclatures de parenté)." *Revue du MAUSS*, no. 11: 132–36.

———. 1992a. "Peut-on mettre la loi au-dessus de l'homme? Sur la philosophie politique de Jean-Jacques Rousseau." In Dupuy, ed., *Introduction aux sciences sociales*, 105–43.

———. 1992b. "Sciences cognitives, matérialisme et anthropologie." In Andler, ed., *Introduction aux sciences cognitives*, 421–46.

———. 1993a. "Vengeance et sacrifice: De l'opposition à la réconciliation." *Droit et Cultures*, no. 26: 77–101.

———. 1993b. "Vers une anthropologie morphogénétique: Violence fondatrice et théorie des singularités." *Le Débat*, no. 77: 102–20.

———. 1998. *Lire Lévi-Strauss: Le déploiement d'une intuition*. Paris: Odile Jacob.

———. 1999. "'Ceci n'est pas un meurtre,' ou comment le sacrifice contient la violence." In Héritier, ed., *Séminaire de Françoise Héritier*, 135–70.

———. 2000a. "Françoise Héritier et l'avenir du structuralisme." In Jamard, Terray, and Xanthakou, eds., *En substances*, 37–45.

———. 2000b. "La place de la nation dans les sociétés individualistes." *Droit et Cultures*, no. 39: 191–210.

———. 2001a. "Mimétisme, violence et éducation: Quelques aspects de la relation maître-disciple." In Barberi, ed., *La spirale mimétique*, 234–46.

———. 2001b. "Nature, normes et démocratie." *Diogène*, no. 195: 76–84.

———. 2002. "Hiérarchie de sexes et hiérarchie des savoirs, ou Platon chez les Baruya." *Cités*, no. 9: 13–24.

———. 2003. "Roi sacré, victime sacrificielle et victime émissaire." *Revue du MAUSS*, no. 22: 197–221.

———. 2004. "Les dimensions religieuses de la déclaration des droits de l'homme et du citoyen de 1789." *Ateliers du LESC*, no. 27: 81–108.

———. 2005. "Le sacrifice a-t-il une fonction sociale?" *Pardès*, no. 39: 143–59.

———. 2008. "René Girard ou la renaissance de l'anthropologie religieuse." *Cahier de l'Herne*, "Girard," no. 89: 105–10.

———. 2009a. "Technology and Culture." In Olsen, Pedersen, and Hendricks, eds., *A Companion to the Philosophy of Technology*, 311–15.

———. 2009b. "L'apport de René Girard à l'anthropologie du sacrifice." *Raison présente*, no. 170: 103–16.

———. 2009c. "A propos du regard éloigné de l'ethnographe, ou les rapports entre la théorie et l'observation." *Ateliers du LESC*, no. 33, at www.ateliers.revues.org/8199.

———. 2011a. "Psychanalyse et anthropologie: Un rendez-vous manqué?" *Revue du MAUSS*, no. 38: 65–86.

———. 2011b. "Le symbolique chez Lévi-Strauss et chez Lacan." *Revue du MAUSS*, no. 37: 223–39.

———. 2012. "De l'échange de femmes' au don des femmes: Le déni de la procréation dans l''atome de parenté.'" *Revue du MAUSS*, no. 39: 79–100.

———. 2013. "Sur une lacune de la théorie mimétique: L'absence du politique dans le système girardien." *Cités*, no. 53: 103–33. [An English translation may be found at www.cairn-int.info/load_pdf.php?ID_ARTICLE=E_CITE_053_0107.]

Spinoza, Baruch. (1675–1676) 2000. *Political Treatise*. Edited by Steven Barbone and Lee Rice. Translated by Samuel Shirley. Indianapolis: Hackett.

———. (1677a) 1995. *Letters*. Edited by Steven Barbone, Lee Rice, and Jacob Adler. Translated by Samuel Shirley. Indianapolis: Hackett.

———. (1677b) 2000. *Ethics*. Edited and translated by G.H.R. Parkinson. Oxford: Oxford University Press.

Tabet, Paola. 1979. "Les mains, les outils, les armes." *L'Homme* 29, no. 3/4: 5–61.

———. 1998. *La construction sociale de l'inégalité sexuelle: Des outils et les corps.* Paris: L'Harmattan.

Tarot, Camille. 2008. *Le symbolique et le sacré: Théories de la religion.* Paris: La Découverte.

Tcherkézoff, Serge. 1983. *Le roi nyamwezi, la droite et la gauche: Révision comparatiste des classifications dualistes.* Paris and Cambridge: Éditions de la Maison des Sciences de l'Homme/Cambridge University Press.

———. (1991) 2000. "Hertz et l'anthropologie britannique." In Bonte and Izard, eds., *Dictionnaire de l'ethnologie et de l'anthropologie,* 324–25.

Testart, Alain. 1985. *Le communisme primitif.* Vol. 1, *Économie et idéologie.* Paris: Éditions de la Maison des Sciences de l'Homme.

———. 1986a. *Essai sur les fondements de la division sexuelle du travail chez les chasseurs-cueilleurs.* Paris: Éditions de l'École des Hautes Études en Sciences Sociales.

———. 1986b. "La femme et la chasse." *La Recherche* 17, no. 181: 1194–201.

———. 1987a. "De la chasse en France, du sang et de bien d'autres choses encore (à propos de Bertrand Hell, *Entre chien et loup*)." *L'Homme* 27, no. 102: 151–62.

———. 1987b. "Réponse à Chantal Collard." *Anthropologie et sociétés* 11, no. 2: 169–71.

———. 1987c. "Réponse à Michel Perrin." *La Recherche* 18, no. 184: 88.

———. 1988. "De la pertinence des homologies: Réponse à François Héran." *Revue française de sociologie* 29, no. 4: 715–18.

———. 1991. *Des mythes et des croyances: Esquisse d'une théorie générale.* Paris: Éditions de la Maison des Sciences de l'Homme.

———. 1995. "Âge et génération chez les Aborigènes australiens." *L'Homme* 35, no. 134: 171–78.

———. 2000. "Quelques considérations sur le temps dans le parenté et le mariage entre cousins croisés." *L'Homme* 40, no. 154/155: 547–58.

———. 2014. *L'Amazone et la cuisinière: Anthropologie de la division sexuelle du travail.* Paris: Gallimard.

This, Bernard. 1980. *Le Père: Acte de naissance.* Paris: Seuil.

Thom, René. (1972) 1977. *Stabilité structurelle et morphogenèse: Essai d'une théorie générale des modèles.* 2nd rev. and aug. ed. Paris: InterÉditions.

Tillion, Germaine. 1966. *Le harem et les cousins.* Paris: Seuil.

Todd, Emmanuel. (1990) 1996. *L'invention de l'Europe.* Paris: Seuil.

———. 2011. *L'origine des systèmes familiaux.* Vol. 1, *L'Eurasie.* Paris: Gallimard.

Tricaud, François. 1977. *L'accusation: Recherches sur les figures de l'agression éthique.* Paris: Dalloz.

Verdier, Raymond. 1980. "Le système vindicatoire." In Verdier and Poly, eds., *La Vengeance,* 1:11–42.

Verdier, Raymond, and Jean-Pierre Poly, eds. 1980–84. *La Vengeance.* 4 vols. Paris: Éditions Cujas.

Vernant, Jean-Pierre. 1972. Introduction to Detienne, *Les jardins d'Adonis,* xxi–xxii.

Vernier, Bernard. 2009. *La prohibition de l'inceste: Critique de Françoise Héritier.* Paris: L'Harmattan.

Viveiros de Castro, Eduardo. 1996. "Le meurtrier et son double chez les Arawete: Un exemple de fusion rituelle." *Systèmes de pensée en Afrique noire* 14: 77–104.

Watzlawick, Paul, Janet H. Beavin, and Don D. Jackson. 1967. *Pragmatics of Human Communication: A Study of Interactional Patterns, Pathologies, and Paradoxes.* New York: W.W. Norton.

Weil, Simone. 1949. *L'Enracinement: Prélude à une déclaration des devoirs envers l'être humain.* Paris: Gallimard.

Xanthakou, Margarita. 1995. "De la mémoire à la méthode: Georges Devereux, tel qu'en nous-mêmes . . ." *L'Homme* 35, no. 134: 179–90.

Index